SURVEYS AND
SOUNDINGS
IN EUROPEAN
LITERATURE

SURVEYS AND SOUNDINGS IN EUROPEAN LITERATURE

BY HERMANN J. WEIGAND

EDITED BY A. LESLIE WILLSON

PRINCETON, NEW JERSEY

PRINCETON UNIVERSITY PRESS

1966

FOREWORD

WHEN A SCHOLAR of the stature and renown of Hermann J. Weigand is privileged to survey the fruits of his research and to make a selection for presentation in a book, an opportunity is extended to his colleagues and to students and fanciers of the wide field of his specialty to renew their acquaintance with—or even more thrilling, for the uninitiated, to meet for the first time—an illustrious literary analyst, a master of critical style, and a keen diviner of sources. With seeming effortlessness Mr. Weigand surveys centuries of literary activity, ranging from the ubiquitous two and seventy tongues of man to the intimate reflections of Broch's dying Vergil. Mr. Weigand is an exemplary scholar who has lent his insight to enrich our understanding and appreciation of a large spectrum of literature. His present admirers, as well as those to come, will surely be grateful to have in a single volume those critical essays written in English which he here presents. The inclusion of a bibliography of his writings is a welcome bonus.

The text of the essays is the same as originally published, except for minimal alterations. Although acknowledgment for permission to reprint the essays is made on appropriate pages in the present volume, I am pleased to reiterate my appreciation to the following: Carl Winter-Universitätsverlag, Heidelberg, for *Euphorion*; *The German Quarterly*, Robert M. Browning, editor; *The Germanic Review*, W. T. H. Jackson, editor; Professor W. P. Lehmann, The University of Texas; the Modern Language Association; the University of Illinois Press, Donald Jackson, editor; the University of Wisconsin Press, Thomas Webb, Jr., director, for *Monatshefte*, J. D. Workman, editor; the Wayne State University Press, Ralph R. Busick, chief editor; and to President Louis J. Long, Wells College.

The abbreviations *PMLA*, for *Publications of the Modern Language Association*, and *JEGP*, for *Journal of English and Germanic Philology*, have not been spelled out in Professor Weigand's bibliography at the end of the essays.

All translations standing within square brackets have been made by the editor.

Austin, Texas   A. Leslie Willson

PREFACE

THE TWELVE ESSAYS that make up this volume constitute about
one quarter of my contributions to scholarly periodicals and collective publications during a career of teaching and incidental writing that extends well over half a century. All of the items here included date from the second half of my professional life.

Since each of these papers owes its origin to a specific impulse
unrelated to any general intellectual scheme or literary method, a
pattern of historical chronology dictated the sequence of presentation. To a certain extent this selection is representative of the range
of my literary interests; however, some of my major concerns have
found no place in the scope of this book. Notably clusters of essays
on Heinrich Heine, Wolfram von Eschenbach, Heinrich von Kleist,
and Rainer Maria Rilke are missing. The Heine papers were excluded as belonging to an earlier vintage. The Wolfram papers
would, perhaps, have given a too specifically medievalist slant to
the volume. The essays on Kleist and Rilke, like many others, were
written in German and would have suffered, some of them greatly,
in translation. An investigation of the sources of Gerhart Hauptmann's drama of the German Peasants' War, *Florian Geyer*, a study
amounting to monograph proportions, which, incidentally, owed
its origin to the felicitous solution of a key word unintelligibly
garbled in all the editions up to that time, would have been meaningless in English translation as it concentrated on sixteenth- and
seventeenth-century German usage. Similarly, two out of four Rilke
essays found in the bibliography deal with the specific poetic
phraseology of a single sonnet-length poem, while a third uses
rhythmical and metrical patterns of the *Duino Elegies* as a key to
textual interpretation.

To account for the reasons why a scholar of bilingual background like myself should have chosen or should have been impelled to alternate repeatedly between the use of English and German in his encounter with literary problems, each of which constituted an adventure in empathy, in critical distance, and in expression, would challenge my powers of self-analysis and is quite beyond the scope of this note of introduction. Since I have had the
rare privilege of teaching primarily graduate courses throughout

the greater part of my professional life, German has been my pre-ferred language for lectures and discussions. Moreover, unlike most writers for popular media, a scholar is apt, I believe, to focus upon the working out of his problem with only a vague idea of the particular audience he may persuade to accompany him in his adventure.

Of the studies included in this volume only the three on Schiller form a unified group. The longest of them attempts to sketch in outline the literary personality of the poet. A second shows his mind, always bent on experiment, emulating his great Athenian model in the genre of fate tragedy. The third attempts to apply the intellectual categories of his brilliant essay on poetry to spell out the meaning of some of his definitions in terms of concrete literary situations.

Formal structure was a prime concern in the essays on Thomas Mann and Hermann Broch, and in dealing with Chamisso's little classic, *Peter Schlemihl*. Readers of these and of my other essays, as well as my books on Ibsen, Thomas Mann's *Zauberberg*, and the little volume on Courtly Love, will be aware of the fact that I have always been particularly fascinated in tracing the devious workings of human psychology. I owe a great debt in this regard to my reading of Heine, Nietzsche, and particularly Sigmund Freud during my years at college and graduate school. This has colored my literary perspective from first to last.

I cannot end these remarks without expressing my heartfelt thanks to the editor of these studies. It was Professor Willson who first urged upon me the idea of collecting my scattered papers in book form; who attended to the necessary correspondence; who scrutinized the text and, with a practiced eye, normalized the references to sources; who supplied the translations to ease the task of the reader unversed in foreign languages; and who read the proofs with dispatch and meticulous care. To Mrs. Willson and to my wife, I am also deeply indebted for their devoted assistance. I want, in conclusion, to express my sincere appreciation to the editors of Princeton University Press and to the anonymous consultants whose judgment contributed to the shaping of this volume.

New Haven, Connecticut   Hermann J. Weigand

CONTENTS

SURVEYS AND
SOUNDINGS
IN EUROPEAN
LITERATURE

THE TWO AND SEVENTY
LANGUAGES OF THE WORLD

MOST OF US know that Julius Caesar built the Tower of London; that the Franks were lineal descendants of the Trojans; that Prague was founded shortly after the building of the Tower of Babel, and that Trier dates back to the time of Abraham and was built by a brother of King Ninus. To everyone who has crossed the threshold of medieval lore at some time or other it is a matter of common knowledge that India harbors many monsters stranger than Caliban, such as that speedy race of men whose feet are put on backwards and whose bodies are surmounted by the heads of dogs; or that headless race that wears its eyes and mouth and nose on the chest; or that dainty breed that nourishes itself on odors only (they always pack an apple in their bags when they travel any distance, Honorius tells us). Any stroll in the medieval landscape is apt to afford us a glimpse of that most elusive and ferocious of beasts, the unicorn, which can be captured only by the pure virgin; and of that rarest of birds, the phoenix, which cremates itself on a pyre once every five hundred years, to be rejuvenated by the flames. As for the movements of the heavenly sphere, it gives one a certain sense of security to remember that the sun, the moon, and the five other planets are wisely provided with a proper motion of their own, diverging from that of the stars fixed in the firmament, in order to act as a brake upon the revolving celestial disc lest it burst by its unchecked speed.

Among the elements that make up the traditional lore of the Middle Ages there is one of peculiar interest to students of language. Today few people know what was once a matter of common knowledge, that the sum total of languages to be found on earth numbers seventy-two. Were this an isolated fact without any bearing on larger issues, there would be no point in stirring up dust to unearth it. But it is an important fact, one with wide ramifications; a fact that illumines the workings of the medieval mind and one not lightly to be omitted from any reliable compendium of medieval knowledge.

The most impressive point of departure for the study of our tra-

Reprinted from *The Germanic Review*, XVII (1942), 241-260, by permission of W. T. H. Jackson, editor.

dition is Wolfram von Eschenbach's *Willehalm*. This is a spirited narrative poem, written about 1220, which deals with the exploits of the warrior-saint Guillaume of Orange, who won fame on earth and a choice niche in heaven by fighting the Saracens in Southern France. In *Willehalm* the seventy-two languages are mentioned three times. The first reference comes at a point where Wolfram wants to impress us with the vastness of the heathen hosts arrayed against Willehalm's stout little band of Christian knights. "There are seventy-two languages in the world," Wolfram tells us, "and as an obvious corollary there are seventy-two lands to correspond to this number. But of this total fewer than twelve adhere to the Christian faith. All the rest are under heathen domination. And it was no mean sample of this preponderant heathen might that gave battle to Willehalm."

> Sît zwuo und sibenzec sprâche sint,
> er dunket mich der witze ein kint,
> swer niht der zungen lât ir lant,
> dâ von die sprâche sint bekant.
> sô man die zungen nennet gar,
> ir nement niht zwelfe stoufes war:
> die andern hânt in heidenschaft
> von wîten landen grôze kraft.
> dâ heten dise ouch eteswaz,
> die dem markîs zeicten haz. (73: 7-16)

Having seen his band cut to pieces to the last man (except for eight captured alive) Willehalm makes his escape. He rejoins his wife and breaks the news to her of the ghastly slaughter. Then she raises her voice in lament, and for a second time our theme is sounded. "Two and seventy languages," she exclaims, "the sum total of speech ascribed to the human race, would not suffice to express in full the measure of my grief and loss!"

> zwuo und sibenzec sprâche,
> der man al der diete giht,
> die enmöhten gar volsprechen niht
> mîniu vlüstebaeren sêr,
> ich enhabe der vlüste dannoch mêr. (101: 22-26)

In the course of time Willehalm collects a new army to meet the heathen, reinforced on their part by immense numbers. This time the heathen are decisively vanquished and the carnage is terrific. Here Wolfram, champion of tolerance, pauses to comment: "All those heathen, to whom the message of the gospel had never been offered—was it a sin that they were slaughtered like wild beasts? It was a great sin, I say; for they that speak the seventy-two languages are without exception God's handiwork."

> die nie toufes künde
> emphiengen, ist daz sünde,
> daz man die sluoc alsam ein vihe?
> grôzer sünde ich drumme gihe:
> ez ist gar gotes hantgetât,
> zwuo und sibenzec sprâche. . . . (450: 15-20)[1]

God's handiwork is, of course, a circumlocution for man, designating his special status, because God shaped him from a clod of earth, whereas he created all other things by his word. We have seen, then, that Wolfram's poem contains three passages that clearly assume it to be a matter of common knowledge that the earth is peopled by seventy-two nations that speak as many languages.

What other evidence of this idea do we find in German literature?

An old song treats the allegory of the Divine Mill in an exchange of questions and answers between King Tirol of Scotland and his son Vridebrant.[2] To the father's question about the two stones of the mill the son answers that the nether stone is the old covenant, and the upper stone is the Christian faith that superseded it. The mill wheel, says the father, has seventy-two buckets, one of them fashioned of lignum aloê, the most precious wood on earth. These signify the seventy-two languages of the world, the son answers, and there is among them one of signal beauty, because it brought forth the maid of Jesse whom the lord of all creation singled out to be his mother. The Hebrew tongue is meant, of course, and the identification of language and people appears automatic.

> Welt ir [wizzen], wie ez umb die kamben stat:
> zwo und sibenzek sprache diu werlt hat,
> Der einen der man da wirt gewar,
> diu da ist von so suezer par,
> Daz ist diu magt von Jesse [her] geborn,
> die got al der werlt herre z'einer muoter hat erkorn. (strophe 15)

---

[1] "zwuo und sibenzec sprâche, die er hât." Thus Lachmann and Leitzmann punctuate this line. The context, however, calls for a full stop after "sprâche." "Die er hât" is a proleptic reference to the languages under the sway of Terrâmêr, mentioned in the next sentence.

[2] Friedrich Heinrich von der Hagen, *Minnesinger* (Leipzig, 1838), I, 6, strophes 14-24.

In the *Younger Titurel*[3] (about 1270), an intricate romance of vast proportions which enjoyed an enormous vogue during the later Middle Ages, there is a detailed description of the Temple of the Holy Grail. Built on a mountain of polished onyx, it has the shape of a rotunda that is flanked by two and seventy chapels (choirs), each of which has an altar of its own that faces east. As the whole poem is saturated with allegory, the seventy-two chapels unquestionably have a symbolic function. The structural design of the Temple suggests, it would seem, that representatives of all the seventy-two nations of the earth are destined to foregather there in the worship of the true God.

The Swabian poet Ludwig Uhland's famous collection of folk songs[4] is headed by a peculiarly archaic one entitled "Trougemund" (preserved in a fourteenth-century parchment manuscript). Trougemund is a wandering minstrel who seems to know everything. Five stanzas of the song pose riddles to Meister Trougemund, and in as many stanzas he supplies the correct answers. Each series of riddles is introduced by the preamble:

> Nu sage mir, meister Trougemunt,
> zwei und sübenzig lant die sint dir kunt.

> [Now tell me, Master Trougemund,
> two and seventy lands are known to you.]

This same minstrel also figures in the old Orendel legend (about 1200), dealing with the vicissitudes of the seamless garment of Christ that is to this day exhibited in Trier. Having been buried in the sands of the sea for nine years, the garment is found by an old pilgrim on his way to the Holy Land, and he is identified as Trougemund, who had seen seventy-two kingdoms.

> Er was geheissen Tragemunt;
> Im worent (zwei und) sübenzig konnigrich kunt.[5] (115-116)

> [He was called Tragemunt;
> (two and) seventy kingdoms were known to him.]

Seventy-two lands in such a context obviously stand for the whole inhabited world. Their languages are not mentioned in either the

---

[3] *Der jüngere Titurel*, ed. K. A. Hahn (Leipzig, 1842). The description of the temple comprises strophes 311-414. See especially strophes 323 and 360.

[4] *Alte hoch- und niederdeutsche Volkslieder*, ed. Ludwig Uhland (Stuttgart, 1845).

[5] Friedrich Heinrich von der Hagen, *Der ungenähte graue Rock Christi: wie König Orendel von Trier ihn erwirbt* . . . (Berlin, 1844).

song or the legend, but we have a right to infer that Master Trougemund speaks them all.

A late echo of just this accomplishment is found in connection
with the *Kaisersage*, the legend according to which Emperor Frederick did not die but withdrew into a mountain (the Kyffhäuser)
whence he would return when the time was ripe to re-establish the
glory of the empire. Impostors arose from time to time claiming to
be Frederick. As late as 1546 an insane tailor was found in the
ruins of the Kyffhäuser castle. Questioned as to his identity he patiently repeated the stock answer that he was Emperor Frederick.
He had dwelt in the mountain for four hundred years, he said, and
he claimed he could answer questions in all seventy-two languages.[6]

In the lay of Siegfried's youthful exploits, *Das Lied vom Hürnen
Seyfrid*,[7] a thirteenth-century composition, the dwarf Euglin shows
Seyfrid the Drachenstein where Grymhild sleeps a charmed sleep,
with the words:

> Ja hettest du bezwungen   Das halbe theil der Erden
> Vnd zwo vnd sibentzig Zungen   Das sie dir dienten gern
> Christen vnd auch die Heiden   Weren dir underthan
> Dennoch must du die schoene   Hoch auff dem Steine lan.

> [Yes, (though) you had conquered   the half-part of the earth,
> And two and seventy tongues,   so that they served you willingly,
> And Christians as well as heathen   were subjects of yours,
> Still you would have to leave the beauty   high up on the rock.]

The reference in the first line to only half the world—a familiar
fairy tale motif—is confusing. But the remainder of the stanza, by
its allusion to two and seventy tongues, Christian and heathen alike,
presumably raises the stakes to include all the world.

Our most abundant evidence, however, comes from books that
present a scheme of history on the model of the biblical Genesis.
Here it is always the story of the Tower of Babel that supplies the
cue. Thus the eleventh-century paraphrase known as the *Milstätter
Genesis*[8] tells us:

> Ez wolden haben gigant gemûret eine stein want
> zir grozzem unheile: ir sprache wart geteilet
> in zwo und subinzich zunge. (p. 32, lines 10-12)

[6] F. G. Schultheiss, *Die Deutsche Volkssage vom Fortleben und der Wiederkehr
Kaiser Friedrichs II* (Berlin, 1911), p. 97.

[7] In Karl Goedeke, ed., *Deutsche Dichtung im Mittelalter*, 2d ed. (Dresden,
1871), p. 555, strophe 54.

[8] *Genesis und Exodus nach der Milstätter Handschrift*, ed. Joseph Diemer (Vienna, 1862).

[Giants wanted a great stone wall to be erected;
to their great misfortune: their language was divided
into two and seventy tongues.]

A few lines later the fact is restated (lines 20-21).

The twelfth-century *Vorauer Genesis*[9] goes into more detail, telling of seventy-two lords building the tower and provoking the wrath of God by carving their names into the "stame" (base columns?) of the tower. Then

> eines nahtes gescah. daz ir neheiner ne wesse waz der andere sprah. si gingen von deme turne. mit micheleme zorne. zvo unde sibenzec zungen gab er in do. inoh stat dev werlt so. (p. 15, printed as rhymed prose)

> [One night it happened that none of them knew what the other was saying. They departed from the tower with great quarreling. Two and seventy tongues He gave them at that time. The world is still that way.]

Similarly the Dutch *Rymbybel* of Maerlant (thirteenth century), after enumerating the offspring of the sons of Noah, continues:

> Van desen volke es ontsprongen
> Twe en seventich manieren van tonghen.[10]

> [From these people there arose
> two and seventy kinds of tongues.]

The ambitious *Weltchronik*[11] of Rudolf von Ems (d. 1254) tells us that the fabulous tower had been raised to a height of 5974 paces and that it had seventy-two corners to correspond to the number of tribes then existing in the world,

> wan der geslehte nah der zal
> alse vil was ubir al,
> alse ih hie vor gesprochin han. (1282-1284)

> [Rather there were many peoples
> and they were everywhere
> as I have mentioned previously.]

Of these, he tells us in the next lines, fifteen were derived from Japheth, twenty-seven from Shem, and thirty from Cham, which makes seventy-two in all. As they were at work on their project God confused their language, with the result that

[9] *Deutsche Gedichte des XI. und XII. Jahrhunderts*, ed. Joseph Diemer (Vienna, 1849).

[10] As quoted by R. Michel, "Zweiundsiebenzig Völker," *Beiträge zur Geschichte der deutschen Sprache und Literatur*, xv (1891), 377.

[11] *Deutsche Texte des Mittelalters*, xx, ed. Gustav Ehrismann (Berlin, 1915).

iegelichim geslehte bleip
sin sunder sprache, die ez treip
und vorstûnt des andern nicht. (1322-1324)

[To every tribe remained
its special language, which it used
and none understood the other's.]

The story grows under the hands of a later chronicler, Jansen Enikel,[12] who wrote about 1280. According to Jansen, the designer of the Tower—his name was Babel—employed seventy-two master masons. When the Tower had reached a height of 5074 cubits God confused their language, so that a foreman calling for mortar was handed stone, etc. Now each spoke a different language. One spoke Hungarian, another Russian, a third Bohemian, a fourth German, a fifth Greek, and a sixth Heathen. It grieves him to think, Jansen comments, that God allotted only twelve languages to Christendom and that all the other sixty should be doomed to perdition. This speculation no doubt represents an inexact reminiscence from *Willehalm*. Wolfram, we remember, had used the figure twelve merely as an upper limit to approximate the relative numbers of Christian and pagan nations. Those fluid proportions have now crystallized into exact figures.

One more of these old biblical paraphrases deserves special attention. It is found in the eleventh-century *Annolied*,[13] a poem justly celebrated for its passages of great rhythmic power. Semiramis, it tells us, wife of King Ninus, founded ancient Babylon from old tiles that the giants had baked when great Nimrod foolishly counseled them to build a tower in sinful pride reaching from the earth up to the heavens. From there God drove them back, when with his power he made a manifold division of them into seventy languages. Thus is the world still constituted.

Sîn wîf diu hîz Semiramis.	[His wife was called Semiramis.
die alten Babilonie stiphti si	She erected old Babylon
van cîgelin den alten,	from the old tiles
die die gigandi branten,	which the giants baked,
duo Nimbrot der michilo	when Nimrod the great
gerîht un dumplîcho,	advised them foolishly
daz si widir godis vorhtin	that not fearing God

[12] *Jansen Enikels Werke*, ed. Philip Strauch, Pt. 1, *Die Weltchronik*, in *Mon. Germ. Hist.*, Deutsche Chroniken, III, 1 (Hannover, 1891). See verses 3245-3398.
[13] Max Roediger's edition in the pertinent section of *Mon. Germ. Hist.*, I, II (Hannover, 1895).

einen turn worhtin	they erect a tower
van erdin ûf ce himele.	from earth to heaven.
des dreif si got widere,	God drove them away from it,
duo her mit sînir gewalt	then with his power
gedeilti si sô manigvalt	divided them thus numerously
in zungin sibenzoch;	into seventy tongues;
sô steit iz in der werlti noch.	thus it is even yet in the world.]
(153-166)	

The figure seventy instead of seventy-two is a departure from the number hitherto encountered. It is an interesting variant that will be touched upon later.

The tradition of a fixed number of languages is not confined to German literature. Without doubt instances similar to those we have mustered could be supplied by students of Old French and Old English literature. An Old French instance is supplied, in fact, by the *Roman de Thèbes*, where a marvelous tent is described as decorated to show the five zones of the earth and their seventy-two languages (ed. Leopold Constans, Paris, 1890, lines 3979-4068, and specifically 4009 f.). A few years ago print shops displayed a British Museum color reproduction of a miniature in a Book of Hours, executed in France for John, Duke of Bedford, about the year 1423. The miniature is a charming illustration of the legend of the Tower of Babel, and the Old French text below the picture, put into English, reads: "How the tower of Babylon was built. And language was altered into seventy-two languages. And the angels broke it [the Tower] to pieces." This confirms the tradition for France. As for England, I recall only a passage from Shakespeare's *King Henry VI: Part I*, act IV, scene 7, a reference to

> The Turk, that two and fifty kingdoms hath.

If the Turk's fifty-two kingdoms are a catchall here for the non-Christian world as a whole, may we not assume that Shakespeare's source thought of an additional twenty kingdoms as professing the Christian faith, to round out the number? That would make the case very similar to that of *Willehalm*, where Wolfram, starting with a total of seventy-two kingdoms, subtracts some twelve as Christian, leaving the remainder to represent the heathen world.

The existence of the tradition having been sufficiently established, the question arises: Where and how did it originate?

So far as there can be an answer, it must be sought in the twilight zone of early Oriental civilization. It seems that the idea of the seventy-two nations can be traced all the way to ancient Egypt. A very learned French Calvinist theologian, Samuel Bochart (1599-1667), pursues our question in his great treatise on sacred geography, *Geographia Sacra seu Phaleg et Canaan*, completed in 1646,[14] and notes that a certain pictograph of Egyptian hieroglyphic writing, the cynocephalus, points to this conclusion. The cynocephalus is a fabulous animal that dies piecemeal over a period of seventy-two days. This idiosyncrasy renders it a fitting symbol for the sum total of the seventy-two inhabited portions of the earth's surface. From Horus Apollo's (i.e., Horapollo's) *Book on the Hieroglyphics*,[15] which the seventeenth century regarded as an authoritative source, Bochart quotes the pertinent Greek passage and then renders it in Latin, according to his custom. In English it reads as follows:

> To designate [in their writing] the orbis terrarum [the concept of the earth as a whole] they [the Egyptian priests] draw [the outline of] a cynocephalus, because they say that the world has numbered seventy-two inhabited divisions from of old. For the cynocephali, when nurtured in the temples with care, do not die on one day the same as do other animals: Rather a certain part of the animal dying each day, is embalmed by the priests, while the rest of the animal continues to perform its functions until seventy-two days are completed; only then does the animal die entirely. (col. 54-55)

Whatever its ultimate origin may have been,[16] the tradition of the seventy-two languages and nations is found as a well-established conception in the early Christian church and reflects notions current in pre-Christian Jewry. As a matter of fact, Jewish tradition leans to the number seventy and has the numbers seventy-one, seventy-two, and seventy-three as variants of the idea. We remark

[14] In Vol. I of Samuelis Bocharti, *Opera Omnia, hoc est Phaleg, Canaan, et Hierozoicon*, Editio Tertia, Lugduni Batavorum (1692). Folio. I owe my knowledge of this remote source to Wilmanns' excellent study, "Über das Annolied," published as No. 2 of the author's *Beiträge zur Geschichte der älteren deutschen Literatur* (Bonn, 1886). See esp. pp. 15ff.

[15] A convenient edition of this famous work, including an English translation, was published by Alexander Turner Cory, *The Hieroglyphics of Horapollo Nilous* (London, 1840).

[16] Hugo Winckler is authority for deriving the significant numbers seventy and seventy-two from the Babylonian calendar, which knew an archaic (astrological) division of both the lunar year (350 days) and the solar year (360 days) into seventy and seventy-two five-day weeks respectively. See *Ex Oriente Lux*, II, 92 (1906). Heinrich Marzell believes the tradition radiated from India. See "Die Zahl 72 in der sympathetischen Medizin," *Zeitschrift des Vereins für Völkerkunde*, XXIII (1913), 71.

upon this only in passing because we are interested in following up the main current of the tradition as it developed in the Middle Ages, and a discussion of variants might get us hopelessly entangled in a web of numerological detail. The fact that variants exist, however, is almost as important as the notion that languages and nations were constituted as a definite number. It shows that ingenious reasoning and a fertile imagination concentrated upon solving what agitated the mind as a very real problem. Thus the existence of variants in itself bears testimony to the vitality of the tradition.[17]

As for the early Christian church, the learned Bochart quotes chapter and verse from several of the Greek fathers in support of the tradition. Saint Clement (of Alexandria, 150-220), Saint Eusebius (of Caesarea, 260?-340?), and Saint Epiphanius (of Constantia, 315?-403) all voice the identical belief. Apocryphal revelations of the Eastern church, such as the Syrian *Cave of Treasures*[18] and the Ethiopian *Book of Adam*,[19] also confirm the same basic idea. Thus the *Cave of Treasures* concludes its narrative of the Tower and the dispersion with the statement: "And there were upon the earth seventy-two languages and seventy-two tribal heads" (p. 30)—this despite the fact that the genealogical tables of this book differ sharply from those of Genesis 10. In some way, as we perceive, the tradition is always linked to the genealogies after the Flood.

But there is definite evidence showing our tradition as already crystallized in the pre-Christian era. The legend current a century before Christ concerning the origin of the Septuagint points in this direction.[20] According to the letter of Aristeas, purporting to have been written in the third century but placed by scholars at around 100 B.C., King Ptolemy Philadelphus (285-246 B.C.) requested the

[17] For a scholarly account of Jewish tradition regarding these numbers see M. Steinschneider, "Die kanonische Zahl der muhammedanischen Sekten und die Symbolik der Zahl 70-73, aus jüdischen und muhammedanisch-arabischen Quellen nachgewiesen," *Zeitschrift der Deutschen Morgenländischen Gesellschaft*, IV (1850), 145-170.

[18] *Die Schatzhöhle*. Aus dem syrischen Text dreier unedierten Handschriften ins Deutsche übersetzt . . . by Carl Bezold (Leipzig, 1883). Alfred Götze, assigning its composition to the middle of the fourth century A.D., says it is based on second- and third-century sources. See A. Götze, "Die Schatzhöhle. Überlieferung und Quellen," *Sitzungsberichte der Heidelberger Akademie*, XIII (1922), 91.

[19] August Dillmann, trans., *Das christliche Adambuch des Morgenlandes. Aus dem Äthiopischen mit Bemerkungen* (Göttingen, 1853). Cf. pp. 116-117.

[20] See the article "Septuaginta" in the Catholic *Lexikon für Theologie und Kirche* (Freiburg i. B., 1931), II, 298ff.

High Priest Eleazar in Jerusalem to send to his court at Alexandria a number of learned men for the purpose of translating the sacred books of the Hebrews into Greek. The High Priest is said to have sent seventy-two, from which number the translation derived its name. (The short form Septuagint, instead of Septuaginta Duo, came into use as a matter of convenience.) It can hardly be doubted that legend selected this number of translators in order to support the conception that the law originally given to the Jews only was to become the rule of life for all races of men. Philo Judaeus and some of the Church Fathers later embroidered upon the legend in a way that gives further point to this meaning. They tell us that King Ptolemy, fearing that the scribes might act in collusion to keep him from obtaining knowledge of some of their sacred arcana, isolated the seventy-two translators in as many different cells and assigned the total work of translation to each. When the seventy-two had finished the task and their work was compared, the translations were found to be identical throughout, and this proved, as everyone will admit, that divine inspiration must have guided the translators.

The New Testament itself shows the influence of our tradition by reporting the mission of Christ's seventy-two disciples. Having dwelt upon the selection of the twelve apostles in chapter 6:13, the Gospel according to St. Luke speaks of the larger group at the opening of the tenth chapter: "After these things the Lord appointed other seventy-two also, and sent them two and two before his face into every city and place, whither he himself would come."[21] Most of us think of only twelve disciples in connection with Christ; but when the Anabaptists in 1524 set out to found the City of God in Saxon Zwickau their prophet, Nicolaus Storch, surrounded himself with twelve apostles and seventy-two disciples in analogy to Christ.[22] Even the most recent German New Testament interpretation[23] says that Christ in selecting this number to send out before him was

[21] The King James version as well as Luther's translation has the variant reading "seventy." But the reading "seventy-two" was that of the Greek text that became the basis of the Vulgate; the Coptic (Sahidic) version also follows the same source.

[22] W. Zimmermann, *Allgemeine Geschichte des deutschen Bauernkrieges* (Stuttgart, 1841-1843), II, 59.

[23] *Das Neue Testament Deutsch*, I, II (Göttingen, 1937), 117. This work adheres to the Protestant reading "seventy" and believes the number to refer to the sum of non-Jewish people, leading to a grand total of seventy-one nations, a variant of the basic figure seventy which in turn alternates with seventy-two.

probably guided by the then current notion concerning the number of existing nations.[24]

Other biblical passages were adduced and ingeniously combined by the Greek and Roman Church Fathers to give circumstantial support to the thesis. After long disputes over divergent theories it remained for Saint Augustine to subject the whole problem to a lucid and exhaustive inquiry and to settle the issue once and for all.

Saint Augustine, Bishop of Hippo Regius (354-430), was not only one of the most commanding figures of the Latin Church, a scholar of vast learning, as keen a thinker as any the Church has produced, an unmatched master of argument, a brilliant stylist, a vivid and dynamic personality. He stands out in addition as the master mind that charted the course of thought for a long chain of centuries to follow. Saint Augustine is the strategically located powerhouse, as it were, that supplied current to a vast number of subsidiaries. Nineteenth-century students of the vernacular literatures of the Middle Ages seem in many cases to have been completely unaware of Saint Augustine's role as fountainhead of the ideas they were intent upon tracing.[25] A more recent generation of scholars has done much to correct this oversight.[26]

In his great doctrinal treatise *De Civitate Dei* Saint Augustine takes up our problem. We find it in Book XVI, which deals chiefly with questions of scriptural interpretation from the end of the Flood down to Moses but which also finds room to inquire into the authenticity of the monsters of the Far East (Chap. VIII) and to air the claims concerning the existence of a race of antipodes on the

[24] For medieval testimony to the same effect see note 36.

[25] Thus Karl Goedeke's note of 35 pages on the Ages of Man, in his edition of Pamphilus Gengenbach's writings (Hannover, 1856), pp. 559-593, presents a wealth of information on the division of the world's history into epochs, as viewed by the Middle Ages, without mentioning Saint Augustine. Wilhelm Wackernagel's treatise, "Über den Ursprung und die Entwicklung der Sprache," *Kleinere Schriften*, III (Leipzig, 1866), touches upon the German tradition of the seventy-two languages and lists a considerable number of passages, but the author is obviously unaware of the Latin sources of the tradition in general and of Saint Augustine in particular. Ignaz V. Zingerle's "Eine Geographie aus dem 13. Jahrhundert," *Wiener Sitzungsberichte*, L (1865), 371-448, also enumerates many instances of the tradition of seventy-two languages, but he has recourse to the old German duodecimal system to explain the popularity of this number. R. Michel (see note 10) also knows nothing of Augustine and the Latin tradition.

[26] Gustav Ehrismann's *Geschichte der deutschen Literatur bis zum Ausgang des Mittelalters*, final volume (Munich, 1935), bears most impressive witness in innumerable instances to this change of focus.

under side of the earth (Chap. IX). Chapters III, VI, and XI discuss the problem of the number of nations and languages. Saint Augustine takes the genealogy of the descendants of the three sons of Noah as reported in Genesis 10 as his text. He makes the fundamental observation that the names recorded in that genealogy do not signify individuals but tribal units. This must be the meaning, he says, in view of the fact that the tables are manifestly incomplete. For when the first table enumerates eight sons of Japheth but lists further offspring from only two, this cannot be taken to mean that the other six died without issue; it must mean, rather, that the other six did not in their turn lead to any further tribal branching.[27] In this way, on the basis of eight tribes stemming directly from Japheth, plus three additional tribes listed as branching from one of these, and four more as branching from another, Saint Augustine arrives at a total of fifteen tribes of the race of Japheth. In the same manner the record speaks of four tribes as stemming directly from Cham which subsequently produce twenty-four additional tribes, and from two of these in turn three more tribal offshoots develop, making a total of thirty-one tribes for Cham. Similarly Shem is credited with fathering six tribes of the first order, plus five of the second, plus one of the third, plus one of the fourth, plus two of the fifth, plus twelve of the sixth order, making a total of twenty-seven tribes for Shem. To us this way of figuring must at first seem a highly questionable procedure, accustomed as we are to think of tribes as originating by a process of division. On that basis, when a parent tribe divides into three, the result is three tribes and not four. Saint Augustine, on the other hand, in designing *his* genealogical tree and computing the total number of points, seems to count not only the shoots at the end, but also the twigs that lead to them and the branches and the big limbs as well, all the way down to where the parent trunk divides!

It is clear that we must discard the image of the genealogical tree if Saint Augustine's computation is to make sense. He obviously had in mind a system of tribal formation other than that of division; for his parent tribes persist as distinct entities while at the same time they throw off subsidiary units which in their turn may repeat the process. We can understand this if we think of it in terms of a mother city that has grown to a point where it can no longer harbor

---

[27] *De Civitate Dei*, in *Patrologia Latina*, ed. J. P. Migne, XLI, col. 481.

its teeming offspring. Then it sends forth colonizing contingents after the manner of the Roman *Ver Sacrum*. Each contingent founds a city of its own while the mother city continues to flourish, and some of the daughter cities may again in due course of time become mother cities. For this conception, of course, we need spaces to fill as well as time to elapse. The process can be visualized only as a succession of tribal crystallizations occurring in multiple localities. But here is a dilemma: The myth of the Tower clearly negates both space and time in so far as it conceives of the whole complex tribal set-up as crystallizing at one point of time and in one locality. To combine Saint Augustine's computation with the myth of the Tower thus amounts to squaring the circle and requires an act of faith, a fact that Saint Augustine would have been the first to concede.

As we count up our grand total a surprise awaits us. Fifteen tribes of Japheth plus thirty-one of Cham plus twenty-seven of Shem add up to seventy-three. But according to the dominant Christian tradition seventy-two is the number wanted, and seventy-two is the number that Saint Augustine is determined to arrive at. How does he do it?

To put a long and intricate matter very briefly, there is in the list of names that make up the genealogy of Shem one Phalech (Phaleg, Peleg), a son of the pious Heber, in whose tribe the original language persisted and from whom it derives its name. Phalech, Genesis tells us, means division, and the name was given to commemorate the division of mankind into a multitude of nations. Because of the meaning attached to this name, it is clear, Saint Augustine argues, that Phalech does not signify a tribe, as do all the other names of the genealogy, but an individual—a son who was born to Heber right at the time of the dispersion. This Phalech, who is in the direct line of Heber leading to Abraham (Genesis 11), founded no tribe of his own and continued to speak his father's language. Hence the name of Phalech must be stricken from the list in order to arrive at the correct total of nations and languages.

We can be sure that Saint Augustine derived no mean degree of satisfaction from his lucid handling of the vexing problem. He took numerology seriously; it was an important element of his allegorical interpretation of Scripture. Why did God take six days to create the world? he asks in one place. Because six is the perfect number, since the prime numbers of which it is composed by addition (1, 2, and 3) are also its factors.[28]

There is one serious catch in Saint Augustine's ingenious reasoning designed to eliminate Phalech as a tribal name. It stands and falls with the chronology of the "begats" as given in that version of the Bible which the Latin Church used during the first centuries—the Vetus Latina or Itala. According to its text, Genesis 11:16, Heber was 134 years old when his son Phalech was born, whose name commemorates the dispersion. This age of Heber at the time of the dispersion could—by stretching things a little—be reconciled with the fact that thirteen of his offspring had teemed to the extent of being themselves listed as tribal heads. The revised Bible text, however, known as the Vulgate (which began to supersede the Itala in Saint Augustine's own day), follows a reading that cuts one hundred years off the ages of the patriarchs at the time of the "begats," giving Heber only thirty-four years when Phalech was born. But as a man of thirty-four Heber could not possibly have been the patriarchal head of thirteen subsidiary clans, such as we find him at the time of the dispersion. How then can Phalech's birth have been coupled with that event?

If we cannot solve this dilemma, the Church was more fortunate. Presumably following rabbinical precedent,[29] it reasoned: Genesis does not say that Phalech was born at the time of the dispersion. He was indeed born long enough before that event for his brothers and nephews to have multiplied and formed clans of their own by that time. If, nevertheless, his father bestowed upon the infant a name designed to commemorate an event that had not yet come to pass, he must have done so by virtue of prophetic power. Thus Hrabanus Maurus (776?-856), Bishop of Fulda, elevates Heber to the rank of prophet.[30]

With the fall of the Roman Empire the great epoch of patristic learning comes to an end. For many centuries to come the chief

[28] *De Civitate Dei*, col. 343-344.

[29] The *Midrasch Bereschit Rabba*, translated into German by August Wünsche (Leipzig, 1881), makes this statement: "Eber war ein grosser Prophet, dass er seinen Sohn nach einem (später eingetroffenen) Ereignis nannte, nämlich Peleg" (p. 167). [Heber was a great prophet in that he named his son after an event (which happened later), namely Phalech.]

[30] In his commentary on Genesis, in *Patrologia Latina*, CVII, col. 529. I do not know whether this is Hrabanus' own contribution. It seems much more likely that it was handed down to him.

business of scholars is now the compiling of data gleaned from the works of the Fathers. Compendia and encyclopedias are written which present systematic summaries of knowledge. Many of these carry an item about the seventy-two nations and languages.

One of the earliest and most influential of these compilers was Bishop Isidore of Seville (d. 633). In Book IX, Chap. 2, par. 2 of his encyclopedia, known as the *Twenty Books of Etymologies*,[31] we read:

> Gentes autem a quibus divisa est terra, LXXIII: Quindecim de Japhet, triginta et una de Cham, viginti septem de Sem, quae fiunt septuaginta tres vel potius, ut ratio declarat, LXX duae, totidemque linguae per terras esse coeperunt; quae crescendo provincias et insulas impleverunt.

The Latin is barbarous and not without a certain ambiguity. The nations by whom the earth was parceled out numbered seventy-three, fifteen from the tribe of Japheth, thirty-one from Cham, and twenty-seven from Shem, making a total of seventy-three. But this figure should be reduced to seventy-two on the basis of rational considerations. A corresponding number of languages began to be spoken, and by increasing the nations and the languages filled the lands and the islands.

Hrabanus, writing two hundred years later, incorporates the paragraph verbatim (except for the word "autem") in his book *On the Universe*,[32] this despite the fact that his *Commentary on Genesis*, mentioned above, uses a revised set of figures from the Vulgate (Japheth 15, Cham 30, Shem 27), which also add up to seventy-two.[33]

A very influential group of books of knowledge has come down to us under the name of Honorius of Autun. They date from about the first quarter of the twelfth century. One of these, the *Imago Mundi*, treats of the physical world, notably its geographical aspect, and among other valuable information it tells us that Phaleg lived 230 years. In his lifetime, languages were divided into seventy-two: "Phaleg vixit ducentos triginta annos. Hujus tempore divisae sunt linguae in septuaginta duas."[34]

The third quarter of the twelfth century produced a much-used compendium of historical knowledge in the *Historia Scholastica* of

---

[31] *Libri Etymologiarum*, XX, in *Patrologia Latina*, LXXXII, col. 328.
[32] *De Universo* (XVI, 2), in *Patrologia Latina*, CXI, col. 437.
[33] *Ibid.*, CVII, col. 526. [34] *Patrologia Latina*, CLXXII, col. 166.

Petrus Comestor (d. 1178). This repeats the statement that seventy-two nations have sprung from the sons of Noah, and that the fifteen deriving from Japheth populated Europe, while the thirty from Cham spread over Africa, leaving the twenty-six from Shem to take over Asia. This compiler quotes Alcuin, the theological adviser of Charlemagne, as his source.[35]

These examples from writings of the seventh, ninth, and twelfth centuries could without question be matched by a great many more.[36] But they amply suffice to show that the Latin learning of the Middle Ages carried the notion of the seventy-two nations and languages from the Church Fathers down through the ages in an unbroken stream of tradition.

This brings us back to our starting point, the numerous references to the seventy-two languages in the German literature of the Middle Ages. It has become abundantly clear that no indigenous Germanic tradition is involved. The vernacular literature is fed by the general stream of sacred tradition.

Now let us pause to see how the use of this tradition reflects the specific temper of the Middle Ages. To do this we must return to Saint Augustine for a moment. He had supplemented his examination of the problem by the following statement:

> Ex illis igitur tribus hominibus, Noe filiis, septuaginta tres, vel potius, ut ratio declaratura est, septuaginta duae gentes totidemque linguae per terras esse coeperunt, quae crescendo et insulas impleverunt. Auctus est autem numerus gentium multo amplius quam linguarum. Nam et in Africa barbaras gentes in una lingua plurimas novimus.[37]

> (Thus from these three men, sons of Noah, seventy-three, or rather, as will be explained, seventy-two nations and as many languages began to

[35] *Patrologia Latina*, cxcviii, col. 1087. Cf. also col. 1089.

[36] Another passage of particular interest is found in Bede's (d. 735) *Commentaries to the Pentateuch*, in *Patrologia Latina*, xci, col. 228: "De Japhet nati sunt filii xv, de Cham xxx, de Sem xxvii: simul lxxii, de quibus ortae sunt gentes lxxii: inter quas misit Dominus discipulos lxxii." [To Japheth were born fifteen sons, to Cham thirty, to Shem twenty-seven, making seventy-two, from which are derived seventy-two nations: the Lord sent seventy-two disciples among them.] Interesting also because of the discrepancy of its figures is the *Chronicle* of Ado of Vienne (b. about 800), which states (*Patrologia Latina*, cxxiii, col. 27): "Fuerunt autem Noe filii tres, Sem, Cham et Japhet, ex quibus septuaginta duae linguae sunt, id est de Sem viginti octo; de Cham, triginta; de Japhet, quindecim." [To Noah were born three sons, Shem, Cham, and Japheth, from whom derive the seventy-two languages, that is, twenty-eight from Shem, thirty from Cham, and fifteen from Japheth.]

[37] *De Civitate Dei*, Bk. xvi, Chap. vi. The wording of Isidore quoted above shows this passage from the *Civitas Dei* to have been his immediate source, unless it was copied verbatim by an intermediary.

exist throughout the lands and by increasing filled also the islands. The number of nations, however, [subsequently] increased to a much greater degree than the number of languages. For [here] in Africa, for example, we know of a number of barbarous nations who speak only one language.)

It is clear from this statement that Saint Augustine regards the dispersion of the builders of the Tower into seventy-two nations and languages as only the starting point of a process of further division that has continued throughout the course of history. But what does this statement wear down to in the Middle Ages? The German paraphrases of Genesis quoted above say that the world was divided into seventy-two nations and adds with emphasis: Even to this day the world is thus constituted. And Wolfram, too, enunciates the dogmatic statement: There are seventy-two languages and nations in the world, once and for all.

Does this not tellingly demonstrate the static character of the medieval world? Things are ordained in a way that will last to the end of time. The world is not in flux, it is fixed securely. The prophet Daniel enunciated his vision of four world empires that span the whole of history—the Babylonian Empire, the Assyrian, the Medo-Persian, and the Roman. The Roman Empire is foreordained to last to the end of time. Thus, although Rome collapsed, the Middle Ages were blocked by this scheme from seeing their epoch as a new development, qualitatively distinct from the classical age. Regardless of the actual European scene, all existing governments and nations had to be viewed as members of the colossus, which, though broken, continued and would continue to exist until doomsday.[38]

Since the numerological tradition stemming from Genesis was so firmly established in the Middle Ages, it is to be expected that its appeal to the fancy would draw other matters into its orbit. The Jewish imagination luxuriates in working out significant aspects of our number and its variant seventy,[39] and most of us are on sufficient speaking terms with the Mohammedan world to remember the two and seventy sects of Omar's quatrain.[40] A case that fairly cries

[38] Cf. Walther Rehm, *Der Untergang Roms im abendländischen Denken. Ein Beitrag zur Geschichtsschreibung und zum Dekadenzproblem.* "Das Erbe der Alten," Zweite Reihe, Heft 18 (Leipzig, 1930), pp. 27-28.
[39] Cf. Steinschneider (see note 17).
[40] The Grape that can with Logic absolute
The Two-and-Seventy jarring Sects confute:
(quatrain LIX, Edward Fitzgerald's translation)

for identification with our tradition is the Pentecostal miracle. When the Holy Ghost descended upon the band of Christian worshipers on that first Pentecostal morning, making the inspired speak the great tidings in a multitude of tongues that they had never learned, would not perfection require that all the seventy-two languages of the world had been heard on that occasion? Up to the present I have not come across any instance of such a version, but it is a fair expectation that one may turn up. (This conjecture is amply confirmed as regards the early Greek church by findings subsequent to the first publication of this paper.) The record of the Middle Ages does, however, contain a considerable number of cases showing the proliferation of our number into other spheres. Thus the legend about the seamless garment of Christ does not content itself with introducing the pilgrim Trougemund who knew seventy-two lands. It has the Jewish owner of the garment sail a distance of seventy-two leagues out upon the sea before he casts it into the water, and Prince Orendel, who is destined finally to bring it home to Trier, sets out with seventy-two sails to court a far-away princess.[41] A considerable number of instances that show no evident relation to sacred tradition are listed by Zingerle.[42]

A definitely related offshoot, on the other hand, is the tradition of the seventy-two names of God. Uhland's *Volkslieder* contains a fourteenth-century song entitled "Sanct Johanns Minne."[43] This sings the praise of the Evangelist and repeatedly implores divine grace in the name of Christ and the seventy-two names of the almighty God.

> bewar und beschirme uns also
> vor schaden der uns mag geschehen
> daz wir dir lobes müssen jehen
> in dem namen der da ist:
> süsser vatter Jesu Crist,
> und in den zwen und sibenzig namen
> des almahtigen godes, amen. (p. 816)

[41] *Op. cit.*, verses 87-88; 241-242, etc.

[42] *Op. cit.*, p. 423. Cf. also W. Knopf, *Zur Geschichte der typischen Zahlen in der Literatur des Mittelalters* (diss., Leipzig, 1902). Further instances of both sacred and profane use are to be found in Reinhold Köhler's "Zwei und vierzig alte Rätsel und Fragen" (1856), in *Kleinere Schriften*, III (Berlin, 1900), 449f.; see esp. 509f. A note by E. Hofmann-Krayer, "Die Zahl 72" in *Zeitschrift des Vereins für Volkskunde*, XXIII (1913), 190, refers to additional literature on the subject.

[43] *Op. cit.*, pp. 814f.

[Preserve and protect us therefore
from misfortunes that may assail us
as we praise thee
in the name of Him Who is there:
sweet Father, Jesus Christ,
and in the two and seventy names
of Almighty God, amen.]

There is good reason to suspect that this notion marks an infiltration of mystical Jewish learning into the medieval Church. The seventy-two names of God were one of the secrets taught by the *Kabbala*, and this was not the least of the attractions that induced the famous German humanist Reuchlin, contemporary of Erasmus and Luther, to take up the study of Hebrew and associate with the Jews. Reuchlin not only obtained the key to the mystical arcana himself, but he taught his friend Laurenz Behaim to deduce the seventy-two unutterable names of God from a single verse of a chapter of Exodus.[44]

This last item has brought us down to the age of Humanism and discovery, an age of fresh intellectual currents that broke up the unity of the medieval Church and dissolved much of the substance of its hallowed traditions into thin air. We are prompted, therefore, in concluding our survey, to ask the question: How long did the tradition of the seventy-two nations and languages survive?

I have not found any reference to it in the writings of Luther; his Latin commentary on Genesis, where one would expect to find it in connection with the account of the Tower of Babel, does not mention it. But Sebastian Franck's *Chronicle of the World*,[45] which appeared thirty-nine years after the discovery of America, is still entirely governed in its outlook by medieval conceptions and retails a great deal of fabulous lore as authentic history. Thus Sebastian Franck divides the span of history from Creation to Judgment Day into six epochs, corresponding to the six days of creation (a scheme inaugurated by Saint Augustine), and the first of these epochs extends from Adam to Noah. Concerning the second period, which includes the dispersion, he writes:

> Das X. Cap. im erstē bůch Mose zeigt an den stam̃ uñ nachkommen Noe aus seinē som̃en / uñ dz Capitel ist voller geheymnus uñ geet fast die gantz schrifft daraus võ mancherley geschlechten uñ zungē. (page x, right)

44 David Friedrich Strauss, *Ulrich von Hutten* (Leipzig, 1858), I, 191.
45 *Chronica zeÿtbůch vnd geschÿchtbibel* . . . (Strassburg, 1531).

(The tenth chapter in the first book of Moses sets forth the stem and descendants of Noah from his seed; and this chapter is full of mystery, and almost the whole body of writing about the sundry nations and tongues is derived from it.)

After touching upon the first kings, Nimrod and Assur, he continues:

. . . ja aus dem geschlecht Noah uñ seinen sünen Sem / Cham / uñ Japhet / sein die Philistei / Jebusei / Ethei / Amorrei / ja lxxij geschlecht herkumen. . . . (ibid.)

(. . . indeed from the tribe of Noah and his sons, Sem, Cham, and Japhet have sprung the Philistines, Jebusites, Hittites, Amorites, in fact seventy-two nations.)

While he does not expressly say that they make up the sum total of mankind, this must be inferred from the story of the Flood. On the matter of language he tells us that at first only the Hebrew language existed. This was preserved in the house of Phaleg and Heber after the dispersion.

For very late surviving traces of our tradition let us finally take one brief glimpse at a famous seventeenth-century narrative, the *Simplicissimus* of Grimmelshausen. At one point of his career the hero meets a philosopher who has many sound ideas. Among other things he wants to bestow universal peace upon the world and a single religion. In pursuance of this aim he plans to call together the theologians of the world and assign a place of deliberation to them, as Ptolemaeus Philadelphus did to the seventy-two interpreters: "Alsdann wird er die . . . Theologos . . . zusammenbringen und ihnen einen Ort, wie vor diesem Ptolomäus Philadelphus den zwei und siebzig Dolmetschen getan, . . . zurichten lassen."[46] There is only one trouble with this wise philosopher. He is insane and fancies he is the God Jupiter!

At a later point of the narrative the hero, who is inclined to tell tall stories, gives us an account of how he descended to the center of the earth via a mysterious lake, the Mummelsee of the Black Forest. For Grimmelshausen, needless to say, the earth is no longer a pancake, but a sphere. Having arrived at the exact center of the earth, he finds it peopled by a very courteous and accomplished race of men who communicate with all points of the earth's surface. Instead of a distinctive garb of their own they wear the national costumes of all the races of men. Thus to Simplicissimus they look like

---

[46] I quote from the edition of the Inselverlag, edited by Reinhold Buchwald (Leipzig: no date), p. 258.

Peruvians, Brazilians, Mexicans, Japanese, Hindus, and islanders from the Ladrones. To his astonishment, however, they speak an excellent German. When he asks how this can be, his informant explains that it is all very simple. They at the center of the earth speak only one language, but all the nations at various points of the earth's surface understand what they say as if it were spoken in their respective languages. These central folk are endowed with this faculty, according to the informant, because their race was not involved in the folly of the Tower of Babel.[47]

We can be fairly certain that in giving this explanation the informant was pulling our hero's leg. It is very much more plausible to suppose that these ingenious people had utilized their strategic location to invent a transformer that gathered all the varieties of speech from the earth's surface, reducing them to a common denominator, as it were, and which conversely brought about a corresponding dispersion of speech sounds directed from the earth's center to its periphery. It seems reasonable to hope that the perfecting of the microphone will one of these days restore us to possession of the lost invention, saving language teachers a great deal of work and perhaps even rendering their existence superfluous.

[47] Als er auch sahe, dass ich mich über ihn und alle die, so mit ihm waren, verwunderte, dass sie als Peruaner, Brasilianer, Mexicaner, Japaner, Indosianer und Insulaner de los latronos aufgezogen und dannoch so gut teutsch redeten, da sagte er, dass sie nicht mehr als eine Sprache könnten, die aber alle Völker auf dem ganzen Umkreis der Erden in ihrer Sprache verstünden und sie hingegen dieselbe hinwiederum, welches daher kömme, dieweil ihr Geschlecht mit der Torheit, so bei dem babylonischen Turm vorgangen, nichts zu schaffen hätte. (pp. 519-520)

FLAMENCA.
A POST-ARTHURIAN ROMANCE
OF COURTLY LOVE

THIS PAPER, dealing with the Provençal romance known as *Flamenca*, is undertaken as a postscript to my *Three Chapters on Courtly Love in Arthurian France and Germany* (Chapel Hill, 1956). Its inclusion there in any capacity but that of a postscript would not have been warranted because there is no longer anything Arthurian about the *Flamenca*. The geographical setting is no longer Arthur's mythical realm, which no cartographer can trace, but the real France and Netherlands of the thirteenth century. The characters, though fictional, are associated with family names that are representative of the French high aristocracy. In this story we no longer find the familiar dwarfs, giants, monsters, enchanted castles, or other grossly miraculous elements of Arthurian lore. Instead of a fanciful "quest" the story presents a rational project. And, we might add by anticipation, the lodestar of the Arthurian ideal has completely vanished. But whereas the *Flamenca* is no longer Arthurian, it revolves about Courtly Love. It centers on the development of a conception of Courtly Love that has the poetry of Chrétien and Wolfram and the dialogues of Andreas Capellanus among its logical and temporal antecedents but differs radically in spirit from them all. Because of this the *Flamenca* has been hailed as the first modern novel and as the crowning achievement of the whole literature of Courtly Love. While I would dissociate myself from both these superlative valuations for reasons that will appear, there can be no question but that the *Flamenca* presents an exemplary treatment of a novel conception of Courtly Love. At the same time the *Flamenca* is so integrally derived from the mode of poetic utterance which we associate with the name of Chrétien as to evoke parallels and prompt comparisons at every turn. Thus, while this paper is written as a postscript, I am persuaded that its subject is an indispensable supplement to any study of Courtly Love.

Let me begin with a word of orientation. The *Flamenca* has been

Reprinted from *Euphorion*, LVIII (1964), 129-152, by permission of Carl Winter-Universitätsverlag, Heidelberg.

preserved in a unique manuscript. It is incomplete. An indeterminate number of pages from the beginning and the end of the volume are missing, and an occasional leaf from the body of the book has been lost. But despite these gaps the more than 8,000 verses (rhymed eight-syllable couplets) that have come down to us tell the whole story. The author of the *Flamenca*, not otherwise known to Provençal literature, seems to have named himself in an aside as one "Bernadet" (1732) writing in the service of the seigneur of Alga (1722). The entire text was first published by the French Romanist Paul Meyer in 1865. In 1901 he brought out a second edition of the carefully revised text and glossary (cited parenthetically throughout this essay), but he did not live to make good his promise of a second volume to contain a commentary and a complete translation. Both before and after Paul Meyer's second edition many studies of the *Flamenca* have appeared in scholarly journals. In 1930 a monograph by Charles Grimm succeeded in rather definitely establishing that the work was written between 1272 and 1300, roughly one hundred years after Chrétien flourished. Also in 1930 there appeared an English translation by H. F. M. Prescott. While this is very readable it rather frequently omits—partly through inadvertence, partly through design—groups of lines which are in some cases of great interest to the scholarly reader, and the dots that designate gaps in the manuscript fail to indicate whether a whole leaf is missing or, as is so often the case, just a single line. Apart from slips of minor importance there are a number of serious inaccuracies which would trip up the reader who depends solely upon this translation.[1] Nevertheless it affords invaluable help to a student with so negligible an ad hoc knowledge of Provinçal as mine. I should also mention Charles V. Langlois' well-annotated extensive summary of the *Flamenca* story in the first volume of *La Vie en France au Moyen Âge* (1924, pp. 128-178). Langlois' account is a retelling rather than an analysis. In the interest of presenting a spicy story to a modern public Langlois deletes with a broad pencil, thereby disturbing the proportions and seriously altering the spirit of the original. Much of what he omits altogether or

---

[1] The really serious ones concern the wrong rendering of days of the week, badly confusing the author's meticulously kept calendar that takes note of all the Sundays and feast days from Easter to August. On page 97, for "On Rogation Sunday" read: On the Thursday following Rogation Sunday [Ascension Day]. On page 109, top line, for "Sunday" read: Tuesday; and again on the same page, line 24, for "Sunday" read: Tuesday.

merely touches upon by implication will be pointed up in these pages.[2]

The story of *Flamenca* is considerably longer than the average work of Chrétien de Troyes. As I have said, its introduction and conclusion are missing, and, considering the leisurely manner in which it gets started and winds up, the lost pages closest to the covers as well as a few from the body of the book may have amounted to another one to two thousand lines. The story is filled with vivid and ingenious detail and it sparkles with wit and humor, but its theme is simple. Reduced to basic terms it might be formulated as follows:

A young knight and a young lady take a course in Courtly Love. It is a long and difficult course that puts their intelligence and character to exacting tests. They pass the course with the highest distinction, and the end finds them enrolled in the register of courtly lovers as honor graduates.

Like the theme, the structure of the *Flamenca* is simple. We shall discuss it in terms of six chapters with the following captions:

1. Introduction: The match, followed by two brilliant feasts
2. Jealousy Rampant: The marriage on the rocks
3. Operation Rescue
4. Operation Pleasure
5. Operation Cure
6. Postlude: Polishing the "hornworks"

1. Introduction

Count Gui of Nemurs[3] has a young marriageable daughter, Fla-

[2] Of the numerous scholarly publications on *Flamenca*, the most recent to have come to my notice is *The Romance of Flamenca*, English verse translation by Merton Jerome Hubert, revised Provençal text by Marion E. Porter, published for the University of Cincinnati (Princeton, 1962). The twenty-page introduction includes among other matters an informative annotated account of the variety of attempts to date the writing of the poem and to ascertain the identity of its author. It discusses a number of treatments of the jealousy theme that show a striking similarity to the *Flamenca* story. It dwells in particular on two specific problems that have taxed the ingenuity of specialists in the field of medieval romance studies: 1) Can the events of the story be identified with a specific calendar year of the thirteenth century? 2) Are the many bearers of prominent French noble family names in the poem to be identified with actual historical personages; in other words, is the *Flamenca* story factual or fictional? I refer the specialist to these discussions and to the four-page bibliography at the end of the volume.

[3] Namur in the Low Countries or Nemours southeast of Paris? This question

menca, whose extraordinary beauty makes her hand sought after by kings. But being an affectionate father, rather than send her away to such distant lands as Slavonia or Hungary, he favors the suit of a French nobleman, Count Archimbaut of Bourbon. The terms of settlement agreed upon, the bridegroom, a handsome man of more mature years, an excellent jouster and a practiced and irresistible lover, arrives for the wedding, accompanied by a splendid retinue. The time is Pentecost, and the bride's father and brother have done everything to make this the most brilliant courtly gathering that the world has ever seen ("since Adam's day," 122). We skim over the description of the vast host encamped in gorgeous tents, the pomp and circumstance of the nuptials, and the unparalleled largess of the bride's father—conventional themes in romances of chivalry. As we would expect, the bridegroom loses his heart to the fair Flamenca at once; he spends three sleepless nights consumed by an inner fever before the union is consummated; and as for the bride, she is well pleased by her father's choice.

The wedding-feast has lasted ten days—the bishops and abbots are the last to depart. Meanwhile Archimbaut has resolved to top this feast by a second, even more lavish and extended celebration set for midsummer day (St. John's) to mark the arrival of his bride in Bourbon. Leaving Flamenca, he returns to Bourbon to make preparations on a vast scale and to dispatch his messengers with invitations to every person of note in Poitou, Berry, Bordeaux, Bayonne, and Blaye. But the highest guest to be invited is the king of France, along with the queen, and the invitation to the king is coupled with the request that he favor Archimbaut by taking his way straight through Nemurs and escorting the bride to Bourbon. He gladly complies, and the ensuing festival comes up to expectations in splendor and magnitude. Here the author indulges his fancy for wild exaggeration, the bastard sister of literary hyperbole. We must not blink at his report that the great hall at Bourbon was spacious enough to seat ten thousand knights and ladies with plenty of room for their domestics to serve up an elaborate dinner (496). As for the entertainment that follows, it is enough to make the most seasoned convention fan reel: fifteen hundred

---

cannot be intelligently weighed without a full knowledge of the chain of events reported in the *Flamenca*. I refer the reader to the Excursus at the end of the essay.

performers of all kinds (503-504) simultaneously juggle, tumble, dance, sing, play a great assortment of instruments, and recite all the stories in the repertoire of the medieval minstrel. In pell-mell fashion the author tosses out some eighty proper names linked with classical myth, with Greek and Roman history, with Bible story, with the lore of Charlemagne, with the Knights of the Round Table, and with the Crusades (592-709). To sample this whirl of names that beat upon our ears, I select from the list, without changing their sequence: Priam, Pyramus, Eneas, Dido, Tydeus, Alexander, Hero and Leander, Jason, Narcissus, Pluto, Orpheus, Samson and Delila, [Judas] Maccabeus, Julius Caesar, Gauvain, Lancelot, Perceval, Tristan, Fénice, the Fisher King, the Assassins and the Old Man of the Mountain, Charlemagne, Lucifer, Dedalus and Icarus. But all this catalog of subjects, highly interesting though it is, is but part of the overelaborate introduction to the story that is about to begin.

2. Jealousy Rampant: The marriage on the rocks

The beginning of the festival is keyed to a programmatic note of gaiety, the king decreeing that no guest must pack up and go home before a fortnight of celebrating. But the atmosphere changes, imperceptibly at first, when the queen notices that the king enters the lists with a lady's favor (a sleeve) attached to his lance. Because Flamenca's beauty outshines that of all the other ladies and because the king singles her out for marked attentions, the queen suspects a clandestine understanding between them. She takes the first opportunity to draw Archimbaut aside and infect him with her jealousy. He protests that her suspicions are baseless, as is in fact the case, but the queen's confident prediction that he will change his mind before the celebration has ended comes true: the poison has begun to work and Archimbaut falls prey to doubts and torments of which—the author anticipates—he was not to be cured until the thing he feared had actually come to pass (905-906). While the festival lasts he does his best to conceal his state of mind, but when the king has departed, on the twentieth day, he loses all his self-control.

Now the author, in the course of more than 400 lines, develops the transformation of that happy and solicitous bridegroom into a monster of jealousy, a querulous tormented fool who succumbs to stupor, an unkempt, unwashed scarecrow in appearance, a tyrant, a very devil. The author uses all the conventional devices of characterization and caricature: when Archimbaut rushes about the house and storms into Flamenca's chamber with intent to beat her and cut her long golden tresses, he is frustrated by the sight of her sitting unconcerned and laughing and gossiping with her ladies. He suspects every visitor to the castle of having designs on his lady. Finally he hits upon an idea for guarding her against all possible opportunity of seduction: he shuts her up in his tower with only two young maids over fifteen for companions. He has her food passed to her through a little wicket. He guards her in person. He keeps the key, and he spies upon her. Even at church, where he conducts her only on Sundays and feast days, he has her stand in a recess with a high screen from which she must not move: the priest's ministrant, a boy, has to bring her the psalter to kiss as the "Peace" is bestowed, and he keeps the same close guard over her on the rare occasions when he conducts her to the baths. By now the whole countryside knows of Archimbaut's transformation and countless ditties are sung at his expense. While Flamenca suffers this inhuman treatment the author again anticipates developments by remarking that Lady Love (Amors) will eventually contrive to initiate Flamenca into Her delights, biding Her own time and place (1413-1414). Thus matters drift for a space of two years. The situation has been fully deployed, and the author is almost ready to begin his real story, the story of Flamenca's deliverance, which takes up more than half of his total account. There is one more preliminary, however, still to be mentioned, namely the specific nature of the locale, which turns out to be an indispensable feature of the plot: Bourbon is famed for its hot mineral springs, piped into well-appointed bathing chambers underground, and the finest of these, with an inn attached, are close to Archimbaut's tower and it is these that Flamenca uses when her jailer permits.

3. Operation Rescue (1561-5808)

A rescue calls for a hero. Accordingly we are introduced to a young Burgundian nobleman who qualifies for the part in every conceivable respect. Guillem de Nivers is a very handsome, tall,[4]

---

[4] The "seven feet" of the text (1635) probably come closer to six as measured by our scale.

and well-built youth of seventeen. We need not follow the author's description of him, feature for feature, from top to toe, to believe that he was indeed a match for Paris in beauty, for Ulysses in shrewdness (*sens*), and for Hector in valor (1575-1578). These and other evocative comparisons (Absalom and Solomon, 1572) belong to the medieval romancer's stock in trade. Guillem had great wealth to dispose of and his liberality was unlimited. The subject of largess to entertainers prompts the author to a fine sally of hyperbole: my own master tries to match Guillem in bounty, he says in an aside; I have known him a hundred times a year to give away in a day his annual revenue (1722-1730). Guillem was not only supple and skilled in all the physical accomplishments of his class, such as being able to kick a distance of two feet above his head and snatching a knight out of the saddle in a charge on horseback (1691 ff.); he not only never stooped to the use of such weapons as a club or mace (1695), but his education, in Paris, also embraced the seven liberal arts, which he acquired so well that he could have taught school (1621ff.). In church he read and sang the service better than the clergy (1626-1627). And as for songs and lais and sirventes which he composed in the vernacular, he was so accomplished a poet that even Daniel[5] would have been no match for him (1706-1710).

All this, of course, leads up to his qualifications as a lover. Guillem knows all that there is to know about the theory of love—he has read all the authoritative writers on the subject (1764) and he knows how to charm women by his discourse on love (1682), but as yet he has not had any practical experience. Now, being learned enough to know that a young man cannot carry on very long without getting involved with love (1767) and being what we would call an exemplary conformist, he makes up his mind to engage in a love that will redound to his credit (1770 ff.). He has heard of Flamenca's plight. He has also heard it said for true that she is the best, the most beautiful, and the most *cortesa* woman in the world, and this puts the idea into his heart that he might love her if he could manage to speak with her (1774-1781). At long last we have arrived at the threshold of the real story. The young man has resolved on the basis of rational considerations to engage in a love

---

[5] Daniel Arnaut, probably, whom Dante did the signal honor of having him speak eight lines of Provençal at the end of Canto XXVI of the *Purgatorio*.

affair, and report has indicated to him the worthiest object to focus upon. He has never seen her.[6] On the basis of report alone he fixes his love upon what appears to be an inaccessible object. To succeed in such an undertaking will indeed be a remarkable exploit.

At this point the author begins to make free and extensive use of the allegory of love which had been one of the most characteristic ingredients in the blend of all chivalric romance for more than a hundred years. Lady Love, *Amor* in French and Provençal, *Frou Minne* in German, steals to Guillem's couch and tells him that she has reserved the richest prize for his delight. The most beautiful and desirable woman in the world is in the tower for him to deliver. The mission is his and his alone, because he is both *cavalliers* and *clercs* (1799). Having received his mandate he sets out for Bourbon without losing a moment. That night in his hostel bed, fifteen leagues from his destination, he tosses about in anxiety: will he succeed or will he fail? He thinks of consulting a fortune-teller, but he decides against this "because a hope too sure does not have so sweet a savor as one that is mixed with apprehension" (1839-1841). This reflection, like a great many that are to follow, shows how well he has studied the theory of love. There can be no doubt but that Andreas Capellanus was among his masters. The next morning, as is proper for a pining lover, he departs without breakfasting, but not before stopping in church to address a fervent prayer to *bel senor Deu* (1851) to help him succeed in his mission. An unquestioning conventional piety is one of Guillem's conformist traits, which it might be all too easy to overlook or forget in view of the ensuing intrigue. He prays on many subsequent occasions for aid in his undertaking. On the morning after his arrival in Bourbon he addresses his prayers to Saint Blaze, Saint Martin, Saint George, Saint Geneis (?), and five or six other saints who had been *cavallier cortes* (2119 ff.); and in church that day, all keyed up at the prospect of catching a first glimpse of his beloved, he prays to God, to the Virgin, and to Saint Michael, and he repeats the Pater Noster several times. Then, sensing the signal importance of the occasion, he ends up with a very efficacious prayer taught him by a hermit: it consists of the two and seventy names of God in Hebrew, Latin, and Greek, and it is so powerful

[6] A parallel to Gramoflanz' passion for Itonje in the *Parzival*, except that Itonje is unmarried.

a charm that a true believer who carries a written copy of it on his person cannot come to grief (2272-2290). But to return to the story.

Guillem arrives in Bourbon the next afternoon and as becomes a man of his station he takes lodgings in the best inn of the town, owned by Peire Guizo and his wife Bellapila, and selects a room from which he can gaze on Flamenca's tower. He is accompanied by two young squires to wait on him. In conformity with his design he conceals his name and station. His alleged purpose in journeying to Bourbon is, of course, to take a prolonged cure at the baths for an ailment. He charms the host and hostess by his beauty, his manners, and his lavish liberality.

The day of Guillem's arrival is the Saturday after Easter (2024). This happens to be the 29th of April, as the following Monday is May Day. The reader should be warned that the author kept exact track of his calendar. A great trial of patience is in store for Guillem. All through May, June, and July he works for Flamenca's deliverance. It is not until the second of August that the lovers have their first tryst. Guillem's ultimate success is, of course, never left in doubt. Lady Love herself commissioned him for the task. No matter how much he may pine and tremble in the process, the reader can have no apprehension as to the outcome. There is in this story the tension of expectation only as to the how of the rescue, but the story follows a unilinear course without complications, without setbacks, without surprises. The scheme of the rescue once hit upon, it unfolds with a maximum of deliberateness according to plan. Similarly, in order to render the flavor of this story successfully, our analysis has to proceed step by step, suggesting— if not actually imitating—the slow-motion technique of the rescue strategy.

That Saturday night to the tune of the nightingales Guillem addresses the first of his interminable apostrophes to Lady Love. Some of his later plaints develop into colloquies between himself and the Goddess, or interior dialogue between the heart and the body. Although they are a conventional feature of chivalric romance, witness *Cligès*, they have in the *Flamenca* a functional justification: they really make us sense the snail-crawl passage of time in the long intervals between the lovers' exchange of signals. This first one, eighty-three lines in length (2035-2117), largely revolves around a conceit of great subtlety, a grammatical play on the words *adimans* (adamant) and *amans* (lover). A true lover must be firmer than adamant, he reasons, because *adimans* is composite, while *amans* is simple: take the *di* out of *adimans* and join the pieces and you get *amans*. Further reasoning in favor of the lover as compared to adamant is based on the premise that composite things are more subject to corruption than simples. Again switching from physics and chemistry to grammar, he demonstrates that *adimans* is a corruption of the Latin *adamas*, whereas the word for lover, *amans*, has retained its true vowel. Taking as another premise that the different vowels are graded in a scale of essential values, he asserts that by as much as the vowel *a* is superior to *i*, by so much is the true lover superior to those who only prate about love.

This discourse, which shows how well Guillem has mastered the idiom of Courtly Love, has kept him awake all night. In the morning, having said his prayers, he looks out at the tower, apostrophizes it, and swoons in exhaustion. But Lady Love rewards his zeal by transporting his spirit to his beloved and letting him caress her. If this spiritual pleasure could be shared by both parties it would be as good as the reality, the author remarks (2162-2164). Guillem awakes refreshed and radiant, to find his face wet with the tears shed over it by his squire, who is very much alarmed.

This is Sunday. Guillem has learned that her keeper will be taking Flamenca to mass. Although it is much too early for the service, which is timed to suit the lady's habits of rising, Guillem persuades his host to take him to the church, where he says his prayers, as already reported. As he opens the psalter, the words *dilexi quoniam* strike his eye and he takes them as a good omen. Then, as they walk out, his host tells him of the close guard under which Flamenca is kept even in church and points out to him the recess in which she is made to kneel and stand. After that they enjoy the air and the song of the nightingales in the garden. When it is time for high mass they return to church and take their seats in the choir. Guillem has seen Flamenca enter, heavily veiled, and he keeps his eye fixed on her during the whole service without his forgetting because of this to sing all the responses. The occasion favors him, for when the holy water is sprinkled she lifts her veil a trifle, and a ray of sun lights up her golden hair. When the gospel is read and she rises to her feet to cross herself, he gets a glimpse of her little hand. Finally, when the acolyte, Nicolaus, a boy of fourteen, takes the breviary and carries it to Flamenca for her to kiss and receive the "Peace," he has the good luck to see her rosy lips. Although these successive revelations have put him into a state of mind bordering on delirium, he betrays his agitation by no sign. By a pretext he gets the acolyte to hand him the book that Flamenca has kissed; by another ruse he learns what page it was that touched her lips, and now he covers it with ecstatic kisses. After the service he makes friends with the priest and asks him to be his guest at dinner during the length of his stay in Bourbon.

This great day is followed by a night of momentous happenings. First Guillem again addresses himself to Lady Love, in a speech of 113 lines. He implores her to come to his aid soon, lest he perish. And Lady Love does not fail him. She spirits him to Flamenca in a second vision that takes 160 lines in the telling, and in the course of this vision the lover's transports of emotion crystallize into a plan of action. After the exchange of their mutual vows of love, the Flamenca of the vision tells him what he must do to win her. First of all he must find a way of communicating with her, but while doing so he must also contrive a place for them to meet. How can he communicate with her? She is under such close guard that no man can approach her even for a moment except the priest's ministrant who brings her the holy book to kiss when the "Peace" is bestowed. Guillem must contrive to get the priest to accept him as ministrant in place of the lad Nicolaus. He is trained for the part because he knows the service as well as any clerk. Now, approaching her to bestow the "Peace," he could whisper two syllables in her ear at the moment that she kisses the book, without arousing her keeper's suspicions, provided he is clever enough. On the next occasion, to be sure, he must be all ears in order to catch the two syllables that she will whisper in reply. By this means a communication could eventually be spelled out between them. But that being accomplished, where can they hope to meet? This is where the underground baths come in. Guillem must find a way to have a passage secretly excavated from his room to the bathing chambers. Then, at the proper signal, she can join him there. After this double plan of action has been sketched, Lady Love quickly terminates the vision and Guillem wakes up in a state of desolation at having been snatched from Flamenca's embrace. For the time being the plan of deliverance has been blotted from his memory.

The next day, being the first of May, is another church festival when Flamenca goes to mass. The two special joys that this day has in store for the distraught lover are reported by the author tongue in cheek, I am persuaded. This day in church Guillem sees Flamenca remove her glove from her right hand, and as she bends down to spit [!] he gets a full view of her mouth (3122-3125). The second incident is of his own devising: pointing out the passage to be touched by the lady's lips in the bestowing of the "Peace," he finds it so appropriate that he instructs Nicolaus to use it every time (3155-3172), thus making sure that he will always be able to kiss the page her lips have touched. (The implied humor of this incident lies in the fact that Guillem's precaution is gratuitous: next time Flamenca goes to mass it will be Guillem who will be presenting the book to her to kiss!)

It is only that night when Guillem, unable to sleep, rises from his bed to gaze at the tower and utter another long discourse on love, that he remembers the plan of deliverance that had come to him in the vision the night before. He rehearses it and it assumes more concrete shape in his mind (3371-3415): he will persuade the priest to take him as his ministrant in place of Nicolaus; he will send for masons to excavate the passage; to effect this in secret, he will feign that he is frightfully ill and in need of complete privacy; he will throw dust in the eyes of his host and hostess and, showering them with lavish gifts, persuade them to move out of their house for a while. Having planned all this, he flings himself on his bed, tormented by hope and doubt of success. He upbraids Lady Love and is gently reproved by her for his impatience.

Now that the plan has been thought out we shall see some action. On Tuesday morning Guillem inspects the bath chambers underground—they are of soft tufa—and he selects the spot where the tunnel is to enter. Next he again bestows costly gifts on his host and hostess and easily elicits an offer on their part to move out and leave him and his squires in possession of the house. It will be for only a little while, he says, gratefully accepting. Then he makes up a story of his once having been a canon in Péronne, and it troubles his conscience that he has neglected to keep his tonsure. The priest is called in to shear his golden locks, which he does very regretfully, while host and hostess weep. The priest is so overcome by the lavish barber's fee which Guillem hands him that he conjures him (using a phrase frequently met with in the *Prose Lancelot*): "Sire, as truly as God may grant you the sight of that thing which you most love, tell me what I can do for you. There is nothing in the world I would not do" (3621ff.). Then take me for your acolyte, says Guillem. Let us send Nicolaus to Paris for another two years of schooling. The priest, seeing that the offer is promptly backed up by a handful of gold, is overwhelmed and delighted. Guillem at once orders a gown made to befit his new station. He is through for good with the flim-flam, the "torris loris" (3682) of courtly ways, he says—at which point the author cannot suppress an allusion to the famous animal story of the wolf, the fox, and the lamb.

On Thursday the host and hostess move out of the house, and Guillem promptly sends to Châtillon for a couple of stone masons who are sworn to secrecy and bribed by sums beyond their dreams. By Saturday the lad Nicolaus is off on his way to Paris and that evening Guillem with the priest rehearses his new duties. Of course the priest refuses to entertain the young gentleman's offer to sleep with him and dress him and wait on him personally, but the offer points up the fact that Guillem is alert to every circumstance involved in the consistent acting out of the role he has undertaken. If money is a prime requisite for such an undertaking, craft and resourcefulness and strength of character and infinite patience are no less required.

The day finally dawns which will put his venture to the first, perhaps decisive test—Sunday, when Flamenca comes to high mass. There is the early matin office first, which he sails through without difficulty. That over with, he lies down at the priest's suggestion, but not to rest, for he asks himself what he shall whisper when the fatal moment arrives. He thinks of a gospel parallel to give him comfort: when Christ sent forth his disciples, he told them not to worry about what they should say in the presence of kings, for the right words would come at the proper time. Like them, albeit with fear and trembling, he will leave it to inspiration. The mass begins. Guillem performs his office without a sign to betray his inner agitation. When at last he steps up to Flamenca with the open psalter to bestow the "Peace," he whispers two syllables, *Hai las* (alas).

So at last Operation Rescue is off to a start! It is quite in order that having hazarded this first step successfully, Guillem should again sway up and down on the teeter-totter of joy and despair, of hope and apprehension, another 117 lines of soliloquy and dialogue with Lady Love; for the inscrutability of women looms as a new unknown factor in his undertaking, and the literature of love, which he has studied so well, supplies plenty of material on this theme for his ruminations. But every reader who has been following Guillem for so long in the preliminaries of his transition from the theory to the practice of Courtly Love must be impatient to learn of the reactions of the feminine partner in his enterprise.

Flamenca, returned to the prison of her tower, is deeply shaken. Nothing has been lost upon her. She distinctly heard the words, she took in the pallor and the blushes and the delicate modesty of the new ministrant whose fine physique is so unlike that of the lad Nicolaus. Yet her first feeling, pretended or real, is that she is being mocked. Speaking aloud, she laments her fate, which is worse, she says, than that of a Greek or Armenian slave. Alis and Margarida, her two maids, have heard the outburst and press her to tell them what has prompted it. The girls, who had not been blind to the cavalierly appearance of the new ministrant either, tell her, what she wants to hear, that this is not a mocker but a soliciting lover who must be answered, and Flamenca is quickly persuaded. But she knows what the proprieties demand of a woman: she must conceal her heart, at least at first, so that her intention be not known, and she must say something so nicely balanced as to make the lover neither hope nor despair. She will know his intentions in two months, she says (underestimating the time!), and if he is in earnest she will yield herself to him. And forthwith she launches into a long diatribe against women who tease a faithful lover and hold out on the *merces*, the reward. Such women are monsters, worse than dragons or vipers (4267-4296). This line is destined to recur with increasing length and vehemence, as the intrigue takes its course. It is an echo of Andreas Capellanus, the antipode of Wolfram. But what is she to say when it is her turn to speak next Sunday? Alis has the answer. Let her reply to his "alas" with a question: for why? This appeals to Flamenca, and during the ensuing week she repeats the words *que plans?* a thousand times.

Thus the success of Guillem's venture is assured in principle from the start. But what a long trial of patience and adroitness lies ahead of the lovers! There will be many weeks without any mid-week festival—the first to look forward to is Ascension Day Thursday. By a slow crawl—no more than two syllables at a time—questions and answers will be pieced together into a communication that will eventually spell out a summons. This game—like a game of chess by mail—will require a total of twenty moves, forty-two syllables by exact count, because at Guillem's last turn to whisper joy breaks through his restraint and he utters four! It was May 7, the second Sunday after Easter, when Guillem whispered his first sigh, and it will be Wednesday, August 2, before the lovers hold each other in their arms. Pursuing his deliberate technique, the author is reluctant to speed things up. In the weeks that drag on we are treated to several more of Guillem's interminable interior monologues and dialogues with Lady Love (with repeated quotations from Ovid) and to a corresponding amount of dialogue between Flamenca and her maids, revolving about love in general and about the specific meaning of Guillem's responses and the appropriate answers to be given. And, as we would expect, each furtive sign of Flamenca's favor, be it a glance or be it a finger extended almost to make contact with his, is developed with relish.

From this long period of patient preparation for THE DAY we shall single out only a few items of special interest. There is a very pretty scene when Flamenca makes a test to find out whether the ministrant-cavalier could have heard her first whispered response. She rehearses it with her maids using instead of the psalter the *Romanz de Blancaflor* (4477) which has helped her to while away the time during her two years of confinement. At another point Alis delivers a great speech to her mistress in praise of letters: what a great thing booklearning is; how only so well-lettered a knight could have devised a plan for Flamenca's rescue; how miserable Flamenca herself would have been without the diversion of reading; and Flamenca takes over, developing the theme further (4804-4838). In the course of these long weeks the two girls learn to discourse on love as fluently as their mistress, prompting Flamenca to exclaim: "Margarida, by the faith you owe me, who has taught you all this dialectic? If you had learned arithmetic, astronomy, and music, you could not better have diagnosed the maladies I have so long suffered" (5441-5447). In the long-drawn-out game we must not overlook the element of pleasure, both in the finesse of playing it as such and at Archimbaut's expense. Flamenca and her girls have a wonderful time laughing at the jealous keeper behind his back; Guillem likewise relishes making love to Flamenca under her husband's very nose. The work of excavation, the tunnel, having been completed in a week and the debris removed without a trace (don't ask me how), Guillem in due time invites his host and hostess to return to their house on the ground that he is much improved. No doubt he enjoys the masterly craft of this act of caution. We are treated to an astonishing climax in Guillem's passion, when he, whom we have known to pray so often and so devoutly, is carried away to the point of addressing the following prayer to God: "*Bel sener Dieus*, I declare to you that you may very easily come to terms with me about my share of Paradise: I'll throw you for it! I take all the prophets and apostles to witness that I will give all the rent I have in France to build churches and bridges,[7] if only you will let me have my lady, with her will and consent" (5056-5065). This is sheer blasphemy by all standards, even though it has neither the flippancy of Aucassin's expressed preference for joining the fine ladies and their knights in hell rather than the poor and the wretched folk in heaven, nor the grief of utter despair as voiced by Clamidé (in the *Parzival*), who would gladly suffer all the torments God has in store for Pontius Pilate and Judas for the price of Condwiramurs' willingly granted embrace. But the fact that such sentiments are uttered by our clerkly cavalier in the form of a prayer gives the passage a peculiar piquancy. A modern reader might easily jump to the conclusion that this prayer shows up Guillem's piety as pure hokum, but I think we should rate it rather as magnificent hyperbole. As for his whole scheme of using the ritual of the church as a ruse to obtain the love of a woman, a married woman at that, medieval as well as modern theology would have condemned it as a sacrilegious farce; yet as a good conformist to the standards of his class Guillem would have repudiated such a charge with indignation. He is first of all a knight, and his conscience does not trouble him in the slightest. His values are not those of a theologian. He renders unto God what is God's and to Lady Love what is Love's. Another piquant passage is Flamenca's discourse to the effect that all women owe feudal servitude

---

[7] Surmounted by the statues of saints, I presume.

to Lady Love. She summons them at the age of thirteen. Any woman who has not rendered service by seventeen, loses her fief unless Lady Love shows mercy. And if she has passed twenty-one without having rendered a third or a fourth or a half of the service due, she will never have her fief entire and she will be demoted to the rank of a common soldier (5591-5605).

This is the point at which we return to the story, for the period of trial and patience is almost at an end when she mentions the fief. This is Monday. Tomorrow is a feast day (August 1), Saint Peter's. Flamenca will give her lover the final signal, and on Wednesday she will proceed to the baths. Is it exhaustion or excitement at the prospect of her imminent deliverance that makes her swoon at the end of her last long discourse? When informed of what has happened, Archimbaut shows signs of concern. He advises her to add a little nutmeg to her diet. No, she declares, she would rather try the baths, not tomorrow, but the day after, when the moon is propitious. But on behalf of her cure he instructs her to dedicate a particularly large and fine candle to Saint Peter, for all the people to see (5695-5696). And with this appropriate symbol to grace the occasion, she goes to mass next day and whispers the final syllables of assignation.

4. Operation Pleasure

Everything works out according to plan. On that Wednesday morning Archimbaut conducts Flamenca and her two maids to the baths. Having sniffed around inside without finding anything to arouse his suspicions, he goes off and locks the door behind them, which they on their part secure by a stout bar on the inside. Shortly thereafter there are sounds of a stone being lifted out of place and Guillem emerges. He kneels before Flamenca, there is an exchange of pretty words and kisses, and then Guillem conducts the three women to his richly furnished chambers. There, after informing Flamenca of his name and high lineage, he and Flamenca enjoy all the delights of love except lying together. Lady Merces (Reward) herself could have done no more for Guillem (5961-5967), as the author says in terms of the allegory of love, and he follows this up with biblical language, closely paraphrasing I Corinthians 2:9: there is no man that could see, no mouth that could speak, no heart that could imagine the bliss they enjoyed (5977-5979).

When the time for parting comes, the lovers weep as though they should never see each other again, carrying on even a bit excessively, as the author remarks, in view of the fact that they are to meet again the next morning and at least four times a week, as Flamenca promises.

Modern readers, and some of the poet's contemporaries as well, may have expected Operation Rescue to take a different turn. Why is there no word of specific plans? Is Guillem not going to spirit his lady away to some safe place, as Cligès had done with Fénice, where the jealous husband will never find her and where they will live happily ever after? But the thought of such a denouement does not enter the mind of either Guillem or Flamenca. Their only plan is to enjoy each other's embraces to the full. There is nothing "romantic" about these courtly lovers. They are conformists, both of them, accepting their social status as the basis of their amours.

The rest of the day is spent by Flamenca with her maids in happy recollections of her tryst. Archimbaut appears at dinner time and has the door shut in his face by Alis who tells him that her lady must not be disturbed. As for Flamenca, she has had the manna from heaven (6095) and requires no food. Neither does she need to cut a reed on Saint John's Day, like plucking a daisy to find out whether her lover's feelings are a match for her own (6192-6194). She yields him dominion unlimited. In the course of a speech of 134 lines she expresses her contempt of women who give themselves airs and hold out on the reward. Given the right time and place, it is much better for the lover to respond to such shilly-shallying tactics with a little resort to force. He can make his peace with her afterwards through a trusty go-between (6252-6258)!

The next morning, at the second encounter, Guillem springs a surprise on the ladies. Flamenca sees that he has something on his mind which he hesitates to come out with. She assures him that whatever it is, his will is hers. He thereupon calls in his two squires, Claris and Ot, cousins of his, who have up to now taken Guillem's illness and his transformation into a clerk in good faith and sadly. It was certainly a feat for Guillem to have executed his whole design without so much as one confidant, even granting that he had unlimited funds at his disposal. Seeing the three ladies, the young men think they are in Paradise. They drop on their knees to Flamenca, who lets them kiss her ungloved hand. And now Guillem makes a suggestion that all parties agree to with alacrity. Let the two maids lead the two squires through the tunnel into the baths, where there are well-appointed chambers for them to disport themselves. Each picks a partner; each squire vows to have only her for his mistress when he is knighted, and each maid vows she will never have another man for a lover after she has become a *domna*. Thus there is no need for Alis and Margarida to return from this encounter as maidens, if they so choose, as the author discreetly puts it. As for Guillem and Flamenca, now left alone in the chamber, they devote themselves to a game at which each wins and neither loses, for they are perfectly matched in their give and take. The technical language of games of dice, a favorite figure in the age of chivalry, allows the author to develop this theme at length without transgressing beyond the confines of delicacy. Quite unlike Wolfram, he is never gross in his reference to sex.

In the tower again after the parting, Flamenca dwells on the delights experienced. But at this point the author feels called upon to insert a long discourse on the text that love that touches the heart via the eyes is finer and purer than that via the mouth; for the eyes pass all the delight they absorb on to the heart, whereas the mouth greedily keeps a share of its sweets for itself. He would caution those who cherish kisses more than the language of the eyes that they are not love's true initiates (6543-6624). Thus he develops the text of Andreas Capellanus, who theoretically gives the preference to "pure" love as compared to "mixed" love.

5. Operation Cure

It was the second of August when the lovers first embraced. Four months have flitted by in ever repeated rounds of pleasure. Now we reach the turning point of the story. If we were surprised when Operation Rescue failed to lead to a romantic abduction, we have reason to be even more surprised at the present turn: with startling suddenness the husband gets cured of his jealousy, and that accomplished, fond and tearful farewells are in order, bringing the episode in the baths to a close; for after all, the full life, as conceived by these conformists, includes the prose of social existence as well as the poetry of love. But how does Archimbaut get cured of his jealousy? How is the ridiculous, blustering scarecrow and devil restored to the estate of a man and a lord who commands the respect and admiration of his fellows?

To accomplish this the author resorts to a very simple procedure. When Archimbaut's jealousy began, Flamenca was a child in experience. She was a cowed thing who submitted to her fate like an inanimate object. But the three months of spelling out the intrigue with Guillem and the four months of pleasure that followed have wrought a profound change in her. She has matured in every way. She has become a woman, wise to the ways of the world, and she no longer fears her husband. A time comes when she decides to make her emancipation known to him. This time she does not rise as he enters. She looks him in the eye and tells him to fold up with his bluster. She will be jailed no longer. Henceforth she will be her own keeper. "And I swear to you a solemn oath on the saints that from now on and forever I'll keep myself as you have kept me guarded here."

At this critical point a leaf is missing from the manuscript. But we should be novices indeed if we could not supply the essential substance of the fine tirade she works herself up to: "I swear to you by all the saints that now and forever I shall keep as close a guard on my own conduct as you have done these past two years. And no man who has not enjoyed intimacy with me during my confinement to the tower shall ever have reason to boast of my favors." Some such trick oath, probably rephrased with many variations and calling of all the saints to witness, she flings into the face of the dumbfounded Archimbaut. It is the trick oath of Iseut, when she submits to the ordeal of the white-hot iron and comes off unscathed by virtue of having told the literal truth; it is the trick oath by which Lancelot, after his night with Queen Guenevere, which left the tell-tale bloodstains of his cut fingers on her sheets, defends her against Meleagant's charge of adultery with Sir Kaye and defeats his adversary, thereby giving the lie to her accuser.

Flamenca's trick oath has worked a miracle. When the manuscript resumes, Archimbaut is a changed man. He is cured forever of his nauseous distemper. He has washed his head and cut his nails and put on dress becoming to the great lord that he is, and there shall be tourneys and feasting again. To signal his cure, he has all the bells rung, the carillon for the knights, the big bell for the townsmen, the little bell for the peasants. He summons them all in witness of his recovery, he announces that the anniversary of this event shall henceforth be celebrated by similar joyful gatherings, and subsequent events show that, like a man who has recovered from a mortal illness, he is completely rehabilitated in the eyes of his social class.

As for Flamenca, she is *sage* and draws the logical consequences from the transformation. She will now be mistress of a great household. Her lover, too, his mission having been crowned with success, cannot remain in hiding forever. He must return home to play that part in the world to which his station, his wealth, and his personal excellence entitle him. Tearful moving farewells are in order. Guillem also accepts the situation. He and Flamenca know that despite their separation, they will always belong to each other as true lovers. Moreover, opportunity may smile upon them again. Archimbaut has decreed a tourney for next Easter which Guillem will be sure to attend, and the lovers rejoice in Easter's coming early that year (6875), the second of April (7024). Nonetheless, their farewells are tearful and long drawn out.

6. Postlude: Polishing the "hornworks"

This section, in which direct discourse is subordinated to narrative, tells a good story full of incidents that make allowance for chance and happy improvisation instead of all falling into place according to plan. The theme of this last part is the complete self-mastery of the lovers when they meet once more, not clandestinely, but with the eyes of the world focused upon them: their craftiness in exploiting every opportunity for intimacy while observing the utmost discretion all around. Having been schooled in all the intricacies of Courtly Love they are put to the supreme test by their staging an unrehearsed play before the flower of chivalry, and they put on a brilliant performance that wins them the award of top honors on the part of the judges. Who are the judges? Author and reader only, for no one in that gay assembly has the faintest inkling that a play is being acted out before their eyes. What gives particular point to the performance is the fact that the husband is unwittingly induced to cooperate as a star performer in the intrigue that is being enacted at his expense. That is why I have captioned the concluding section "Polishing the hornworks," with apologies to *Tristram Shandy.*

To illustrate these general remarks, I shall limit myself to essentials. A pre-Lenten tourney at Louvain, where Archimbaut and Guillem carry off highest honors between them, provides the opportunity for the two men to make each other's acquaintance and become close friends. Guillem, of course, accepts Archimbaut's invitation to his forthcoming tournament at Bourbon: any tournament goes the better if one is friends with the husband, the author wryly remarks (6975-6976). When Archimbaut gets home he overflows with praise of his new friend's prowess to Flamenca. But can such a great fighter also be a gentle lover? Alis pertly asks. He is also without a par as a lover, Archimbaut replies, and to prove it he takes from his pocket a superbly written and illuminated rhymed epistle of love addressed to "the Lady of Belmont." Guillem has given him this copy as a favor, he explains, enjoining him not to show it to unworthy eyes. You must read it aloud to us, says Flamenca, for knowing it already you can recite it with the proper expression. Thus Guillem has contrived to make the cuckold the bearer of his love letter to Flamenca. Two leaves are missing at this point, so that we do not have the text of the missive, but only the description of the fine symbolic miniatures that adorn the text: there is a knight kneeling before his lady; the stem of a flower issues from his mouth and touches the verses; another flower describes the passage to the ear of the lady, to whom the goddess of love also stoops to whisper. Flamenca recognizes the portrait likeness of herself and her lover, and having obtained the precious parchment from her lord she spends the intervening weeks in sweet and fanciful play with the priceless treasure. When the preparations for the tournament are complete—the King of France is again among the guests with all the nobles of the realm—Archimbaut's first act in welcoming Guillem is personally to knight his two squires, the lovers of Alis and Margarida, and to belt their swords. Then he takes Guillem to present him to *vostra domna* (7307), who happens to be gaily chatting with the king. There is an exchange of gallant courtesies. The king, rising with his following to attend to his duties and greet the endless train of guests still arriving, regretfully remarks that he will soon be forgotten when Flamenca has such a paragon of a lover to entertain her. The noise and confusion of the departing crowd allow Flamenca, as she bestows an ostentatious kiss on the newcomer, to whisper a promise of more intimate rewards into his ear. The two squires are not forgotten either. Flamenca orders her two maids to decorate them with pennants. This is a ruse authorizing them to pay court to the girls whereas the rules normally limit such attentions to the married ladies. The situation comes to its improvised climax that evening. Guillem, with a presentiment of going to a hazardous tryst, has taken the precaution to wear a shirt of mail under his clothes and a stiletto in his belt, even though he is not stealing furtively into the castle, but riding at the head of thirty followers with great torches to light their way. His arrival is again observed by all the gathering and he engages Flamenca in gallant conversation. At this point Archimbaut, who has a thousand things to attend to, quietly approaches Flamenca with a request: two cousins of hers are to be knighted the next day, and he would like her to select some gifts from her store of jewels. But what shall I give them? she asks. Take Guillem and his two squires and your two maids, Archimbaut replies, they will assist you in your selection. So the obliging husband conducts the party of six to Flamenca's chamber, but he must be off on other business. There are three of you women, and three men, he says, in haste to leave, so agree among yourselves how you will distribute your favors (7620-7622). The dramatic irony of his words is not lost on them. They abandon themselves to love's delights, with one of the couples keeping guard at the entrance, and "neither bliaut nor chemise interfered with their bliss" (7648-7649). We overlooked one characteristic little touch in the preparation of this scene. When Archimbaut approached his wife and her lover, Guillem moved to rise. Don't get up, he said, putting his hand on Guillem's knee, but with so light a touch that he did not feel the mail beneath his hose.

The next morning sees the opening of the tournament with the king and Flamenca stationed on the spectators' platform. At the signal for the first charge Flamenca loudly proclaims that her sleeve will be the favor to reward the knight who is first to unhorse an opponent. At almost the same instant Guillem has thrown his opposite number out of the saddle, and the platform rings with shouts acclaiming the winner of Flamenca's prize. In the best fashion of Lancelot Guillem sends his captive to Flamenca for her to determine his ransom. He kneels to her and makes an appropriate speech, whereupon she hands him her sleeve with instructions to take it to his captor and inform him of what a prize he has won. The favor, publicly bestowed, is tucked by Guillem on the inside of his shield, with only a little of the edge showing over the top; and with such a favor to brace his arm, he downs sixteen more knights that morning, and allows them all to go off scot-free along with their horses. Thus Flamenca has succeeded in decorating her lover publicly without incurring the slightest risk of gossip or scandal.

After a few more paragraphs of who throws whom in the tourney, all uninteresting filler, the manuscript breaks off. But for all practical purposes the story is complete. I can fancy the author as working up to a spirited conclusion by having Archimbaut address a grateful speech to the king and Flamenca to this effect: A lady's sleeve—not *my* lady's—was the means of my undoing when I was a newly wed bridegroom. Now again a lady's sleeve—this time truly *my* lady's sleeve—is worn by the best knight in the world, and I am proud to see it peek over the edge of his shield. Lucky man that I am, to have the best man in the world for my friend![8]

This conclusion—if my hypothesis may be entertained—would tend to shift the accent of the story rather sharply in the direction of low comedy: the cuckold as the butt of ridicule. This feature is undeniably and unavoidably present, but the ripples of laughter extending from this center rock the whole glittering surface of courtly society duped by the lovers' clever game. Yet the work as a whole is not pointed in the direction of satire. On the contrary, the values of courtly society are positively affirmed as the framework for the unfolding of so sparkling an intrigue. The elation of the lovers, themselves securely anchored within this framework, reflects rather their consciousness of supreme virtuosity in the bold, adroit, impeccably sustained execution of their amorous enterprise. The intellectual pleasure deriving from this source so nicely matches the ardor of their sensuous rapture that the two notes blend into one chord of perfect dynamic balance.

Is, then, the *Flamenca* the supreme example of the novel of

[8] It is intolerable to imagine the *Flamenca* as ending with a slip leading to the exposure of the clandestine love affair. The form of the story as well as the ideal conception of the characters require that only the author and his audience be partners to the perfectly kept secret—quite apart from the consideration that to associate a scandalous ending with the name of one of the most powerful families of France would have been too foolhardy for any writer to venture.

Courtly Love with a distinctly modern slant? To my way of thinking, grave reservations to qualify so superlative an estimate are in
order on two counts.

1) As has long been recognized, and implicitly demonstrated by
our analysis, the *Flamenca* is not a novel at all but a short story, a
novas, a *novella*, a *Schwank*, blown up to the length of a novel. It
lacks the breadth and scope that we associate with a novel, such as
the *Yvain*, the *Lancelot*, the *Parzival*. It develops a single theme
in a unilinear way. There are no complications, no surprises,[9] no
unforeseen major turns or retardations to flavor our suspense with
the quality of apprehension as to the outcome. There is no quest of
the unknown; there is, instead, a calculable enterprise undertaken
by a hero completely qualified for his project. The plan is outlined, moving for the most part at a snail's pace, and the whole
intrigue develops according to plan with minute and often exquisite
attention to detail. This is true even of the last part, where the
element of improvisation, brilliantly employed, is strictly limited to
the means for working out a preconceived design. There is no current of fresh air about this story. It is contrived throughout. Conceived in a cleric's study, it is a perfect illustration of the theory of
Courtly Love as put into practice by a hero who is perfectly
schooled in its theory. Thus it is essentially didactic without the
spontaneity of life, and its length makes for tediousness. Now we
come to the second point:

2) Granted the distinctly modern note, we raise a fundamental
question: Does the passion of our two lovers really conform to the
definition of Courtly Love as understood by the *Flamenca*'s Arthurian prototypes? Even so viscous a writer as Andreas Capellanus
had based his treatise on Courtly Love on the axiom: *Amor est
fons et origo omnium bonorum.* [Love is the source and origin of
all good.] He as well as the Arthurian poets of France and Germany
had interpreted this axiom to mean: A knight's love of a lady is a
celestial force which inspires him to rise above himself and perform superhuman feats of valor in the service of the oppressed. Such
was the quality of the flame that glowed in Yvain, in Lancelot, in
Parzival and Gawan. But what of this idealistic doctrine in its application to Guillem? It is completely forgotten! What excruciating

[9] If we discount the lack of a plan for an abduction and the cure of the jealous
husband by the time-worn device of the trick oath.

sufferings does Guillem endure except the pangs of love? What superhuman feats of valor does he rise to by virtue of his love? There are none to report. Being perfect to begin with in prowess and valor, in craft and patience, in learning and piety as well, he demonstrates these qualities in his exploit but he does not exceed himself. He is the ideal conformist representative of his class who decides on rational grounds to engage in a love affair, and he singles out Flamenca because she is beautiful and because the winning of her will subject all his capacities, physical, mental, and moral, to the most rigid tests. There is no getting around the fact that the conception of love as the divine stimulus has yielded to love as the pleasure principle, though still disguised by elaborate allegorical trappings. Love, no longer the ideal stimulus but the pleasure principle—this, together with the greatly expanded role of the woman partner, constitutes the modern note of the *Flamenca.*

Excursus

Namur or Nemours? There is a geographical problem to plague us. The locale of the intrigue is *Borbon* (Bourbon Archambault, as it is called on the present-day map in the *Guide Bleu*), situated in almost the exact geographical center of France. This is the domain of the bridegroom, soon to be transformed into a monster of jealousy. But where does the bride, Flamenca, hail from? Does the *Nemurs* of the story mean Namur in the Low Countries or Nemours in France? We must look at the map to visualize the two locations. The Namur of present-day Belgium is situated roughly 470 km to the northeast of Bourbon, as the crow flies, and some 200 km northeast of Paris, by the same handy reckoning. The Nemours of France, on the other hand, lies approximately 200 km due north of Bourbon, and it is another 70 km northwestward from Nemours to Paris.

Our story presents two sets of geographical facts which are difficult or impossible to reconcile. The preparations for the wedding party at the beginning of the story (as well as some later references to the hero's exploits) clearly point to the Low Countries. The bride's father wants all the knights "from here to Alamainna" (125) to come to his feast; "guests are to be summoned from near and far" (138); and he sends invitations to all the knights in Flanders (144). Germany and Flanders are the only geographical names mentioned in connection with this celebration. Here we ask: Why is Flanders singled out? The duchy of Namur lies far to the east of Flanders. The duchies of Hainaut (Hennegau) and Brabant lie in between. Are these ignored for simplicity's sake? I have no ready answer.

The second set of facts concerns the bridegroom's preparations for a second, even more sumptuous feast to celebrate the bride's arrival at her new home. The wedding took place after Pentecost (187-188), while this second feast is scheduled for Saint John's Day, midsummer day, June 24 (471 ff.). In this context the name *Nemurs* seems to point as strongly to Nemours in France as it did to the Low Countries in the earlier context. For this occasion the bridegroom wishes to assemble all the nobility of France. Poitou, Berry, Bordeaux, Bayonne, Blaye, are mentioned. But the chief guest of honor to be invited is the king of France, along with the queen. And—here is the point—Archimbaut couples his invitation to the king with the request for a signal favor: he entreats the king to take his way "straight through Nemurs" (372) and conduct the bride to her new home. Now Nemours, as I said above and as a glance at the map will show, lies directly on the road from Paris to Bourbon; so there is nothing extraordinary about this request, if Nemours in France is meant. If we think of the Namur of the Low Countries, on the other hand, we would have to suppose that the king of France had been engaged in some business way up there and beyond, so that it could suit his convenience to pick up the bride on his way back. No vassal in central France, surely, would have the cheek to request his sovereign to set out on a long expedition to the northeast and fetch his bride for him. Since there is no mention to the contrary, I think we must assume that the invitation was sent to Paris, and that the king set out from there, picking up the bride on his way. Clearly, the two sets of circumstances seem based on incompatible geographical assumptions.

Since we are concerned with a realistic story that challenges us at every point with specific data of real geographical space and real time as measured by the church calendar, we have the right to weigh the relative distances of the two Nemurs in terms of the time scheme underlying the introductory portion of the novel. This time scheme places the wedding at Nemurs on the day after Pentecost (187-188) and continuing for ten days, and it fixes the opening date of the second feast, at Bourbon, on June 24 (471 ff.). Allowing for the great variability of the Easter season, on which the date of Pentecost (the fiftieth day) is dependent, the time interval between the end of the first and the beginning of the second celebration is also subject to a variation of more than four weeks; but however we stretch the time, the greater proximity of the French Nemours to Bourbon as compared with the far more distant Namur will allow of a much more reasonable interval for making adequate preparations. Supposing Easter to have occurred on the first of April in the year of our story, much earlier i.e. than its average occurrence, Pentecost would have fallen on May 20 and the wedding feast on May 21. In that case the bridegroom could not have taken his departure and set out for Bourbon before May 30. Arrived there after perhaps five days of sharp riding—or twice that number, depending on which *Nemurs* he set out from—he would have had to allow a similar time for his invitation to reach his guests plus a much greater time to be consumed in their more leisurely journeying to his estate. By any realistic computation, I think, the Namur of the Low Countries is ruled out under the circumstances.

Our perplexity grows when we turn to the last part of the story and its geographical data. Here we learn (1) that Guillem, after returning home from Bourbon, distinguished himself in a war in Flanders (6930 ff.), (2) that Flamenca's father reports having seen this knight Guillem accorded the highest honors at the court of Flanders (6942-6947), (3) that Archimbaut and Guillem made each other's acquaintance at a pre-lenten tournament held by the Duke of Braiman (Brabant) at Lovan (Louvain) (6982 ff.), and (4) that after this tournament Archimbaut first accompanied his brother-in-law Jauselis to his home Nemurs before his own return to Bourbon (7033-7035). Here, not only the repeated mention of Flanders and the one mention of Nemurs in that context but also the references to the neighboring Duchy of Brabant and its capital Louvain leave no shadow of doubt as to the fact that the Nemurs here referred to must mean the Namur of the Low Countries.

Thus the data pertaining to the wedding feast at the beginning and to Guillem's exploits before his second visit to Bourbon clearly point to Namur of the Low Countries, whereas the data pertaining to the second wedding feast as clearly point to Nemours, south of

Paris. What does all this add up to? Are we not forced to the conclusion that the author, a southerner, had only a hazy idea of geographical locations and distances as regards Northern France and the Lowlands? I see no escape from this without doing violence to one or the other set of data.

This settled, let us speculate for a moment on how the confusion of the two *Nemurs* could have occurred.

First there is the fact that this story has the structure of a *novas* or *novella*—a type of which the stories of Boccaccio provide some of the best known examples. It has long been recognized that the *Flamenca* is in essence a short story (a *Schwank*, in German) which has been blown up to give it the length of a novel. Now to recognize this fact is tantamount to saying: the author of the *Flamenca* did not invent the subject matter of his story; he took a story already existing and, using the general form, the allegory, the sentiment, and all the poetic figures familiar to versifiers since Chrétien, he expanded it greatly—overexpanded it to a degree all out of proportion to its inherent substance—and this involved altering it and inventing new features of detail. It is more likely than not, I would say, that the original story knew only one Nemurs with specific and definite associations. And this brings me to my second point:

The heroine's name is Flamenca. This is not an exotic or poetic name like that of the Arthurian heroines. It designates its bearer's origin as Flemish, and this name surely could not have attached itself to her by whim or chance. Her father was Duke of Namur. [In his youth, when he cast about for a mate, he found a suitable partner at the court of Flanders. The daughter born to them was named Flamenca to express the mother's pride in her ancestry. It is on this account that] the knights of Flanders are mentioned as specifically invited to the wedding, whereas the father's expansive mood makes it clear that he is inviting all his upper-class neighbors, west and east, all the way to Germany. Thus the name Flamenca supplies a strong link to the reading Namur. Let us not forget that an indeterminate number of pages from the beginning of the *Flamenca* are missing. Is it not highly likely that this account of Flamenca's origin, which I have conjecturally sketched (in the lines enclosed in square brackets) was actually reported on the pages which have been lost?

Now if we try the same hypothesis but read Nemours for Namur, we get into difficulties at once. True, a French nobleman, lord of Nemours, could equally well have picked his bride in Flanders and named his child Flamenca. But when it comes to marrying her off to a lord in central France, is it conceivable that he, a vassal of the French crown, surrounded on all sides by French-speaking lands, should have ignored his own kin, singling out only the Flemish, way to the north, and the Germans (to the far northeast) with whom he has no discernible ties!?

The reading Nemours in our story is predicated only on the circumstance that the King of France picks Flamenca up on his way from Paris and conducts her to her new home, Bourbon. But this circumstance is by no means an essential part of the story. Nothing significant is reported as happening during their common journey. There was no clandestine understanding between the king and Flamenca, and the queen's jealousy is aroused—not during the journey but—only during the festivities at Bourbon by the king's marked attention to the bride and by the queen's false suspicions regarding the sleeve which the king carried on his lance. The situation would have been just the same if Archimbaut had himself conducted his bride to his home and if the king had first laid eyes on the fair Flamenca after his arrival at Bourbon.

This makes it extremely likely that our poet, having only a hazy notion of locations and distances to the north of central France but knowing that Nemours was somewhere between Paris and Bourbon, invented the circumstance of having the king pick up Flamenca and conduct her to her new home, thus causing the confusion of the two Nemurs, which has been a headache to scholars.

SHAKESPEARE
IN GERMAN CRITICISM

CONTRARY TO THE continuity of English literary tradition that never lost sight of Shakespeare, Shakespeare's name and work were still all but unknown in Germany up to the middle of the eighteenth century. But, as in England during the last third of that century the interest in and admiration of Shakespeare's work acquired a momentum that culminated in what Professor Babcock has happily labeled as Shakespeare "idolatry," the advance guard of literary Germany, eagerly receptive to English thought and animated by a strong anti-French bias, felt and quickly responded to the groundswell of this movement. By 1766 Wieland—at the age of thirty-three—had completed his prose translation of Shakespeare's plays. Two years later, Lessing, the redoubtable critic, in his *Hamburgische Dramaturgie*, extolled Shakespeare in exposing the artificiality of the conventions of French classicistic drama, and by 1770 Herder, aged twenty-six, was preparing to proclaim to the world the incomparable vastness of Shakespeare's genius, veritable creator of a second universe. The German *Sturm-und-Drang* movement of the 1770's owed its impetus and direction primarily to Shakespeare; to the prose Shakespeare of Wieland, it must be remembered, a hasty, faulty, incomplete rendering of Bishop Warburton's revision of Alexander Pope's edition of 1725. Some of the young men of this generation knew enough English to realize how far Wieland had fallen short of doing justice to the original; but their enthusiasm for the turgid elegiac rhetoric of MacPherson's allegedly Gaelic *Ossian*, quickly suspect to the English as a forgery, shows how far they were from understanding the specific poetic value of Shakespeare's language.

In spite of all his shortcomings, Wieland performed a great service for the young men of the 1770's in making even so distorted an image of Shakespeare available. At that time a translation that could do justice to Shakespeare was out of the question, not only that there was no one to do it, but the German language as such was not ready for the task. The literary language of a people is a

Reprinted from *The Persistence of Shakespeare Idolatry*, ed. Herbert M. Schueller (1964), pp. 107-133, by permission of the Wayne State University Press.

collective treasure house of phrasing that determines its users' maximum range of human experience. Any new intensity, any new subtlety of the life of the spirit remains private and becomes lost unless and until it is captured by some verbal turn of unique configuration. Only then does it become re-experienceable, transmittable. This cardinal insight is developed with great lucidity in Friedrich Gundolf's early work on the reception and assimilation of Shakespeare by Germany (*Shakespeare und der deutsche Geist,* 1911). In the 1760's, the German language, collectively considered, had not yet accumulated a wealth of phrasing that could cope with the infinite varieties of emotional play encountered in Shakespeare's plays. By 1800 the climate of literary Germany had undergone a momentous change. Poetry had come into full flower. The native German poets, Goethe above all, had enormously expanded the potential expressiveness of the German language. It had become an instrument capable of a range hitherto unheard of for expressing the inner life of man in words permeated with sensuous imagery, in words that make their appeal to the inner eye of the imagination. When this had been achieved, it happened by a singular piece of good fortune that a man, sensitive to all the nuances of the poet's language and adept in their use, but untroubled by any real creative urge of his own, dedicated four years of his life to the translating of sixteen of Shakespeare's plays with meticulous fidelity to rhythm, phrasing, and poetic imagery. That man was the critic August Wilhelm Schlegel. His translation of Shakespeare has been hailed as the greatest single achievement of the German Romantic movement. It is an exaggeration, of course, to claim that the translation measures up to the original, but it is this translation (later supplemented by Ludwig Tieck and his family) that has supplied the spoken word for most Shakespeare productions and adaptations on the German stage for a century and a half, and it is thanks to this translation that the cultured people of prewar Germany claimed to know Shakespeare better than the British. Insofar as this is true, there is a historical reason to account for it. Schlegel's translation, though difficult, is more easily intelligible than the original. Schlegel wrote in the elevated poetic medium of his German contemporaries Goethe and Schiller, which, though obsolescent in many respects today, is still readily understood. We English readers, on the other hand, are separated from Shakespeare's productive era by three and a half centuries, and the difficulties encountered by our teen-agers in coping with Shakespeare's inexhaustible and very motley vocabulary are enormous. The vocabulary of the translation is smaller and much more homogeneous; and where, in English, a passage will stubbornly retain a flavor of obscurity, the translator is bound to render it in a way to make sense. The simplification and reduction inherent in any translation of Shakespeare also help to account for the fact that more Shakespeare plays are produced and seen by more people every year in Germany than in England.

These sketchy remarks about the reception of Shakespeare in Germany are needed as an introduction to the subject of my essay, Shakespeare criticism in Germany. This subject, however, is much too large to be profitably condensed into an essay. Also, I am not a specialist in the field. If my interest in Shakespeare has remained very much alive since my college days, it is because the work of the great German poets and philosophers testifies to Shakespeare's abiding presence. German drama, from Goethe to Hauptmann, including Schiller, Grillparzer, Hebbel and Otto Ludwig, bears the imprint of Shakespeare. Since I want to speak of Shakespeare as a living force in German literature rather than as an inexhaustible subject for the investigation of scholars, I shall limit myself in the main to the impact of one particular play, the play that has aroused the most widespread interest and has called forth the greatest variety of interpretation—*Hamlet*. We begin with Goethe.

We are told that Goethe's enthusiasm for Shakespeare was kindled by Herder. This is true insofar as Goethe's horizon expanded enormously during his association with Herder in Strasbourg in 1771. Shedding the rococo manner of his early youth, Goethe found himself transformed into a Titan, affirming strength and intensity as his supreme values and assigning to beauty, equated with charm and prettiness, a subordinate role. It is only after he had caught the pulse of Herder's *Lebensgefühl* that he hailed Shakespeare as the incomparable genius. But the fact is that Goethe had begun to know and admire Shakespeare at the age of sixteen, shortly after his arrival at the University of Leipzig. Dodd's *Beauties of Shakespeare* fell into his hands. He straightway began to quote from this book of excerpts in his long, rambling, multilingual letters to his sister (passages from *As You Like It, The Merchant of*

Venice, Romeo and Juliet). He began to try his hand at writing English, and, like many college students today, he made a stab at writing verse in the new language. It is amusing to read in one of these letters "A Song over the Unconfidence Toward Myself." Such lines as "In moments of meláncholy" or "I hum no súpportable tune" show his unfamiliarity with English accent, and the following stanza is a real gem of German word order:

> Hah, when my child, I love thee, sayd,
> And gave the kiss I sought,
> Then I—forgive me, gentle maid—
> She is a false one, thought.

At this early time Goethe sensed that the German imitation of the French six-beat Alexandrine verse, practiced for over a century in tragedy, was on its way out, about to be replaced by the more flexible iambic pentameter of English usage, and in his characteristic manner he communicated this information to his sister in lines of this five-beat pattern. But that Shakespeare had made more than a superficial impression on young Goethe even before he met Herder, we learn from a letter of February 20, 1770, addressed to Philipp Emmanuel Reich. Expressing his high regard for a Leipzig etcher, Oeser, who had taught Goethe the rudiments of his craft, Goethe goes on to say that except for Oeser and Shakespeare he will acknowledge only Wieland as his genuine teacher. All others have shown him what mistakes to avoid. These three, on the other hand, have shown him the way to positive improvement ("wie ich es besser machen könnte") [how I could do it better].

The inclusion of Wieland in this trio is significant. In Goethe's commemorative address on Shakespeare, written under Herder's influence in the fall of 1771 ("Zum Schäkespears Tag"), he couples a disparaging remark on Wieland with a vicious thrust at Voltaire (whose *English Letters* had first made Shakespeare known on the Continent). There was, indeed, one more such episode, two years later, when Goethe poked fun at the rococo spirit trespassing upon the ancients, in his *Götter, Helden und Wieland*, but from the time of his arrival in Weimar, in 1775, throughout the rest of his life, Goethe treated Wieland with great cordiality and respect. Whenever he mentions Wieland's translation of Shakespeare in his writings, he does so in terms of high praise, even going so far in his

Dichtung und Wahrheit as to express his preference for the prose version over Schlegel's masterly verse rendition. If we find that whole passage embarrassing and almost incredible in its peculiar reasoning and obvious bias—seeing that the young critics of 1770 had torn Wieland's work to shreds and that Gundolf's great twentieth-century study, *Shakespeare und der deutsche Geist,* is scandalized by the frivolity of Wieland's engaging in an enterprise so alien to his temperament and so vastly beyond his capacity—it shows how deeply Goethe felt indebted all his life to the image of Shakespeare presented by Wieland to himself and his companions of the era of Storm and Stress.

When Goethe first discovered *Hamlet* I do not know. It is hard to think that the effervescent and volatile enthusiast should have thought of himself as kin to the melancholy Dane. It is much more likely that he identified with the escapades of Prince Hal, and I suspect that he cultivated his love of disguise and his talent of impersonation with a conscious eye to his illustrious model. But there is no reason to doubt his account in *Dichtung und Wahrheit* (Bk. XI), where he tells of reading the whole Hamlet play aloud in one sitting to Friederike Brion and her sister, when the two girls from the village of Sesenheim visited him in Strasbourg. He dwells on this reading, addressed to the girl he loved, as a memorable experience.

For Goethe's critical preoccupation with *Hamlet* we have to turn to his novel, *Wilhelm Meisters Lehrjahre,* published a quarter of a century after the effervescent address "Zum Schäkespears Tag." The hero, a poet by temperament, a cultivated young man of bourgeois origin, has a passion for the stage that dates back to his childhood. In his early twenties, having left home for extended travels, commissioned by his father to look after his business interests, he makes the acquaintance of some players that have strayed from a troupe, and before he knows it and almost against his will he finds himself deeply involved in their affairs. First participating in their enterprise in an amateur capacity, Wilhelm is eventually induced to become a professional actor. What decides him is the fact that Serlo, the astute, practical manager of a well-organized standing troupe in a North German city, has promised to stage a production of *Hamlet,* unaltered and uncut, in which Wilhelm is to act the part of the prince. Long before this, a man whose personality greatly impressed Wilhelm had put a copy of the German Shakespeare into his hands (Bk. III, Chap. 8). On beginning to read, his prejudice against an author notorious for his "strange monstrosities" had given way to amazement and boundless admiration. After reading his way into the plays, his interest had concentrated on "the incomparable *Hamlet*" (Bk. IV, Chap. 3).

Goethe develops his interpretation, appraisal, and criticism of Shakespeare's *Hamlet*, the play and its hero, in the novel, begun in 1777 but radically recast fifteen years later and published in 1795-1796. In the published version, separated from young Goethe's heady enthusiasm for Shakespeare by a quarter of a century, the discussion of *Hamlet* forms the core of Wilhelm's intellectual and practical preoccupation with drama and theater. *Hamlet* is the subject to which Wilhelm returns in chapter after chapter of Books III-V, and this interest culminates in a production of *Hamlet* on the stage of a North German city under the direction of an experienced producer who attempts to combine fidelity to Shakespeare's poem with regard for the interest and understanding of his German audience.

Since Wilhelm's development and his ideas coincide with the decade during which *Hamlet* achieved popularity on the German stage, Goethe's novel is deliberately focused upon the reception of Shakespeare by the German literary public. To read the discussion of *Hamlet* in *Wilhelm Meister* as if it were a critical essay, and to systematize the observations on *Hamlet* scattered throughout hundreds of pages, is to take a false approach. The discussion of *Hamlet* is imbedded in a novel. It is begun and sustained by the enthusiasm of the novel's hero. But a variety of views are voiced by various characters, the discussion is essentially dialectic, and the hero's views on *Hamlet* undergo modification in important aspects. Moreover—and this must not be overlooked—Goethe, the author, does not fully identify with Wilhelm Meister. Goethe always treats Wilhelm with a certain benevolent condescension. Goethe projects Wilhelm as an incorrigibly naive idealist, full of poetic enthusiasm, generous to a fault, ready to be taken advantage of by people whose association with the stage invests them with an aura of glamor in his eyes. He is virtuous but not prudish. He is a great talker, snatching every opportunity to deliver himself of fine generalizations on human life with little or no regard for the temper of his captive audience.

It is clear that such a personality, granting Wilhelm's good will, the intensity of his approach and his great intuitive capacity, would tend to see the young prince, whose fine soliloquies first kindled his admiration, through the distorting medium of his own temperament. Wilhelm, vastly more simple and homogeneous than his creator, is no match for Hamlet's erratic complexity; and when he characterizes Prince Hamlet as "ein höchst moralisches Wesen" (a man of the highest moral integrity) (Bk. IV, Chap. 13), we may suppose that Wilhelm rather smugly sees himself reflected in his favorite hero. In another passage of the same chapter, on the other hand, where Wilhelm sees Hamlet at his uncle's court reduced from heir presumptive to a mere nothing, the phraseology is definitely Goethe's and unmistakably dictated by echoes of Schiller's *Don Carlos*, where the status of the prince at King Philip's court is just that,[1] whereas King Claudius' throne speech in Act I accorded the highest possible position of honor to his nephew.

The general formula to express the theme of the play: "the mandate of a great deed thrust upon a soul [a sensitive temperament] that is not equal to it," ("eine grosse Tat auf eine Seele gelegt, die der Tat nicht gewachsen ist"; Bk. IV, Chap. 13) is obviously Goethe's and Wilhelm's. This also applies to its elaboration. The maturing of Wilhelm's penetration into Hamlet, after his first attempts to identify piecemeal with all the prince's moods have led him to a dead end, is shown in the new method of his approach. The study of an individual role in isolation will lead to nothing; for a key to Hamlet's character the whole play must be studied in all its complexity. In particular, every lead must be explored to make us see the prince as he was before the double shock of his father's death and his mother's hasty remarriage threw him into the turmoil from which he never recovered (Bk. IV, Chap. 3). Proceeding on the assumption that Shakespeare's "incomparable" *Hamlet* is an organic product of the poet's genius, this method offers the only sound approach to the work. It is universally valid as a heuristic principle of literary interpretation. The endeavor to be objective

---

[1] The line "in seines Nichts durchbohrendem Gefühle" [pierced by the sense of his own nothingness] is addressed by Prince Carlos to Duke Alba, but the phrasing is what counts here, not the context.

and all-embracing in the imaginative identification with the poet's work is basic. Wilhelm has this endeavor, in contrast to Aurelie and her brother Serlo. Aurelie is an emotional subjectivist who projects her own tortured soul into the role of Ophelia without regard for the specific image created by the poet (Bk. IV, Chap. 14). Serlo, on the other hand, is the practical man of the theater who is willing to go to any lengths in departing from the poet's text in order to satisfy the demands of his public for an effective performance. Thus Wilhelm's approach is the only one concerned with doing justice to the poet's intent.

That the subjective factor of the recipient's personality and *Weltanschauung* intrudes despite all attempts at objectivity is apparent from Wilhelm's and Serlo's discussion of the over-all upshot of the catastrophic denouement. "The hero has no plan, but the play has a plan," Wilhelm insists (Bk. IV, Chap. 15). What appears on the surface like a freak series of accidents, a crazy play of chance, is in reality the working out of an immanent design, an ineluctable fate. Wilhelm experiences a lofty feeling of edification in seeing one royal house mowed down by death the reaper, and a new race of kings, represented by Fortinbras, arising to take over in its place. Serlo counters ironically that the wholesale destruction of the innocent along with the guilty would seem to do little honor either to Providence or to the poet's sense of a moral order. He might have added that the same kind of catastrophe terminates the crude pre-Shakespearean *Hamlet* performed by the English players in Germany and adapted for a German audience under the moralistic title "Der bestrafte Brudermord" [Fratricide Punished]. The distinction between chance and fate, and the feeling that only the latter was appropriate to elicit a sense of the tragic from reader and audience (Bk. V, Chap. 7), is something that Wilhelm and Serlo agree on. And this conformed to Goethe's ideas as formulated in a letter to Schiller shortly after the completion of *Wilhelm Meister*. Here, again, we have to be on our guard, however, against a dogmatic approach. Throughout the novel, Wilhelm has a great penchant for seeing the design of a higher fate directing his own life, where the reader sees an interplay of chance and the interference of a mysterious group of well-wishers at work, and Wilhelm is taken to task repeatedly for his subjectivism in attributing the course of his life to a higher supernatural guidance. Thus dialectic undercurrents of the novel leave Wilhelm's enthusiasm for the sublimity of the tragic denouement as the work of fate colored by a substantial ingredient of his emotional subjectivism.

In much of the *Hamlet* discussion in *Wilhelm Meister* the ordinary reader is likely to take Wilhelm's observations on *Hamlet* as Goethe's own, unaware of the fact that these observations are projected through the medium of an immature personality. The difference between the author and his hero emerges quite unmistakably where the construction of the play is discussed. Wilhelm is still in a stage of development, Goethe remarks, when we cannot think of an admired author or a girl we are in love with as anything but absolutely perfect (Bk. v, Chap. 4). He is impatient of any criticism leveled at the diffuseness of the last two acts. But when he is confronted with the alternative of either cutting away indiscriminately what he calls the scaffolding of the edifice, or of shoring up the structure more economically in accordance with the available talent and the capacities of the audience, Wilhelm makes a startlingly quick and radical turnabout. A few days of concentrated thinking on the subject convince him that Shakespeare's close adherence to the diffuse action of his novelistic sources is responsible for grievous errors in the handling of the denouement. He has found a way to remedy all this; he is sure, in fact, in the heat of his enthusiasm, that Shakespeare, with a little more time to devote to the problem, would have hit upon the identical solution proposed, and he develops his plan to Serlo, who enthusiastically approves of the changes. Later, to be sure, Wilhelm retracts much of his adverse criticism: he comes to realize that much of what he found unsuitable for his German eighteenth-century audience would not have disturbed the Elizabethan English public, accustomed as a seafaring nation to the widest geographical perspective (Bk. v, Chap. 5). In thus presenting an adaptation of *Hamlet* that he prides himself upon as an improvement on Shakespeare, and then conceding that the adaptation is valid for his *ad hoc* audience only, Goethe is seen wrestling with the problem of *Hamlet* as a practical man of the theater (he had been director of the Weimar stage since 1792) and at the same time as vindicating Shakespeare in terms of his own historical situation and perspective.

When we look closely at the changes suggested by Wilhelm—the elimination of all reference to Wittenberg, the elimination of Hamlet's embassy to England and his capture and release by the pirates, the elimination of Fortinbras' expedition against the Poles, the substitution, in place of all this, of a naval operation against Norway, headed by Horatio and participated in by Hamlet—we see that this simplification of the plot has brought in its wake far-reaching alterations in some of the principal characters. Horatio, no longer a poor gentleman, stranger to the court at Elsinore, is advanced to the status of an older, experienced officer, who enjoyed the favor of the old king. He is the soul of the expedition, and it is to him that Hamlet, dying, gives his vote for the succession to the Danish throne. By the elimination of Wittenberg, the basis of Horatio's friendship with Hamlet is undermined and left hanging in the air. King Claudius is referred to as "saumselig" (Bk. v, Chap. 4), a dilatory reveler, in sharp contrast to the initiative attributed to him by Shakespeare in the feverish preparations against the expected invasion from Norway and his statesmanlike diversion of Fortinbras' hostile enterprise into channels that would make Denmark the indirect beneficiary of his success. Queen Gertrude's personality also undergoes a change in the adaptation: Hamlet is allowed, contrary to his mother's earlier wishes, to join Horatio and the fleet "weil er dem König und der Königin zu gefährlich wird" (because he becomes too dangerous to the king and the queen). Shakespeare's queen never wavers in her deep attachment to her son. When she reports to her husband that Hamlet killed Polonius, she not only stresses Hamlet's madness, in obedience to his entreaty to do so *and* believing him to be mad, but also, in order to shield him, she makes it appear as though he had been devastated with remorse over having killed "the good old man," whereas Hamlet had reacted to the corpse with annoyance and callous disgust.

The image of the prince himself is profoundly changed. Even in his analysis of Shakespeare's play Wilhelm-Goethe had conceived of Hamlet as a man not deficient in will power as such, but not equal to the mandate of the great deed thrust upon him. But now, in the adaptation, the "hero without a plan" is about to act planfully by seizing the opportunity to put himself at the head of an armed force and exact vengeance; it is only the contrary winds that keep the fleet from sailing, that rob Hamlet of the opportunity to carry out his plan. Such initiative does not at all conform to the image of Hamlet, as I see it. The sense of relief evidenced by Serlo by the elimination of Wittenberg (Bk. v, Chap. 4) is somewhat puzzling. I believe that Wilhelm and Goethe wanted to think of Hamlet as a young but mature man, who spoke his soliloquies on the basis of a wealth of practical observation and not as the precocious derivative wisdom of the adolescent who had been the pride of his teachers before being called home by his father's death. The elimination of the embassy to England was due, I believe, to considerations that had very little to do with the alleged aim of simplifying the plot. We remember Wilhelm's characterization of Prince Hamlet as "ein höchst moralisches Wesen." This estimate is never revised, and it is fair to assume that Goethe's view of the hero coincided with Wilhelm's. But the trick Hamlet plays on his escorts, in forging a commission to send them to their doom "not shriving time allowed" is unworthy of a man of noble character. The insertion of the phrase "not shriving time allowed" makes the order clearly an act of vengeance rather than of planful policy, and it is ignoble for vengeance to find gratification in taking it out on the instrument rather than the agent. (Antony whipping Octavius' messenger is a case in point.) Goethe and Wilhelm, in their disparaging references to Rosencrantz and Guildenstern (Bk. v, Chap. 5), identify with Hamlet in assuming these two, Hamlet's closest boyhood friends, to be guilty of consciously collaborating with the king for Hamlet's destruction. There is not one shred of evidence in the play to give substance to this assumption. But in any case Hamlet's cunning trick disfigured the image of the hero like a "vicious mole." Hence the whole episode was eliminated as out of keeping with the noble Hamlet. In the same way, Polonius had to be disparaged, not merely as senile, but as an unsavory politician. A "Halbschelm" (Bk. v, Chap. 6), a half-crook, Serlo calls him, to take the edge off Hamlet's outrageous treatment of the old snooper and his abuse of the corpse.

As would be expected, the discussion of *Hamlet* in *Wilhelm Meister* leaves many questions unanswered. Goethe showed great artistic tact in not freighting the novel with too heavy an intellectual load and in distributing the cargo over many areas. There is flexibility in this approach. The image of the play and its hero are developed as emergent and constantly opening up new aspects as the interpreter's insight progresses.

Generally speaking, there is projected an image of Hamlet, the hero, as a young idealist of the highest moral integrity and a sensitivity of sentiment that conjures up the image of Goethe's own Werther. Hamlet's unparalleled afflictions, including the obligation that runs ineluctably counter to his contemplative disposition, plunge him into a constantly darkening mood of *Weltschmerz* and make him fall victim to the evil machinations of his entourage. Insofar as any guilt attaches to him, it results not from his disposition but from the fatal situation in which he is placed. His apparent madness is only a mask which he is driven to assume under pressure of intolerable anguish. If I understand Goethe aright, no stigma of moral insanity attaches to Hamlet in his last phase. The blighting of his love for Ophelia is sentimentalized—inadvertently by Wilhelm; deliberately by Goethe?—in Ophelia's being pictured as a suitable marriage partner for the prince (Bk. IV, Chap. 14), contrary to the precise pronouncements of her brother and father, with nothing but Queen Gertrude's tearful words at Ophelia's grave to lend support to this view. Despite earnest attempts at objectivity, it is Hamlet's image of himself which dominates the unqualifiedly sympathetic approach of the German interpretation.

We cannot leave Goethe without touching upon his three-part essay, "Shakespeare und kein Ende" (literally and enigmatically, Shakespeare and no End). This essay reflects Goethe's views on that inexhaustible British author two decades after the publication of *Wilhelm Meister*. Its last part reduces the significance of Shakespeare for the modern theater. Its middle portion attempts to define the tragic aspect of man peculiar to Shakespeare, as differentiated from that of both the ancients and the Romantics (the moderns). But the upshot of this philosophical approach, in the manner of Hegel and his followers, is more entangling than enlightening, particularly in its application to the dilemma of Hamlet. The first part, on the other hand, is most notable in its grave and deliberate reaffirmation of the supremacy of Shakespeare's poetic genius. Shakespeare speaks far less to the outward senses than to the inner eye of the imagination. His word has the magic power of making the universe of man transparent. All his characters "wear their hearts on their sleeves." They verbalize all the crosscurrents of their drives and emotions to a degree incomparably in excess of actual life. They make us feel the pulse of the forces that move the world with an intensity, a range and clarity that our own experience cannot provide. Goethe's homage to Shakespeare is summed up in the following remarkable sentence: "There is no higher and no purer pleasure than to listen with eyes closed to the reading of a Shakespeare play, rendered, not declaimed, by a natural expressive voice." I can never read that sentence with its reverent approach to poetry without recalling an equally notable sentence epitomizing, by contrast, the alien mood of the age of reason. In his *Decline and Fall of the Roman Empire* Edward Gibbon wrote: "Among a polished people a taste for poetry is rather an amusement of the fancy than a passion of the soul."

In Germany the discussion of Hamlet—the play and the character—begun by Goethe, continues to this day. The number of books, essays, and papers on Shakespeare's *Hamlet* by poets, philosophers, and critics is staggering. A recent analytical study of major German trends of *Hamlet* interpretation and criticism reports at length on some fifty of the more significant attempts to come to terms with the problem of *Hamlet*. I refer to the book of a young Swiss scholar, Hans Jürg Lüthi: *Das deutsche Hamletbild seit Goethe* (Bern, 1951). This informative and well-documented account will be found highly stimulating by the Shakespeare specialist. But to list chronologically the names and dates of even the major figures and their publications with succinct comments and appropriate quotations would turn this occasion into what perceptive audiences refer to as a telephone-directory lecture.

As is well known, during much of the nineteenth century German intellectual life was largely dominated by speculative philosophy. The philosophers seized upon *Hamlet* as the philosophical drama par excellence, and adherents of the most divergent schools saw in the play and its hero a model exemplification of their *Weltanschauung*. Hegel and his school, seeing the world as the progressive realization of the spirit by an immanent dialectic movement of thesis, antithesis, and synthesis, saw the man Hamlet as the exponent of reflective thought, a noble, but rigidly restricted position that invokes as its corrective counterpart the antithetical principle of action. Hamlet being unable to act himself, the initiative of action devolves upon his antagonist, Claudius, who acquires a contingent justification as the defender of the status quo, that is of the actual world, in contrast to mere abstract thought. In the tragic denouement, where both parties perish, the pendulum has completed its swing in both directions. Equilibrium is restored on a higher level, in the accession of Fortinbras. In this Hegelian view, most precisely elaborated by Eduard Gans, a close friend of Heine's, the world spirit uses the individual to achieve its aim of restoring the moral order, but the individual functions less as an agent than as a tool. Hamlet defaulted in the performance of his assignment. Retribution is achieved, not by Hamlet but via Hamlet. Thus the optimistic Hegelian can point to the tragedy of *Hamlet* as a source of high philosophical edification.

But the same is the case in the camp of Hegel's most bitter antagonist, the pessimist Schopenhauer. To the mind of Schopenhauer the outcome of the play most forcefully demonstrates the fact that this is the worst of all possible worlds and that life is not worth living. Hamlet's gaze has pierced the veil of Maya, the world of appearances. His eyes have penetrated to the central mystery of life, the process of individuation, as the unending source of suffering. He knows there can be no surcease from the torturing drives, no *Erlösung*, except by the unqualified renunciation of the will to live and the return to the matrix that has spawned all the horrors of individual existence. Schopenhauer attributes to the Hamlet of the last act that serene renunciation of the will to live that is the mark of the true sage and the saint.

A half century later, Nietzsche reaffirms the view of his master Schopenhauer regarding Hamlet. In the blazing brilliance of his *Birth of Tragedy* (1871) it is the figure of Hamlet that exemplifies cognition, insight, carried to its ultimate limits and resulting in total paralysis of the will. Activity, the case of Hamlet teaches us, is possible only against a background of illusion. Where true insight has dissipated illusion and penetrated to the hideous core of existence, motivation leading to action has become inoperative; there remains only the longing for death. As we know, Nietzsche sets up this image of Hamlet as the prototype of philosophical pessimism only to repudiate it. Negation and despair become the foundation on which Nietzsche builds a philosophy of the most ecstatic affirmation of life. In a late reference to Shakespeare, prompted by the thought of his own *Zarathustra*, Nietzsche muses: "What must a man have suffered for him to feel the need to indulge in such clowning!" (*Ecce Homo*)

Regardless of school, philosophers were interested in the figure of Hamlet only as a type which could serve to illustrate their own basic theories of life, positively or negatively. They had none of the literary scholar's passionate respect for the poet's work as an organic creation. They treasured the abstraction to which they reduced it.

Another type of unliterary *Hamlet* interpretation, encountered throughout the first half of the nineteenth century, shows a political orientation. Post-Napoleonic Germany, the land that prided itself on being known as the land of thinkers and poets, politically an unwieldy conglomerate, invited comparison with the figure of Hamlet on many points. Any number of *Hamlet* interpreters, August Wilhelm Schlegel, Adam Müller, and the Hegelian Rötscher among them, pointed to the imbalance between thought and action, reflection and performance, as characteristic German traits. Ludwig Börne, the most effective radical journalist of the 1820's and '30's, a great admirer of Shakespeare, gave his analysis of Hamlet's personality a totally negative slant. In picturing Hamlet as indolent, incompetent, egocentric, a moral coward, Börne aimed his shafts at the reactionaries, the Romantic poets, and at Goethe. Börne felt that the salvation of Germany lay in following the course of the French Revolution. But the great majority of intellectuals and poets turned a deaf ear to the summons of the times because their comfort accorded with the maintenance of the status quo and they had no love for the people.

But it remained for a poet, an ardent democrat and nationalist, Ferdinand Freiligrath, to make the most pointed, tendentious identification of Germany with Hamlet. He voiced the fears and aspirations of thousands when, in 1844, he wrote his famous verses beginning with the words: "Deutschland ist Hamlet." The theme sounded in the first line is carried through all nine stanzas. Clad in shining armor, the ghost of buried Freedom stalks nightly in the citadel. It beckons to the guards and summons the dilatory doubter Germany-Hamlet to draw his sword and be the avenger of her foul murder: "They poured poison into my ear." Dumbfounded, he is slow to comprehend. Then he accepts his task. But he meditates and dreams. He wilts, unable to plan the deed that calls for initiative and courage, for his soul is capable of neither. By reading too much, by lying in bed, by fussing with abstruse learning, he has lost his vigor. He has become a thinker, not a doer. He spent too much time at the university in lecture halls and beer halls. He has become fat and short of breath, his blood runs sluggishly through his veins. The verses that follow are full of topical allusions: If for once he is provoked to draw, his lunge kills the wrong man, Polonius-Kotzebue. (Kotzebue, the prolific Weimar playwright, reputedly a spy for the Holy Alliance, was assassinated in 1817 by a young idealistic firebrand.) But now, the poet continues, we are moving into the fifth act. Let us hope that the parallel will not hold to the end. The poisoned French rapier is prepared for a treacherous thrust. (This refers to French aggressive designs against the Rhineland and danger of war in the 1840's.) Should Hamlet-Germany succumb, there is a northern army on the march, ready to take over the realm, but this time it would scarcely hail from Norway. (This alludes to the dispute over Schleswig-Holstein which eventuated in the two Danish wars of 1848 and 1864.)

In these verses the German body politic is castigated for its indifference toward the achievement of free political institutions within and for its failure to marshal its strength effectively against attacks from without. Despite the passionate invective that exposes the weakness of Hamlet-Germany's moral and physical character, these verses are not without an undertone of hope, even admiration. After all, the designation of hero is still applied to Hamlet. And the poem ends with the soul-searching realization on the part of the writer that he is himself a piece of that dilatory dreamer Hamlet-Germany.

When we now glance at the mass of German books, essays, and articles seriously concerned with the problem of *Hamlet* during the last hundred years, we find something of a composite image emerging despite the continuation of sharp debate concerning the temperament of the hero, his motivation and purposes, his involvement in tragic guilt, and the reading of the catastrophe as the working out of a transcendental design. Apart from crackpots, some highly respected voices made themselves heard in radical dissent. Thus Hermann Grimm (1875) propounded the view that Shakespeare deliberately posed an enigma defying solution. And Gustav Rümelin (1865) arrived at the conclusion that in *Hamlet* Shakespeare's artistic powers did not succeed in reshaping the traditional material into a new coherent whole. In our day, this view has been most impressively restated by T. S. Eliot.

By and large, however, German *Hamlet* criticism has tended to arrive at agreement on a number of basic points. These points, implicitly assumed as guide lines in Hans Jürg Lüthi's survey of the field, I would summarize as follows:

1. In *Hamlet*, Shakespeare's deepest insight into the tragic situation of man has found expression. *Hamlet* is Shakespeare's greatest work. Any deviation from this view bears the brand of heresy.

2. The hero is seen in very positive terms from beginning to end. He is noble throughout, and the range of his imagination stamps him with the mark of genius.

3. Hamlet's madness is all simulation, partly a ruse to confuse his enemies, partly a defensive device to keep himself sane in the face of excruciating torture.

4. Hamlet is desperately in earnest about carrying out his father's mandate.

5. The integrity of Hamlet's personality is vindicated by his death. He appears in a light of transfiguration in the last act. We follow his course with love and admiration.

6. The catastrophe leaves us with a sense of tragic edification. Through the exposure of the king's heinous crime and the exaction of retribution, the world has returned to a state of moral equilibrium.

The image, of which these six points are constituent features, has found its supreme elaboration in the *Hamlet* chapter of Friedrich Gundolf's monumental study of Shakespeare (2 vols., 1928). Gundolf, the most gifted exponent of the cultural movement that had its center in the poet Stefan George, demonstrated his incomparable mastery of the literary essay by a profusion of books on key figures of the Western World's cultural heritage. As a writer of intellectual prose saturated with sensuous imagery, he is without a peer in the German language. He seems to have had the gift of total recall along with the magic touch of evoking in three-dimensional substantiality every figure that he discusses. He is a prodigy of verbalization, recasting the conventional coin of the German language in an inexhaustible abundance of new variants unrecorded in any dictionary. The pulse of emergent creativity is to be felt in each of his long, apparently effortless sentences that toy with the plasticity of his medium. In following his discussion of Shakespeare the reader is under the illusion that all the great host of figures peopling the pages of Shakespeare's plays are simultaneously present at every moment in the writer's mind. It is as though his eye encompassed the whole starry expanse and could at will bring a star of whatever magnitude into the focus of the dazzled reader's vision. The reader is hypnotized by Gundolf's formulations and awed by a conviction of his infallibility. This has always been my experience when yielding to the persuasive magic of Gundolf's intuitive characterization and criticism. Gundolf's spiritual ties to the Romantic critics of a century and a half ago, the Schlegels in particular, are close enough for him to espouse their faith in Shakespeare's infallibility.

There is another side to the picture, especially as it applies to *Hamlet*. When one has made a long and concentrated effort to penetrate into the fabric of Shakespeare's text, shutting out as far as possible all those handed-down prejudgments that blur the receptive faculty, when one has sunk his teeth into some of the problems arising (and possibly lost some teeth in the process), when one then returns to a reading of Gundolf, the spell of his evocative eloquence no longer works. Then one comes to feel at point after point of his 25,000-word essay that he has ignored problems that clamor for discussion or obscured them by a flood of facile verbiage. By slightly retouching Shakespeare and elaborating on the background in a rhapsodizing style that throws critical caution to the winds, Gundolf fashions a portrait in which Prince Hamlet emerges as the ideal Renaissance man of genius. The range of his imagination, the variety of his moods, his capacity for suffering, and the complexity of the tensions joined in his nature, make his personality an enigma for all the lesser figures in his entourage. This image of Hamlet presupposes an intellectual climate that disdains the morality of the herd as a standard by which to judge the individual of superman stature. Gundolf's Hamlet owes its inspiration to the vitalism of Nietzsche. It is a distorting monumentalization of the hero, passionately partisan in its slant and scarcely remarkable for psychological penetration. It is not my image of Hamlet. It is, nevertheless, a brilliant chapter in a discussion that shows no signs of abating.

SCHILLER:
TRANSFIGURATION
OF A TITAN

I

AMONG GERMAN WRITERS of the first rank there is no one so easy to make fun of as Schiller, no one who has provoked so many quips from his own day to ours. Yet Schiller's stature is not dwarfed by his being seen standing alongside of Goethe. Despite Nietzsche's railing against the Germans for chanting Goethe *und* Schiller, to which he opposes his Goethe *aber* Schiller, the two men form a mutually compensating team. But there is this curious difference about them in the period of their friendly rivalry and collaboration: while Goethe was attacked from many quarters, Schiller was ridiculed by the sophisticates of his day. They thought they had him catalogued and classified once and for all as one of the lesser lights, this, when he was just on the point of rising to his full stature. When one of the distichs that appeared under the joint names of Goethe and Schiller challenged the ingenuity of the critics to identify its author, Friedrich Schlegel, with a pointed allusion to Schiller's terminology of naive and sentimental poetry, exultantly quipped: Here is a truly naive challenge, for who can fail to see that it is the other, "der für sein Heil zu dreiste Patroklus" (Patroclus, too brash for his own safety), who has donned the armor of the great Achilles in the vain hope of deceiving us Trojans? His brother August Wilhelm wrote a witty verse mocking Schiller's Swabian rhymes by punning on the verb "schillern":

> Wenn jemand Schosse reimt auf Rose,
> Auf Menschen wünschen und in Prose
> Und Versen schillert; Freunde wisst,
> Dass seine Heimat Schwaben ist.

> [When someone rhymes womb with rose,
> wish with mankind and scintillates
> in prose and verses: know, friends,
> that his homeland is Swabia.]

Reprinted from *A Schiller Symposium*, ed. A. Leslie Willson (1960), pp. 85-132, by permission of W. P. Lehmann, Chairman of the Department of Germanic Languages, the University of Texas.

Schillern, a word of common use for dazzling, shifting, iridescent light and color effects (*Schillertaft,* changing taffeta)—*schillern* is a word that Schiller seems to have studiously avoided. Was it that his conscience stirred every time it offered itself? Was it that he was sensitive to its too aptly spotlighting the great weakness of his middle period when he so often put on a brave and dazzling eloquent show of apostolic conviction to hide the fact that he knew himself to be skating on very thin ice with regard to those philosophical premises he was proclaiming with such bold assurance? The Schlegel circle rocked with laughter over Schiller's poem "Würde der Frauen," August Wilhelm remarking that it reads equally well if one begins with the last stanza and works up to the beginning. We feel the same way today about these alternating dactylic and trochaic stanzas, and the effect of these rhythms contrasting the male and the female temperament is irresistibly funny. One is tempted to set them to music by putting two instruments alternately to work during the song: a whirling eggbeater to accompany the ladies' voices and a puffing toy steam engine for the rude storming of the males.

> Ehret die Frauen! Sie flechten und weben
> Himmlische Rosen ins irdische Leben,
> Flechten der Liebe beglückendes Band
> Und in der Grazie züchtigem Schleier
> Nähren sie wachsam das ewige Feuer
> Schöner Gefühle mit heiliger Hand.
>
> Feindlich ist des Mannes Streben,
> Mit zermalmender Gewalt
> Eilt der Wilde durch das Leben
> Ohne Rast und Aufenthalt.
> Was er schuf, zerstört er wieder,
> Nimmer ruht der Wünsche Streit,
> Nimmer, wie das Haupt der Hyder
> Ewig fällt und sich erneut.
>
> [Honor the ladies! They braid and weave
> heavenly roses into earthly life,
> braid the enrapturing bond of love
> and in the modest veil of grace
> they nourish vigilantly the eternal fire
> of beautiful feelings with a holy hand.
>
> The striving of a man is hostile,
> with crushing power
> the wild one hurries through life
> without rest and sojourn.

Whatever he creates, he destroys again,
the battle of wills never ceases,
never, as the head of the hydra
eternally falls and renews itself.]

One modern critic cannot restrain his mirth when in the enormously popular *Song of the Bell,* "Das Lied von der Glocke," he hears the horses that draw the mother's hearse break into a trot. As we know, the German language is full of sententious familiar quotations of Schiller's coinage that come to everyone's lips, but almost invariably in a jocular context. Theodor Fontane's novels abound with instances of this, furnishing evidence both of Schiller's popularity and of the middle class social stratum that idolized Schiller for a hundred years. I remember as a boy reading a German life of Napoleon that taxed my patience by quoting at least two lines of Schiller verse on every page. This struck me even then as the deadly mannerism of a crank. As to the use made by nineteenth-century foreigners of Schiller quotations in a serious context —I think of Balzac and Dostoevski—the effect on a person familiar with German literary tradition is very peculiar. When Dmitri Karamazov in one of his emotional flights goes into transports as he quotes copiously from "An die Freude," it is not only the slowly dawning discovery that this turgid bombast, done into English on the basis of a Russian translation, paraphrases the sentiments of the *Ode to Joy* that breaks the mood of empathy, but the original German song itself embarrasses a sensitive ear by its extravagant crudity. As we all know, Beethoven used part of it as the text of the fourth movement of his Ninth Symphony, but a great musician is not necessarily sensitive to the art of words, and vice versa. We need not chime in with Klopstock who termed the poem "das Abscheulichste, was man sich auf der Welt denken kann" [the most abominable thing that one can imagine in all the world]; we may side with Schiller's own judgment, fifteen years after penning this youthful effusion, to the effect that, despite its recommending itself by a certain fiery emotionalism, it is a bad poem. Soberly viewed, it is the effervescent product of a bacchic mood, wallowing in shoddy rhetoric, whirling in a cosmic tantrum, reaching a ridiculous climax in proposing a toast to God:

Dieses Glas dem guten Geist
Überm Sternenzelt dort oben!

[This glass to the good spirit
over the starry canopy above.]

The previous stanza had sworn off every grudge and included "our mortal enemy" in a gesture of universal embrace; the one that follows the toast to God switches the theme from joy to manly virtue and ends on a thunderous note of: "Untergang der Lügenbrut!" [Down with the pack of liars!]. A final stanza, deleted in later printings, attuned the mood of the chorus to a grave *memento mori* and a serene posture in expectation of the verdict that will decide man's fate in the Beyond. By the time Schiller wrote this poem he had unquestionably cast overboard the conventional Christian notion of reward and punishment in an after-life. He had said this explicitly in his poem "Resignation," written a year earlier but published in the second issue of his journal *Thalia* along with "An die Freude." In "Resignation" the dialectical clash of conflicting attitudes with regard to a life to come had been resolved with the explicit conclusion: The world is eternal; there is no world judgment other than the immanent course of the world's history. The voice of Genius cried out to the poet's bewildered soul:

Geniesse, wer nicht glauben kann. *Die* Lehre
Ist *ewig wie die Welt*. Wer glauben kann, entbehre.
Die Welt*geschichte* ist das Weltgericht. (italics mine)

[Let him who cannot believe enjoy. *That* precept
is *eternal like the world*. Let him who can believe do without.
The *history* of the world is the Last Judgment.]

Yet Schiller ended the *Ode to Joy* with the discarded notion of a day of resurrection. Why did he do this? For dramatic effect, without doubt, to light up the poem with a final burst of cosmic fireworks. If challenged on this, Schiller would have protested against being taken seriously. He would have pleaded poetic license as to the idea, just as it was second nature to him to resort to personification in dressing up in verse the general ideas that were his stock in trade.

Poetic language was to Schiller only so much decorative drapery, never bearing too close an examination. A touch of the figurative was his way of giving a graceful turn to a sentiment, and the same conventional imagery could as often as not be given a twist to make it equally applicable to a contrary sentiment. (We could trace the ever-recurring image of "picking flowers," now with a negative, now with a positive connotation, to illustrate the arbitrary mobility of Schiller's conventional imagery.) That is the weakness of Schiller's flowery language. He had come early to think of poetic language as an embellishment superimposed on a reality that needed the embellishing touch to make it bearable. Poetic language was an attractive façade to cover up the sober prose of "truth," to conceal the distasteful tissue of material existence, which his study of medicine had taught him to see in terms of organic decay and nauseous odor. To put it crassly, the function of poetry was for Schiller, among other things, that of the Hollywood master mortician, who decks out the corpse to give a deceptive semblance of smiling prettiness and cheer. Schiller, the student of medicine, the "Regimentsarzt," did not have to fall back merely on the baroque tradition of *memento mori* for this view: he knew the stench of disease, death, and decomposition from the anatomical laboratory and the hospital. One of his poems to Laura anticipates Baudelaire's "Une Charogne" in projecting a view of his beloved, a few years hence, as a rotting carrion. Life, tending inevitably to hideous dissolution, must not be viewed at too close a range. The poet who covers it with a flowery mantle is a benefactor of mankind.

This view of poetry came to young Schiller as a matter of first-hand experience. Coupled with it was the theoretical idea, presented in the science course of the *Akademie*, that Nature, taken in its largest aspect, the stellar universe, is a dead, soulless aggregate of mechanical processes. Likewise, except for man, all the teeming life on earth, the trees and the flowers, the tiger, the maggot and the microbe, are soulless phenomena, products of the interaction of physical and chemical law. It is the function of the poet to endow all these with human desires and emotions on a strictly make-believe basis in order to comfort man with a deceptive sense of intimacy. The more effectively the poet succeeds in deceiving us into accepting this false, humanized, soul-endowed picture of Nature in place of the monstrously ticking mechanical clock of the universe, the more he deserves the gratitude of mankind. This profoundly pessimistic view of life and this view of poetry as an opiate and intoxicant determines, to a large extent, Schiller's outlook, his *Lebensgefühl*, during the whole of his short span of life. They become modified and blended with optimistic crosscurrents as Schiller's faith in man's inalienable metaphysical freedom emerges; but his optimism is reserved for man's innermost drive and for a realm of absolute values beyond space and time.

As a type, Schiller is the poet of general ideas. His imagination never dwells on particulars. Schiller has no eyes, but his eye has a commanding sweep. Intimate personal experience contributes a minimal share to the tissue of his poetry. It is always in bold fresco style that he conjures up his pictures of Nature. He knew a lily from a rose, but it is to be doubted whether he could tell a violet from a pansy, an oak from a beech. In the animal world, it is always the tiger and the worm that turn up as his stock examples. When one reads the body of Schiller's poetry in chronological sequence, from his juvenilia to the great philosophical poems of his maturity, one keeps constantly asking: What does Schiller believe in? How does Schiller view man's place in the cosmos? What is the meaning of human life? Schiller started out in his youth with the ready-made values of Christian tradition. They were quickly discarded in favor of a scientific, mechanistic view of the universe; but the temper of the Enlightenment, religiously oriented despite its rejection of re-vealed religion, exposed Schiller to a great variety of mutually contradictory philosophies on which his imagination seized and with which it experimented. During the turbulent years of his Storm and Stress, Schiller felt free to play with all manner of extravagant hypotheses. After his life had taken a more settled turn, he was constrained by circumstances to adopt the preceptorial pose of an apostle of the Enlightenment and to pretend to serene assurance of insight regarding the course of human history and the providential plan unfolded in its stages. But while he entered into his role with gusto and flattered himself with the elegance of his performance, he did so with a bad conscience. He was well aware of the fact, if his readers were not, that he was trafficking in glittering phrases for the edification of simple minds; that his pretended insight was just another phase of poetic make-believe, offering a colorful imaginative show that masqueraded as truth. It was only when he came into contact with the philosophy of Kant (in the early 1790's) that he found a platform on which he could henceforth stand with assurance. He had saved his soul at last, and the words he hence-forth uttered had the ring of conviction.

Let us attempt a brief survey of Schiller's development up to the point of his encounter with Kant's abstract critical doctrine.

There is first the traditional Protestant outlook implanted in the boy by family and teachers. The chill of shrinking fear and the warmth of expanding love appear blended in this austere faith reared on a base of unquestioning submission to paternal and political authority. The uneasy symbiosis of these ingredients is vividly exhibited in the career of his father, a remarkable man who left us a straightforward and highly revealing account of his life. His talents, his practical mind, and his tenacity won out over his limited education and made him rise from very humble beginnings to honestly earned middle-class prosperity in the service of Duke Karl Eugen of Württemberg. An apprentice barber and field surgeon in his teens, he was repeatedly taken prisoner in local wars and forced to don the uniform of his captors. He saw his share of engagements, he fought, killed, and took booty. Later he managed the tree nurseries of his Duke. He has to his credit the planting of tens of thousands of fruit trees on the Duke's estates, and he published a treatise on his specialty. The fact that his son's spectacular insubordination and flight did not cause him to lose the favor of the Duke speaks for his integrity and his close-mouthed caution. His character suggests the hardy stamina of the best of the American pioneers. In his son we see the same unflagging energy, ambition, and capacity for self-discipline; also, in his later years, a sense of diplomatic tact and a skill in negotiating practical matters which come as a surprise in the idealistic poet. The female side of the family stayed within the bounds of mediocrity. Schiller's sister Christophine, the poet's elder by two years, who lived to a ripe old age, is largely responsible by her sentimental anecdotes for the legendary image of the gentle poet that made him the idol of the German middle class in the nineteenth century. She exhibits the limitations of her matter-of-fact endowment rather cruelly in her account of her own unromantic marriage. It was, as she puts it, the presence of so many cavalry officers at the court, and all their horses and the indelicacy of the stables that prevailed on her sensitivity to cast her lot with the hunchbacked Meiningen librarian Reinwald, twenty years her senior, who befriended Schiller during the months he spent in hiding after his flight.

The first stage of naively innocent acceptance of traditional piety came to an end when the adolescent Friedrich was assigned a place in the Duke's *Akademie*. This was an honor, but it came as a keen disappointment to the boy that he had to renounce his wish to become a preacher, as the school did not provide for a theological education. First enrolled as a student of law, he was later permitted to switch to medicine. Whether his awakening from innocence took a gradual or an abrupt course is rather obscure. We know that he conformed to the strict discipline of the Academy. For years he was in great personal favor with the middle-aged Duke who, after a dissolute youth, had one day surprised the country with the announcement, read from all the pulpits, that he had resolved henceforth to be a real father to his people. Education became his particular hobby, and he loved to attend class exercises and other functions in the company of his young, pretty, and popular mistress. The Duke was not slow to discover Schiller's oratorical talent, and he fostered it by competitive assignments for orations on set topics dealing with moot aspects of virtue—performances in which young Schiller starred. Some of Schiller's exercises, presenting a glittering show of empty dialectics, have been preserved for us. They abound in passages lavishing the most extravagantly fulsome praise on the Duke, his foster-father, to whom, as he puts it, he owes an infinitely greater debt of gratitude and reverence than to his physical father, and whom he adores as the incarnation of true virtue. This was the tone prescribed for such occasions, and Schiller no doubt took it up with gusto at first, giving rein to his faculty of polishing phrases, and ending up his elaborate periods with effective flourishes. Was he sincere in any of this? Most likely the question of sincerity did not enter the adolescent mind at all for some time: he simply gloried in the opportunity to show off his gifts. But as his critical maturity developed he took a cynical joy in mouthing these phrases tongue in cheek. Later, when the seething revolt of his heart made this tone of flattery nauseous to him, he branded this false cult of virtue as "lächerliche Tugend, die—Hanswurst erfand" [ridiculous virtue which—a clown invented]. He came to regard the moral training aimed at by the school and its ducal preceptor as a systematic corruption of youth. He resented bitterly not only what it had done to the whole academic community, but what it had done to him personally. The passage of the years after he had escaped from this atmosphere did not still his rancor. As far as public utterance was concerned he kept a dignified silence: after all, the Duke had ignored his flight instead of sending his henchmen to trap him, and the Duke had generously ignored the Jena professor's nine months' visit to his native land. But after the Duke's death in 1793, nine years after the poet's rebelliousness had burst into open flame, Schiller vented his rancor in a letter by referring to the late Duke as "der alte Herodes." The moral slaughter of the innocents still preyed on his mind. (We are reminded of Rilke's vehemently denunciatory reaction to a friendly letter addressed to him in later years by one of his one-time teachers at the military academy at St. Pölten.)

Once kindled, the spirit of inner revolt against the prevailing atmosphere of sycophantic subservience festered in young Schiller the more violently, the more carefully it had to be concealed at first from his mentors. At this time Schiller was experiencing an enormous upsurge of his oratorical and poetic powers. His clandestine preoccupation with literature produced his first drama *Die Räuber*, and spawned the poems of the "Anthologie." They inaugurated his phase of titanism, which carried over from his last years before graduation into his term of service as "Regimentsarzt," through his flight from the Duke's territory, and through three succeeding years which began with fantastic hopes and brought crushing disillusionment, insecurity, acute want, starvation, a mountain of debts, and a radically disordered existence in their wake. What we call his titanism is a sense of intoxication with his creative power, an overwhelming inflation of his ego. He, the individual, feels himself cut adrift from society and perceives all its values as mere conventions. He, the titan, is the measure of all things. His creative urge disports itself among a welter of ideas; his imagination plays with all the philosophical attitudes that come into his ken. During this stage of his titanism Schiller has no point of view that can be called his own; he experiments with them all.

Schiller's titanism is a sustained exhibitionistic pose. In a literary way it was a late wave of the tide of the Storm and Stress movement that swept across Germany in the 1770's. But the personal experience that touched it off in Schiller was the physical maturing of his sex. The male sex drive, now naked, now cerebrally masked, exhibits itself to full view in the most characteristic poems of this period. Actual contact with the opposite sex played a minimal part in this intoxicating expansion of his ego. The counterpart, the opposite pole of what he felt surging within him, was, on the other hand, the image of woman in general, and, on the other, nothing less than the physical universe. As could not but be the case in a youth reared in the Christian tradition, this drive manifested itself as a welter of desires and taboos. It raised him up to heaven, it plunged him into hell. It was the forbidden fruit of Paradise that now put him on a par with the gods and now made him tremble as at the perpetration of sacrilege. In the experience of sex the moral dichotomy of duty and impulse confronted Schiller in the core of his personality. The poems of Schiller's youth, though crude and raw as poems, are, psychologically considered, the most interesting product of Schiller's career. In a sense, their turbulent dynamics and crass antitheses anticipate everything that the later Schiller formed with more conventional restraint. Desire stalks through all of the later Schiller's poems and essays as the contaminating drive to be renounced in favor of disinterested contemplation. It is always referred to in general terms and embroidered with mythological allusions, because direct reference to the facts of life violates the code of prissy gentility insisted on by his wife; but whenever the concept of desire is evoked the sex drive is meant.

When we approach the poems of Schiller's youth with the question, what did he believe, we get a great variety of contradictory answers from them. His mind, stored with a host of half-assimilated literary and philosophical ideas, is in a state of flux and experiment. A great many of the early poems operate on a base of traditional Christian belief. Poems like "Der Abend," "An die Sonne," sing the praise of the Creator by glorifying His works. They display a theatrical panorama of Nature in which the poet manipulates the show, with its lights and shadows, with the roll of thunder, the roar of the waterfall, the ripple of the brook, the myriad tiny voices of the insect world. The poet prostrates himself before the Almighty, but it is his own self-conscious touch that really makes creation arise out of chaos. The piety of these poems, unlike that of their model, Klopstock, is a matter of showmanship. There is a very revealing passage where the poet, overwhelmed by the spectacle of sunset, apostrophizes the Lord in the lines:

> Vater der Heil'gen vergib.
> O vergib mir, dass ich auf mein Angesicht falle
> Und anbete dein Werk!

[Father of the saints, forgive,
O forgive me, that I prostrate myself
and adore thy works!]

He transgresses against the Lord's command to worship the Creator and not His creation, but is not his confessing to his transgression a gesture of flattery no different in kind from those that his Duke would have graciously acknowledged? He may surely be pardoned for letting his theologically trained reason be overcome by the magnificence of the spectacle. The lines quoted, moreover, have been the subject of an unresolved controversy: Is a printer's oversight responsible for the omission of a "nicht" in the middle line?

Vergib mir, dass ich *nicht* auf mein Angesicht falle
Und anbete dein Werk!

[Forgive me, that I do *not* prostrate myself
and adore thy works!]

Such a reading would certainly enhance the subtle dialectics of flattery with the poet saying: Forgive me, father, for remembering your injunction in the face of such rapture.

There are funeral odes, occasional pieces, some of them done to order, in which Schiller, after the manner of an accomplished pulpit orator, plucks the heartstrings of the bereaved survivors, now making them sob and groan over their loss, now inducing a flood of sparkling tears at the thought that the departed has entered upon the bliss of Paradise. There is a stanza in which Schiller does not shrink from having the bereaved father rail in blasphemous fury against a "barbarous" deity that has blasted his hopes—to return, of course, from this paroxysm to humble acceptance of the dictates of an all-wise Providence. But when it is General Rieger, one of Karl Eugen's top officers, who is carried to the grave, Schiller exploits his privilege of religious oratory to deliver a blow below the belt. First he employs all his transfiguring rhetoric to paint the deceased in the guise of an angel. Then, shifting the scene to the bar of divine judgment where man is stripped of all earthly accessories, he exclaims: What are all Karl's decorations now but trash and tinsel! As a general reflection this was unexceptionable, but the personal twist made it highly offensive, the more so as Schiller had been foxy enough to introduce the Duke's name early in the poem by addressing the mourners as "Krieger Karls" [warriors of Karl]. He could play the innocent, then, in reverting to the personal note at the end as in keeping with the rest of the poem. But we can be sure that Karl Eugen was not fooled. It is safe to assume that he resolved not to let his stripling creature's insolence go unpunished.

The scales of judgment, so prominently displayed in Klopstock's odes, Schiller learned to employ as the heaviest brass of his lyric orchestra. He uses them with telling effect in "Der Eroberer." This is among the most interesting of Schiller's youthful poems by virtue of the extreme involvement of its dynamic build-up and the bizarre emotionalism of its climax. The Conqueror is pictured as a fiend of colossal stature who has trodden humanity into the dust. Then Schiller imagines the sounding of the trumpet of Judgment Day to bring the enemy of mankind to book. There, suspended between heaven and earth is the scale in which the Conqueror's deeds are to be weighed. This scale is empty while the Conqueror sits enthroned in his purple in the other. First, the host of the Conqueror's victims, an endless throng, file past and hurl their cry of vengeance into the empty scale. Then the sun, the moon, and all the spheres throw their weight into the scale. They are followed by all the celestial hosts who do the same. Weighted with all these curses, the scale begins to sink and the other scale slowly rises to bring the malefactor into the presence of God. And now comes the climactic gesture to complete his doom: a thundering curse issuing from the poet's lungs contributes the deciding weight to make the scale of the Conqueror's crimes plunge to the abyss of hell. The final scene shows the poet rolling in the dust with convulsive joy and chanting through all eternity his praise of the beautiful Day of Judgment. This is juvenile titanism foaming at the mouth. But in the middle of the poem he came so close to identifying with the Conqueror's dreams of grandeur as to all but confess: If I cannot be God I would be Lucifer. The Conqueror is Milton's Satan thinly disguised. It is pointless to ask what human figure he had in mind, an Alexander, an Attila, a Ghengis Khan. His own age supplied no model for the colossus. A generation later there was a real conqueror, Napoleon, whom the frenzied hatred of a Kleist execrated as "ein der Hölle entstiegener Vatermördergeist" [a patricidal spirit risen from hell]. But young Schiller had to spend his anathema on a straw man of the imagination, just as he, like Klopstock before him and Hölderlin a little later, had to glory in the posture of dying for the fatherland without there being anything on the contemporary map to warrant that exalted name. The fatherland Schiller longed to die for was the brainchild of the German humanists of the sixteenth century, and it was the Roman legionaries of Varus in whose blood he longed to bathe.

In a piece cautiously entitled "Die *schlimmen* Monarchen" [The *bad* Monarchs] (italics mine), Schiller directs his fire against potentates and princes whose mad orgy of power, pomp, and lust has come to a halt in the silent stench of the tomb. His lips curl with a sneer as he repeatedly apostrophizes the fallen mighty as "Erdengötter" [gods of earth]. (How different the temper of Goethe in his *Tasso* where, eight years later, the princes of the Renaissance are still referred to as "Erdengötter" without any satiric overtone!) Schiller wallows in offensive imagery, he inflates his nostrils to savor the pus of decomposition. He pulls all the registers of pointed insult, and the last line of each stanza rhetorically cracks the whip over his silent victims. No vindictive proletarian has ever gloated with more ghoulish glee over his reduced exploiters. There is the difference, of course, that Schiller's sadistic resentment vents itself within a framework of holy religious zeal. He poses as the mouthpiece of divine wrath annihilating the perverters of true virtue.

There is a poem on Rousseau apotheosizing the saintly martyr who fought against the three monsters of the age: religious fanaticism, prejudice, and egotism. Schiller couples his fate with that of Socrates as he lashes out against the Christian world in the poem's most pointed stanza:

Wann wird doch die alte Wunde narben?
Einst war's finster—und die Weisen starben,
   Nun ist's lichter—und der Weise stirbt.
Sokrates ging unter durch Sophisten,
Rousseau leidet—Rousseau fällt durch Christen,
   Rousseau—der aus Christen Menschen wirbt.

[But when will the old wound heal?
Once it was dark—and the wise men died,
   now it is lighter—and the wise man dies.
Socrates perished because of sophists,
Rousseau suffers—Rousseau falls because of Christians,
   Rousseau—who recruits men from Christian ranks.]

In this poem there is an undercurrent of high hopes in the dawn of the Enlightenment, which Schiller, a few years later, so eloquently hails as the new era that has achieved the enthronement of the dignity of man. But for the time being Schiller's imagination is involved in other topics.

I have already remarked on the dominant role of sex during Schiller's phase of titanism. We must now turn to the working out of this theme in the poems. In its simplest aspect we see it in a piece called "Kastraten und Männer," an exuberant panegyric on raw, ithyphallic masculinity. "Ich bin ein Mann," he shouts. He exults in being able to show in his male organs "den Stempel zu Gottes Ebenbild" [I am a man, the stamp of God's own image]. He boasts of being able by virtue of this to put to flight even the emperor's daughter should he meet her alone. He pours scorn upon castrates. He sums up the glory of his status in the lines:

> Wer keinen Menschen machen kann,
> Der kann auch keinen lieben.
>
> [He who cannot make a human being,
> also cannot love one.]

Except for its allusions to figures of Roman history this piece sounds like the blatant exhibitionism of a young savage, and the crudity of its versification is in keeping with this posture:

> Ich bin ein Mann, das könnt ihr schon
>   An meiner Leier riechen,
> Sie donnert wie im Sturm davon,
>   Sonst müsste sie ja kriechen.
>
> [I am a man, that you can surely
>   smell from my lyre;
> it thunders off as in the storm,
>   else it would have to creep.]

But this jubilant, uncomplicated proclamation of male potency becomes involved with philosophic speculation in a long series of poems addressed to the idea of woman under the name of Laura. In the Laura poems sex is the central mystery of life. A number of these culminate in the depiction of the physiological orgasm. But it is scarcely a man and a woman, it is rather a pair of cosmic forces that we see celebrating the mating act in the lines:

> Wenn dann, wie gehoben aus den Achsen
> Zwei Gestirn', in Körper Körper wachsen,
>   Mund an Mund gewurzelt brennt,
> Wollustfunken aus den Augen regnen,
> Seelen wie entbunden sich begegnen
>   In des Atems Flammenwind —

[When then, as though lifted from their orbits,
two stars, grown body into body,
    burning rooted mouth to mouth,
rain sparks of voluptuousness from their eyes,
souls meet as though released
    in the flame-wind of breath.]

Quite literally, they whirl through space as companions and co-equals of suns:

Aus den Angeln drehten wir Planeten.

[We hove planets from their hinges.]

The earth is left behind. They soar among stars. The scene of their orgies is always the stellar universe—and not just a poet's but a scientist's universe, a universe governed by the inviolable laws of celestial mechanics as evidenced by the repeated invocation of Newton's name. Gravitation is the spring that keeps the wheels of the universe turning.

So far science; but philosophy enters into the picture by contributing the idea that the prime law of attraction and repulsion also governs the universe of spirit. What operates as gravitation in the physical world is experienced in the world of spirit as *Sympathie*. Schiller takes over this favorite term of Wieland's as the name of the binding universal force, and he still uses it to conjure with in "An die Freude":

Was den grossen Ring bewohnet
    Huldige der Sympathie!

[Let whatever dwells in the great ring
    do homage to sympathy.]

Thus Schiller tries to bridge the dualism of matter and mind by a monistic synthesis. We should refer to this as mystical (and at moments it is mystical!) if the imagined unity were not so patently cerebral. Leaving aside passages where labored allegory stamps it as a mere exercise of abstract reflection, the best example to reveal this monism as essentially cerebral is the first strophe of "Die Freundschaft." The poem exhibits some of Schiller's finest *Schwung* and enthusiasm, but the comprehension of the first strophe hinges on the impossible stressing of a dative plural ending:

Freund, genügsam ist der Wesenlenker—
Schämen sich kleinmeisterliche Denker,
    Die so ängstlich nach Gesetzen spähn—

Geisterreich und Körperweltgewühle
Wälzet Eines Rades Schwung zum Ziele,
    Hier sah es mein Newton gehn.

Turned into prose, this says: Friend, Economy is the Creator's maxim. Shame on petty thinkers who try to discover a plurality of fundamental laws. It is the momentum of but one single wheel that governs both the realm of spirits and the whirl of the world of matter. It was in this latter area that the great Newton observed its workings.

Crosscurrents of dualism and monism that fail to integrate play across the most ambitious, artful, and psychologically revealing of the Laura poems. "Das Geheimnis der Reminiszenz" begins with a subconscious wish fantasy for an erection of eternal duration:

Ewig starr an deinem Mund zu hangen,
Wer enträtselt mir dies Wutverlangen?

[To hang forever rigid on your mouth,
who can unriddle me this furious desire?]

But the psychological core of the brilliant imagery of the next two stanzas is a sense of being rendered impotent when confronted with the physical presence of the object of his desire. He experiences a desperate sense of frustration and inner conflict: the unity of the self is reduced to a battleground of conflicting forces. Soul and senses are at loggerheads. The mastering will of the soul is betrayed and deserted by a host of treacherous vassals and recreant slaves. Brooding on this dualism, his overheated fancy takes a flight into pre-existence to picture himself and his Laura whirling through space as a single entity of free spirit. Plato had started Schiller on his flight, but Archimedes and Milton help to sustain it; for that free spirit-force glories in "heaving planets out of their hinges" and shattering worlds (the answering rhyme to "dein Dichter" is "ein Weltzernichter"!) [thy poet—world annihilator]. This couple is the greatest pair of delinquents on record: *our* delinquents, on Hallowe'en, overturn garbage cans and set barns on fire; these pranksters throw a wrench into the cosmic works from sheer excess of energy—all in the spirit of good, clean fun, with no idea of Satanic opposition to the Creator. No wonder that the spirit-force becomes the victim of the Deity's jealous wrath. It is fissioned into a male and a female half and both are imprisoned in bodies. Henceforth their existence exhausts itself in fruitless tormented desire to recapture the primal state of union. This is the sex drive, but it is checked by a sense of taboo, taint, and sin. The final scene of the poem drops the cosmic stage to revert to the myth of Genesis. It pictures the glee of the devils as they see the *innocently* whirling creatures trapped by the toils of lust.

In another of these poems Schiller holds out to his Laura the prospect of an enduring nuptial night. This will come about when Time and Eternity are locked in embrace as the world is consumed by fire.

All these poems are the product of a superheated brain feeding on cosmic and apocalyptic imagery. Sex in search of an object exhausts itself in gigantic dynamics. As poems they are monstrous. Most of them are much too long. They cannot sustain the fire of their initial *élan*. The white-hot rhetoric of their turgid blocks of phrases forbids any intimate identification. Yet close analysis is rewarding. What at first reading seems nothing but a foaming, disordered orgy turns out, more often than not, to follow an ingenious structural plan. Despite their bombast they are not formless effusions but works of calculated art. If they do not appeal as music, this is because the melodic theme is drowned out by an excess of orchestration.

Leafing through the poems of the "Anthologie" and trying to extract from them the outline of a *Weltanschauung*, the positive yield is very limited. The twenty-three-year-old poet believed in his own powers, in his freedom, and he believed in the facts of natural science. Everything else, all the notions derived from religion and philosophy were so many theatrical properties for him to set up at will and rearrange and discard, as it suited his fancy. But perhaps the most important observation regarding the cerebral display is this: He not only puts on a spectacular show but he reserves for himself the star part in the performance. In the love poems, he does all the whirling and the talking, Laura is only a dummy. In the religious poems, it is the flame of his voice that sears the culprit. In a poem about the vastness of the starry universe, "Die Grösse der Welt," it is he who shoots through cosmic space with the speed of light. It does not occur to him that the grandiose effect aimed at may boomerang. It is no small feat of course to exchange a word with a wanderer coming from the opposite direction and bent on the same errand. And whereas the poet is awed by the report of the limitless spaces left behind, are we not more likely to remark in the face of such a meeting: What a small world it is, after all! Or, returning to the poem about the Conqueror, where Schiller wants us to feel that the weight of *his* curse matches that of the victims, the sun, moon and stars, and the heavenly hosts combined, we may be tempted to think of it rather as the straw that breaks the camel's back.

Before leaving the lyric theater of Schiller's titanism, let us dwell upon one of his grandiose built-in pieces of imagery to illustrate the intoxicating pomp and glitter of his youthful style. There is a superlative purple passage in "Vorwurf an Laura," a poem that develops the theme of a feigned reproach but is really an extravagant gesture of homage to Laura. The first three stanzas have stated in general terms (involving the imagery of piled-up mountains, pyramids and the river of Hades) that he is no longer the giant he was before he succumbed to Laura's spell. Now he begins to develop by more specific examples the change she has wrought in him. The first of these, rendered in sober prose, would say: Formerly, when the sun rose, I leapt to greet it, but what of me now! Schiller uses a whole six-line strophe to introduce the idea of sunrise as a build-up before asking the fatal question. He begins with a dazzling image in which the thunderous clash of lances arouses victorious warriors from the embrace of beautiful courtesans. He suggests the glint of steel armor reflecting the rosy glow of female nudity—all this as an elaborate simile for the mythological image of the Sun-god leaving the rosy bed of Dawn to bring joy to an awakening world:

> Siegern gleich, die wach von Donnerlanzen
> In des Ruhmes Eisenfluren tanzen
>   Losgerissen von der Phrynen Brust,
> Wallet aus Auroras Rosenbette
> Gottes Sonne über Fürstenstädte,
>   Lacht die junge Welt in Lust.

> [Like warriors, who awakened by thunderous lances
> dance into the steely meadows of fame,
>   torn from Phryne's breast,
> there seethes from Aurora's bed of roses
> the sun of God above princely cities;
>   the young world laughs for joy.]

This grand preamble is followed by the question:

> Hüpft der Heldin noch dies Herz entgegen?
> [Does this heart still leap toward the heroine?]

"Die Heldin" is the sun, not Laura, as Schiller would have made abundantly clear in oral recital by an outstretched arm and an eye focused on a point of the horizon. But the reader is likely to miss this all-important point without a footnote to unmask the baroque eroticism of the passage as an allusion to Schiller's favorite verse from the nineteenth psalm, reading in Luther's translation: "Die Sonne gehet hervor wie ein Bräutigam aus seiner Kammer und freuet sich wie ein *Held* zu laufen den Weg." Schiller's transformation of the bridegroom and hero of the original into a "Heldin" conforms to the sun's grammatical gender, but it is motivated also by the erotic ardor of his context. In *Die Räuber* the allusion to the same biblical passage retains the masculine gender. "So stirbt ein Held" [That's the way a hero dies], says Karl Moor, his gaze lost in the splendors of the sunset. And it recurs in masculine form, a few years later, in one of the really fine passages of "An die Freude":

> Froh, wie seine Sonnen fliegen
> Durch des Himmels prächtgen Plan,
> Wandelt, Brüder, eure Bahn,
> Freudig wie ein Held zum Siegen.

> [Joyfully, as his suns fly
> through the splendid design of heaven,
> wander, brothers, your path,
> exultant as a hero to victory.]

It is fitting to conclude this sketchy survey of Schiller's poetry of titanism with the *Reproach to Laura*. The poem builds up to a highly effective climax when the poet throws off the transparent mask of reproach in order to fling himself at Laura's feet and proclaim that he owes his all to her love. Without her he would have been just a superman, but thanks to her he has become something higher, a lover of mankind:

> Über Menschen hätt ich mich geschwungen.
> Itzo lieb ich sie.

> [I could have soared above mankind,
> but now I love them.]

In its context, this seems no more than a glittering phrase uttered for dramatic effect. But this sentiment, here voiced for the first time (unless the logic of "Männerwürde": Wer keinen Menschen machen kann, der kann auch keinen lieben, be taken in this spirit!), is destined to become the keynote of Schiller's next phase. The titan, the iconoclast, the scourge of society blossoms into an ec-static lover of humanity in general. When he is in his cups, he flings his arms around mankind:

Seid umschlungen, Millionen,
Diesen Kuss der ganzen Welt!

[Be embraced, millions,
this kiss for the whole world!]

And when he is sober, his heart beats for the human race in the lyrical eloquence of Marquis Posa that all but moves the hardened tool of the Spanish Inquisition to turn the grim prison of his empire into an earthly paradise.

II

The yeasty ferment of titanism seethed in Schiller's blood from the first stirring of revolt against arbitrary authority until the end of his second sojourn at Mannheim. He fled his homeland with extravagant hopes of immediate fame and success as the new German Shakespeare, but his expectations were shattered at the first contact with reality. There followed years of a wretched, disordered existence that undermined his health, saddled him with debts, and taught him the hard elementary facts of social intercourse. He had written three plays, *Die Räuber, Fiesco,* and *Kabale und Liebe,* the last of which was great theater, if not great drama. But all this had done nothing to set him on the road to a secure career.

He was at the end of his resources when he launched his first literary journal, the *Rheinische Thalia.* The tone of the leaflet in which he announced this venture veered sharply away from his earlier cult of notoriety. This was a new voice speaking. With measured pride and manly self-assurance the author introduced himself as "a citizen of the world," attached to no prince or patron, making his appeal solely to an intelligent public whose friendship he hoped to gain by dedicating his talents to the elevation of mankind. In this posture frankness and flattery were subtly blended. That it amounted in part to a whistling in the dark is shown by the fact that the first issue to appear (in the spring of 1785) was dedicated with fulsome praise to Goethe's patron, Duke Karl August of Weimar, who had meanwhile conferred on Schiller the title of *Rat* after attending a reading of the first act of his newly begun drama

Don Carlos. The title carried no stipend; it was of value in giving Schiller a status in a world of graded class distinctions. But what saved him from ruin is the well-known fan-letter and gift from a circle of admirers in Leipzig. For six months Schiller neglected to acknowledge this tribute, but when he finally wrote, the response brought him an invitation that put all of Gottfried Körner's resources at his command and offered him a haven for an unlimited time. This unparalleled generosity marked the turning point of Schiller's career. It gave him two years of leisure to finish his Spanish tragedy and elaborate his dream of a noble, happy, and free humanity.

Schiller never wrote with more inspiration than when he plotted the tortuous dramatic web of the conspiracy of Marquis Posa for the cause of tolerance, enlightenment, and the brotherhood of man. The youthful extravagance of Posa's fabulous pleading and plotting is matched by his equally fabulous eagerness to sacrifice his life for the great cause and the friend to whom he transmitted his mission. Juvenile idealism has never been pictured in a more winning light. Though proved premature by the grim course of events, it was a glorious dream, but more than a dream: it verged on fulfillment, as Schiller persuaded himself now, in his own day, at the end of the eighteenth century. This is an astounding about-face, considering the lurid picture of social and political conditions that *Kabale und Liebe* had placed in a setting of contemporary Germany not more than five years earlier. But is it surprising that Schiller should have been carried to such a crest of optimism when we consider the way his personal fortune had turned? When a reader who had been a complete stranger to him extended a gesture of fabulous generosity to Schiller and made it good, how could he take it as other than a symptom of a new era of universal brotherhood in the making?

With the completion of *Don Carlos* (in 1787) a new Schiller emerged. All traces of the turbulent titan vanished. He now addressed the world as the noble, suave, eloquent, polished, optimistic apostle of universal enlightenment. He had become respectable too. He had established contacts with the literary lights of Weimar, Wieland in particular. Within a few years he married into a family with connections at court. He was installed as professor of history at Jena. Four years more, and Goethe's aloofness gave way to a friendship which Schiller referred to in after years as the most

significant event of his life. That period of friendly rivalry and collaboration, spanning the last decade of Schiller's life, produced the
brilliant philosophical essays, the masterly stories in verse (that go
in German under the name of ballads), and, beginning with *Wallenstein*, the proud line of his great dramas in a historical setting—
achievements of a trenchant intelligence, a disciplined craftsmanship, an indomitable creative drive that have made Schiller's genius
a source of inspiration to succeeding generations. The triumph of
the spirit over constantly besetting illness, which cut him off in his
forty-sixth year, gives Schiller a unique stature in the history of
German literature and thought. If this essay does not sufficiently
dwell on these aspects, it assumes them as the basis for the interest
it solicits for the earlier, formative and experimental stages of Schiller's career.

The first significant product of the new Schiller that took shape
after *Don Carlos* is his long poem "Die Götter Griechenlands." The
choice of subject comes as a surprise because Schiller's early work
had given no evidence of passionate devotion to Greek antiquity;
but his development of the subject by sustained antithesis, an over-
abundant flow of mythological allusions, rhetorical figures, and
fluent, graceful versification makes it a very characteristic product
of Schiller's pen. It is an impassioned *elegy* (in the sense of the
terminology he later developed), contrasting the idyllic beauty of
the Greek view of life with the austere gloom of Christian doctrine,
on the one hand, and the illusionless prose of the modern mechanistic, deistic view of the universe, on the other. He has no scruples
about lumping the Christian and the scientific view together as if
they were one, because they both strip life of beauty, but his sharpest barbs are aimed at Christianity. The service that pleases the
Christian god is mortification of the flesh practiced in chill edifices
where a hushed gloom reigns. Christianity has turned life into a
torment, it has made death a grinning skeleton, it scourges man
with the whip of demands that stamp his spontaneous impulses with
the taint of sin. Enthroned above this world of misery is a "heiliger
Barbar" [holy barbarian] whom human tears do not move. As to
the outlook into the beyond, it affords a glimpse of unfamiliar, abstract joys that he can do without, "die ich missen kann." In contrast to this, Schiller parades all the mythological inventory of ancient Greece, as relayed in Ovid's *Metamorphoses*, to conjure up

the life of the Greeks as one continuous festival of a people attached to their gods by the closest bonds of affection, gratitude, and consanguinity. There was then no sharp dividing line to separate men from gods, whereas now man's only distinction is to rank highest in a graduated series of worms that grovel at the feet of a master wholly beyond their reach. Schiller points up the conclusion by apostrophizing the composite deity of the Enlightenment and of revealed religion ("Werk und Schöpfer des Verstandes" [the work and creator of intellect]) with the antithetical plea: either give me power to attain to absolute truth, or reinvest the world with the beauty that you have made vanish. Truth and beauty as mutually incompatible divine sisters—the dichotomy was never more sharply stated. Never was Schiller's fluctuation between intellectual conviction and willing illusionism more clearly revealed. From the outset he had made no secret of the fact that the mythical picture about to be painted in such lively colors was only a figment of the imagination. "Schöne Wesen aus dem Fabelland" [lovely creatures from fairyland], he had apostrophized the gods of Greece in the opening stanza. In the poem as a whole the will to surrender consciously to illusion is at odds with the will to understand the meaning of life. Revealed religion parades in the mantle of truth only on a make-believe basis; it is to Schiller just another mythology, negatively valued when compared to that of the Greeks. What seriously troubles him is the mechanistic view of the universe which his reason compels him to accept as "truth" while his heart protests against it because it leaves out beauty. Like many others, this poem was revised and softened by Schiller in later years. The final rebellious apostrophe to the deity is replaced by a new stanza which shows the poet reconciled to the idea that the gods of Greece, removed from the realm of time, endure as eternal images:

> Was unsterblich im Gesang soll leben,
> Muss im Leben untergehn.
>
> [That which will live immortal in song
> must perish in life.]

Although Schiller's poem is one of the most eloquent glorifications of the Greek view of life, the poet never came under the spell of the Greeks, unlike his younger compatriot Hölderlin. The lectures on the Greek city states which Schiller delivered as professor of history at Jena show that he was critical of their civilization as founded on slavery. Speaking soberly, he was convinced that his own enlightened century marked an enormous advance, moral as well as material, over the age of Pericles. Later indeed, in his philosophical essays, he conjured with the idea of Greece as a golden age of the past. But this was strictly a figure of speech, a philosophical fiction employed in order to anchor the abstract concept of limited perfection ("Vollendung") in a make-believe space and time and thereby contrast it more effectively with the idea of modern man's growth as a process of limitless spherical expansion ("Unendlichkeit").

Having, in "Die Götter Griechenlands," produced an exemplary poem in the mode of the elegy, Schiller followed it up with an even more ambitious exercise in the mode of the idyll. "Die Künstler," Schiller's longest poem, written just a year before the outbreak of the French Revolution, is a versified essay on the evolution of man. It is a superbly elegant performance, one of the great show pieces of Schiller's muse. Freedom and discipline combine in its artfully rounded periods to exhibit a temperament in which grace and dignity are poised in the nicest balance, persuading us as much by the restrained fire of its delivery as by the content of its message that the Kingdom of Man is at hand. Can it really be the same man speaking who, but seven years earlier, poured his scorn upon this "tintenklecksendes Saekulum" [ink-daubing century], this "schlappes Kastratenjahrhundert" [flabby century of castrates], and who now salutes the final decade of the eighteenth century as the fulfillment of man's coming of age? Was the dawn of an age of universal peace and brotherhood ever hailed with a greeting that can match the tempered mellifluence of Schiller's opening stanza?

> Wie schön, o Mensch, mit deinem Palmenzweige
> Stehst du an des Jahrhunderts Neige,
> In edler stolzer Männlichkeit
> Mit aufgeschlossnem Sinn, mit Geistesfülle,
> Voll milden Ernsts, in tatenreicher Stille,
> Der reifste Sohn der Zeit,
> Frei durch Vernunft, stark durch Gesetze,
> Durch Sanftmut gross, und reich durch Schätze,
> Die lange Zeit dein Busen dir verschwieg,
> Herr der Natur, die deine Fesseln liebet,
> Die deine Kraft in tausend Kämpfen übet,
> Und prangend unter dir aus der Verwildrung stieg!

[How splendid, o Man, with thy palm frond
dost thou stand at the turn of the century,
in noble, proud masculinity
with open senses, with abundance of mind,
full of mild earnestness, in stillness rich in deeds,
the maturest son of time,
free through reason, strong through law,
through gentleness great, and rich in treasures,
which thy breast kept concealed from thee a long time,
Lord of Nature, which loves thy fetters,
which tests thy strength in a thousand battles,
and resplendent under thee rose from barbarism.]

Every line of this stanza hails the millennium of human dignity as achieved. Its confidence matches that of Saint Paul proclaiming that the Kingdom of God is at hand, that the time is fulfilled, and that every believer is in actual possession of the full fruit of salvation. Who can read this idyllically optimistic paean, this beautiful dream, without turning with a shudder to the grim face of reality that was even then on the point of emerging: a wild burst of oratory and emancipation, followed by a reign of terror, an era of conquest, rampant nationalism, class war, global wars styled "crusades," a fissioned world of two power blocs poised for mutual destruction! In this our age, that has seen horrors stalk on a scale the world has never known before, our age, whose prime concern centers on infernal machines for man's extermination and equally infernal machinery for manipulating mass emotion,—who in this age can let himself dwell on the picture of man sketched by Schiller as even the outline of a dream destined to achieve limited fulfillment in ever so distant a future? The dream of millennialism has been too radically shattered by the harnessing of forces that would make incredulous eighteenth-century eyes gaze upon us as a race of supermen for any sober present-day thinker to revive it. Perhaps we have been hardened by our experiences even beyond the wish to revive it; for even as we no longer share the Romanticist glorification of childhood as the age of innocence, even so we cannot, within our hearts, wish ourselves transplanted to any previous stage of human history. We accept our existence as rooted in this our age, for better or worse.

Did not Schiller know that his picture of the Kingdom of Man achieved was only a glamorous bubble? Without question. The whole poem moves on the plane of idyllic anticipation, not of reality. The mode of the idyll gave him general license to endow reality with the color of his hopes. But in part he was also indulging in that false poetic license which says things merely for rhetorical effect. Among the dazzling jewels with which he adorned the image of man, Schiller smuggled in a piece of paste. When he hailed man as Lord of Nature, which loves thy fetters—"Herr der Natur, die deine Fesseln liebet"—he was fully aware that he was introducing a spurious sentiment. Nature was for Schiller a soulless mechanism, and to represent it as in responsive contact with man was sheer make-believe.

"Die Künstler" is the first of Schiller's systematic attempts to trace, by deductive reasoning and the experience of history, the course of mankind's development. This remained a favorite theme to which Schiller returned from a variety of standpoints and widely varying premises. There is the academic lecture which draws for source material on the early chapters of Genesis to embroider freely on them in the eighteenth-century manner. There is the broad survey of cultural history offered by "Der Spaziergang," one of the finest poems of Schiller's maturity. In "Das Eleusische Fest" the founding of human institutions is portrayed in mythological terms, and the Rütli scene in *Wilhelm Tell*, recapitulating the founding of the Swiss Confederacy, shows the same interest at work in a restricted field. In "Die Künstler," the rise of man from infantile savagery to his present high estate is exclusively attributed to the development of his sense of beauty and the awakening of his creative energies. This sense and these energies cooperate in the setting up of an endless chain reaction of ever-growing complexity. Seeing always leads to doing, and vice versa. The theoretical and the practical sides of man's nature are engaged in constant intercourse for mutual enrichment. Concretely speaking, the sense of beauty begins with the first perception of form in natural objects as distinguished from their substance. The perception of an outline detached from the thing and traced against the sky or reflected in the water is the initial revolutionary experience which promptly evokes the drive to imitate it with the hand. Having once begun, man is launched on a course of infinite progression. His powers of abstraction grow, leading him to discover and use simple geometrical forms, which he then learns to arrange and combine in a multitude of ways. In this manner the fundamental concepts of order, design, symmetry and harmony, and so forth, become part of his mental organization, and as this grows in complexity he learns more and more to emancipate himself from slavish imitation of Nature's models. The same exercise of the power of abstraction on a higher plane leads to the birth of sentiment and soulful love by dissociating the image from the object of carnal desire. Gradually man's reason, by cultivating the sense of form and fitness, is led to the concept of justice, and this in turn, owing to the deficiency of its realization in Nature, leads him to posit a second, invisible world, the other half of the sphere, where imperfectly seen design is revealed as perfect order. We are, of course, reminded of the similar construct of Alexander Pope's *Essay on Man*, more than half a century earlier with its famous formulation:

> All Nature is but art, unknown to thee,
> All chance, direction, which thou canst not see,
> All discord, harmony not understood,
> All partial evil, universal good,
> And, spite of pride, in erring reason's spite,
> One thing is clear: whatever is is right.

But there is this difference: Schiller, instead of writing a theodicy, sees the construction of a world of the Beyond as a development of man's own inherent aesthetically guided activity.

The idyllic flight of Schiller's imagination now soars to one of its greatest heights in projecting the image of man as ennobled to such a degree that even the experience of death has lost its sting. His impulses are completely reconciled to the law of higher necessity. Behold the unsurpassed elegance of the picture that Schiller presents to our eyes at this point:

> Mit dem Geschick in hoher Einigkeit
> Gelassen hingestützt auf Grazien und Musen,
> Empfängt er das Geschoss, das ihn bedräut,
> Mit freundlich dargebotnem Busen,
> Vom sanften Bogen der Notwendigkeit.

> [In high unity with fate
> calmly leaning on Graces and Muses,
> he receives the arrow that threatens him,
> with a breast amicably presented,
> from the gentle bow of necessity.]

The idyllic mode is sustained. Grace and dignity are in perfect accord in this tableau of man's supreme posture depicted as achieved in the here and now. But if we think the ultimate climax has been reached in this portrayal of man, Schiller raises a hand to stay our applause. He has one further trick in reserve. For now, abandoning the idyllic present, his imagination soars into the space of a limitless future. The orator becomes a conjuror, a magician. The chain reaction of the aesthetic drive has not yet reached its ultimate goal. The dizzying process of man's ennoblement continues. More and more, his gross earthly substance is pruned away, he comes closer and closer to a life of pure spirit. What can eventuate from this process but his final divestment from the trammels of the flesh? And indeed, Schiller performs the miracle before our eyes: with a final *élan*, after a piled-up sequence of escalations, the wholly transfigured spirit of man is wafted into the cosmic spaces. To our modern eyes this dazzling spectacle is touched off by an all but inaudible jet-puff, as we dwell on Schiller's final apostrophe to the practitioners of art to carry man to his ultimate destiny:

> So führt ihn, in verborgnem Lauf,
> Durch immer reinre Formen, reinre Töne,
> Durch immer höhre Höhn und immer schönre Schöne
> Der Dichtung Blumenleiter still hinauf —
> Zuletzt, am reifen Ziel der Zeiten,
> Noch eine glückliche Begeisterung,
> Des jüngsten Menschenalters Dichterschwung,
> Und — in der *Wahrheit* Arme wird er gleiten.

> [So lead him, in a hidden course,
> through ever purer forms, purer tones,
> through ever higher heights and ever more beautiful beauties
> quietly up the flowered ladder of poetry —
> finally, at the ripe goal of the ages,
> one more happy enthusiasm,
> a poetic leap of the youngest age of man
> and — he will slip into the arms of *truth*.]

This conclusion—for we can disregard the stanzas still to follow as the descending spirals of oratory returning to earth—this conclusion does not come as a total surprise. The groundwork for the climactic miracle was unobtrusively laid in the second stanza where there was an allusion to incorporeal spirits (angels) as included in the diverse host of animate creation. There Schiller had cautioned man, the composite creature of flesh and spirit:

> Im Fleiss kann dich die Biene meistern,
> In der Geschicklichkeit ein Wurm dir Lehrer sein,

Dein Wissen teilest du mit *vorgezognen Geistern*,
Die Kunst, o Mensch, hast du allein.

[The bee can outdo thee in industry,
the worm can be thy tutor in dexterity,
thy knowledge thou sharest with *preferred spirits*,
but art, o Man, hast thou alone.]

And the fifth stanza had restricted man's mode of cognition on earth to the colored light of beauty, reserving the apprehension of the white light of truth for the Beyond as too dazzling for human eyes:

Was wir als Schönheit hier empfunden,
Wird einst als *Wahrheit* uns entgegengehn.

[What we have here beheld as beauty,
will one day approach us as *truth*.]

Thus there can be no quarrel with Schiller's preparation of his final coup. It has a built-in motivation. But what disturbs is the fact that the idyllic evangelist cannot bring himself to forgo the pleasure of moving us by a mirage. For a mirage he knows this jet-puff ascension to be, no less than the cosmic fireworks of his earlier titanism. For all his manly posture of idyllic didacticism, he knows that the "preferred spirits" of the second strophe and the divine sisters of the fifth are in his mouth just stage properties he manipulates for effect. He knows that in presenting man as poised for the ascent "am reifen Ziel der Zeiten" he is just using another meaningless phrase, for he had long come to regard the world as *ewig*. His rationalism had come to regard all eschatology as childish attempts to come to terms with the mystery of existence. But the vapors of his oratory still go to his head. The same temperament that turns the political spellbinder into a demagogue makes Schiller succumb to the lure of achieving a spurious edification.

The upshot of this fabulous sermon is a glittering blend of Christian and Platonic myth-making—"ein schillerndes Gemisch" would be the cruel but appropriate phrase in German. Our concern is not over the fact that Schiller says these things (countless poets have done the same), but over the fact that he says with such persuasive elegance and apostolic zeal things that he does not believe in. It is exceedingly hard for Schiller to break out of this vicious circle, but when he has eventually broken out of it, under the guidance of Kant's critical philosophy, the ambiguity of his position is gone.

In what I am tempted to regard as his greatest poem, "Das Ideal und das Leben," the new point of view has fully emerged. This poem contains the finest mythical image that Schiller ever sketched —the vision of the company of brand new stainless souls poised in the Beyond before entering upon the long cycle of contamination by fleshly bonds and eventual purgation, this vision in which the Platonic mythology of Vergil is reborn in sublime language. But this time it is projected as an ideal vision. There is no longer any sleight-of-hand trick to confuse us as to its ideal visionary character and to raise false hopes as to its perfectionistic realization in life in any ever so distant future.

The sleight-of-hand quality that marks the idyllic panorama of "Die Künstler" also pervades all of the historical prose which absorbed most of Schiller's energies during the five-year period extending from 1788 through 1792. Seen in broad outline, the motivation of this quality is fourfold. First, there is the carry-over of the spirit of Christian idealism, the Christian perfectionist urge, the saving of the soul as the supreme concern, even after the theoretical, other-worldly orientation of Christianity has been abandoned. This is what we commonly refer to as the secularization of the Christian point of view. Regardless of his intellectual position, Schiller always remained a Christian at heart. His impulses continued to respond to Christian motivation, and his ideology suggests the pattern of Saint Paul in a host of respects. There is, secondly, the constant temptation to exploit his great talent in an exhibitionistic way, to give rein to his imagination and substitute heroic drama for sober history—a tendency that still stamps his history of the Thirty Years' War as a brilliant performance. There is, thirdly, the pressure of an academic office for which he is ill prepared. Speaking to youth from the academic platform, he feels an enormous burden of responsibility. These young minds expect him, the teacher, to unfold to them the book of universal history, to trace out for them a pattern of Providential design and—subject to reservations—pretend to a superior insight which he does not possess. There is, lastly, the pressure of the economic situation, compelling Schiller to feed a steady stream of marketable literary material into the printing presses. All these considerations combine to make Schiller's historical essays a very uneven performance. They are aglow with faith in progress. They abound with the far-flung idealistic gesture, with flashy fluency, and a plethora of superlatives. These afford respite from the tedious recital of the flow of events by building up effective climaxes. The stage is peopled with heroes and villains as in Schiller's dramas. On occasion we are taken behind the wings of the cosmic stage to glimpse the hand of Providence shaping events. The exposition tends to be rhetorical rather than searching, often spinning out a meager skein of fact into a very thin thread of surmise and speculation. Judgments often seem to be dictated by *ad hoc* expediency and haste. Generally speaking, the late eighteenth-century temper of this writing is so pronounced that the age of Rousseau is often more clearly reflected in it than the personality of our author.

A few examples must suffice. Schiller's inaugural lecture on the study of universal history is a great paradox: History should be studied as a free pursuit. The great exemplars of mankind it puts before us to emulate and the inspiring view of man's progress are infinitely rewarding. The student who enters the field as a means to earn his livelihood, the *Brotstudent*, is told with withering scorn that he is unworthy to enter these portals. Young Schiller had indeed devoured Plutarch's *Lives* in the spirit of this idealistic message. But what of Schiller now? Had not the emergency of need put him into the professorial chair as a *Brothistoriker*? And was he not even now reading history with an ulterior purpose, scanning its pages for figures and situations to be used as so much raw material to be modified at will and cast into the form of effective drama? And what about Schiller's conclusion, conjuring up before the mind's eye a picture of Universal History as a goddess all-knowing, all-wise, all-just, enthroned in the majesty of Homer's Zeus? No doubt an impressive theatrical ending to befit the solemn occasion. But we know that Schiller had in reserve an alternate slide that pictured the goddess as the Sphinx with sealed lips and an inscrutable smile.

There is a very interesting lecture on early man that uses the account of Genesis as its point of departure but replaces the incomparably colorful myth of the Garden of Eden by elusive eighteenth-century allegory. Instead of the God who set man in the Garden with a specific prohibition, Schiller shows us Mother Nature guiding the first steps of infant man by her leading-strings. Then, by some fore-ordained miracle, his instinctual docility gives way to a stirring of nascent reason: he breaks away from Nature's leading-strings and strikes out on a quest of the unknown. This, Schiller's version of the fall of man, is a philosophical idea which he sells us under the label of a historical event. Schiller hails the metaphysical miracle as the greatest event in human history, for, though catastrophic in its immediate effects, it marked man's first assertion of his freedom, his first step on the path of infinite progression destined ultimately to make him the equal of the gods.

Of greatest interest among Schiller's shorter historical essays is his account of the mission of Moses. Seen in its broadest aspect, this mission was a decisive step in an all-embracing providential scheme to prepare mankind for the truth of a purely rational religion that accepts the world as the creation of a Universal Deity who is at the same time the fountainhead of the moral law. This Deity manifests itself to the mature mind through the agency of Nature by an automatic process, without recourse to special revelation or miracle. The positive religions of Judaism, Christianity, and Islam represent approximations to the pure truth of rational religion mingled with error. This lofty idea of universal monotheism, heretofore grasped by only the most advanced sages in a group of Egyptian priests and carefully guarded as a dangerous esoteric secret, it was the mission of Moses to instill for the first time into a whole nation. In the fulfillment of this mission Moses appears in the double role of an enlightened eighteenth-century philosopher and of a national leader. In his characteristic way, Schiller presents the historic situation confronting Providence as a problem that poses what appear to be insurmountable difficulties in order subsequently to show how these difficulties are neatly resolved, one by one, through the agency of purely natural means. He portrays the Hebrews, an alien population of two millions, segregated from the Egyptians who despise and fear them; a nomadic shepherd people, yet living somehow in conditions resembling a European ghetto; an ignorant, stupid, brutish people ravaged by leprosy and venereal disease, yet pullulating with vigorous offspring. They are an abomination to the Egyptians, who try to cope with their numbers by brutal exploitation and mass murder, yet somehow the humane instincts of the Egyptian midwives prevail over Pharaoh's order to kill all the male children at birth. Moses is saved by his mother's ruse of hiding the infant in a basket among the rushes of the Nile, to be found and adopted by Pharaoh's daughter. In this way he comes to be initiated into the highest mysteries of the Egyptian priesthood but without losing touch with the traditions of his people. What reads as beautiful legend in Exodus bristles with a host of unresolved contradictions when presented in the historian's language. If Schiller sensed this, he betrays no awareness of it.

As for Moses, Schiller is hard put to reconcile the figure of the enlightened sage with that of the national leader. The religious insight of Moses is equated with pure, unadulterated truth; yet he can transmit this insight to his people only by phrasing it in terms that they will be bound to misunderstand. In order for the idea of the true God to become an active force giving them the hope and strength to break the chains of their bondage, they must reinterpret the universal God in terms of a national god of whose special solicitude they are the object. Moses foresees the inevitable misunderstanding and reckons with it in his strategic plan. Schiller insists that Moses was far too noble a man to stoop to fraud, but it was impossible on the political level to operate without accommodating his pure message to the unenlightened minds of his people. For this reason he embroidered the purity of the true worship with the trimmings of ritual, he invented the account of his meeting God in the burning bush, and he resorted to the performing of magic tricks in order to brace the faith of his blind followers. Throughout all this Moses appears as the superlatively sagacious man of reason, always calculating his means to achieve his ends. There is no trace in his make-up of the dark forces that sway the mystic and the prophet. The portrait strikes us as thin and unconvincing, like all the speculative history of the Enlightenment. But we note the evident pleasure with which Schiller takes us behind the scenes to demonstrate the workings of an all-wise Providence within a framework of history that requires no tampering with the economy of Nature in order to achieve its ultimate ends.

The story of the exodus of the Hebrews from Egypt and the birth of the first great monotheistic religion afforded the speculative historian a particularly fine opportunity for tracing the hidden design of Providence. The same temptation to lift the curtain of history and display the divine hand manipulating the welter of events animates Schiller at times in dealing with the more limited sphere of the Thirty Years' War. Here, in a full-length monograph written for a ladies' historical almanac, Schiller builds up Gustavus Adolphus as a shining knight and champion of the good cause of German liberty. Gustavus is removed from the scene, by death in battle, at the very moment when it has become apparent that he has begun to pursue selfish, ambitious ends. All of a sudden the constitution of the moribund Holy Roman Empire is represented by Schiller in terms of a sacrosanct institution endangered by the foreign conqueror, and Schiller contrives to make Providence take a very vital interest in the upholding of the sanctity of that dying realm. In indulging in these nationalistic speculations Schiller was skating on very thin ice, and he knew it. There is good reason to think that in all this it was Schiller's main object to capture for his recital some of the spirit of the Homeric epic, which owes its great fascination to the fact that the action moves on a double plane, human and divine.

Since the note of nationalism is rarely sounded by Schiller (except to proclaim the newly achieved pre-eminence of art in the age of Goethe), this is the place to mention a nationalistic poem, "Deutsche Grösse," which Schiller sketched but never executed. Fortunately; for what to Hölderlin was a flame of living faith and to Fichte an elemental passion rationalized would have been in Schiller's mouth no more than another glittering rhetorical exercise. Underlying the draft of the poem are a series of general historical propositions which, firmly believed in by some of the world's great thinkers, merely served Schiller as tentative points of departure. These are: (1) Human history moves toward a goal that will be achieved at the end of time. (We know that the concept of time's having an end has long ceased to have meaning for Schiller.) (2) In the evolution of the pattern of history every nation has a specific mission. (This is a key concept of many philosophers, including Saint Augustine and Hegel, and it is used to conjure with by Heine and Renan, among others in the nineteenth century. The "manifest destiny" of America is another example on the same pattern.) (3) The last nation to arrive on the scene will mark the culmination of mankind's achievements. Using these three propositions as a springboard, Schiller proceeds to specific conclusions: The Germans are the slowest people to arrive, "das langsamste Volk," hence they are reserved by Providence for the role of star performer in the final, most glorious phase of man's history. Other nations have sprouted leaves and flowers, the Germans will produce the yield. This is said without political overtones. Schiller is thinking purely in terms of moral and aesthetic culture. Proof of the mission reserved for the Germans is the fact of the German language. The German language has developed a flexibility which makes it the adequate vehicle for the deepest thought and the most delicate sentiment. "Unsre Sprache wird die Welt beherrschen" [our language will be dominant in the world], is Schiller's confident prediction. The course of history has already invalidated Schiller's conclusions. But if his propositions are still on the agenda, we shall have to ponder the question whether it is the Russians who are the slowest people, or the Chinese, or some other nation still to emerge from the teeming equatorial belt.

III

The years that Schiller spent in the writing of history stand out as a period of bondage. There was the exhausting labor of assimilating, sifting, and shaping an enormous mass of dry source material. There was the constant temptation to enliven the tedious record by dancing adroitly on the precarious tightrope of providentialistic philosophy. The chief compensation lay in the fact that he stored up in his mind a vast array of figures and colorful incidents which his imagination eventually welded into the tragedy of *Wallenstein*, Schiller's most monumental achievement.

It is with relief that we turn from these years to the final decade of Schiller's maturity. Thanks to Kant, he had at last arrived at a point of view, a *Weltanschauung*, that put an end to his backing and filling and, thanks to the friendship of Goethe, he could turn again to the writing of poetry and drama. This new phase brought to perfection Schiller's specific endowment. It began with a series of philosophical treatises that examine the interrelations of morals and the sense of beauty, the function of art in society, and the specific difference between the poetry of the ancients and that of the moderns. By their clear yet often inspired prose these treatises bridged the gap between the esoteric language of Kant's critical philosophy and the aesthetic humanism of the age of Goethe. They combine a unique gift of popularization with a pioneering zest for exploring uncharted areas of the mind. There is no room in a sketch such as this to embark on any discussion of their content.

As for Schiller's poetic work, the last decade of his life produced a number of poems in which the fusion of form and content is achieved with a skill that is no longer to be distinguished from inspiration. They deal with general ideas, but thought appears transmuted into living experience. They are the work of a virtuoso, but their sincerity refutes the charge of empty virtuosity.

One such gem—I would call it the finest—is "Das Ideal und das Leben." Here, after five introductory strophes that develop in general terms the contrast between the life of contemplation and the life of involvement in material desire, four pairs of strophes apply the thematic polarity to specific areas of human interest, and the whole is capped by a final pair of strophes that focuses the thought into a grandiose symbol: the labors of Hercules on the one hand, and his death and transfiguration on the other. Involvement with the dark forces of life followed by transfiguration in death is also the most succinct formula for Schiller's practice as a writer of tragedy, and thus the symbol of Hercules takes us to the very core of Schiller's tragic view of life.

An equally compelling symbol for the spirit of indomitable idealism prevailing against overwhelming odds is the epigram "Columbus" that summarizes its message in the lines:

> Mit dem Genius steht die Natur in ewigem Bunde.
> Was der eine verspricht, leistet die andre gewiss.

> [Nature stands in eternal bond with genius,
> what the one promises, the other will assuredly accomplish.]

The whole epigram is afire with zeal, whereas the same sentiment as voiced in the sing-song stanzas of "Hoffnung" strikes the ear as so much edifying claptrap:

> Und was die innere Stimme spricht,
> Das täuscht die hoffende Seele nicht.

> [And whatever the inner voice promises,
> does not disappoint the hoping soul.]

"Der Tanz," like "Columbus" cast in the form of the classical distich, is another superb example of immanent symbolism: a sensuous phenomenon, spontaneous movement governed by an inner law of order, reveals itself in the end as a symbol of the harmonious interaction of freedom and law in both the material and the spiritual universe.

"Der Spaziergang," taken as a whole, is a felicitous symbol of the course of human civilization. Individual phases of the wanderer's ascent to steeper heights are full of spontaneous symbolic overtones. Take the following lines:

> Tief an des Berges Fuss, der gählings unter mir abstürzt,
>   Wallet des grünlichten Stroms fliessender Spiegel vorbei.
> Endlos unter mir seh ich den Äther, über mir endlos,
>   Blicke mit Schwindeln hinauf, blicke mit Schaudern hinab;
> Aber zwischen der ewigen Höh und der ewigen Tiefe
>   Trägt ein geländerter Steig sicher den Wandrer dahin.

> [Deep at the foot of the mountain, which plunges dizzily below me,
>   the greenish stream's fluid mirror flows past.
> Endless below me I see the ether, above me endless,
>   with dizziness I look up, look with a shudder below;
> but between the eternal height and the eternal depth
>   a railed path bears the wanderer safely along.]

There is not a trace of contrived symbolism in this recital, yet it inherently expresses a serene confidence with regard to man's place in the universe, a secure sense of location, of belonging, so utterly lost to us of the atomic age. We cannot leave "Der Spaziergang" without touching on that superb line in which the meter of the distich itself becomes the vehicle of symbolism. The wanderer, oblivious now of the landscape about him, his attention engrossed by an inner vision, sees the turbulent forces unleashed by the French Revolution and sums up the revolt of the intellectuals and that of the masses in the line:

> Fre*i*heit ruft die Vernunft, Frei*heit* die wilde Begierde.

> [Reason cries *free*dom, wild cravings free*dom*.]

What could more effectively render the seething of blind fanaticism than the distortion of the accent of Fre*i*heit to Frei*heit!* This distortion was not the result of a happy accident; moreover, it is revealed as a flash of inspiration when we compare it with the line's original reading:

> Freiheit heischt die Vernunft, nach Freiheit rufen die Sinne.

> [Reason demands freedom, the senses call for freedom.]

And, in the context of Schiller's verse in the form of the classical distich, who could omit mention of that golden page entitled "Das Glück," the most generous act of homage to the greater endowment of his friendly rival, Goethe? He, Schiller, had earned his place beside Goethe by indefatigable striving, by tireless self-criticism. He had pulled himself out of the mire of his youthful extravagance by his bootstraps. There was none more proudly conscious than he of what can be accomplished by a keen intellect and an inflexible will. But this poem testifies to an unqualified acknowledgment of Schiller's realization that there are limits to such achievements, that grace from above freely bestows its highest gifts, and that rivalry must yield to love in the unequal struggle:

> Alles Höchste, es kommt frei von den Göttern herab.
>
> [All that is highest comes freely down from the gods.]

This was Schiller's way of coming to terms with the basic Christian antithesis between salvation by works and salvation by grace. Here he sided with Saint Paul as he had done in the essay "On Grace and Dignity," where the ideal of the beautiful soul had made him plead against Kant the freedom of "the children of the house" as rising above the severity of the Old Covenant and the motive force of fear. Although he had repudiated Christian dogma and all its metaphysics, and the conception of Christ as redeemer is significantly absent from his thinking, Schiller's message was essentially that of a secularized Christianity, as an abiding faith in things unseen.

Also Christian in origin was Schiller's acute sense of responsibility to mankind, what we might call a sublimation of the sense of sin implanted in the child by his religious teachers. The final paragraph of his inaugural lecture at Jena dwells on the high obligation imposed upon us by a survey of history and the wish thereby engendered in each of his hearers, "an das kommende Geschlecht die Schuld zu entrichten, die er dem vergangenen nicht mehr abtragen kann" (to acquit himself to the rising generation of the obligation he owes to that which has passed away). It is not enough, moreover, to pass on to the next generation the accumulated capital of human values; it must be our aim rather to transmit it enriched by a specific contribution. Schiller returns to the same idea in his poem "Die Ideale," where it is developed in its double aspect of an infinite accumulation of capital in terms of the eternal flow of time and of a constantly pressing debt in terms of the living generation. The sober upshot of the elegiac poem is that all the sparkling ideals of his youth—the unbounded dreams of love, happiness, glory, truth—have dissolved into thin air leaving him only two abiding companions, Friendship and Tireless Industry. These two, endowed with the shadowy outlines of female allegorical personages, he addresses, singling out Industry for his final apostrophe:

Und du, die gern sich mit ihr gattet,
Wie sie, der Seele Sturm beschwört,
Beschäftigung, die nie ermattet,
Die langsam schafft, doch nie zerstört,
Die zu dem Bau der Ewigkeiten
Zwar Sandkorn nur für Sandkorn reicht,
Doch von der grossen Schuld der Zeiten
Minuten, Tage, Jahre streicht.

[And thou, who gladly joins her (friendship),
and like her conjures the storm of the soul,
Industry, which never wearies,
which slowly creates, but never destroys,
which for the structure of eternities
uses grains of sand for grains of sand,
but from the great debt of ages
erases minutes, days, and years.]

Turning now to Schiller's dramas, we enter the field that was most congenial to Schiller's creative imagination, the field in which his genius proved itself pre-eminent. We must limit ourselves, in the scope of this essay, to some very general observations regarding his characteristic way of coming to terms with the form of drama and its living presentation on the stage. Since all of his dramas with the exception of *Wilhelm Tell* are tragedies, shaping an action that leads to the death of the protagonists, our discussion will concentrate on Schiller as a writer of tragedy. Four main topics will engage our interest: (1) the general structure of his dramas, (2) his strategy in the grouping of the dramatic forces, (3) the psychology of his characterization, and (4) the tragic catharsis. As to the subject matter, we note that seven of the nine dramas—all, that is, except *Die Räuber* and the bourgeois tragedy *Kabale und Liebe*—have a historic or legendary setting in a period remote from Schiller's own time. *Fiesco* takes us to sixteenth-century Genoa, *Don Carlos* to the Spain of Philip the Second, *Wallenstein* to the Germany of the Thirty Years' War, *Maria Stuart* to Elizabethan England, *Die Jungfrau von Orleans* to fifteenth-century France, *Die Braut von Messina* to medieval Sicily, and *Wilhelm Tell* to fourteenth-century Switzerland.

Turning to structure first, we note two distinct types. Three of the dramas, *Die Räuber, Die Jungfrau von Orleans* and *Wilhelm Tell*, present the whole design of the action from its beginning to its conclusion. This means that the stages of the action are separated by intervals of time that may amount to weeks or many months. But the structure that Schiller favors is the closely knit analytic form. In all of his other six dramas the curtain rises at the point of impending catastrophe, and in a matter of one, two, or three days the catastrophe rolls swiftly and inexorably to its conclusion. This is the case in *Wallenstein*. In retrospect, as our memory roams over the colorful scenes of the Prologue, the *Lager*, and over the breath-taking multitude of scenes that constitute the ten giant acts of the *Wallenstein* tragedy proper, it may seem incredible that the whole complicated panorama of sixteen years of war should have been unfolded in a matter of days. But this is indeed the case. Not only has the Emperor's decision to remove Wallenstein from his command been worked out to the last detail and the machinery for its execution been set in motion before the play begins, but also the documents proving the generalissimo's treasonable intercourse with the enemy have already fallen into the Emperor's hands. We find out about the go-between's capture only near the close of the fifth act, and it is not until the sixth that Wallenstein himself learns that the trap has been sprung, that a free decision is no longer possible, and that he is at the mercy of the new allies whom he had planned to manipulate for his own aggrandizement. Schiller's timing of this denouement and of the retardations that make us hold our breath until the very moment of Wallenstein's murder is a magnificent display of dramatic planning. The whole play is traceable as a descending line of action. The same structural scheme is to be seen in *Maria Stuart*. The Queen of Scots is already under sentence of death as the curtain rises and the schemes set in motion for restoring her to liberty and power serve but to precipitate the catastrophe of her execution all the more swiftly. Schiller achieves all this without streamlining the action. The interaction of a multitude of plots and counterplots is managed with consummate mastery. From the completion of his first play Schiller had aimed at compressing a swiftly descending action into a coherent time-sequence of minimal duration. The flaws in the timing of *Kabale und Liebe* are likely to pass unnoticed. But the vertiginous web of plot and intrigue in *Fiesco* leaves us dazzled rather than convinced, and *Don Carlos* occupied him so long and grew to such unmanageable proportions that the perspective got confused. These were works of his youth, separated by an interval of twelve years from his *Wallenstein*. The last of Schiller's tragedies to be completed, *Die Braut von Messina*, again shows the poet's tight hold on the reins of the dramatic action, which runs its course in the limits of a single day.

So much for the structure. Now for the strategy. To Schiller, every theme for dramatic treatment presented itself as a conflict of forces, a clash of opposing wills, well balanced in strength, spurning compromise. Schiller deals in bold contrasts, in black and white. His protagonists are heroes, his antagonists are villains. We are never in doubt as to which side we are to identify with. The issues are fought out on the stage, and each play, except the first, has a series of climactic scenes in which the opponents face each other in brilliant verbal fencing bouts, where thrust is followed by counterthrust in rapid succession. Schiller always has an eye for strong stage effects. His characters are conceived as parts that call for star performers. There is always a strong element of intrigue, abounding in surprises. But for the most part, *Fiesco* excepted, the participating audience is prepared for these surprises in advance of the performers, so that we experience the shock of startling revelations in terms of their effect on the characters concerned, in terms of empathy and increased tension. The advantage we enjoy in always seeing the dramatic situation in larger perspective than the characters involved also allows the most extensive use of the device of tragic irony. Again and again a phrase of limited purport, innocently uttered by a protagonist, reveals itself to us as charged with sinister overtones foreshadowing the speaker's doom. It is as though the breath issuing from these lips took on the shape of a boomerang silently flitting into space and tracing its deadly curve back to its point of origin. Most famous example among scores to be found is Wallenstein's admonition to the guards to insure quiet for the night, at the moment when the murderers are about to strike: "Ich gedenke einen langen Schlaf zu tun." [I intend to sleep a long time.]

Schiller always surrounds the core of his action with colorful pageantry for the eye to feast on. There is the austere figure of King Philip among his grandees; there is Wallenstein surrounded by glitteringly uniformed generals and dignitaries; there is the pomp of Queen Elizabeth's court; there is the great triumphal procession leading the Dauphin, Charles, to be crowned at Rheims; there is the double chorus of knights flanking the two princely brothers in *Die Braut von Messina.*

There are weaknesses, to be sure, not to be overlooked. In three of his plays Schiller has one of the principals resort to an unmotivated fit of hysteria, to keep the web of dramatic suspense from being prematurely broken—when Ferdinand, in the bourgeois tragedy, throws down his pistol and rushes from the presence of the panicked Hofmarschall who is already stammering his confession of the villainous intrigue of which Ferdinand is the deluded victim; when Don Carlos rushes out of Princess Eboli's apartment under similar circumstances; and when the Queen Mother, in *Die Braut von Messina,* with a gesture of wild panic brushes off her elder son's inquiry as to the place from which his sister has myteriously vanished.

This leads us to the topic of character portrayal, Schiller's psychology. If Schiller is one of the world's greatest masters of dramatic architecture and theatrical effect, a sober appraisal cannot accord him the same high status as to the figures with which he peopled his dramas. This is said without questioning the fact that his figures are vividly conceived, that their contours are clear and bold, and that their behavior shows a high consistency of motivation. The point is rather that Schiller is not a pioneer as regards insight into the depth of the human soul. Unlike Goethe, Kleist, Heine, Nietzsche, Ibsen, and Thomas Mann, Schiller is not an intuitive precursor or exponent of the depth psychology associated with the name of Freud and the whole modern school. The life of Schiller's characters is restricted to the conscious level. There is very little suggestion of pre-conscious or unconscious strata of the soul. Schiller sees his figures from without. They are constructs composed of the conventional virtues and vices—substantive qualities, mixed in differing proportions. These substantive qualities bear clear labels. They are easily recognized as vanity, ambition, greed, lust, vindictiveness, courage, fear, pettiness, honor, fidelity, generosity, magnanimity, emulation, and so forth. Each of the characters responds to motivation in terms of his specific blend of these qualities. Each responds to situations with the mechanical precision of the wheels of a well-constructed clock. This creates the illusion of a living action so long as we surrender to the dramatist's lead and do not allow ourselves to stray into lower depths in the attempt to identify with the characters. Once we do that, the supports of some of the most brilliant scenes fall and leave us dismayed. Take for example the showiest scene Schiller ever wrote, the confrontation of Ferdinand with Lady Milford—he, the young, aristocratic idealist, lover of Luise, that paragon of middle-class virtue and piety, face to face with the Duke's incomparably beautiful, dazzling mistress, whose passion is focused upon winning the young man and returning by this means to the path of virtue she has forsaken in yielding to the seduction of power and adulation. Ferdinand, proud and cool, his lips curled in disdain, has no inkling of the passionate assault to which his senses, his mind, and his heart are about to be subjected, an assault which all but triumphs over his tottering virtue. What begins as a forensic debate in which German virtue is pitted against British pride turns into a fearsome emotional contest fought by two champions superbly matched in dialectic skill. Their hearts ablaze, they stage an exhibition game of dialectics played so fast that the subtlety of an individual thrust is often brought home to us only by the deadly accuracy of the riposte. The logic of their dialectics and the passion of their all but irresistible mutual attraction are as psychologically incompatible as fire and water. Yet on the stage the display of fireworks is so dazzling that we are held enthralled, and only when it is over do we emerge from the spell to protest: this is as false from first to last as it is showy. Let us not think for a moment that Schiller did not know this as well as we. As we know from his criticism of *Die Räuber* and his letters on *Don Carlos*, he enjoyed bringing his analytic mind to bear on his own works and exhibiting the machinery of his dramatic constructions. And let us not think that he took Ferdinand's "virtue" as anything more than theatrical currency!

What has been said above about Schiller's seeing his characters from the outside calls for one reservation regarding the dramas of his youth. He has infused his titanism into them all. In all of them he dazzles us with exhibitions of psychological grandeur that rises sky-high over the level of mediocrity. Magnanimity, emulation, not virtue, is the ideal that shapes the contours of his heroes. Regardless of orientation in the direction of what conventionally passes for virtue and vice, the characters he loves are attuned to a display of grandeur. Karl Moor, the robber, whose first key word is the name of Plutarch, has an ego that makes it inconceivable to him that the world should harbor a second man to match his own stature. Fiesco impulsively jeopardizes his whole, long-prepared plot to make himself master of Genoa, because he cannot bear the idea that old Andrea Doria should surpass him in magnanimity. Even Lady Milford, having been worsted in a contest of high-mindedness by the simple fiddler's daughter, cannot bear this humiliation of her pride: she must even the score, tossing into the scales her wealth, her power, her very existence in exchange for a single superbly reckless moment of personal triumph. And in *Don Carlos* the relation of the two young idealists is keyed to the note of mutual emulation. The bond of their friendship is the tension of a jealous rivalry, each striving to outdo the other in selfless heroic devotion to the cause of his friend and that of humanity. They are like two track runners, each trying to better the world's speed mark, each trying to make the victory in the race the more difficult for the other, each hoping to win, each hoping even more to make the other wrest the palm from his hands.

In his mature dramas Schiller no longer dazzles us with such exhibitions of juvenile emulation. Heroism is no longer equated with the spectacular gesture. Having sublimated the totalitarian titanism of his own ambition into the polarity of his friendly rivalry with Goethe, Schiller appears as a powerhouse of creative energy, free to turn to any task of his choosing without being pressured by private psychological complexes. He now works out his dramatic plans, including the roles of his heroes, with complete objectivity and detachment. How well he succeeded in creating full-bodied, complete characters that engage our sympathies without his dissembling as to the dubious quality of their moral status, we learn from a study of Wallenstein and the Scottish Queen, among others. But Schiller was also a restless experimenter with dramatic form. Twice he constructed his plots against a background of beliefs quite alien to those of himself and his contemporary audience. When the theme concerned the working out of a Providential design, in the legendary story of the Maid of Orleans, he subordinated psychological plausibility to miracle and pageantry. And when, with his eye on Greek drama, he presented the sinister working out of an ancestral curse, he all but ignored psychological motivation.

Our survey finally turns to the question of the tragic catharsis in Schiller's dramas. Given a reader or audience ideally attuned, what is the over-all effect of a cycle of action that has run its course with the death of the hero? We are not concerned with the hopeless attempt of working out a generally valid definition of what constitutes tragedy and of judging Schiller's tragedies in terms of it. There are many mutually incompatible types of end situation and of human response that are labeled as tragic, and the problem for esthetics in this field is to differentiate the varieties of tragic experience. There are great authors who are not limited to a single type. In the case of Schiller, however, we can confidently trace the variations of a single underlying pattern more or less clearly worked out.

All of Schiller's dramas are centered on the career of one or more individuals whose stature vastly exceeds that of the average man. Schiller's protagonists are heroes in the traditional sense. They are endowed with an emotional and sometimes intellectual capacity for experience that makes them exemplars of mankind. Their striving and suffering is of a range and intensity that stamp them as great. They are governed by passions and ambitions that make them engage in life's struggles with an uncommon zest. They play for the highest stakes, and even when involved in crime they present a spectacle of basic nobility and high-mindedness. Take the greatest example, Wallenstein. He is ruled by a towering ambition that subordinates everything to his personal ends. But in working out his scheme of colossal treason he has a perspective of the desperate total situation. Old loyalties have become meaningless in a war that has come to be fought by the opposing armies as the end in itself. The most drastic remedy is called for if the civilization of Central Europe is to be saved. Wallenstein is fully aware of the fearful weight of the imponderables of sentiment and morals that will brand him with the stigma of an arch-traitor if he fails in his gamble. He does not flinch from the realization that personal ambition, even more than the general good, tempts him to pursue his reckless course. When he balances the weight of morals against his contemplated treason we are made to feel the power of morals not only as a political factor to be weighed with detachment, but also as a deeply ingrained force in his own character. He is most nobly moving when the death of the young idealist, Max, his most devoted friend, whom he has sacrificed to his ambition, makes him speculate: Had I known that this would be the outcome, perhaps I would have renounced my plans; perhaps not. How much greater he appears in thus pondering this question than if he had uttered the cliché of facile repentance: Had I known this, I would never have embarked on my course! But Wallenstein's figure owes its awesome grandeur above all to the irrational factor in his make-up, his mystical faith in the stars. It is his imperturbable confidence in the connection of his career with the heavenly constellations that blinds and deludes him and leads directly to his downfall. Wallenstein's star-gazing faith in an objective order of the universe beyond human calculation raises his stature above that of a mere ambitious schemer. For the reader, too, ultimate reality is shrouded in mystery. There may be no more than uncanny coincidence at play in the dream that confirmed Wallenstein in his blind trust in Octavio. The drama never leaves the plane of naturally motivated action. Yet the mysticism of Wallenstein in its serene assurance is infectious. We are left pondering.

The death of Wallenstein is an event of retributive justice, both morally and esthetically satisfying. But when he has paid the supreme penalty, the contours of his personality stand out in awesome greatness. There is atonement in death for the grosser part of his impulses. There was something in the man's essence that would have made him accept his doom as just and proper. Death has a transfiguring effect. The career of Wallenstein can be summed up in a two-part formula: Involvement with the dark forces of life; death and transfiguration. But does not this formula apply, in greater or lesser degree, to every one of Schiller's tragic heroes? The very first of them, Karl Moor, a noble hot-headed titan, plunged by blind impulse into a career of robbery and murder, struts as a tool of divine retributive justice until he is brought up short by a series of emotional shocks. When his eyes are opened and he sees his deeds in the ghastly light of reality, he implores heaven's mercy and surrenders to earthly justice, still every inch a man. Fiesco, all but too noble to pluck the prize of his plotting, finds his victory rendered meaningless at the moment of success: he has unwittingly stabbed the wife he worships, the woman whom he had schemed to surprise and glorify by his dazzling coup. If this is cruel punishment, his assassination a few moments later at the hand of a counter-plotter, appears in the light of a merciful fate. Ferdinand, least heroic of Schiller's heroes, high-minded but flashy and impetuous, becomes the dupe of a fiendish plot that leads him, in jealous rage and desperation, to poison the angelic Luise and himself. When it is too late, he learns the truth and makes his peace with heaven. In the Spanish tragedy the three idealistic conspirators, the Marquis, the Prince, and the Queen, take their exit from the human scene purged of all earthly dross and trailing a cloud of glory. Mary, Queen of the Scots, goes to the block an innocent victim of a rigged court. But she feels it a privilege to atone by her martyrdom for the crimes of passion with which she had offended Heaven in her youth. In Schiller's version of the Maid of Orleans Johanna is a warrior saint and a martyr without a flaw. What looks like an act of disobedience to her heaven-ordained mission is only a visitation jointly contrived by the powers of heaven and hell to test her mettle in a period of tribulation. Heaven disavows her by ostentatious signs. Her friends abandon her. She is a prey to confusion. Where we see only a foreordained mysterious catastrophe, she translates what has befallen her into a sense of sin, and she bears her fate meekly and without a murmur, trusting in the fatherly design of an inscrutable Providence. When the foreordained period of her trials is completed her faith is vindicated. Filled with supernatural power she breaks her chains and, leading the French forces to victory, she dies on the battlefield. Here we have death and transfiguration in purest conjunction though only on the superficial level of theatrical legend. In *Die Braut von Messina*, finally, the sagacity of the noble Queen Mother and the most earnest good will of the two princes, her sons, are of no avail to avert the fulfillment of an efficacious ancestral curse that began working itself out by dreams and ambiguous oracles many years before. On the very day when the lifelong feuding of the two brothers has yielded to sincere reconciliation, the younger brother impulsively stabs the older only to learn that the woman whose attraction had worked on them both like a magnet was their own sister, brought up in a distant convent in ignorance of her ancestry. As in *Oedipus Rex* all the designs of men to nullify what has been foretold have worked to bring about the family's fated doom. But the surviving brother, finding himself thus trapped by fate, his hands stained with his brother's blood, his passion unquenched by the sexual taboo, rises above the foreordained horrors of the situation to atone by a freely willed death for his part in the guilt of the doomed house. In dying by his own hand he shows that no force of fate can break a free man's spirit. He dies a hero, cleansed.

This brief sketch of Schiller's tragedies has revealed a uniform pattern governing their course. In all of them the action is centered around men and women of highly superior emotional range, strength, and ingrained nobility. They get involved with the dark forces of life through headlong impulse or ambition. They engage in the struggle for highest stakes, boldly, courageously, generously. They perish. But in each case the figure of the protagonist, the *Gestalt*, is enduringly stamped upon our inner eye as the incorporation of timeless human values. They are heroes, exemplars of human freedom within the framework of a higher moral law to which they pay tribute in their very transgression. The net effect of each of Schiller's tragedies is to leave us with a quickened sense of life as a proving ground of personality. Our response to the heroic struggle of the protagonists and the vindication of the moral law in their downfall is affirmative. A life that affords room for personalities of such scope to develop is good. We are impelled to emulate them in the hope of ourselves leaving a significant mark for posterity. Thus Schiller's pattern of tragedy is basically optimistic.

If it sounds paradoxical to speak of the net effect of tragedy as an optimistic affirmation of life, we need only glance at the tragedies of Shakespeare, of Grillparzer, Hebbel, and Ibsen to see how totally different the effect of a tragic action can be.

Contrast the heroine of Hebbel's providential drama *Judith*, for example, with Schiller's Johanna. In both plays Providence uses a woman to work out its ends. Johanna's death is an apotheosis. Judith, prepared for her task of slaying Holofernes by the mysterious fate of virginal widowhood, likewise has fulfilled her mission, but at the end she finds herself left a piece of human wreckage. The divine plan used her as its vessel and it tossed the vessel upon the scrap-heap after it had served its purpose. Judith's final act is to exact a promise from the city she has delivered: If I find myself pregnant by Holofernes, kill me. A similar piece of human wreckage is all that remains of Mrs. Alving in Ibsen's *Ghosts*.

If we turn to Grillparzer's tragedies, the contrast that the Austrian dramatist presents to Schiller is nothing less than stunning. In most general terms, the outcome of Grillparzer's tragedies finds the protagonists reduced to victims, battered, exhausted, shorn of their pride and strength if they survive; ingloriously wrecked if they do not. There are no heroes to emulate. Even Sappho, seemingly secure in her aura of glory when she makes her entrance, alienates us by the abuse of her privileged social status as soon as she leaves the charmed circle of her divine art to compete in the arena of life. We are relieved to see her choose death as the only means of obliterating the otherwise ineffaceable stain on her character. King Ottokar, a strong and progressive leader at the outset, despite his crudity and lack of *Pietät*, overreaches himself and goes down to abject humiliation and defeat. Jason, a figure of brilliant daring, resourcefulness, decision, and irresistible personal magnetism in his quest of the Golden Fleece, is unnerved by his success. He undergoes a process of attrition that leaves him stripped of all his dash and glamor, an ignoble schemer and moral coward, while Medea, irresistibly drawn into unwilling partnership in his exploits, is the innocent victim of an excruciatingly cruel chain of circumstances. Bancban, the Hungarian regent, unimpeachably noble and upright, has a responsibility thrust upon him for which he is temperamentally unfitted. He emerges from the upheaval of the civil war a quavering broken reed. If a kindlier fate allows Hero to expire on the body of her drowned lover Leander after one night of rapture, her confidante Ianthe has the last word in turning to the statue of the God of Love with the disillusioned query: Versprichst du viel und hältst du also Wort? [You promise much, and this is how you keep your word?]

Of Grillparzer's three posthumous tragedies only *Libussa* marks an exception to the general tone of defeat without, in its final scene, coming any closer to Schiller's type of the heroic catharsis. In full knowledge of the fact that she is too frail a vessel to sustain the spirit of prophecy, Libussa accedes to the ordeal thrust upon her in order to become the tutelary genius of the city of Prague at whose founding she officiates. But her final blessing is bestowed in a muted deliberately sub-heroic strain. In the final scene of *Ein Bruderzwist in Habsburg* we see Matthias, when his scheming for power has finally won him the imperial crown, beat his breast with the cry:

"Mea culpa, mea maxima culpa!" And at the end of the tragedy of the Jewess of Toledo, though King Alfonso may make a brave and fluent speech consonant with his inalienable role of king, it is the sister of the lightheaded girl whose bloody corpse lies in the adjoining room, it is Esther who sums up the action in words that sound like the dirge of a tragic chorus: forgiveness all around, because we are all sinners in need of mercy. In all these tragedies the affective state of the reader or spectator resembles that of Esther. We are bowed down, unnerved, unstrung; we are left debilitated and helpless in the wake of spectacles that have seen human will, pride and glory ground to pieces in consequence of the unleashing of passions. The only refuge to hope for is a life of quiet obscurity. As at the end of a morality play we tremble lest we be set up on high and exposed to the temptations that have played havoc with the mighty. How unlike the emulative tension we feel at the exit of Schiller's heroes is the subdued hush at the end of a Grillparzer tragedy! We identify not with heroes, not even with victims. We identify with the chorus of survivors in the realization of our frailty.

Schiller's particular conception of the tragic was never more happily formulated than in one of the great stanzas of "Das Ideal und das Leben." Let us recall the beautiful lines that follow upon a stanza that dwelt on the horror of human suffering evoking tears of sympathy and anguish. Having conjured up the agonies of man in the symbol of Laocoön in the coils of serpents, Schiller turns to the contrast of death and transfiguration in tragedy:

> Aber in den heitern Regionen,
> Wo die reinen Formen wohnen,
> Rauscht des Jammers trüber Sturm nicht mehr.
> Hier darf Schmerz die Seele nicht durchschneiden,
> Keine Träne fliesst hier mehr dem Leiden,
> Nur des Geistes tapfrer Gegenwehr.

> [But in the more serene regions,
> where the pure forms dwell,
> the sad storm of wailing sounds no more.
> Here pain cannot cut through the soul,
> no tear is shed here now for suffering,
> only for the brave resistance of the spirit.]

Unlike the audiences of Schiller's day, we are not given to weeping over tragedy, not even to tears of admiration, but the mood of heroic admiration prevails as the upshot of Schiller's tragedies, then as now. In the concluding lines of the stanza Schiller develops the net effect of a calm serenity possessing us, by the image of the rainbow limned against the thundercloud:

Lieblich, wie der Iris Farbenfeuer
Auf der Donnerwolke duft'gem Tau,
Schimmert durch der Wehmut düstern Schleier
Hier der Ruhe heitres Blau.

[Lovely, like the fiery colors of Iris
on the fragrant dew of thunder clouds,
shimmers through the gloomy veil of melancholy
here the serene blue of peace.]

OEDIPUS REX
AND *DIE BRAUT VON MESSINA*

I

THE *Oedipus Rex* is concerned only with a prediction fulfilled, not with the visitation of any punishment for willful transgression of divine law. As to any design to account for the horrible chain of circumstances revealed, the tragedy of Sophocles contains not a word, not a hint. It makes manifest the omniscience of the god Apollo and the mysterious chain of necessity to which human life is subject. It evokes the tragic responses of pity and fear, of awe and submission in the face of this demonstration of how little man's conscious intent avails him in the shaping of the pattern of his life.

The *Oedipus Rex* is a fate play insofar as the *events*, twice foretold by the all-seeing god, are revealed as having come to pass long ago despite the attempts of the mortals involved to avoid them.

The *Oedipus* is not a fate play as to the *action* performed, when contrasted with the revelation of past events. There is no supernatural agency binding Oedipus' will to act in any way that does not conform to the natural impulses of his strong, resourceful, boldly aggressive personality—the personality of the good ruler who identifies the welfare of his people with his own. All the action performed is the automatic development of a situation initiated by the oracle's answer as to the cause of the pestilence; with one exception: the messenger's arriving from Corinth with the news of King Polybos' death is a coincidence. The death of Oedipus' putative father at this juncture, divinely foreseen without doubt, is a chance feature not organically connected with Oedipus' present concern, the investigation of the identity of King Laïos' murderer. The fact, however, that the messenger is the same shepherd who delivered the exposed foundling to King Polybos long ago is very plausibly motivated: he, having saved the infant, expects a commensurate reward as bringer of the glad tidings that Oedipus is now summoned to Corinth to succeed the late king.

The fact that during the course of the drama Oedipus moves

Reprinted from *Schiller 1759/1959*, ed. John R. Frey (1959), pp. 171-202, by permission of the University of Illinois Press.

with the same degree of free will as does Hamlet, for instance, is brilliantly demonstrated by Bernard M. W. Knox in his book *Oedipus at Thebes*.[1] Neither Oedipus nor the other characters that participate in the action of the play are visibly subject to any supernatural pressure in the governance of their behavior. Jocaste's suicide after she has divined the dreadful truth and Oedipus' blinding of himself after it has been spelled out for him are the reactions of their personalities to the situation.

Nevertheless, the parricide and mother incest of Oedipus as foretold—once to King Laïos and Jocaste, a second time to Oedipus himself—make the *Oedipus Rex* a fate play in a peculiar sense, differentiating it from anything modern in spirit (which is to exclude the genre of German Romantic fate tragedy). In Shakespeare's plays there are also elements of mysterious prediction that come true, such as the witches' prophecy to Macbeth, or that which told Henry Bolingbroke he would die in Jerusalem, and found ambiguous fulfillment in the fact that Jerusalem is the name of the palace chamber in which he died; and we could point to strong elements of the same sort in Ibsen's *Emperor and Galilean*—not to mention a host of others. But in *Oedipus* the weight of the fact that a terrible and fantastically improbable prediction has turned out to be true despite all human efforts to circumvent it is disproportionately greater than any elements of ambiguous prediction in modern drama. There is the additional fact that in contrast to the ambiguous oracles of the moderns there is no ambiguity about Apollo's oracle in the *Oedipus*. Knox objects to the label of fate play as tending to downgrade the dramatic human appeal of the *Oedipus*. He even makes a point of insisting that the god predicted only the events themselves and not their coming to light. True; but what meaning is there in any prediction of untoward events without the proof of fulfillment?! Such a prediction would not differ in kind from those biblical predictions that foretell the end of the world and the Day of Judgment.

Christ's prediction to Peter that he would deny him thrice before the cock crew is cited by Knox as an analogous case of divine foreknowledge without any implication of the act predicted as being imposed or fated. The case of Peter resembles that of Oedipus in the divine foreknowledge of precise detail, but in all other respects

---

[1] New Haven, 1957.

it differs: (1) it is a minor incident in a divine drama foreknown by Christ in general terms; (2) it is a psychological prediction based on Christ's intimate knowledge of the human frailty of his staunchest disciple and as such does not exceed the limits of human insight; (3) there is no devious attempt on Peter's part to dodge the fulfillment of the prediction.

These things established, let us see how Apollo's oracle and the characters interact to subject our emotions eventually to an over-whelming assault. We begin by focusing upon the middle of the play, where Jocaste appears for the first time and wants to know from Oedipus what his fierce quarrel with her brother Creon is about. Learning that it is the seer's charges against Oedipus that have put her brother in danger of his life, she impulsively discloses a heretofore closely guarded secret, hoping by this means to settle the issue. But her disclosure has the opposite effect of that intended. It leads Oedipus in the course of his questions prompted by her story to make a series of disclosures of his own that ultimately lead to the discovery of the facts hidden from them both.

Thus, at the middle of the play, a new layer of exposition begins to be unfolded. Through the communications exchanged and the inferences we are forced to draw, we learn that during the long years of their married life together Jocaste and Oedipus have each kept from the other some vital area of his past, and certain other equally vital matters have been covered by the silence of a sacred taboo. All these years Jocaste has never told Oedipus that she and her first husband had consigned their infant son to death by ex-posure in consequence of Apollo's oracle predicting that his son would be his father's slayer. This was a jealously guarded secret known only to herself, to King Laïos, and to the shepherd whom they commissioned to do away with the child. We can well under-stand that she could never bear to mention the fact that she had consented to a decision that so outraged her maternal feelings. And resentment against the god who prompted it must have continued to rankle in her heart under the mask of conformist piety forever after. We must also infer that Jocaste never discussed the circum-stances of King Laïos' murder with her second husband. Did she fear that to do so would prompt her to reveal her secret and vent her spite against the deity, whose power she has nevertheless not ceased to dread? Such is the irrational ambivalence of her *Gottes-*

furcht [fear of God] that she supplicates at his altar, later, before apprehension has yielded to wild despair. A further surmise concerns Oedipus' perforated feet or ankles. Was it by tacit mutual agreement that no mention was ever made of his foot trouble? Were not those scars also intolerable reminders to her of the dark blot on her life?

As for Oedipus, upon coming to Thebes he had declared himself son of King Polybos of Corinth (the chorus refers to him in these terms in its second ode); but, after marrying the late king's widow, he had never told her of (1) the doubts concerning his parentage raised by a drunken reveller's remark, (2) the failure of his parents' angry protestations to reassure him, (3) his recourse to the Delphic god who, instead of answering his questions, staggered him with the prediction that he would kill his father and marry his mother, (4) his precipitous flight, and (5) his encounter with the noble traveler whom he slew shortly before the miraculous change of fortune that made him savior of Thebes and brought him the crown and the queen. In addition he had also refrained, like Jocaste, for good reasons of his own, from discussing with her the circumstances of King Laïos' murder and the condition of his feet.

All these concealments come to light either by word of mouth or by inference from the general context. That they constitute an enormous factor regarding the inner motivation of the principals during the play cannot be denied. Attempts to explain away all or some of them as not real concealments but as merely a technical device for stimulating the curiosity of the audience to fever pitch must be dismissed as superficial. Taking these concealments at face value, we say: There is a terrible block of unassimilated experience in the lives of both Oedipus and Jocaste. Each of them, while not having forgotten certain frightful experiences and certain disquieting signs extending into the present, carefully keeps all this block of unassimilated experience concealed from both the world and the mate. It is treated by each of them as nonexistent, forgotten. Jocaste lets out her secret on seeing Oedipus beside himself with rage and threatening the life of her brother.

As for Oedipus, we have a right to let our imagination dwell on what happened to him. When his unstilled doubts as to his parentage (always: why those scarred feet?) had led him to Delphi, to learn the dreadful pronouncement of the oracle, he took flight in a state of panic, resolved never to set foot in his homeland again. He made his way roaming through forest and mountains by night, more like a beast than a man. Then at a threeway the distracted desperado stumbled into the way of an aging nobleman's conveyance accompanied by a herald and three servants. Rudely ordered to make way for his betters, he, the king's son, felt hot anger flare up in him. He struck the insolent coachman. The nobleman himself retaliated by striking him on the head with his double-pronged goad. Then, in an access of blind, manic frenzy, Oedipus laid about him with his staff and slew them. He was in a "black out." He did not even notice that one escaped. He himself escaped from the event, it seems, without counting his victims. What had befallen him was an event, not a deliberate act. This was probably the first blood to stain his hands. He now erred on, with a second ghastly experience to add to the horror of the prophecy. It was soon after this that he came upon the winged monster, the riddling Sphinx. With nothing but his life to lose, a life branded by a dire prediction and a beastly multiple murder, he faced up to her riddle, solved it, saw the monster destroy itself, and found himself hailed as the savior of the City and raised to the vacant throne by popular acclaim. It is understandable that he did not breathe a word about his recent past either to Jocaste, or to anyone else, and if any dark surmises arose in his mind as to the identity of the murdered travelers he kept them to himself or rather, from himself.

If we are correct in the way we have delimited these blocks of unassimilated—repressed—experience in the lives of the two principal characters, we must ask ourselves: To what extent could the awareness of this factor have affected the first Athenian audience? The answer is that this audience could have been aware of what was heaving in Oedipus during the first half of the play only very faintly, if at all. They were familiar, from Homer and Aeschylus, with the basic outlines of the myth—the oracle, the exposure of the infant, the young man's parricide, and his incestuous union with his mother. And they knew that these facts would somehow come to light. But they could not have understood, except in retrospect, to what extent Oedipus' and Jocaste's repressions were unwittingly contributing to bring about the ultimate discovery of their ghastly situation. The participation of the first audience must to a large extent have consisted of curiosity as to the how of the outcome.

In this respect our type of participation is fundamentally different. Having read or seen the play, and retracing its course, we are vastly more aware, for one thing, of the tragic irony that permeates every portion of Oedipus' and Jocaste's part in the dialogue. But beyond this, we soon become aware of a tremendous obscurely felt undercurrent of pressure exerted on Oedipus by the repressed block of his past. It is heaving and fermenting in Oedipus' viscera and his blood, clamoring to come into the open and be recognized as something that will fit into the pattern of his life and tie its loose ends together. The further Oedipus progresses in his inquiry and the more determined he is to get at the bottom of the truth, the more desperately he fights against admitting to himself that the facts hidden up to now in a sealed-off compartment of his self are an integral part of the mysterious ups and downs of his fortune. His anger against Teiresias' stubborn refusal to speak is motivated in part, to be sure, by the surface situation: what else but irrational malevolence could keep the renowned seer, having responded to the summons to appear, from opening his mouth and revealing the key information sought in order to make the pestilence come to an end?! But when the prodding of his violence has at last provoked Teiresias into replying:

"Des Manns Mord, den du suchst, ich sag, auf dich da fällt er!"[2]

[The murder of the man whom thou seekest, I say it falls on thee!]

he shuts his ears to the words that designate him as Laïos' murderer and brand him as living in incest with his wife. He has comprehended and not comprehended. In his desperate fight to keep the

---

[2] This, Hölderlin's rendering, falls on Oedipus' head like a crackling flash of lightning. This trimeter of thirteen monosyllables—its staccato rhythm not prefigured by the polysyllabic words of the Greek original line—is a marvel in the context of the German language, where, contrary to English, verses consisting entirely of monosyllabic words are almost impossible to find. Thirteen monosyllables, each with a ringing vowel, moreover! There is a comparable line in Goethe's *Faust* (broken by a caesura, however, without the headlong rush of Hölderlin's), spoken by Mephisto, after Faust has fallen dead:
"Der mir so kräftig wiederstand,
Die Zeit wird Herr, der Greis hier liegt im Sand."
[He who resisted me so mightily,
Time becomes his lord, the old man lies here in the sand.]
And additional examples of such lines, counteracting the up-and-down pulse of the German language, can be found chiefly in Stefan George's poetry. This one Hölderlin line gloriously compensates for all the errors, the overliteralness, and the obscurity of much of his translation.

horrible truth fermenting within him from welling up to the surface of his consciousness, he levels his attack against Creon: Teiresias and Creon must be accomplices in a political plot to destroy him! Only later, when Jocaste's chance remark about the threeway, at which Laïos was murdered, has led him to pursue the other threads of the web—the exact place, the time, the number of the King's companions, and the King's age and stature, he has all but fully realized that it was Laïos he had slain. At this point, in the depths of despair, he clutches at a single straw of hope—the messenger's report that it was a band of highwaymen, not one individual, who did the killing. His speech, as he awaits the coming of the messenger, does not express a sense of triumph, as Knox would have us believe; it is, rather, a desperate, delirious outburst of manic euphoria—the victim's frenzy in expectation of the final crushing blow. All this before he has any inkling of that other message from Corinth, the news of King Polybos' death. Before he hears that message he is already branded in his own sight as the murderer of his predecessor and the desecrator of his nuptial bed. By the curse his own mouth has pronounced upon the King's slayer, he is already toppled from his rule and committed to execution or banishment from his home and his family.

Thus, knowing Oedipus' heretofore carefully guarded secrets, we see him throughout the play waging a fierce fight against two sets of antagonists, an outer set—Teiresias and Creon—falsely accused of a plot, and an inner set: he is fighting against himself; he is fighting to prevent the concealed threads of his past from revealing themselves to complete the pattern of his disjointed life. Our empathy with a hero, shown intrinsically noble, intelligent, quick, resourceful, and bent on saving his city at all costs, is vastly heightened by our realization of his struggle against the forces within him.

Dwelling on Oedipus' reaction to the truth as finally revealed, Knox insists (and we fully agree) that the greatness of Oedipus' personality becomes most manifest in the hour of his total catastrophe. But in his emphasis on Oedipus' active determination to get to the bottom of the truth, Knox all but ignores the psychological factor of repression as regards both Oedipus and Jocaste.[3] While

[3] Among the few references to that factor, this, from page 92, is significant: "The fullness of his account has often been censured as dramatically implausible, for Jocasta, though it is conceivable that she does not know of Oedipus' fight at the crossroads or the oracular response (one can well imagine that Oedipus sup-

other aspects of Sophocles' drama, elaborated by Knox—Oedipus as a symbol of Athens, *tyrannos* of Greece, and Oedipus as a paradigm of man's limitations—may go unchallenged, the *Oedipus Rex* is psychological drama of overwhelming intensity.

II

With this sketch of *Oedipus Rex* as a background let us look at *Die Braut von Messina*. The fact that Schiller wrote his drama with an eye on Sophocles' most famous work is too well known to require elaboration here. A recent, highly rewarding study of Schiller's relation to Sophocles in all its aspects, by Florian Prader,[4] supplies ample documentation. Both the analytical technique and the experimental use of the chorus show a studied attempt on Schiller's part to compete with the Athenian masterpiece on its own ground by imitating its most conspicuous technical features. In order to assess Schiller's success or failure we must focus upon these particulars. At the same time we must compare the over-all conception of human life in the general order of things, as it appears in the two dramas. To take this up first, we cannot but be aware of the radical divergence of the religious outlook. Sophocles' tragedy both reflects a deep personal piety, and appeals to the piety of his characters and that of his audience by demonstrating the unerring prescience of the gods, whereas Schiller relativizes all religious beliefs: against a heavily underscored background of surviving classical polytheistic conceptions and imagery, medieval Christian institutions, ritual and faith determine the religious life of the Messina community. As a third factor, the Moslem outlook on life and certain Moslem practices persist as an undercurrent. Schiller's creation of a composite, noncommittal religious atmosphere has, of course, been noted by all commentators, but the degree to which it radically shifts the fundamental assumptions underlying the two plays has escaped even so discerning a critic as Prader; and Ernst Müller's essay on *Die Braut von Messina*,[5] in his recent

---

pressed and even tried to forget these uncomfortable facts), surely knows the identity of Oedipus' supposed parents." ". . . surely knows"? Since the chorus knows it (referring to him as Polybos' son in the second ode), it is certain that Jocaste knows it.

4 Florian Prader, *Schiller und Sophokles* (Zürich, 1954).

5 In Friedrich Schiller, *Ausgewählte Werke*, ed. Ernst Müller, 6 vols. (Stuttgart, 1954), IV, 622-637. The edition shows signs of hasty preparation accounted

edition of Schiller's works, leaning heavily on Prader and, repeating his errors, shows a disquieting reliance on secondary sources coupled with a painfully superficial acquaintance with Schiller's text.

Schiller's fundamental point of divergence from Sophocles is this: underlying the dark web of events brought to light in the *Oedipus Rex* is a prediction on the part of the all-seeing god; and the events of the play show the prediction to have been fulfilled to the letter. As has been pointed out above, there is no reference in Sophocles' tragedy to any act of primal guilt on the part of Oedipus or his ancestors as responsible for his terrible fate. Schiller, on the other hand, bases the dire events of his play on a primal crime—a collision between father and son in the area of sexual competition— followed by a paternal curse the sinister working out of which is revealed in both the *Vorgeschichte* and the action of the play. The key disclosure of the initial situation that starts the House on the road to ruin is made by the chorus, not as a revelation but as a matter of common knowledge, at a point just before the first change of scene:

> Auch ein Raub war's, wie wir alle wissen,
> Der des alten Fürsten eh'liches Gemahl
> In ein frevelnd Ehebett gerissen,
> Denn sie war des Vaters Wahl.
> Und der Ahnherr schüttete im Zorne
> Grauenvoller Flüche schrecklichen Samen
> Auf das sündige Ehebett aus.
> Greueltaten ohne Namen,
> Schwarze Verbrechen verbirgt dies Haus.　　(ll. 960-968)[6]

> [It was also a rape, as we all know,
> which dragged into an outraged marriage bed
> the lawful wife of the old prince,
> for she was the choice of the father.

---

for, no doubt, by the urgent postwar need for new editions. It is marred by an excessive number of misprints, and the copious editorial apparatus is very uneven. The essay on *Die Braut von Messina* is poorly written, abounds in errors, and refers to the text by act and scene, although the text as printed shows no such divisions. The treatment of young Schiller is on a much higher level, and Ernst Müller's separately published study, *Der Herzog und das Genie: Friedrich Schillers Jugendjahre* (Stuttgart, 1955), deserves honorable mention for the freshness and objectivity of its presentation.

[6] All quotations from the play refer to Vol. v of *Schillers Werke*, in collaboration with Robert Petsch, Albert Leitzmann and Wolfgang Stammler, ed. Ludwig Bellermann, 2d ed. Bibliographisches Institut (Leipzig, n.d.).

And the ancestor cast in anger
the ghastly seed of gruesome curses
upon the sinful marriage bed.
Loathsome deeds without name,
dark crimes does this house hide.]

Prader alludes to this passage once, in order to derive from it the idea of an "Erbschuld," an ancestral guilt (p. 77). He does not quote it, and although he speaks of the fated curse, "schicksalhafter Fluch," he never spells out the terms of the situation, while Ernst Müller, in his glib and obscure philosophizing about this play, never mentions this key passage at all! How was it possible for it to be thus slighted? The position in which it stands is indeed puzzling and may account in part for its neglect. Only the chorus is on the stage at the time, Don Manuel, the last of the principals to leave, having taken his exit after line 860. And the chorus has meanwhile delivered itself of a hundred lines of florid speculation on a variety of pursuits that may appeal to men's desire for action and excitement before it squarely focuses upon the ominous open secret. Thus the veil of the past is lifted at a time when the attention of reader and audience, wearied by ornate rhetorical embroidery, is least likely to grasp its full significance. It is imperative now to analyze the purport of the passage.

When the late King[7] of Messina was a young man his father decided to marry a second time. But the young man (perhaps fearing that such a step might endanger his right of succession) seized his father's intended bride and married her himself.[8] In terms of the patriarchal setup this was a heinous act of filial insubordination, a "Frevel,"[9] and the father reacted to it in a terrible way. If the passage is to be taken literally, the father invaded his son's residence and cursed his marriage-bed, accompanying the curse by an obscene act of pollution. However Schiller may have visualized it, he probably felt that the potentially offensive passage would evoke

---

[7] I hope I may be pardoned for rendering "Fürst" and "Fürstin" as king and queen in the absence of any simple title in English for the heads of a ruling house.

[8] As we see, the situation is that of *Don Carlos* in reverse.

[9] Cf. the Queen Mother's words, lines 2503-2505:

Dies Haus. Ein Frevel führte mich herein,
Ein Frevel treibt mich aus. Mit Widerwillen
Hab' ich's betreten und mit Furcht bewohnt.

[This house. An outrage led me into it,
an outrage drives me out. With disgust
did I enter it and dwelled there with fear.]

only a mood in the reader without conjuring up anything approaching an image. "Grauenvoller Flüche schrecklichen Samen": this involves a metaphor without any doubt. The dire curses *are* the seed that brought forth a baleful harvest. But the chain of terms, *schüttete* (= cast, not scattered), *Samen* (= semen as well as seed), and *Ehebett* (the bed itself, standing for the relation), combine in their aggregate to conjure up an image of horror. Since no further mention is made of the frustrated sire throughout the play, it would not be going too far to assume that he succumbed to a fatal stroke during his cursing, leaving his son in undisputed possession of the realm. He continued to govern Messina with a stern hand, curbing the feuding of the two sons born to him, until his death some two or three months[10] before the day on which the action of the drama takes place. Another thing to puzzle us about this passage is its last two lines. What are these deeds, monstrous beyond naming, these black crimes harbored by the royal house? Is it the son's bold snatching of his father's bride, along with the curse that followed this rash act, that warrants so terrible a designation? Is it also the command to do away with the infant daughter? This was kept secret, of course, and is revealed by the Queen Mother to the chorus at a very late point of the action (ll. 2335ff.). Is it also, perhaps, the brother-sister incest and the fratricide prophetically seen and anticipated by the chorus? Or does the chorus have in mind only the ancestor's curse, inflating it with rhetorical effect by the plural form and the repetition in the manner of Vergil and other classical writers?

While there is no definite answer to any of these questions, one thing is certain: the curse pronounced by the grandfather of Manuel, Cesar, and Beatrice is the *primum agens* that sets in motion the chain of events leading to the destruction of the royal line. It is Schiller's intention without a doubt that everything we hear and witness until Don Cesar's suicide[11] is to be experienced by us as the methodical, ineluctable working out of the grandfather's curse— everything: the two dreams and their divergent ambiguous interpretation, the meaningful actions of all the members of the royal house as regards both the remote and the recent past and also the

---

[10] Two months, according to line 13; three months according to line 1368.

[11] Whether Don Cesar's suicide is to be included is a question to be determined by later discussion.

day of the play itself; everything, including even the fateful timing of the entrances and exits, the "machinery" of the plot. All these are part of the sinister, inescapable web in which mother, sons, and daughter are helplessly, hopelessly caught. We shall pick up all the salient strands of this web in due course. But the matter to be taken up first, a matter not even touched upon by Prader's and Müller's interpretations, is the paternal curse as a favorite vehicle of development in Schiller's dramatic plots.

In every one of Schiller's first three dramas the idea of the paternal curse as an agency invested with supernatural power is prominently featured. Bound up with religious notions of awe and reverence due, it is credited with a magic efficacy. In *Kabale und Liebe* the idea of the father's curse is twice used with telling effect to influence the course of the action. In act III, scene 4, Ferdinand tries to prevail upon Luise to flee with him. For him to continue to submit to his father's jurisdiction is impossible, he tells her. Fury and despair would compel him to reveal the fact that his father rose to the presidency by the murder of his predecessor; he would be delivering his own father to the executioner. But to Ferdinand's "wir fliehen" Luise replies:

> Und der Fluch deines Vaters uns nach?—ein Fluch, Unbesonnener, den auch Mörder nie ohne Erhörung aussprechen, den die Rache des Himmels auch dem Dieb auf dem Rade hält, der uns Flüchtlinge unbarmherzig wie ein Gespenst von Meer zu Meer jagen würde?—Nein, mein Geliebter!

> [With the curse of thy father after us?—a curse, thou heedless man, which even murderers never utter without effect, which the vengeance of heaven pledges even to the thief on the wheel; which would chase us fugitives unmercifully like a ghost from sea to sea—No, my beloved.]

Ferdinand turns a deaf ear to this motivation. He finally works himself into a rage of suspicion: "Schlange, du lügst!" [Serpent, thou liest!]—and he rushes out in a state that makes him an easy prey for Wurm's intrigue of the planted letter. A second time (in act V, scene 1), the threat of her own father's curse provides the decisive motivation that makes Luise abandon her plan to commit suicide and inform Ferdinand by a posthumous letter of how he had been deluded. After Miller has exhausted all his theological arguments in the attempt to dissuade Luise from suicide as the sin not to be forgiven, he rises to a climax with the words:

Bring deinem schlanken Jüngling ein Opfer, dass deine Teufel jauchzen und deine guten Engel zurücktreten.—Zieh hin! Lade alle deine Sünden auf, lade auch diese, die letzte, die entsetzlichste auf, und wenn die Last noch zu leicht ist, so mache mein Fluch das Gewicht vollkommen!

[Bring a sacrifice to thy slender youth, so that thy devils will jubilate and thy good angels retreat.—Go away! Take up all thy sins, take up also this, the last, the most horrible, and if the burden is still too light, then let my curse make the weight complete.]

A few more words in this vein, and Luise tears up the letter that would have restored Ferdinand's faith in her.

In *Fiesco* the father's curse is employed not as a dreaded anticipation; rather, we hear it roll with the most turgid rhetorical thunder. The daughter of the one stalwart republican, Verrina, has been brutally raped by Gianettino Doria. When her father has learned of the outrage from the victim's lips, he pronounces the most awful curse upon her—a provisional curse—in order to steel his nerves for the assassination of young Doria, which accomplished, the curse would automatically be annulled. In the presence of his daughter and his co-conspirators Verrina strikes his pose and speaks as follows:

Verflucht sei die Luft, die dich fächelt! Verflucht der Schlaf, der dich erquickt! Verflucht jede menschliche Spur, die deinem Elend willkommen ist! Geh hinab in das unterste Gewölb' meines Hauses. Winsle! Heule! Lähme die Zeit mit deinem Gram. Dein Leben sei das gichterische Wälzen des sterbenden Wurms—der hartnäckige zermalmende Kampf zwischen Sein und Vergehen!—Dieser Fluch hafte auf dir, bis Gianettino den letzten Odem verröchelt hat.—Wo nicht, so magst du ihn nachschleppen längs der Ewigkeit, bis man ausfindig macht, wo die zwei Enden ihres Rings ineinandergreifen. (act I, scene 12)

[Cursed be the air which fans thee! Cursed the sleep which refreshes thee! Cursed every human trace which is welcome to thy misery! Go down into the lowest cellar of my house! Whimper! Wail! Lame time with thy grief. Let thy life be the most gouty writhing of a dying worm —the stubborn, crushing battle between existence and perishing! May this curse cling to thee until Gianettino has breathed out his last breath. If not, then mayest thou drag him after thee into eternity until it is learned where the two ends of its circle mesh.]

All this bombast, regardless of its missing its effect on a modern audience, would be sheer nonsense if the solemn pronouncement of the father's curse were not credited with a magic automatism of fulfillment in the minds of Verrina and those who hear him.

Turning back now all the way to *Die Räuber*, we find here also

the idea of the father's curse as an instrument of heavenly vengeance lavishly exploited. To be sure, we never hear the old nobleman pronounce a curse upon the head of his wayward son Karl;
and it is inconceivable that this weakling without a trace of stiffen-
ing in his temperament, a man whose goodness reacts with pious
imbecility to the most heinous outrages, should ever have pronounced such a curse. Yet this is the burden of the torments of his
conscience. "Mein Fluch ihn gejagt in den Tod! gefallen in Verzweiflung!" [My curse has driven him to death! Fallen in despair!], he
moans when Hermann, disguised, brings him the fictitious message
of Karl's death in act II, scene 2—the message that charged him
with having compassed his son's destruction by his curse. In the
further course of the scene the villain Franz turns the knife in his
father's wound, making him exclaim: "Und du hast mir den Fluch
aus dem Herzen geschwätzt—du—du!" [And thou hast chattered
my curse out of my heart—thou—thou!] After his rescue from the
dungeon of his living death by Karl, whom he does not recognize (act IV, scene 5), the old man still broods on the alleged
curse, ". . . dass ihn mein Fluch gejagt hätte in Kampf und Tod
und Verzweiflung" [. . . that my curse had driven him to battle and
death and despair]. And the psychological effect of the parental
curse upon its victim is attested by Karl himself, first in act I, scene
2, where the impact of his brother's letter makes him spew forth
a flood of wild hyperbolic images, all of them embroidering on the
text of the father's curse without the word "Fluch" being mentioned, and again in act v, scene 2, when he exclaims: "Zu spät!
Vergebens! Dein Fluch, Vater! Frage mich nicht mehr! Ich bin—
ich habe—dein Fluch—dein vermeinter Fluch!" [Too late! In vain!
Thy curse, father! Ask me no more. I am—I have—thy curse—
thy presumed curse!] This is the prelude to his confessing that he
is the leader of a robber band, as the old man succumbs to the
shock of the revelation and gasps his last.

The concept of the father's curse in Schiller's first three dramas
does not appear quite the same in each instance. In *Die Räuber*
its primary function is psychological as regards both father and
son; but it is also felt to be an instrument of retributive justice conceived both in impersonal terms as Nemesis and in personal terms
as the deity of Christian tradition. In *Fiesco* the father's curse is
supposed to function as a magic automatism pure and simple. In

Kabale und Liebe the threat of a father's curse operates as a (subjective) psychological motive upon Luise, but its ability to do so is predicated on her conviction that such a curse destroys its intended victim regardless of the moral qualifications of the parent who utters it. We see, thus, that the idea of the parental curse as infallibly efficacious is a key device employed by Schiller in each of his early dramas. I call it a device because it is not to be believed for one moment that the writer himself held any such belief. But as for reader and audience, Schiller doubtless counted upon their yielding to that willing suspension of disbelief which would lead them to empathize with the characters in their way of conceiving the curse.

For, to sanction this lurid theatrical exploitation of the father's curse, Schiller had a great fund of hallowed tradition to point to; chiefly biblical, but also classical. The stories of the Patriarchs abound with examples of both the curse and the blessing as automatically efficacious. It is enough here to recall the curse that Noah pronounced on his son Ham when he had irreverently exposed his father's shame. Every child in Schiller's day was brought up to know that the skin of Ham's descendants had turned black as the result of this curse. A much more horrible example from the world of classical myth was at hand in the story of Oedipus' ill-fated sons. In the version of Statius' Latin epic, the *Thebais*, which won the distinction of supplying the story for the first medieval romance of chivalry, the *Roman de Thèbes*, Oedipus not merely blinds himself but tears his eyeballs out of their sockets. His sons, who witness this bloodcurdling self-mutilation of him who is also their half-brother, trample upon his eyeballs in derision. Oedipus thereupon pronounces a terrible curse upon their heads, and their lifelong feuding and eventual mutual fratricide spell out its fulfillment. In *Die Braut von Messina* Schiller has the Queen Mother allude to the story (also used by Dante in Canto XXVI of the *Inferno*) that even the flames issuing from their joint funeral pyre, refusing to mingle, rose in two separate tongues:

> Leib gegen Leib, wie das thebanische Paar,
> Rückt aufeinander an, und wutvoll ringend,
> Umfanget euch mit eherner Umarmung!
> Leben um Leben tauschend, siege jeder,
> Den Dolch einbohrend in des andern Brust,
> Dass selbst der Tod nicht eure Zwietracht heile,

Die Flamme selbst, des Feuers rote Säule,
Die sich von eurem Scheiterhaufen hebt,
Sich zweigespalten voneinander teile,
Ein schaudernd Bild, wie ihr gestorben und gelebt. (ll. 450-459)

[Body against body, like the Theban pair,
move to one another and, furiously wrestling,
receive each other with brazen embrace!
Exchanging life for life, may each be victorious,
thrusting the dagger into the other's breast;
so that even death may not heal your dissension,
may the flame itself, the red column of fire,
which rises from your funeral pyre,
separate and split in two,
a terrible symbol of how you died and lived.]

And six years earlier one of the *Xenien* had pointed to Statius'
version (or Seneca's tragedy) in the lines satirically captioned
"Die höchste Harmonie":

Oedipus reisst die Augen sich aus, Jokasta erhenkt sich,
Beide schuldlos—das Stück hat sich harmonisch gelöst.[12]

[Oedipus tears his eyes out, Jocasta hangs herself,
both blameless—the play has ended harmoniously.]

For good measure we could also point to Shakespeare's *The
Tempest*, where Prospero enjoins Ferdinand under threat of a dire
curse not to "break her [Miranda's] virgin knot before / All sanc-
timonious ceremonies may / With full and holy rite be minister'd"
(act IV, scene 1).

After all that has been said we are not surprised to see the efficacious paternal curse reappear—this time as the key motif—in the

---

[12] Schiller's epigram contaminates Sophocles' tragedy with one of the Roman
versions—probably Seneca's *Oedipus* tragedy (das Stück!) which was the source
of Statius' epic. Seneca has the messenger report in gory detail on Oedipus' digging
his eyeballs out of their sockets and then ripping away the dangling orbs. Jocaste
is still alive when Oedipus returns to the stage. But his prodding makes her seize
the dagger and plunge it into her womb in the presence of chorus and spectators.
The father's curse is, of course, already a feature of Sophocles' *Oedipus in
Colonus*. Here, after his twenty years of wandering, their callous indifference to
the dreadful lot of the blind outcast prompts Oedipus to curse his two sons and
even predict their death by each other's hand. But here there is nothing to indicate
that the curse derives its efficacy from the fact that he is their father. The fact is,
rather, that Oedipus, though still a mortal, has evolved into a demon-deity with
unlimited arbitrary power to bless and to curse, and he lavishly indulges his power
in both directions (to the benefit of Athens and the detriment of his native
Thebes) before he undergoes a mysterious translation not unlike the biblical
Enoch or Elijah.

one fully executed analytical dramatic plot of Schiller's own invention.[13] In *Die Braut von Messina* the idea of the curse occurs in closest conjunction with the popular ideas of Nemesis and Fate working through the agency of supernaturally inspired dreams and ambiguous oracles. For the deceptive operation of the divine oracle, in contrast to the straightforward prediction in Sophocles' tragedy, Schiller had a host of examples from Herodotus to draw on, such as the story of Cyrus and that of Croesus. And this feature largely contributes to the predominantly classical flavor of *Die Braut von Messina* despite its medieval setting. We recall that Schiller used the idea of Nemesis as a quasi-personal agency of retribution in *Wallenstein*, through the mouth of Octavio, in lines set off from their blank verse context by the use of the classical trimeter:

> Mit leisen Tritten schlich er seinen bösen Weg,
> So leis und schlau ist ihm die Rache nachgeschlichen.
> Schon steht sie ungesehen, finster hinter ihm,
> Ein Schritt nur noch, und schaudernd rühret er sie an.[14]

> (ll. 3584-3587)

> [With quiet steps he slunk his evil way,
> thus softly, slyly did revenge slink after him.
> It stands unseen already, ominous behind him,
> just one more step, and shuddering he touches it.]

While Nemesis suggests the idea of retribution catching up with crime in rather general terms, the idea of Fate, as exemplified in Romantic drama in Schiller's own day and for more than a decade after his death, is conceived as a sinister supernatural agency plotting a diabolically ingenious maze of interlocking coincidences that eventuate in the destruction of the victims. The victims may have no suspicion of the trap to be sprung, thereby permitting of the use of tragic irony on a large scale. Or, as in Grillparzer's *Ahn-*

---

[13] For another—ultimately abandoned—attempt of Schiller's to build a modern crime-thriller drama on the idea of Nemesis, see Prader's illuminating chapter: "*Narbonne* oder *Die Kinder des Hauses*," pp. 37-55.

[14] I fully subscribe to Prader's concluding summary of Schiller's use of Nemesis: "Wir finden ihn [den Gedanken der Nemesis] in den Fragmenten und auch mit Bezug auf den *Wallenstein* häufig erwähnt. In der *Maria Stuart* gewinnt er in den letzten Szenen, in denen sich nach Marias Tod auch Elisabeths Vernichtung darstellt, eindrückliche Gestalt. Nun lässt sich aber nicht daran zweifeln, dass Schiller keineswegs an das Wirken der Nemesis glaubt" (p. 140). [We find it (the thought of Nemesis) in the fragments and also frequently mentioned in reference to *Wallenstein*. In *Maria Stuart*, in the last scenes, in which Elizabeth's destruction is depicted after Maria's death, it takes on an impressive shape. However, there is no doubt that Schiller in no way believed in the effects of Nemesis.]

frau, the dialogue may be keyed from the first words spoken to a sense of impending inescapable doom, thereby severely curtailing the use of verbal irony. Whichever method is used, we have the mechanics of the horror thriller. That *Die Braut von Messina* makes sense only in terms of such a frame, is my thesis.

We return to our starting point, the outraged sire's curse upon his son's marriage bed. To us, who have just witnessed the reconciliation of the feuding brothers, this disclosure comes as a surprise, but the chorus refers to it, almost casually, as a matter of common knowledge ("wie wir alle wissen" [as we all know], l. 960). Having exposed the open secret of the royal house, the chorus adds another twelve lines of comment. It points an interpreting finger, to drive home the full import of the curse in the statement:

> Es ist kein Zufall und blindes Los,
> Dass die Brüder sich wütend selbst zerstören,
> Denn verflucht ward der Mutter Schoss,
> Sie sollte den Hass und den Streit gebären. (ll. 973-976)

> [It is no accident or blind lot,
> that the brothers destroy themselves in rage,
> for their mother's womb was cursed;
> she was to give birth to hate and quarrel.]

Thus, in the most authoritative terms, through the mouth of a collective spokesman, the curse is referred to as operative. Now, no one could have been more familiar with the curse than the Queen Mother, but her introductory speech drops no hint of this fact. In her very first mention of the fraternal discord she is at pains to declare that it grew "aus unbekannt verhängnisvollem Samen" (l. 24) [out of unwitting portentous seed]. It is only very much later when the news of her daughter's disappearance has thrown her into a state of panic that she owns up to the fact that anxiety regarding the old curse had been weighing on her mind all the time:

> Wann endlich wird der alte Fluch sich lösen,
> Der über diesem Hause lastend ruht? (ll. 1695 f.)

> [When will the old curse finally be dispelled,
> which rests burdensome upon this house?]

Like Jocaste, who makes a brave show of slighting the oracle which she believes to have been successfully circumvented, Isabella discusses the feuding of her sons in wholly rationalistic terms. Because it dates back to their earliest infancy it is only a carry-over of childish behavior which should be overcome by the boys now grown to manhood. "Nur dieses eine leg' ich euch ans Herz," she begins her impassioned appeal:

> Das Böse, das der Mann, der mündige,
> Dem Manne zufügt, das, ich will es glauben,
> Vergibt sich und versöhnt sich schwer. Der Mann
> Will seinen Hass, und keine Zeit verändert
> Den Ratschluss, den er wohlbesonnen fasst.
> Doch eures Haders Ursprung steigt hinauf
> In unverständ'ger Kindheit frühe Zeit,
> Sein Alter ist's, was ihn entwaffnen sollte.
> Fraget zurück, was euch zuerst entzweite;
> Ihr wisst es nicht, ja fändet ihr's auch aus,
> Ihr würdet euch des kind'schen Haders schämen. (ll. 405-415)

> [Just this one thing do I enjoin upon you:
> The evil which a mature man
> inflicts upon a man—this I must believe—is
> forgiven and reconciled with difficulty. A man
> wills his hate, and time does not change
> the resolution which he prudently makes.
> But the origin of your dispute rises
> from the early time of imprudent childhood;
> it is its age which should disarm it.
> Think back upon what first estranged you;
> you know it not, indeed, were you even to find it out,
> you would be ashamed of your childish dispute.]

On the plane of rational motivation this plea of the Queen Mother, whose nobility of utterance throughout is as spotless as her beauty is immaculate, should succeed, the more so as her sons, in the reconciliation scene that follows, give proof of a high-mindedness that has spurned treachery even during the feuding. "Du willst nicht meinen Tod," Don Manuel says to his younger brother,

> ich habe Proben.
> Ein Mönch erbot sich dir, mich meuchlerisch
> zu morden; du bestraftest den Verräter. (ll. 479-481)

> [Thou desirest not my death, I have the proofs.
> A monk prevailed upon thee to murder me
> most dastardly; thou didst punish the traitor.]

And the whole exchange makes it clear that they both subscribe to the same chivalrous code.

The reconciliation scene takes place with the Queen Mother off-stage (after l. 459). The machinery required her absence for a space of 800 lines in order that the revelations with which she is eager to surprise her sons be timed in keeping with the foreordained catastrophe. The expected, natural thing after the reconciliation (which it would have been most natural for the mother to witness) would have been for both sons to announce the happy tidings to their mother at once. Instead, in consequence of a message, Don Cesar leaves rather hurriedly on an important errand of his own, and Don Manuel eventually goes to the bazaar with two of his followers. By the time the mother appears again, in the company of her sons, these events have happened: (1) Don Cesar has entered the retreat of the long-sought girl and impulsively declared her his wife; (2) we, together with the chorus, have learned all about Don Manuel's happy romance including his abduction of Beatrice from the convent the night before; (3) from the chorus we have learned of the grandfather's curse and its fateful significance; (4) and, lastly, Don Manuel has been spending his time at the bazaar making purchases for his bride.

The Queen Mother's long-deferred announcement to her sons is to the effect that they have a sister whose return to the household, momentarily expected, is to climax the joy of the reconciliation. But this announcement involves the recounting of a mysterious train of events, hitherto her jealously guarded secret. These comprise (1) her husband's portentous dream during her third pregnancy and its sinister interpretation by an Arabian astrologer, (2) her own corresponding dream and its optimistic interpretation on the part of a Christian monk, (3) her husband's order, after the birth of a daughter, to cast the child into the sea, and (4) her success in secretly saving the infant and having it reared in a convent. One additional item of importance that she has not the time to mention is the fact that she once yielded to her desire to see the small girl—a fact that we learn from Beatrice in her soliloquy (ll. 1026 ff.); and it is her description of this encounter that clinches Don Manuel's realization of her identity moments before he is stabbed (ll. 1841 ff.). The sons greet their mother's announcement with joy and add to her rapture by each confessing that he is going to augment the happy household with a bride that very day.

These are the bare facts regarding past events. We must now take a closer look at the circumstances surrounding Beatrice's birth and her rescue from death. There are two symbolic dreams, divergently interpreted. The father's dream:

Er seh' aus seinem hochzeitlichen Bette
Zwei Lorbeerbäume wachsen, ihr Gezweig
Dicht ineinanderflechtend—zwischen beiden
Wuchs eine Lilie empor—sie ward
Zur Flamme, die, der Bäume dicht Gezweig
Und das Gebälk ergreifend, prasselnd aufschlug
Und um sich wütend schnell das ganze Haus
In ungeheurer Feuerflut verschlang. (ll. 1308-1315)

[He saw out of a wedding bed
two laurel trees growing, their branches
tightly interwoven—between the two
a lily grew aloft—it became
a flame which, seizing the thick branches of the trees
and the joists, shot up crackling
and raging all about quickly devoured
the whole house in a monstrous flood of fire.]

The mother's dream:

Ein Kind, wie Liebesgötter schön,
Sah ich im Grase spielen, und ein Löwe
Kam aus dem Wald, der in dem blut'gen Rachen
Die frisch gejagte Beute trug, und liess
Sie schmeichelnd in den Schoss des Kindes fallen.
Und aus den Lüften schwang ein Adler sich
Herab, ein zitternd Reh in seinen Fängen,
Und legt' es schmeichelnd in den Schoss des Kindes.
Und beide, Löw' und Adler, legen fromm
Gepaart sich zu des Kindes Füssen nieder. (ll. 1336-1345)

[A child, lovely as gods of love,
I saw playing in the grass, and a lion
came from the forest, carrying in its bloody maw
the freshly caught prey, and it let it fall
fawningly into the lap of the child.
And from the sky an eagle soared
down, a trembling doe in its claws,
and laid it fawningly into the lap of the child.
And both, lion and eagle, lay down innocently
together at the feet of the child.]

From the Arabian astrologer the father received the interpretation:

wenn mein Schoss von einer Tochter
Entbunden würde, töten würde sie ihm
Die beiden Söhne, und sein ganzer Stamm
Durch sie vergehn. (ll. 1321-1324)

[if my womb were to produce
a daughter, she would kill his
two sons, and his whole tribe
would perish through her.]

The Christian monk, on the other hand, told the mother:

> Genesen würd' ich einer Tochter,
> Die mir der Söhne streitende Gemüter
> In heisser Liebesglut vereinen würde. (ll. 1349-1351)

> [I would be delivered of a daughter,
> who would unite in the hot breath of passion
> the quarreling hearts of my two sons.]

In view of the catastrophe that has begun to unfold with Don Manuel's happening upon Beatrice in the convent garden five months previously and with Don Cesar's encountering Beatrice at their father's funeral, when for a moment his hand lay in hers (l. 1123)[15] and his breath mingled with hers (l. 1538); and in view of the play's bloody denouement, which finds both sons dead as a result of the fatal magnetic attraction of Beatrice upon them both, what is there to say other than that both dreams presaging the same course of events, have turned out to be fulfilled to the letter! Beatrice has innocently brought both her brothers to their death. The lily's incendiary flame is the same as the hot breath of passion which the mother mistook to mean devoted affection. Whether the monk spoke with guile in giving his phrasing of the interpretation the ambiguous twist "in heisser Liebesglut" is beyond knowing and altogether irrelevant. He is certainly identical with the Old Man of the Mountain (ll. 1347 f. and 2105 ff.), who is unquestionably gifted with second sight on the day of the catastrophe.

The mother's action in saving her infant daughter is motivated by natural feeling and by a deep Christian faith in the rule of a kindly Providence. Of the monk's interpretation she says:

> Im Innersten bewahrt' ich mir dies Wort;
> Dem Gott der Wahrheit mehr als dem der Lüge
> Vertrauend, rettet' ich die Gottverheissne. (ll. 1352-1354)

> [In my inmost being did I preserve his words;
> trusting more the god of truth than him
> of lies, I rescued her whom God had promised me.]

The genuineness of her faith is not contradicted by her sense of fatalistic resignation despite the studiedly ominous ring of her words a little later in the scene, where she uses the word "Verhängnis" to characterize the fortunes of her house (l. 1552) and sums up her feelings in the words:

[15] "Die Hand, die in der deinen zitternd lag" [The hand which lay trembling in thine own]—a perhaps significant reversal of the usual man-woman handclasp.

So unterwerf' ich mich—wie kann ich's ändern?—
Der unregiersam stärkern Götterhand,
Die meines Hauses Schicksal dunkel spinnt. (ll. 1557-1599)

[So I submit myself—how can I change it?—
to the inordinately stronger divine hand
which darkly spins the destiny of my house.]

These lines, saturated with the flavor of ancient polytheism, like so many pronouncements of the chorus and the other characters, simply show her piety as imbedded in that of her time and her locale. How ghastly, then, her awakening at the end to the fact that she, a not unsaintly sufferer, has unwittingly been instrumental in bringing unspeakable horrors to pass!

It has been argued that the prophetic dreams and the ambiguity of their interpretation in *Die Braut von Messina* constitute only a subjective factor and not an objective fate, as though events really hinged on the free decision of the characters.[16] This is simply to

---

[16] Ernst Müller writes: "Bei Schiller aber muss der Zuschauer bis zuletzt dadurch in Spannung gehalten werden, dass er so wenig wie die Figuren weiss, was zuletzt noch geschieht, weil das Geschehene nicht vorausgesagt ist. Der Zuschauer weiss erst nach der Tat, wo die Handlung hinauswill. In der Exposition, deren Hauptinhalt im Ödipus das Orakel ist, sind die beiden Morde nicht vorgesehen gewesen, eben nur ein allgemeines Unglück" (IV, 627-628). [In the case of Schiller, however, the observer must be kept in suspense to the last moment because he knows as little as the characters about what will happen finally—because what happens is not predicted. The observer knows only after the deed where the action is headed. In the exposition, whose main content in Oedipus is the oracle, the two murders are not foreseen but are simply a general misfortune.] This is palpably wrong. The violent death of the brothers through the agency of their sister is mentioned as explicitly predicted by the Arabian soothsayer not once but twice, in lines 1320 ff., by the mother to her sons, and in lines 2346 ff., by the mother to the chorus. Ernst Müller's failure to heed the text leads him to continue a little later: "Genau so wie in der *Jungfrau von Orleans* oder im *Wallenstein* (warnende Stimmen) äussert sich die Weissagung subjektiv als Traum; es unterstützt also nur die tragische Situation, führt sie aber nicht notwendig, als wie von Göttern gesandt herbei, ist also nur ein notfalls wegzulassendes Stilmittel, aber kein objektiver Bestandteil der Tragödie" (*ibid.*). [Just as in the *Jungfrau von Orleans* or in *Wallenstein* (warning voices), the prediction is expressed subjectively as a dream; it therefore supports only the tragic situation, however does not necessarily bring it about as though it had been sent by the gods. It is thus only a stylistic mode, to be left out if necessary, but is not an objective ingredient of the tragedy.] All this is in flat contradiction to Schiller's play and must be attributed to too superficial a reading of Prader (pp. 66-68). Almost everything Prader says here is well thought through, but there are a few sentences on page 66 that strike me as unfortunately phrased. Prader says: "Bei Sophokles hat das Orakel eine tragende Funktion. Ohne Orakel könnte der *König Ödipus* nicht bestehen. In der *Braut von Messina* dagegen hat es diese Funktion verloren. Die auf Isabellas Bericht folgende Handlung könnte sehr wohl auch ohne die Prophezeiungen durchgeführt werden." [In the case of Sophocles the oracle has a sustaining function. Without the oracle *Oedipus Rex* could not exist. In the *Braut von Messina* on the other hand it has

remain blind to the fact that everything here fits into the pattern of a diabolical maze. Unseen supernatural forces have been at work on every hand to guide the behavior of the characters into a pattern of compulsive automatism. Let us review these features in the sequence of their occurrence: (1) The Queen Mother succumbs just once to the compelling urge of motherly feeling to see her child in the convent. This "natural" act is designed to contribute to the horror of the anagnorisis on the day of the play in two ways: Don Manuel recognizes the Queen in Beatrice's description of her mother's features moments before he is stabbed (ll. 1843-1850), and when carried before the Queen Beatrice recoils in horror upon realizing that those features, indelibly engraved on her memory as the result of that single visit, are those of the Queen of Messina, mother of Don Manuel and Don Cesar (ll. 2216-2246). (2) Don Manuel's coming upon Beatrice in the convent garden in his pursuit of the white doe reproduces the situation of Isabella's dream where the lion lays his prey at the feet of the beautiful child. (3) The hasty incestuous union of brother and sister must be read as evidence of a fated irresistible mutual attraction. (4) Beatrice's irresistible urge to attend the late king's funeral despite her lover's veto springs not from her character (l. 1659) but from a fated compulsion (ll. 1889 ff.), and (5) the same is the case with the trusted servant's connivance in her wish (ll. 1642-1657). (6) Isabella's decision to have her sons attend the funeral incognito is part of the same pattern. (7) Don Cesar's coming upon Beatrice in the throng of mourners and the mutual instant attraction that grips them both is likewise the work of fate. Although Beatrice felt a convulsive shudder at her encounter with the stranger (whose presence obscured the image of her lover), we are told that his hand lay trembling in hers (l. 1123) and that their breath mingled (l. 1538). (8) If we agree to regard Don Manuel's abduction of Beatrice as a neutral feature motivated by his fear of her removal (despite questions arising from his reluctance to inquire about her family, ll. 755 ff.), there is something strange about Diego's antici-

---

lost this function. The action which transpires following Isabella's report could probably be carried out even without the prophecies.] It is literally true that the plot of Sophocles' drama could not be conceived without the oracle, whereas in Schiller's case one *could* imagine a story of brother-sister incest, fratricide and suicide, hinging on the concealed identity of a sister, without any of this being predicted. In this sense, Schiller's ambiguous oracles are a secondary feature.

pating Isabella's order to bring Beatrice home on the day set for the reconciliation: his disclosure of the impending change in her status (ll. 781 ff.) was clearly unauthorized, as the order to bring her home is given to him in the first scene (ll. 116 ff.).[17] (9) Beatrice's leaving of her retreat the next morning to pray in the nearby church, where she was discovered by Don Cesar's spies, must also be chalked up as the work of fate. (10) The reconciliation scene is interrupted by the messenger telling Don Cesar that the long-sought girl has been found. Don Cesar checks his first impulse to join her at once. Looking at his brother he is eager to confide to him the secret of his happiness. But Don Manuel dissuades him: he will learn it later. Had he let his brother speak he would have learned that it was his own bride Don Cesar had discovered. (11) After the news of Beatrice's disappearance the mother's hysterical response to Don Manuel's question as to the locale of the convent (ll. 1634-1637), in contrast to the reasonable answer she gives to the same question when asked by her younger son, a few moments later, clearly shows the manipulation of her emotions by fate. (12) On top of all this, Don Cesar's fatal dagger thrust, the instant he sees his brother in the embrace of the woman he has designated as his wife that same day, is as compulsive and automatic as the mutual magnetism that marks the relation of brothers and sister.

As I have said earlier, even the timing of the entrances and exits must be read in the light of the whole action as cunningly built-in devices contributing to the flawless functioning of the fated mechanism: had not Don Manuel rushed from the scene right after the return of his brother—Don Cesar has time to speak but a single line entreating him (such is the irony of fate!) to stay that they may undertake the search for the lost sister together (l. 1671)—he would have learned at once that the convent from which his sister Beatrice (he knows her name by now, l. 1571) has disappeared is the identical place from which he abducted *his* Beatrice (ll. 1680-1685). The revelation would have exposed the horror of their incest, but the more horrible fratricide would have been avoided.

[17] Whether or not the hand of fate shows in Diego's indiscretion can be argued. The chorus remarks apropos of the old servant: "geschwätzig ist das Alter" (l. 756) [old age blabbers], thereby supporting a natural interpretation. But the insurmountable fear that kept Don Manuel from even approaching Diego (ll. 757-774) points the other way.

Much has been made of the alleged difference of temperament between the two brothers with a view to reducing the element of fate and making personal individuality largely responsible for the catastrophe. In this view the elder brother, Don Manuel, is marked by a saturnine disposition while the younger, Don Cesar, is sanguine and impulsive.[18] This view is utterly mistaken. The two brothers are scarcely differentiated representatives of one and the same type. As Prader correctly remarks (p. 57), Schiller's prime concern in this play was the action, not the characters. Their different behavior springs from the radically divergent situation in which the two brothers find themselves. Don Manuel has enjoyed the furtive possession of his beloved for five months. Forewarned of her impending change of status, he acted on sudden impulse and abducted her. By morning he may well have begun to wonder whether he had been wise in acting with so much haste. The news that he has a sister introduces a factor of potential uneasiness. And when pressed by his mother to give particulars as to the bride whom he has promised to present to her before the close of the day, he puts her off with a few brief lines that express his embarrassment (ll. 1445-1449). But after a silence of nearly a hundred lines he seconds his brother's passionate recital with an aria on the power of love in the best grand opera manner (ll. 1542-1550). How different is Don Cesar's situation. He is in a state of almost uncon-

---

[18] To quote Ernst Müller: "Rational symmetrisch sind . . . die Kontrastcharakteristiken der feindlichen Brüder, wobei Don Manuel der finster verschlossene Melancholiker und schenkende Realist ist, Don Cesar dagegen, der nehmende und aggressive Idealist, der sanguinische Draufgänger und grosse Leidenschaftliche, der sich durch Selbstmord vom Verhängnis losspricht" (IV, 624). [The contrasting characteristics of the hostile brothers are rationally symmetrical: Don Manuel is the morosely close-mouthed melancholiast and the outgoing realist, but Don Cesar on the other hand is the grasping and aggressive idealist, the sanguine daredevil, and the man of great passion who frees himself from fate by suicide.] Müller returns to this later, contrasting two sharply divergent portrayals of Beatrice by the two brothers: "Da sind das ritterliche Mittelalter, das bazarfreudige Maurische, das streng Antike und das Christliche beieinander. Don Manuel zaubert der Mutter seine Geliebte, I, 7 in den buntesten Farben und im Geschmack einer Idealtürkin vor Augen, während Don Cesar sie in den Weihen einer erhabenen Klosterdame malt" (IV, 630). [There the cavalier Middle Ages, the bazaar-lusty Moorish atmosphere, severe antiquity, and the Christian quality are all together. Don Manuel conjures up his beloved for his mother (I, 7) in the brightest colors and in the taste of an ideal Turkish woman, while Don Cesar paints her in the raiment of a stately nun.] Müller has forgotten that it is not the mother but the chorus to whom Don Manuel confides the detailed story of his love, and that his resolve to deck out his bride in festive array is part of this story. Note in passing that on page 625, ten lines from the bottom, Müller writes Don Cesar when he means Don Manuel.

trollable joyous excitement. It was only that morning that his two months' search for the woman of his dreams was rewarded. He broke away from his brother to rush to her and declare her his wife. He is now bursting with eagerness to tell his mother all about his fateful encounter at the funeral with the divinely beautiful stranger who has changed the whole orientation of his life, and of his having discovered her in Messina that very day. Surely the difference in their respective situations fully accounts for the fact that the emotional tone of the two brothers, both of them impulsive sons of an impulsive father, shows up in such sharp contrast. After Don Cesar has stabbed his brother it is his turn to be reflective.

In keeping with the whole character of Schiller's play as an action engineered by a fiendish fate, a time bomb set ticking by the grandfather's curse, Don Cesar's suicide is managed by Schiller with an eye to maximum theatrical effectiveness. The mother's pleas, functioning as a retardation, have fallen on deaf ears. Now Beatrice, called by the mother to reinforce her own pleading, returns to the stage. Her own emotions at first seek a different solution. You must live, she tells Don Cesar. I am the one destined to die, having been prenatally foredoomed to be the instrument of the ancestral curse. But Beatrice's wish to die only arouses Don Cesar's smouldering jealousy. The only thing that matters to you, he tells her, is to be reunited with your dead lover. Gradually Beatrice is softened, she renounces her will to die, she promises to live for her mother and for him, her brother; and with this she inclines toward him and he enfolds her in his embrace. Now the chorus raises its jubilant shout: They have won, Don Cesar will live! But at that moment the portals of the cathedral open, the strains of a dirge are heard, and Don Manuel's coffin, surrounded by lighted tapers, is exposed to view. This scene stiffens Don Cesar's wavering resolve to be true to his original purpose. His eyes on his brother's coffin and continuing to hold Beatrice in his embrace, he stabs himself "und gleitet sterbend an seiner Schwester nieder" [and slides down, dying, against his sister]. Thus the theatrical effect of the funeral scene is fully exploited in Don Cesar's voluntary death of atonement.

In his interpretation of the funeral scene Florian Prader commits a very grave error.[19] He begins by observing quite correctly that in

---

[19] In which he is echoed by Ernst Müller (IV, 627).

addition to the "analytische Handlung," the unravelling of the past, *Die Braut von Messina* has an "aktuelle Handlung"—the reconciliation, the fratricide, and Don Cesar's atonement by suicide. He would have done well to recall—a matter effectively stressed by Bernard Knox—that *Oedipus* too has an "aktuelle Handlung" that goes beyond the uncovering of the past: Jocaste's suicide and Oedipus' self-mutilation. He would then have been bound to remark that in contrast to Oedipus' and Jocaste's acts of violence committed against themselves—acts in no way intimated by the god's prediction—the destruction of the brothers through the agency of their sister was part of the foreordained scheme. Now, with the differentiation of an "analytische Handlung" and an "aktuelle Handlung" in mind, Prader quotes from Schiller's letter of January 26, 1803, to Goethe in a way designed to equate Schiller's reference to "die theatralische Zeremonie" with the analytical action and Schiller's term "die ernste Handlung" with what Prader calls "die aktuelle Handlung," with special reference to Don Cesar's suicide. Despite the length of the passage it is necessary to quote Prader in full on this point. Prader writes:

> Dass in dieser Weise am Schluss zwei verschiedenartige Entwicklungen nebeneinander hergehen, hat Schiller selber gemerkt, wie wir das einem Brief an Goethe entnehmen können: Schiller schreibt: ". . . und das letzte Sechsteil, welches sonst immer das wahre Festmahl der Tragödiendichter ist, gewinnt auch einen guten Fortgang. Es kommt dieser letzten Handlung sehr zustatten, dass ich das Begräbnis des Bruders von dem Selbstmord des andern jetzt ganz getrennt habe, dass dieser jenen Aktus vorher rein beendigt als ein Geschäft, dem er vollkommen abwartet, und erst nach Endigung desselben über dem Grabe des Bruders, geschieht die letzte Handlung, nämlich die Versuche des Chors, der Mutter und der Schwester den Don Cesar zu erhalten, und ihr vereitelter Erfolg. So wird alle Verwirrung und vorzüglich alle bedenkliche Vermischung der theatralischen Zeremonie mit dem Ernst der Handlung vermieden." Es ist für Schiller sehr bezeichnend, dass er die spezifisch theatralische Wirkung der von Sophokles beeinflussten Erkennungsszene zuschreibt, während der nicht antike Sühnetod Don Cesars mehr den realen als theatralischen Ernst der Handlung ausmacht. Für den Schluss des Dramas ist die Trennung der beiden Handlungen im Sinne der dramatischen Klarheit und Wirkung wohl ein glücklicher Kunstgriff des Dichters. (pp. 64-65)

> [That in this manner, at the end, two different developments proceed next to one another Schiller himself remarked, as we can see in a letter to Goethe. Schiller writes: ". . . and the last sixth, which usually is the true feast of the poet of tragedy, also gains a favorable continuation. It proves very useful to this last action that I now have completely sep-

arated the burial of the one brother from the suicide of the other, so that the latter has finished the rite previously just as a matter of business which he attends to completely, and only after its termination over the grave of his brother does the last action take place, namely the attempts of the chorus, the mother, and the sister to preserve Don Cesar, and their thwarted success. Thus all confusion and especially all questionable mixture of theatrical ceremony with the seriousness of the action is avoided." It is very characteristic of Schiller that he attributes the specific theatrical effect to the recognition scene influenced by Sophocles, while the propitiatory death of Don Cesar, not in accordance with antiquity, forms more the real than the theatrical gravity of the action. For the close of the drama the separation of both incidents, in the sense of dramatic clarity and effect, is probably a fortunate device of the poet.]

Unquestionably right as Prader is in taking Schiller's term "die ernste Handlung" to refer to Don Cesar's suicide, he is just as definitely in error in equating Schiller's "die theatralische Zeremonie" with the analytical action. The fact is that "die theatralische Zeremonie" refers not to the analytical action at all but to the solemn rites of Don Manuel's funeral! Prader was led into his error by his failure to observe a number of things. First, the passage quoted by him is *immediately* preceded by the remark: "Ich habe ein missliches und nicht erfreuliches Geschäft, nämlich die Ausfüllung der vielen zurückgelassenen Lücken in den vier ersten Akten nun beendigt." [I have now completed an awkward and not enjoyable task, namely the padding out of the many holes which I left in the first four acts.][20] Clearly, "die vier ersten Akte" take the play to the point where Don Cesar orders the solemn funeral for his brother to be arranged, but do not include it. At this time Schiller evidently had in mind a division of the play into five acts, for what the letter, in estimating its probable length, refers to as "das letzte Sechsteil" is termed in the next sentence "diese letzte Handlung," which can only mean the fifth act. The play as printed has no act divisions, but the action takes place in five symmetrically arranged settings: (1) Colonnade, (2) Garden, (3) Palace Room, (4) Garden, (5) Colonnade. These would readily be equated with five acts. However, in terms of Schiller's letter, most of the action that takes place in the second colonnade setting—the anagnorisis scenes successively involving Beatrice, Don Cesar, and finally Isabella herself—must be identified with the fourth act. To say that it was Schiller's original

---

[20] Quotations from Schiller's letters are taken from *Briefwechsel zwischen Schiller und Goethe*, ed. Franz Muncker, 4 vols. (Stuttgart, n.d.).

intention to stage the fifth act in the cathedral, "über dem Grabe des Bruders," is to anticipate.[21]

To come to the second point, Schiller, in the passage quoted by Prader, speaks of the funeral and the suicide as strictly separated. The funeral is to be completed first: "Jenen Aktus, vorher rein beendigt als ein Geschäft, dem er vollkommen abwartet, und erst nach Endigung desselben, über dem Grabe des Bruders, geschieht die letzte Handlung, nämlich die Versuche des Chors, der Mutter und der Schwester, den Don Cesar zu erhalten" [the rite previously finished just as a matter of business which he attends to completely, and only after its termination over the grave of his brother does the last action take place, namely the attempts of the chorus, the mother, and the sister to preserve Don Cesar]. This is certainly not the case in the drama as we have it. The funeral ceremony is in progress in the background when Don Cesar stabs himself.

In the third place, Schiller's reference to the final sixth as still to be written must mean that he expected at this time to treat the final phase of the drama at much greater length than he acually did in the end. Prader overlooks the fact that in the letter from which he quotes, Schiller continues: "Schwerlich aber werde ich mich vor vierzehn Tagen am Ziel meiner Arbeit sehen. [Only with difficulty do I see myself at the goal of my labors within two weeks.] Actually, however, Schiller wrote to Goethe on February 4, eight days after his earlier letter: "Mein Stück ist fertig. . . . Ich habe mich in der Katastrophe viel kürzer gefasst, als ich erst wollte, überwiegender Gründe wegen." [My play is finished. . . . I was much briefer in the catastrophe than I first intended, for preponderant reasons.]

All these points, taken together, lead to the inescapable conclusion: Schiller radically revised his original plan concerning the catastrophe. Instead of using the cathedral as the setting, first of the funeral ceremonies to the point of their completion, and then having the mother and finally the sister enter to make their retarding but unavailing pleas to prevent Don Cesar's suicide "über dem Grabe des Bruders" [on the grave of his brother], Schiller decided to have the funeral and the final pleas take place simultaneously,

---

[21] Schiller originally had six sittings in mind, but as the conventions of his day limited a play to five acts he solved the dilemma by grouping settings 2 and 3 together as act II. This is what the Hamburg theater manuscript has, but it arrives at a total of only four acts as a result of the final shift of scene being abandoned by Schiller. See the textual variants in Bellermann's Schiller edition, v, 473-474.

keeping the colonnade setting of the anagnorisis scenes. He achieved this by having the cathedral portals flung open when the final point of retardation has been reached. In this way he acted in the interest of economy: even as we have it, the play exceeds 2800 lines. And he decided on second thought to exploit the theatrical effectiveness of the visual confrontation of the living and the dead to the full. The play was keyed to such exploitation in every scene, and it is only fitting that the final scene should not deviate from this essential character.

With the voluntary atonement of Don Cesar the play ends as it must. No conclusion leaving him as a survivor would have been acceptable. He feels that his rash deed can be expiated only with his own blood. He is at least dimly aware, furthermore, that his sister's fatal sexual attraction has not ceased to be operative. There is, in fact, an element of voluptuous ecstasy in the manner of his suicide. Considering the situation from the angle of his subjective consciousness, his suicide is the free act of an idealistic youth, and it is to himself and his abiding after-image that his fine words about the purifying power of death apply in fullest measure:

> Der Tod hat eine reinigende Kraft,
> In seinem unvergänglichen Palaste
> Zu echter Tugend reinem Diamant
> Das Sterbliche zu läutern und die Flecken
> Der mangelhaften Menschheit zu verzehren. (ll. 2731-2735)

> [Death has a cleansing power,
> in his everlasting palace
> to refine the mortal
> to the pure diamond of genuine virtue
> and to consume the flaws of imperfect man.]

This, the finest formulation of the tragedian Schiller's credo of transfiguration in death, assures to Don Cesar a place among the stars. So much for the subjective aspect of his suicide. But, objectively considered, the deed also completes the fulfillment of the ancestral curse. Don Cesar thinks he speaks as a free agent when he says:

> Den alten Fluch des Hauses lös' ich sterbend auf,
> Der freie Tod nur bricht die Kette des Geschicks. (ll. 2640-2641)

> [Dying, I dissolve the old curse of this house;
> only a voluntary death breaks the chain of destiny.]

But the import of these words is completely ambivalent. "Auflösen" [dissolve] is equated in our minds with "erfüllen" [fulfill]; "die Kette des Geschicks brechen" [to break the chain of destiny], with "die Enden der Kette zum Ring zusammenfügen" [to join the ends of the chain into a circle]. From our vantage point, perceiving as we do the ticking of the infernal mechanism of fate in all the dire events, we cannot hold him guilty; we see both his crime and his death as foreordained. His "free" death of expiation confronts us with an irresolvable antinomy. The most that we can say is: Don Cesar could have died less nobly. His unstilled incestuous desire might have forced the dagger into his sister's hand to put an end to his life.

What are our feelings, then, with regard to the play as a whole? Can we think of the upshot of the tragic denouement in terms of pity and fear and awe, as we do in the case of *Oedipus Rex*? Our answer is an unqualified No. In place of pity and fear we experience horror and revulsion—not as regards the characters, who are noble throughout, but as regards the supernatural forces that have engineered their destruction. If faith and trust in "the god of truth" avails so little against the power of an ancestral curse, if all that is good in the Queen Mother proves to have been used with fiendish subtlety to contribute to the ghastly outcome, then it is indeed a cunning demon who pulls the wires and makes the human marionettes perform their dance of death. Beside this hellish demon the god of truth is either powerless or nonexistent. When we think of how the mother's faith and trust have been rewarded and when, after all the horrors except the last have already come to pass, the same appeals to a kindly and forgiving Providence are urged once more to deflect Don Cesar from his resolve to end his life,[22] we can

---

[22] By the chorus:

Beschliesse nichts gewaltsam Blutiges, o Herr,
Wider dich selber wütend mit Verzweiflungstat:
Denn auf der Welt lebt niemand, der dich strafen kann,
Und fromme Büssung kauft den Zorn des Himmels ab. (ll. 2630-2633)

[Resolve on nothing violently bloody, my lord,
raging against thyself with a desperate deed:
for no one is alive in this world, who can punish thee,
and pious penance undoes the rage of heaven.]

By Don Cesar:

Nicht auf der Welt lebt, wer mich richtend strafen kann,
Drum muss ich selber an mir selber es vollziehn.
Bussfert'ge Sühne weiss ich, nimmt der Himmel an,
Doch nur mit Blute büsst sich ab der blut'ge Mord. (ll. 2634-2637)

think of these people only as so many rats in a maze, persisting in the same automation of habit in exploring the cul-de-sac in which they are trapped. The infernal powers take a diabolical delight in watching the blind scurrying of their hapless victims. And, it must be said, the imagination of the dramatist, in devising a plot of such fiendish ingenuity, catered to the same impulses as does the present-day sex and murder thriller. How different the tragedy of Sophocles! Let us remember that in the story of Oedipus, as unfolded by the Athenian master, the gods are presented only in their aspect of un-erring prescience. The all-seeing Apollo has only foretold a dread-ful chain of events that is discovered, in the course of the play's action, to have been fulfilled many years ago. The consequences that Jocaste and Oedipus draw from the discovery are their own free acts. The truth of the gods has been vindicated, and Jocaste's skepticism and Oedipus' hybris of self-reliance are shown up as a blasphemous error. In *Die Braut von Messina*, by contrast, it is the supernatural powers who devise the diabolical trap.

There is a lurid discrepancy between Schiller's infernal plot, the working out of the ancestral curse, and the magnificent, stately, superbly rhythmical language of Schiller's chorus that draws upon every device of baroque pomp and classicistic rhetoric. Without question Schiller counted upon the chorus and the sustained lofty

---

[No one is alive in this world, who can punish me in judgment,
therefore I myself must exact it from myself.
Contrite atonement, I know, heaven will accept,
but bloody murder is expiated only with blood.]

By the mother:

Reich ist die Christenheit an Gnadenbildern,
Zu denen wallend ein gequältes Herz
Kann Ruhe finden. Manche schwere Bürde
Ward abgeworfen in Lorettos Haus,
Und segensvolle Himmelskraft umweht
Das Heil'ge Grab, das alle Welt entsündigt.
Vielkräftig auch ist das Gebet der Frommen,
Sie haben reichen Vorrat an Verdienst.   (ll. 2709-2716)

[Christianity is rich in images of grace,
to which a tortured heart can flutter
and find peace. Many a heavy burden
was thrown off in Loretto's chapel,
and the blessed power of heaven flows
down upon the holy grave which absolves the whole world from sin.
Manifold in power also is the prayer of the pious;
they have a rich store of merit.]

style of the dialogue throughout the play to offset and counterbalance the bloodcurdling thrills of the plot and make a mood of solemn edification prevail. That he correctly sized up his reading public and the theater audience is shown both by a large body of critical comment and by a study of the performances from Schiller's day to the present.[23]

Let us examine Schiller's chorus. But let us first sketch the character and functioning of the chorus in *Oedipus Rex* in order to see how radically Schiller diverged from his model in this regard too.

In Sophocles' play the chorus represents the citizens of Thebes. They are bound to their ruler by ties of gratitude and loyalty verging on veneration. They are now joined in a common affliction, the pestilence. Oedipus has proved himself their savior by ridding them of the taloned virgin monster, the Sphinx, many years before, and they again pin their hopes on him, the wisest of men, in their present plight. And not in vain, for the affliction of them, his "children," weighs most heavily upon him. The chorus participates in the action in two ways. It takes part in the dialogue through the person of its leader, speaking a line or a few lines at a time. It implores Oedipus to help in the present crisis. During his heated exchange with the seer Teiresias it counsels him to observe moderation. Later, it intercedes for Creon when Oedipus would condemn him for treason without evidence. It directs the messenger from Corinth to Jocaste. It reveals that the shepherd summoned is an old slave of King Laïos.

But its major function is to express the mood of the City, in its choral odes. There are five of these, and these chants are couched in dark and mystical language that is difficult to interpret, in contrast to the lucid quality of the dialogue. Now the mood of the chorus shifts as the action progresses. Each chant reflects a different stage of the dramatic situation. First there is a prayer for deliverance addressed to Athena, Artemis, and Apollo, and Zeus and the local divinity Bacchus are also invoked. The second ode, after Teiresias has been provoked into hurling his unintelligibly fearful

---

[23] Prader (pp. 91 ff.) summarizes the results of a study of *Die Braut von Messina* on the stage by Karin Dieckmann. Reporting on a variety of attempts "zu kürzen, vereinfachen, vereinheitlichen" [to shorten, simplify, unify], he says: "Interpretationen, die uns von Schiller aus gesehen am befremdlichsten erscheinen, haben sogar bis zu fünfzig Vorstellungen erlebt" (p. 93). [Interpretations, which from Schiller's viewpoint seem most strange to us, reached up to fifty performances.]

charges against Oedipus, reflects a mood of consternation and bewilderment, but their loyal faith in Oedipus remains unshaken. After Jocaste has stated her outright disbelief in oracles and divine prescience, telling the story of her child's death by exposure to prove it and inducing Oedipus tentatively to second her view of these matters, the chorus sings its third ode. This time the tone is ominous. It sings of law as divinely ordained and immutable. It warns that the tyrant who flouts it in his self-confident pride will be brought low. It affirms its faith in the gods and their truthfulness in the strongest terms by saying in substance: if the oracles of the gods are proved false there is no sense in our worship and sacred dance. Meanwhile Oedipus' confidence has been dealt a mortal blow by his coming to realize that the chain of circumstantial evidence almost inevitably fastens the crime of King Laïos' murder upon himself. He is in a state of uncontrollable anguish regarding both the past and future consequences of his deed, when he is struck a second blow by the revelation that he is not the son of King Polybos of Corinth but a foundling. This second blow, while destined to annihilate him utterly, when its implications are spelled out, makes him rebound for the time being in a frenzy of delirious euphoria. He proclaims himself a son of Fortune. And the chorus, catching the contagion of his mood, in its fourth ode exults in the anticipation of some great revelation that will prove their revered king to have been sired by one of the mountain gods. Then, with Oedipus' cross-questioning of the old shepherd, the whole ghastly truth is revealed to Oedipus and the chorus. Now there is nothing left for the chorus to do in the final ode but to bewail the gruesome fate that has overtaken their ruler and savior. Thus the character of the chorus, grounded in its attitude of immutable piety and reverence for the gods, while identifying with all the stages of their beloved ruler's ordeal, has been sustained throughout the tragedy.

To this chorus the chorus in *Die Braut von Messina* stands in sharp contrast in a number of ways. Perhaps the first thing to be remarked is the sheer length of its assignment. I count 767 lines spoken by the chorus in Schiller's play against 301 in the *Oedipus*. Of course, Schiller's play is nearly twice as long as that of Sophocles, so that the difference is not proportionately as great. Schiller's chorus accounts for a little over twenty-seven per cent of the lines, while that of Sophocles has just under twenty per cent. In the very long action of the first colonnade setting, however, the chorus speaks 386 lines out of a total of 980, which is a little under forty per cent. In the second place, the highly ornate diction of the chorus may foster the fallacy of our seeing this group, or rather the two symmetrically ranged groups, in terms of an ideal timeless spectator reflecting on the vicissitudes of the principals and of life in general. The fact is, however, that Schiller's chorus has a very specific character of its own, conditioned by the circumstances and the locale. We have but to listen to the remarks of the Queen Mother, first in the presence of the elders, then in that of the chorus itself, to the tenor of the chorus' own utterances, and finally to the comments of the two brothers as they make up their feud, to see that the sentiments of this Sicilian community have nothing in common with those of the Thebans. These Sicilians are a subject people (l. 222) held in thrall by a foreign race whose presence they resent: "Es hat an diesen Boden kein Recht" (l. 205). [They have no right to this soil.] Too weak to protect themselves, having long learned to regard their island as a coveted prize, they have learned to dissemble and bow to the foreign yoke. But their loyalty is not to be trusted. Theirs is a slave mentality. While they are willing with a certain fatalism (ll. 178-180) to spill their blood in their masters' feuds, the weal and woe of the ruling house leaves them basically indifferent. Their masters may come and go, but they, the native race, will survive (ll. 253-254). It is in the light of these sentiments, in support of which the whole choral passage from line 175 to 254 could be quoted, that we must evaluate the strains of homage and adulation that greet the Queen Mother's entry. She, certainly, is not deceived by this extravagant acclaim of her beauty as rivaling that of the sun and the moon, and of her issue as "Einen blühenden Baum . . . Der sich ewig [!] sprossend erneut" (ll. 279-280) [a tree in blossom / which eternally budding renews itself]. A moment before her entry this same chorus had summed up its sentiments in the lines:

Die fremden Eroberer kommen und gehen,
Wir gehorchen, aber wir bleiben stehen. (ll. 253-254)

[The foreign conquerors come and go,
we obey, but we remain.]

Accordingly, in addressing herself to her sons, Isabella speaks her sentiments regarding the chorus with a pride of majesty that can afford to ignore the presence of those being discussed. She refers to them as "die fremde Schar" (1. 331) [the foreign host], "diese wilden Banden" (1. 336) [these wild bands]. She reminds her sons that to these vassals they are foreigners, intruders (1. 341). She warns them against their Sicilian subjects, "dies Geschlecht, das herzlos falsche" (1. 349) [this race, this heartless, false one], its "Schadenfreude" (1. 350) [malice] in the face of their strife, and its basic enmity (1. 356). All this as a preliminary to imploring her sons to remember the bond of nature that has made them brothers. And the chorus, instead of wincing under the lash of her characterization, is true to form by seconding the mother's sentiments the moment she pauses:

> Ja, es ist etwas Grosses, ich muss es verehren,
> Um einer Herrscherin fürstlichen Sinn:
> Über der Menschen Tun und Verkehren
> Blickt sie mit ruhiger Klarheit hin.
> Uns aber treibt das verworrene Streben
> Blind und sinnlos durchs wüste Leben. (ll. 370-375)

> [Yes, there is something mighty, I must respect it,
> about the princely mind of a ruling woman:
> with calm clarity she surveys
> the comings and goings of men.
> But muddled striving drives us
> blind and senseless through desolate life.]

And after the mother has resumed her plea the chorus once more underscores its own basic indifference:

> Höret der Mutter vermahnende Rede,
> Wahrlich, sie spricht ein gewichtiges Wort!
> Lasst es genug sein und endet die Fehde,
> Oder gefällt's euch, so setzet sie fort!
> Was euch genehm ist, das ist mir gerecht,
> Ihr seid die Herrscher, und ich bin der Knecht. (ll. 433-438)

> [Harken to the admonishing words of the mother,
> verily, she speaks momentous words!
> Let it be enough, and end the feud,
> or if it please you, continue it!
> Whatever contents you, is satisfying to me,
> you are the rulers, and I am the slave.]

Having defined the character of the chorus, we look at the functions assigned to it in the development of the play. These are varied.

After the reconciliation scene, when Don Manuel is left alone on the stage with his followers, the chorus is employed in the traditional role of the confidant[24] who is used as the medium for communicating the salient facts of the exposition to the audience. Responding to the chorus' repeated overtures, Don Manuel, in a scene of nearly three hundred lines (597-860), makes a full confession of his five months' romance including his bride's abduction. If the role of the confidant is a somewhat awkward device at best, it is doubly so when a whole band of followers is made the repository of so intimate a secret; triply so, in the light of the dubious attachment of these vassals to their master. After Don Manuel's exit the chorus takes on another function, as it poses the question of what they are going to do, now that the fraternal strife has been ended, and suggests a variety of alternatives. In a series of free lyrical improvisations it extols the blessings of peace, the sturdy virtues of war, the delights of love, the joys of the chase, and the adventure of life at sea with its tempting but uncertain stakes. These one hundred lines (860-959) are inserted to give us a sense of the passing of time, both to keep us occupied and to evoke a growing sense of impatience to learn how matters will develop. Here the chorus functions as a clock, ticking off the minutes, that is to say the hours in terms of an action stretched to extend into the night. The last of the alternatives enumerated is developed at greater length than the others. It skillfully prepares a mood of uncertainty and foreboding as a springboard for the chorus to take over a whole new set of functions: through its individual speakers the chorus first criticizes Don Manuel's rash act and expresses apprehension as to the outcome; then it reveals the dark cloud of the ancestral curse that hovers over the royal house; and, finally, it speaks with the authority of a seer in interpreting the lifelong feuding of the brothers as the fated result of the curse. While the transition of the role of the chorus from time-marking entertainer to prophet of doom is very skillfully managed, it also tends to defeat its own purpose because, having succumbed to a sense of boredom during the exhibition of so much verbal pageantry, we are scarcely in a properly receptive frame of mind for the portentous announcements that follow.

Since the further behavior of the chorus is an extrapolation of its

24 Prader, p. 88.

character and function as hitherto analyzed, we are now ready for its over-all appraisal as an integral factor in Schiller's play. We are bound to ask ourselves: This chorus, representing the Messina community torn by factional strife,—this chorus, lavish in flattering praise of and professions of loyalty to the ruling house,—this chorus, cowed into submission by the stern rule of generations of foreign masters but knit in a bond of fundamental indifference and potential enmity against the master race,—has this chorus any warrant for assuming the function of prophet, monitor, and moralist with which Schiller has gradually invested it? Is this chorus qualified to represent the higher principle of divine law over against the blind and erring behavior of mortals, as it does so impressively in *Oedipus Rex*? The answer is No. It is disqualified by its own testimony and by that of mother and sons. That it can support the semblance of such a role is wholly due to its formal disciplined presentation and the stylized quality of its utterance. Stripped of its discipline and the purely formal embroidery of its classical religious concepts and images, this community is no more than a cunning mob whose smouldering resentment against their masters needs only a spark to flare into open rebellion. The reflections of this chorus, blowing now hot, now cold,[25] as the occasion suits,

[25] Early in the play, the high and mighty had been extolled for escaping the oblivion that is the lot of common mortals:

> Völker verrauschen,
> Namen verklingen,
> Finstre Vergessenheit
> Breitet die dunkelnachtenden Schwingen
> Über ganzen Geschlechtern aus.
> Aber der Fürsten
> Einsame Häupter
> Glänzen erhellt,
> Und Aurora berührt sie
> Mit den ewigen Strahlen
> Als die ragenden Gipfel der Welt. (ll. 283-293)

> [Peoples pass on,
> names fade away,
> dark oblivion spreads its night-enfolding wings
> over whole generations.
> But the lonely
> heads of princes
> gleam with illumination,
> and Aurora touches them
> with the eternal rays
> like the towering peaks of the world.]

Toward the end of the play the chorus, in its praise of the humble life of the peasant and the sheltered life of the cloistered recluse (ll. 2561 ff.), develops a

carry no weight. The character of this chorus is fundamentally at odds with its suprahuman function.

This is an irremediable flaw that the fine words of Schiller's preface[26] can do nothing to explain away. Whereas Sophocles made of his chorus an ideal instrument to accompany an action performed by characters of sharply outlined individuality, Schiller did just the reverse: his characters are simple, idealized types that would not interest us but for the fate visited upon them; his chorus, on the other hand, is stamped on our minds as a realistic collective portrait. Despite Schiller's brilliant foreword he did not succeed in restoring to modern tragedy the ancient chorus as a factor of suprapersonal weight. Schiller was certainly wrong in thinking that as a contemporary of Sophocles he would have rated a prize with his *Braut von Messina* in Athens.[27] As for us, while admiring it as the most ambitious representative of the questionable genre of Romantic fate tragedy, we write it off as a noble experiment that failed. There is a consolation in the fact that, as an attempt to revive the mode of classical ancient drama, it is in distinguished company: Goethe's *Die natürliche Tochter* was completed and performed in the same year 1803, a few months after *Die Braut von Messina*.

---

curiously inappropriate image in view of the fact that we are witnessing the destruction of a royal house:

Nur in bestimmter Höhe ziehet
Das Verbrechen hin und das Ungemach,
Wie die Pest die erhabenen Orte fliehet,
Dem Qualm der Städte wälzt es sich nach. (ll. 2581-2584)
[Only to a certain height does
crime proceed, and trouble—
just as plague flees the lofty regions—
rolls after the smoke of cities.]

These lines, together with those that immediately follow,

Auf den Bergen ist Freiheit! Der Hauch der Grüfte
Steigt nicht hinauf in die reinen Lüfte,
Die Welt ist vollkommen überall,
Wo der Mensch nicht hinkommt mit seiner Qual!
[Freedom is on the mountains! The breath of tombs
does not rise up into the pure airs,
the world is perfect wherever
man does not go with his torment!]

show Schiller already straining to escape from the artificially overcharged atmosphere of *Die Braut von Messina* to the clear mountain air of the Switzerland of *Wilhelm Tell*.

[26] Written in May, three months after the completion of the play. See his letter to Goethe, May 24, 1803.
[27] Letter to Wilhelm von Humboldt, February 17, 1803.

ILLUSTRATIONS
TO HIGHLIGHT SOME POINTS
IN SCHILLER'S ESSAY
ON POETRY

THE REMARKS HERE offered are a wholly unpretentious attempt to illustrate some ideas developed in Schiller's essay, *Über naive und sentimentalische Dichtung*. This paper consists of two parts. The first deals with the psychological analysis of a type of moral behavior—the Naive. The second is concerned with Schiller's three types of sentimental[1] poetry, more particularly with the third, the Sentimental Idyll.

1. The Naive

The cultivated eighteenth-century man took an eager interest in the analysis of moral behavior. Today such interest is restricted largely to the professional philosopher who specializes in ethics.

The Naive, as analyzed by Schiller in the first section of his essay, is a phenomenon of moral behavior. It involves both an agent and a qualified observer. To speak of the observer first, Schiller himself has all the representative qualifications of status and interest that mark the class: eighteenth-century man, the product of a high degree of intellectual, aesthetic, but above all, moral culture, "der reifste Sohn der Zeit"; no longer living in a state of simplicity and innocence; moving, rather, in a highly conventionalized sphere, but fired with zeal to face toward the goal of simplicity and innocence regained, undeterred by the realization that the path of progression is infinite and the goal will never be reached. Such an observer, worldly-wise but sincere, derives a complex satisfaction from the exhibition of naive moral behavior.

As for the agent, naive behavior presupposes the presence of two contrasting ingredients in his make-up: Nature and Art. These highly flexible terms correspond roughly to good and evil, or to

---

[1] Professor Elizabeth M. Wilkinson has felicitously coined the term "sentimentive" to apply to Schiller's essay to differentiate it from "sentimental," which is charged, in our usage, with pejorative associations.

Reprinted from *Monatshefte*, XLVI (1954), 161-169, by permission of the University of Wisconsin Press.

plus and minus values. Nature as here used is identified with a behavior pattern of warmth, spontaneity, impulsiveness, candor, truth, simplicity, wholeness. For Art we can substitute such terms as coolness, reserve, calculation, artifice, deception, conventionality, insincerity. Schiller's typology has reference to the adult individual in whose personality both Art and Nature are potentially present in varying degree. In any conduct situation either one or the other of them can become operative and take the lead. (By way of a symbol we may think of Plato's charioteer and his horses in the *Phaedrus*.)

All cases of naive behavior show conduct governed by Nature in contrast to Art, and in all cases the observer feels that Nature is in the right, while Art would be in the wrong (448, 19 ff.).[2] But naive behavior can be of two kinds: either it may be prompted by surprise, or it may reflect the dominant character of the agent.

In the case of naive behavior prompted by surprise the individual is caught off guard, and as soon as he comes to his senses he is shocked at what he has done (449-450). Such candid, spontaneous action is not to the individual's credit as a Person, and we feel amused at the Person's expense (*Schadenfreude*). But because it is Nature's candor breaking through the shell of artifice, our feeling of *Schadenfreude* is mingled with a higher satisfaction; for "Nature in contrast to artifice, and truth in contrast to deception must always evoke respect" (450, 10 ff.). Thus our satisfaction partakes of a positive moral quality.

I can think of no finer example of the complex reaction evoked by naive behavior under pressure of surprise than Schiller's own Maria Stuart in her meeting with Elizabeth. Had this play been written by the time Schiller was at work on our essay, he would doubtless have analyzed that crucial scene at this point of his exposition. (Remember the keen delight he took in picking apart his *Räuber* and *Don Carlos*!) He would have said something like this:

It would be a grave fallacy to identify the Mary who meets Elizabeth in the park with the Mary who has renounced the world and made her peace with God the following morning, the morning of her execution. In that short interval her personality has undergone

[2] All references are to Volume VII of the fifteen-volume Bellermann–Petsch edition of Schiller.

a fundamental (an infinite) development. Up to the time of that fateful meeting with Elizabeth she schemed to win freedom, love, and power. In this her scheming Mary is the object of our warm sympathy because of her beauty, her cruel plight, her condemnation on unjust grounds and under circumstances that denied her a fair trial. But our sympathy for her must not blind us to the fact that she is a great schemer and a brilliant actress. We had a compelling demonstration of her capacities in the latter regard in the scene with Burleigh, when this minister of state announced to her the verdict of guilty. There she fenced with superb adroitness, having been prepared for the verdict of a rigged court by the lapse of a month since she was summoned to the bar and having been specifically prepared for Burleigh's coming by Mortimer.

In the case of her meeting with Elizabeth the situation is wholly different. During the years of her captivity (and specially since her transfer to the rigorous confinement of Fotheringhay) she had schemed, if all else failed, to bring about a meeting with her hated rival. She had rehearsed that scene in her imagination as she wanted it to develop: she would play the part of the broken reed, bereft of her beauty and her ambition, a mere shadow of her former self, no longer a challenge to the woman or the queen in Elizabeth; she would humble herself (without sacrificing her dignity), and her blandishments would trick Elizabeth into compassion and generosity. She would owe her liberty, she hoped, to the artful execution of a well-rehearsed act of dissembling. To what extent she had actually probed all the dangers that would have to be adroitly skirted in the acting out of such a scene we do not know, and this need not concern us. The important thing is that her request for the meeting is granted under circumstances that render her psychologically incapable of acting out any rehearsed role. So much has happened to alter her situation during the twenty-four hours that have elapsed since she put into her keeper's hands her letter soliciting this favor that she has quite dismissed that letter from her mind: she has learned of Mortimer's plot to free her; through him she has found access to Lord Leicester, on whom she pins her most extravagant hopes involving life, liberty, love, and the return to power; added to this anticipation of an imminent complete turn of her fortunes is the sudden relaxation of her confinement; she is allowed to stroll in the park, and the soft breezes and the sight of the spring green have raised her excitement to the highest pitch. She has presented the spectacle of a woman utterly unnerved; we have seen her in a state of extreme euphoria, of uncontrollable rapture, when the fateful announcement of Queen Elizabeth's presence in the park is conveyed to her. Completely taken by surprise, she all but collapses, and a moment later the scene between the two queens unfolds under auspices that rule out the resort to artifice and stratagem. "Nature" takes over. Mary's temperament triumphs over her prudence. Her accumulated hate and scorn gush out in a torrent of barbed words that leave her rival annihilated but also seal her own doom.

Mary's behavior illustrates the naive of surprise. The effect of her behavior on the cultivated beholder corresponds to the pattern delineated in Schiller's essay: it is not to Mary's credit as a Person that she has had her fling. It was an elemental outburst quite contrary to her plan. Her temperament doublecrossed the mature design of her scheming will. If the implications were not tragic, our involvement in the situation would include a strong undercurrent of amusement at her expense; even so I would maintain that an overtone of *Schadenfreude*, though muted by sympathy, is part of the ideal spectator's response. The other angle of Schiller's observation applies with full force to the scene in question: our moral sense sanctions the triumph of Nature over artifice, of spontaneity over scheming, of elemental candor over the lie of hypocrisy.

From naive behavior induced by surprise Schiller distinguishes naive behavior that emanates from the character of the Person. Again there is a choice between conduct governed by Nature and conduct governed by Convention, and the agent's response in line with Nature ranges him on the side of the angels. Naive behavior of this kind, "das Naive der Denkart" (446) [the naiveté of sentiment], "der Gesinnung" (448) [of conviction], is meritorious and presupposes a high degree of moral cultivation. In the beholder of this phenomenon respect for Nature is joined with respect for the Person. The peculiar earmark of such conduct is, in present-day parlance, lack of sophistication. As an example, Schiller quotes Pope Hadrian the Sixth's frank admission of corruption having infiltrated the Church all the way up to the Holy See itself, but there is an unresolved doubt in his mind whether this was truly a case of naive conduct or whether it was dictated by practical strategy (451 ff.). (We had a somewhat similar case during the 1952 electoral campaign when Adlai Stevenson was maneuvered into admitting that he intended to clean up the "mess in Washington.")

For one excellent literary instance of "das Naive der Denkart" Schiller could have pointed to Goethe's Egmont as he walks into the trap laid by the Duke of Alba. A very interesting case is presented in Schiller's own *Wilhelm Tell*. When Tell explains to Gessler why he thrust a second arrow into his doublet before he aimed at the apple on his child's head, is his candid explanation prompted by surprise, or does it stem from his character? Both types of motivation are involved, without doubt. On the one hand Tell had no time to weigh the situation, and on the other he was so congenitally lacking in guile that he interpreted the captious promise of the ruthless tyrant to spare his life in broad generous terms. We admire Tell's simplicity, but at the same time we feel he should have known better. That his capacity for judging human motives is so limited, in view of the drastic proofs of unscrupulous violence that he and his countrymen have witnessed, detracts from the stature of his personality. His intelligence is not on a par with his integrity. At this point he is only half a hero. Schiller realized this, and it was with a view to restoring his protagonist to full heroic stature that he enveloped Tell's subsequent exploit of the leap from Gessler's ship in an aura of mythical hyperbole.

For the finest example of "das Naive der Gesinnung," however, he could have pointed to Fouqué's *Undine* if he had lived to see the publication of this story (1813). The chain of events had begun with the exchange of two children in pursuance of a far-reaching plan: Undine, the little mermaid, had been left with a lowly fisherman and his wife to console them for the disappearance of their infant daughter Bertalda, for whom the masters of the sea had provided a foster home at the court of a duke. The plan had matured; a doughty knight-errant had been decoyed to the fisherfolk's deserted tongue of land and kept prisoner by the elements long enough to make him fall in love with Undine and marry her. She had thereby acquired a human soul and the object of the watery power's scheming had been accomplished. Now the knight has escorted his mermaid bride to that same court where Bertalda, all the time thinking of herself as the child of the noble couple, dominated the scene, and the two young women have become fast friends. Undine, fully aware of Bertalda's identity, has so far kept her secret. But Bertalda's approaching birthday provides the occasion for Undine to plan a surprise that she thinks of as the crowning feature of the festival. On the day of celebration Undine produces the humble fisherfolk couple and, the light of purest heavenly joy upon her countenance, she effects the reunion of the parents with their long lost child. But instead of sharing Undine's transports, Bertalda is stunned by her change of fortune and goes into hysterics. All the good people at court are shocked by such wicked, unfilial behavior, and the unwary reader finds his emotions moving in the wake of their disapproval. The fact is, of course, that Bertalda behaved as any normal person would have done in similar circumstances. Undine's projection of the situation was a naive miscalculation based on the purest motives and a lack of knowledge of the world. Why was she so different from all the rest of us? The answer is: since she was not of the seed of Adam, the gleaming new soul that entered into her through marriage with a man had no part in original sin. We must think of Undine as theoretically capable of a choice between good and evil like Adam and Eve (how else could she interest us as a human being!), nevertheless her spontaneous impulses are without any primal taint.

Schiller says, the naive character evokes laughter as well as esteem by his lack of guile (451). That is because we postulate a knowledge of disingenuous human behavior on the part of people who have lived in this world and share the common human *Anlage* in that direction. But can we laugh at Undine? Certainly not. The reason is that she impersonates in full perfection that moral cultivation which for Schiller exists only as a theoretical ultimate, a limit to be approached but never realized in human life. But is humor then completely absent from this paradigmatic situation of naive behavior? Not quite, I would say. Is it not amusing to find the courtiers frowning on Bertalda for a behavior which they would have shown in the same situation? Is it not amusing to catch oneself and others, on first reading, sliding into this same pattern of moral judgment? And is it not amusing to detect how Fouqué baits his trap for us by the cultivation of a style that makes us forget all about any sophistication?

(The above analysis is based, of course, on the premise that Fouqué's axiomatic assumptions are left unchallenged—the assumption, in particular, that the discovery of his true parentage should be a matter of the utmost joy to the heart of any good child. "Nature" calls for such spontaneous joy, automatically registered, whereas the response of Convention would be qualified by circumstances.)

It is characteristic of Schiller's whole approach, that the theoretically perfect example to illustrate it has to be supplied by fairy tale.

2. The Sentimental Idyll: An Exercise in Optics

The meaningful basis of Schiller's essay is the experience of a fundamental dualism. The modern poet matures in a world that shows a sharp cleavage between his poetic ego and Nature. The term Nature, as here conceived, is charged with all the connotations it has acquired in the writings of Rousseau and the Return-to-Nature movement associated with Rousseau's name. Nature in this sense is not a definable concept, but an idea of life under auspices of perfection, embodying wholeness, spontaneous growth in conformity with law, the resolution of struggle, harmony, beauty, truth, goodness, in short, the human community and its environment conceived as divorced from all negative aspects, all evil. The idea of Nature is projected backwards to the beginning of time (a golden age of the past) and projected forward to the end of time as the ideal goal of human development. Over against this luring phantom there is the hard core of reality with all its struggle, its imperfections and dissonances. The sentimental poet is identified with all the conflicts and imperfections of Reality, but he is filled with an ardent longing for the phantom that dazzles his eyes as Nature, or the Ideal. Once, he reflects, *before* the dawn of Time, the poetic spirit and the Phantom were one. Nay, once *upon* a time, even, he goes on to reflect, they were one. Although Nature, strictly speaking, never existed in perfect purity since man's arrival upon earth, yet the blue haze persuades his dazzled eye to all but identify pure Nature with a historical phenomenon—the flower of Greek civilization. So he is emboldened to continue: the poet of ancient Greece, then, *was* a piece of Nature, not an outcast like his modern brother. The Greek poet knew not the experience of fundamental dualism. He was whole. He was *naive* (nativus: to the manner born).

Having established this fiction of the naive poet (both as an *ideal* type and a type that once existed), Schiller, the modern (the sentimental) poet takes his stance somewhere in the void, as it were, where his gaze can simultaneously encompass the two objects of his speculation, the Ideal on the one hand, and Reality on the other. But now the act of focusing, as an aspect of two-eyed vision, comes into play. As his eye fixes upon the one object, bringing its features into clear focus, the other object recedes into the periphery of the field of vision and loses its distinctness. The choice of focus will determine the basic mood or character of the poetic product that results from such contemplation. If the poet focuses upon Reality and sees all its imperfections in clear and bold detail, then of necessity the Ideal will enter into the whole picture only as a more or less blurred and hazy peripheral element. The net effect will be Satire (anger, scorn, derision, laughter). If, on the other hand, the finder eye focuses upon the Ideal, imperfect Reality will recede and become a factor of only marginal awareness. In that case the poetic product will be elegiac, expressing emotions that lift the soul.

Now, strange though it seems, there is a third possibility of focus, but very difficult to attain for the naked eye (we have all experienced it with the aid of the stereoscope). It is possible so to control the muscles of the eyes that two objects, ranged at some distance from one another, can be made to approach each other until they coincide. If the gaze of the poet's soul, shifting between Reality and the Ideal, is sufficiently intense and compelling, he can—theoretically—achieve a perfect fusion of the two. As the goal of such fusion Schiller postulates the Sentimental Idyll. He can point to no satisfactory example, but he is sure that it is within the range of destined human achievement.

Schiller is at pains to point out that there exists a well-represented genre of the Sentimental Idyll (Gessner) but that it does not conform to what he is projecting. The pastoral idyll of the moderns (508 ff.), looks backward, whereas the idyll he has in mind looks forward. There are times in Schiller's essay when the terms Nature and the Ideal are used as interchangeable synonyms; but here they are contrasted, ranged at opposite points of the horizon: Nature is infra-civilizational, the Ideal is ultra-civilizational. The popular Idyll conjures up the fiction of a golden age of primitivism, whereas Schiller's programmatic Sentimental Idyll calls for the interpenetration of the Ideal with the highest achievements of culture. The ethical climate of the projected Sentimental Idyll will be pastoral innocence,[3] but this innocence will be domiciled in a setting involving vitality, intellectual range, aesthetic culture and social refinement, all to the highest degree. Its password will be not Arcadia, but Elysium. It will be the ideal of beauty made applicable to real life. Satiric and elegiac poetry derived all their themes from the contrast between the real and the ideal. In the projected idyll every vestige of such contrast will have vanished. All conflicts having been resolved, there prevails an atmosphere of tranquility—the tranquility of perfection, not of inertia; the result of equilibrium, not of stagnation; of saturation, not of inanity. This calm must be tantamount to a sense of infinite potentiality, a difficult feat to accomplish in the absence of any play of opposing forces. This type of poetry must contrive to achieve the maximum of unity without any sacrifice of diversity.

Here we have Schiller's program for a genre of poetry in which modern man's experience of a basic dualism between the real and the ideal is conceived as transcended, as *aufgehoben* (513). It is interesting to note that Schiller finds the nearest approach to the realization of the Sentimental Idyll in *Paradise Lost*, in Milton's depiction of the ancestral human pair before the Temptation and the Fall (511). Schiller could have found no better example to drive home his point. For there is nothing remotely primitivistic about Adam's sentiments or his faculties of reasoning. They find expression, on the contrary, in a language modulated and disciplined to the highest degree. Adam's discourse keeps constantly reminding us of the fact that the refining process of untold ages has converged upon the shaping of this tool of the spirit despite the fiction that he received it brand new from the hand of the Creator. Wits have asked the question, "Who was the first man to quote Aristotle" and answered "Milton's Adam." And for Milton there was nothing incongruous about the idea that the first man should

[3] I am paraphasing and condensing p. 513.

not only have been endowed with all human potentialities in the germ but that he should have possessed them rather in their fullest deployment, to a degree, in fact, which the seventeenth-century poet, himself suffering from the taint of the Fall, could no more than falteringly adumbrate in the finest flights of eloquence that he put in Adam's mouth.

We now ask: Has modern literature produced any works that qualify as a fulfillment of this program of what I would call the ultimate in contrast to the primitivistic Sentimental Idyll? The answer is Yes. Schiller's program has found both a limited and a total realization.

First a limited realization; but not in Schiller's own subsequent work. His *Tell* is often referred to in this context, but the social setting of *Tell* is an idealized primitive society of peasants, hunters, and fishermen. The one, the only name that comes to mind among Schiller's contemporaries as the exponent of the ultimate Sentimental Idyll is Hölderlin. In Hölderlin's great hymns we find the mood of the ultimate idyll—not as a sustained temper, however, but rather as a series of rapturous flashes piercing an elegiac background of somberest hue. These flashes, cataclysmic in their intensity, overwhelm us with the suddenness of miracle. Sometimes the miracle is achieved by a complete reversal of course in the middle of a sentence that began with deepest brooding despair. Greatest example, the sixth strophe of *Menons Klage um Diotima*, where the "bis" initiates the miraculous turn and has achieved a total reorientation before we have become aware of even a change. Examples of pure ultimate idyll we find in the last four strophes of *Der Rhein*, in the middle and end of *Gesang des Deutschen*, and in all those pivotal passages of Hölderlin's other hymns where "ausgeglichen / Ist eine Weile das Schicksal" [for a while destiny is in balance]. There, again and again, what was grief and lament over what is lost, what was longing, hope, and apprehensive expectation perilously poised, is "othered" into full realization of the divine presence. But only for moments. In Hölderlin's poetry we have the ultimate Sentimental Idyll imbedded in a magma of elegy and serious satire.

There is one mid-nineteenth-century work, however, which meets all of Schiller's programmatic specifications and sustains the mood of the ultimate Sentimental Idyll over many hundreds of pages. There is only one such work to my knowledge. I refer to Stifter's

Nachsommer. This curious novel, for many years all but forgotten and reputed to be unreadably tedious, has emerged in our century as one of the most treasured prose masterpieces in the German language. There is a very large literature about it. I do not know whether any of the monographs and essays that deal with the *Nachsommer* have established its connection with Schiller's essay, but I am positive that this is the right approach. In Schiller's program of the ultimate Sentimental Idyll we have the theoretical foundation for a work that represents a conscious and radical departure from anything ever before attempted in the field of the novel. Here we have vitality, profound thought, aesthetic culture, and social refinement of the highest degree, not in a fairy-tale projection but in a here-and-now setting of mid-nineteenth-century Austria. We become party to a progressive harmonious development of all the human faculties, intellectual, scientific, artistic, moral, aesthetic, political, social, but without struggle, back-tracking, or error. We see the unfolding of infinite potentialities in an atmosphere of tranquility—the tranquility of equilibrium and saturation. Here the ideal flowering of human relationships is depicted, not as a dream or a vague hope, but as an unfalteringly emergent achievement. There is a constant tension, the swell of which becomes richer and richer, but there is no note of passion, violence, or acute surprise. Error, agony, and renunciation are introduced only as muted echoes of a distant past in the one retrospective chapter of the novel. In all this the *Nachsommer* is unique and it is bound to remain so. The real as coinciding with the ideal—to depict this with the unerring exactness of the disciplined stylist, so that we come under the spell of the characters and their milieu and take them as real on a make-believe basis, this was a prodigious *tour de force.* Any second attempt of the sort would be a monotonous duplication, because the ideal is essentially an abstraction, and all approximations to the ideal have a very strong family resemblance. As Victor Hugo said, in sounding the keynote of the anti-classicistic revolt in the preface to *Cromwell* (1827): Beauty has only one face, but ugliness has a thousand facets;[4] and after him Schnitzler's Anatol in praise of the morbid, "Es gibt so viele Krankheiten und nur eine Gesundheit" [There are so many illnesses and only one health].

[4] Le beau n'a qu'un type; le laid en a mille.

GOETHE'S *FAUST.*
AN INTRODUCTION FOR
STUDENTS AND TEACHERS
OF GENERAL LITERATURE

I

THE HISTORY OF Doctor Faustus, the celebrated magician who sold his soul to the devil in return for a stipulated term of personal services, the revelation of occult mysteries, and diversified entertainment, was a thrilling horror story with an edifying moral. First published in 1587, it was sold like other "chapbooks" at country fairs year after year, undergoing a variety of versions. Without any pretension to literary form, it catered to the undiscriminating taste of a growing middle class reading public in an age of printing, discovery, and religious controversy. It was immediately snapped up by Christopher Marlowe and turned into a play for the Elizabethan stage. Before long the theme supplied one of the lasting attractions with which troupes of travelling puppet players diverted their audiences. In the third quarter of the eighteenth century, young Goethe made the acquaintance of both the chapbook and the puppet show. Child of an age that experienced the world in terms very different from those of the age of the Reformation, Goethe sensed that the theme of Doctor Faustus harbored unlimited possibilities for expressing the altered and expanded aspirations of the human soul. In the early 1770's he began to toss off the first scenes of a projected *Faust* play. When in the fall of 1775 he came to the little duchy of Weimar, where he was destined to spend the rest of his mature life, he brought with him a substantial number of worked-out scenes which luckily have come down to us in an unauthorized copy discovered more than fifty years after Goethe's death.

The theme had implications beyond what Goethe had first imagined. He worked at it intermittently, but despairing of rounding it

Reprinted from *The German Quarterly*, xxxvii (1964), 467-486, and xxxviii (1965), 1-13, by permission of Robert M. Browning, editor.

out, he published an unfinished version in 1790, *Faust, ein Fragment*. Under the prodding of Schiller, during the next decade, he set to work afresh and finally published *Faust, Part One* in 1808, carrying the work to the death of Gretchen, the Gretchen action constituting the most poignant episode in the *Faust* drama, but an episode only. Long before this, he had gotten to work on a second part, enormously differing from the first in style, setting, and perspective. Portions of Part Two were published during Goethe's lifetime. But when he finally put the concluding touch to his manuscript, in the year before his death, he sealed it up for posterity. The complete *Faust* drama was given to the world in 1832, some sixty years after Goethe had first set to work on it. *Faust* has become the legacy of a lifetime. It embodies the most mature distillate of the wisdom of Germany's greatest poet.

The age of the Reformation saw the career of Faust as an object lesson and a warning. To the age of Goethe it was natural, on the other hand, to look upon the doctor-magician as a blurred and distorted prototype of man's ideal aspirations. This is the premise that explains Goethe's abiding attraction to the theme. Faust appealed to Goethe as a symbol of man's emancipation from authority. Regardless of whether Faust's path would eventually lead him to perdition or to salvation, his courage in daring to trespass upon the realm of the forbidden makes him a heroic figure charged with positive value. This is the age of the Enlightenment, and obedience is not one of its watchwords. The Judaeo-Christian pattern of thought continues to persist as the general framework of the philosopher's speculations and the poet's imaginings, but for the free spirits of the age it has lost the sanction of any ironclad dogmatism. A century earlier, Milton still founded his great poem of *Paradise Lost* on the theme of "man's first disobedience." This involved the axiomatic acknowledgment of divine arbitrary authority. The eighteenth century, on the other hand, was set to challenge all arbitrary authority, in the spiritual as well as the secular sphere. Mere power as such could compel submission but not induce reverence. Thus what had been branded as sin could take on the aspect of a higher glory. The criterion of moral value must now be sought in the essential nature of reason. Thus Schiller, lecturing to his students on the fall of man with the biblical story as his text, is ready to concede that the fall precipitated a catastrophe. But he takes pains to point out that the fall was also an absolutely necessary first step in the higher development of mankind. With the fall, the mind of man embarks on the realization of its limitless potentialities. Without it, he would forever have remained a child of Nature, innocent but ignorant, unable to develop the faculties of distinguishing between good and evil. And let us recall in this context the famous emancipatory gesture of Goethe's older contemporary, Lessing: If God were to stand before me, holding in his closed right hand the absolute truth, and in his left hand the unceasing search for truth but with the proviso of being doomed to stray from it for ever and ever, —if, thus standing before me he would ask me to choose, I would humbly say: Father, the absolute truth is for you alone, give me what your left hand holds. Autonomy as the premise of human dignity was never more pointedly formulated.

Autonomy involves pride, and pride, we remember, was the cardinal sin of the fallen angels. Their rebellion sprang from "superbia." But even Milton could not refrain from endowing Satan, archfiend and seducer of man, with qualities of strength, steadfastness, and endurance that lent him more than a tinge of the heroic. Faust also exhibits a pride that the Church would have branded as sinful, though it is by no means nihilistic in its aim. All in all, the situation conspires to make us approach the personality of Faust with a highly favorable prejudice.

Let us go afield a moment longer before entering the portals of Goethe's poem.

The spirit of Faust stops at nothing in its quest for self-realization. An exponent of this spirit, Faust, the individual, assumes symbolic significance as the extreme exemplar of the deepest drives of western civilization. Self-realization, properly considered, is a program without inner or outer limits. It is the spirit of total experiment probing the recesses of the individual soul, the relation of the individual to society, the relation of man to his terrestrial environment, the relation of man to the universe. The hazard of self-destruction in the pursuit of this quest is a risk to be faced. In a supreme moment of his career Faust exclaims: "Dasein ist Pflicht, und wär's ein Augenblick." Total self-realization is imperative, even if it were only for a moment. This is the drive that made Nietzsche speak of himself as the flame that glories in consuming itself. It is the drive that Oswald Spengler, in his *Decline of the West*, saw as the central force that distinguishes the present cultural sphere from those of all former ages. In a subtle way it pervades one of the great books of our age, *The Magic Mountain* of Thomas Mann. Although its hero, Hans Castorp, seems simple, tame and even lethargic at first sight, and far removed from the temperamental titanism of Faust, yet his surrender to disease is a decision involving, in his case, an infinite dynamic expansion and spiritual escalation. It is in essence the same as Faust's pact with the devil. At key points of the novel we ponder the recurring leitmotif: "It is more moral to lose oneself and even abandon oneself to perdition than to preserve oneself." The word "moral" in that sentence has an ambiguous ring. It certainly carries no connotations of social adjustment. It stands rather for the response to an inner summons that transcends all considerations of personal "security." It spells experimentation in the widest ideological sense, involvement with the realm of the forbidden. If we substitute "nobler" for "more moral," this thinly disguised New Testament dictum (Luke 9: 24) stands out as the formula for a heroic ethic, a Faustian ethic.

Without question, Goethe projected in the personality of Faust a sublimely noble aspiration of the human spirit. This does not mean, of course, that Goethe glorified Faust uncritically. That he was not blind to his dark and sinister side no thoughtful reader of the play can overlook. Even before his association with the Evil One, Faust is labeled a "superman" in a deeply ironical context. And with a deliberate eye to restoring a balance, he again employs the word "Übermensch" in one of those very personal stanzas which he set at the head of his collected poems, in "Zueignung," 1784.

In this poem Goethe uses the device of allegory to report on a vision during an early morning walk. When the mists that contested the power of the rising sun have vanished, the poet is dazzled by an apparition hovering in their place. He recognizes the female form as the Goddess of Truth and hails her with passionate joy. She has been his intimate since his childhood days, whereas his companions preferred to stray in pursuit of error. After this outburst the Goddess indulgently smiles upon him and replies: "Thou seest how wise, how necessary it was to reveal only a small part of my essence to you [she lumps him with his companions]. Scarcely having overcome the crudest error, scarcely having mastered thy first childish wilfulness, thou deemest thyself straightway a superman who can afford to ignore the ordinary duties. Art thou really so different from the others? Get to know thyself. Live in peace with the world."[1]

This poem, acknowledging Goethe's identification with Faust's immoderate aspirations, at the same time reduces his own stature to modest proportions and avows his dedication to a life of cooperation and service.

After these preliminaries are we ready to enter the portals of Goethe's dramatic poem? Almost, but not quite. Like a stately edifice, the *Faust* drama has a gate, a portico, and an elevated platform which we must traverse before passing into the interior.

The gate takes the form of a poem in which the poet, at an advanced stage of his life, invokes anew the airy shapes that haunted the young man's imagination and now press in upon him demanding that he endow them with substance. While the poem is cast in a melancholy mood, the portico, entitled "Prelude in the Theater," treats us to a spirited improvisation in which the director, the poet, and the clown discuss the impending production from a variety of angles, mixing business sense, seriousness, and fun along with satirical shafts aimed at the expectant public. We pass right on to the elevated platform, the "Prologue in Heaven." Here we pause, to note the scene, the songs of glory, and the ensuing dialogue with the utmost care, for this is our initiation, in the heavenly regions, into the action that will take place on earth. The Prologue at once characterizes the *Faust* poem as epic drama, for as in the epics of the ancients, Homer, Vergil, Statius, and the rest, down to Dante, Milton, and Klopstock, the terrestrial action has its counterpart in the councils of the supernatural powers.

[1]   "Du siehst, wie klug,
Wie nötig war's, euch wenig zu enthüllen!
Kaum bist du sicher vor dem gröbsten Trug,
Kaum bist du Herr vom ersten Kinderwillen,
So glaubst du dich schon Übermensch genug,
Versäumst die Pflicht des Mannes zu erfüllen!
Wie viel bist du von andern unterschieden?
Erkenne dich, leb' mit der Welt in Frieden."

The "Prologue" is a brilliant stage scene revealing the heavenly powers in the best anthropomorphic tradition—the Lord, flanked by three archangels, with the lesser hosts in the background. The paeans of praise deserve the student's closest attention in their blending of the old and the new astronomy (the sun and the lesser planets revolving around a motionless earth, and the earth in rotation), their Pythagorean reference to the music of the spheres, their simple mythology (the setting of the sun at journey's end), their literary synesthesia (the rendering of light in terms of sound), their references to the forces of the tides and meteorology, and finally their climactic allusion to the still, small voice of the prophet Elijah's vision (I Kings 19: 12). The setting is solemn and dignified, but the ensuing dialogue is at once shot through with satire and humor.

We see the Lord of the universe engaged in an inspection tour that has brought him to the vicinity of the earth. Closely following the analogy of the Book of Job, Satan-Mephisto, the wag ("der Schalk"), to the Lord the least distasteful of all the spirits of negation, comes to pay his respects to the Lord with guarded mock reverence for the Almighty, with jibes at the "domestics" ("das Gesinde") and a parodistic echo of their strains of praise, and he launches into a tirade of criticism leveled at man, the diminutive god of creation, and at the Creator for having endowed him with the ambiguous gift of reason. When the Lord interrupts with a reference to Faust, the most exalted exemplar of the breed, Mephisto gives full rein to his satirical vein, characterizing Faust as mad and proposing a wager to the Lord that, granted permission to ply him with his arts of seduction, he will succeed in deviating this soul to his own ends. The Lord, with great tolerance and unperturbed confidence in the sound kernel of Faust's soul, grants the desired permission for the duration of Faust's sojourn on earth, implying that there is more to come. The Lord's generalization about "a good man," with obvious application to Faust, his "servant," shows that his concept of the "good" transcends the standards that associate the term with divinely and socially sanctioned norms of moral behavior. His unfathomable tolerance of the self-assertive spark differentiates him radically from the biblical Jehovah whose wrath doomed disobedient man to perdition.

Inasmuch as the Lord of the "Prologue" must be taken as the

source of infinite goodness, power, foreknowledge, and wisdom, there can be no doubt as to the ultimate discomfiture of Mephisto. That Faust will be saved in the end is programmatically certain. It may be puzzling in terms of this view that Goethe entitled his poetic drama a tragedy. Would not the outcome have equally justified the title of comedy in the sense used by Dante? But the solemnity of the action, in analogy to Greek drama, may have been decisive in warranting this label. This, however, is a question that the reader of the whole drama may be left to ponder.

The first four scenes of the human drama, a unified sequence spanning two nights and two days, show how the impatient, frustrated idealist is induced to form with the "spirit of negation" an association that is destined to cast its shadow over the rest of his earthly life. The first scene develops Faust's situation and his personality in a dazzling variety of facets. It unfolds chiefly by way of a very extended dramatic monologue, interrupted by dialogue passages that allow no monotony to develop—the apparition of the Earth Spirit, the dialogue with his assistant Wagner, and the pealing of the bells and the chorus of Easter voices at the climactic moment. On stage the dramatic monologue usually suffers drastic cuts. Its extreme length and subtlety overtax the capacities of both the average theater audience and all but the greatest actors. But for the reader who yields to its spell every line carries its own emotional charge born of Faust's situation and the visible and tangible associations that stream down from the clutter of the high, musty study. With two exceptions: (1) The opening paragraph is a deliberately archaic piece of exposition, evoking the age of the Reformation and the verse form of its most popular poet, Hans Sachs, by its prosy diction and the mechanical rhythm of its four-beat couplets. (2) Later on we come across one more passage where Faust, in the trough of the emotions that toss him, reflects in general terms on the theme of anxiety as the most corroding affliction of the human race. This does not seem to relate to his immediate state of mind, but we are forewarned of what is coming when Anxiety, in the guise of a spectral sister, confronts Faust on the last night of his life as his most sinister assailant. But apart from these two passages all the rest of Faust's monologue has the compelling power of spontaneous improvisation. This effect is achieved by a most felicitous blending of form with content that has been the despair of all translators. The lyrical pitch of the diction, vocabulary, and sentence structure varies from mood to mood. The lines are not of a set length but swell from four- to five- and six-beat waves to return at will to lesser undulations. The rhyme scheme operates with equal freedom, now joining lines in couplets, now looping two pairs, now circling an inner by an outer pair, now binding triple lines or triple pairs together, employing a free alternation of one syllable rhymes with those of two. These few remarks on form must suffice. They apply in large measure to the whole of Part One of the drama. In Part Two the problems of form are far too complex even to be touched upon here.

The middle-aged scholar, who recapitulates his career in the opening lines, is a man wearied and exhausted to the breaking point. He has mastered all the substance and all the techniques of the total medieval university curriculum. The intangible abstractions of logic, metaphysics, and theology have left him disillusioned. He is equally fed up with the procedures and yields of the practical professions, law and medicine. The satirical colloquium to which Mephisto treats the eager Freshman in a later scene merely transposes all of Faust's feelings on these matters into a humorous key. Faust is in deadly earnest. Words have assumed a hollow ring. Words are a device to conceal fundamental ignorance. Words provide no tool for a breakthrough from the world of appearance to the world of essence. In scene after scene Faust harps on this central fact. This is his frustration. He conceives of the world in terms of a pantheistic reinterpretation of Scripture. Creation (God, Nature) is a divine, eternally emerging process. He affirms it with all his soul. Is he not cast in the Creator's own image, part of His essence? Is it not his birthright, then, to participate consciously in the sublime dynamic process? Is he not higher than the angels— mere ministrants they? This is the repeated starting point of his broodings after his rejection by the Earth Spirit. Meanwhile, in the opening passage, he gives only a passing glance to the thought that riches and honors, attending the pursuit of worldly success, have passed him by. In his frustration he has taken recourse to magic as a possible shortcut to the spiritual revelation he longs for with every fiber of his being. Impatience dictates this bold and forbidden course, a fever pitch of frenzied affirmation. At this stage the spirit of negation is utterly foreign to him ("Ein guter Mensch" [a good man], the Lord termed him). Faust is a rebel only as regards the barriers of sense that keep him from communing directly with the divine spirit. Philosophically speaking, he storms against being hemmed in by space, time, and causality. Rationally considered, Faust's behavior is quixotic, but a kindred spirit, Heinrich von Kleist, in the age of Kant, clutched at the same motivation in exhibiting the tantrums of a total nervous collapse, and in our own century Rainer Maria Rilke directed the hysterical drum fire of his "Spanish Trilogy" and the bleak despair of the eighth Duino Elegy against the intransigence of the subject-object relation as conditioning man's communication with the universe.

Yet even while overreaching himself, Faust tempers his folly with some discretion. Contemplating the magic symbols drawn by the renowned master's own hand, he turns from the figure suggesting the workings of the universal spirit as too vast for his comprehension. He hails the Earth Spirit, the lesser deity that dwells in the earth like the soul of man in the body, as the more fitting object for his empathy. His ardor is rewarded by a manifestation. Recoiling in terror from the insupportable light, he hears himself gently reassured and chided with mild irony. Then, with a superhuman burst of courage Faust rises to the challenge of the unique moment to proffer himself to the apparition's embrace, only to find himself put in his place by a terse, definitive rejection. But before Faust has time to come to terms with his humiliation his assistant's knock at the door dispels the mood.

Faust dislikes and despises Wagner's fawning airs and his careerist aspirations. That he reveals no trace of these personal feelings either in the midnight discourse or on the next day's afternoon walk, bears testimony to his generosity and humanity. Faust is no cynic. He does not vent his pessimism in taunts and sarcasms leveled at his fellow man. He strives to educate by example and precept. Throughout the dialogue, the issue is sharply drawn between sincerity and scheming, simplicity and pretension, dedication and self-seeking, between earnest self-examination and easy complacency.

After Wagner has left, Faust's mind returns to the vision, to assess its impact. His ego has suffered an annihilating deflation. His buoyant feeling of participating in the creative pulse, on a par with the gods, has been cruelly exposed as brash presumption. Sharp despair yields to the softer hurt of self-pity, inducing a mood of quieter, almost impersonal meditation on the theme of anxiety. But his brooding soon reactivates the sting of his having been called a worm. He indulges in self-laceration as he develops the parallel between the worm groveling in the dust and his own life. Now the paraphernalia of his cluttered study meet his eye to mock his existence. Item after item—the stacked books and rolls, the grinning skull, the obsolete and useless machinery on which his misguided father pinned his faith—stare him in the face as so much dust. But when he spies the vial that harbors the potent poison that he has decocted, his mind veers to a different tack. In a twinkling he has rebounded from his despair to salute suicide as the most thrilling of all adventures. His imagination straightway paints the exploit in the most glowing poetic colors. All his manly self-esteem is revived at the thought of setting his course to the Unknown, of facing a Beyond that childish imaginings have invested with unspeakable horrors, of facing, what might prove to be total annihilation, not in a frenzied access of blind impulse, but open-eyed, calm, serene. In a state of tempered euphoria Faust takes from the shelf the precious chalice, removes its case, and, reminiscing on its festive function in the days of his youth, he pours the poison and raises the cup to his lips. The Easter bells and chorus stay his hand. Though they cannot rekindle his faith in the miracle of the resurrection, memories of the fervent piety of his childhood crowd in upon him. His mood is softened, and the momentum for taking the irretrievable step is lost.

The scene of the Easter walk reinforces some important aspects of Faust's personality that were only lightly touched on in the initial scene. Faust's deep love of Nature, already glimpsed in his invocation of the moon, finds full expression in the rapturous lyric passage with which he greets the spring landscape and its festive human throng. He mingles with the simple folk and receives the tribute of their love and respect with unaffected modesty. Their praise of his dedication and success during the plague he counters with the admonition to give credit where it is due, to the Helper above. To infect them with irreverent skepticism is the last thing he desires. But most important, the allusion to the plague has touched in Faust's soul a complex of confused and bitter grief. He confesses the young man's importunate piety, the ascetic zeal with which he tried to bend the will of Heaven to his desire. Evidently, Faust is of the stuff that great saints are made of. Then he speaks with guarded criticism of his father as having been deluded into the blind alley of alchemy: dispensing his nefarious concoctions in good faith, he and his colleagues perpetrated wholesale murder surpassing the ravages of the plague. The honest intent may exonerate his father, but it cannot efface a deep sense of guilt on Faust's own part. And the extreme emotional outburst about "the impudent murderers" helps us to see two enigmatical lines of scene 1 in perspective. The lines, "What you have acquired from your forefathers, assimilate it in order to possess it," had seemed to interrupt the expression of a desire to be rid of all that had been handed down to him, with a puzzling *non sequitur*. Those lines make sense as the quoting by Faust of a familiar adage. But in his mouth the adage has the ring of bitter irony as the repudiation of his traditional heritage. The end of the scene introduces the poodle in the guise of which Mephisto is to make his debut.

Returned to the study that on the previous night had twice seen the superman poised on the brink of annihilation, Faust is about to make the acquaintance of his satanic companion. Scene 3, a theatrical show-piece, unfolds in three stages—the problem of scriptural translation, the exorcism, and Faust's dialogue with the travelling scholar. This scene shows Faust at his best. Having bathed in the fresh air of the woodland hills, he is cleansed and tranquil, at peace with himself, and aglow with the love of God and his fellow men. In this mood he yields to the impulse to translate a New Testament passage from the Greek. No believer in the dogma of the Church, but in search of revelation everywhere, he finds its purest spring in the New Testament. Characteristically, he turns to the opening chapter of the Gospel According to Saint John which, in contrast to the three "synoptic" gospels, exhibits a blend of Hellenistic mysticism with the Jewish ideas of the promised Messiah. The very first verse stymies Faust's efforts: "In the beginning was the word." The word, the "logos," a term of the most elusive connotations, is not fit to be rendered by the prosy German equivalent, "das Wort," an empty husk against which he had railed bitterly. He casts about for a term that might more adequately spread its aura over the page. In this his effort he appears as the double of Martin Luther, who set his aim to render the spirit of the gospel rather than the letter. Faust's concentration is disturbed by the antics of the restless poodle.

When repeated attempts to quiet the animal fail, Faust senses that there is something wrong, and the transformation of the dog into a monster presently confirms his suspicion. Not for a moment at a loss to meet the challenge of what he assumes to be an elementary spirit, he recalls the magic formulas that are applicable in such a case. He proceeds to smoke out the spirit with a systematic series of exorcisms. Readers who wish to inform themselves on the nature, appearance, and habits of the elementary spirits as well as on their commerce with mankind, will find their curiosity satisfied by a highly ingenious "scientific" tract on the subject (available in English translation) by the renowned Swiss physician, naturalist, and philosopher Paracelsus, a contemporary of our Doctor Faustus. If readers wish to pursue the matter further, they will find a highly instructive and tragic application of Paracelsus' doctrines as regards the inhabitants of the watery realm in a celebrated Romantic tale, *Undine*, by the German poet Fouqué.

When his sundry exorcisms all fail to work, Faust changes his diagnosis: since this is not a neutral elementary spirit, it must be a demon out of hell. This calls for more potent incantations. Working himself up to a fever pitch of excitement, Faust cudgels the recalcitrant monster with spells that circumscribe the mystery of the eternal only-begotten and his passion. These, and the threat of the irresistible Trinitarian thunderbolt, take effect: in place of the shapeless monster there stands the harmless figure of a travelling scholar.

Do we find this confusing? This man, who had dismissed hell as a figment of morbid fantasy, this man, who had expressed his disbelief in the glad Easter tidings—this same Faust has now worked a miracle with magic spells that derive their potency from the assumption of the Christian mysteries as valid realities! This is paradoxical. We note this only in passing; for Faust is not the man to solve the riddle of the Beyond. His mind dwells in a kind of limbo swarming with mutually contradictory images and concepts. For the moment he is completely occupied with his visitor.

What strikes us throughout the ensuing dialogue is Faust's composure, his superior control in the presence of the infernal emissary. The first interchange establishes Faust as master of the situation. Assuming a condescending tone, he displays active curiosity without a trace of nervousness: he listens to the riddling answers, the boasts, and tantrums of his visitor with grave concern and mild amusement. To the spirit of negation he opposes his deep, positive reverence for the eternal mysteries of Nature's creative workings. The professor even lectures the devil on the folly of his impotent negativism and admonishes him to mend his ways.

To his surprise Faust discovers that the devil has allowed himself to be caught in a trap. The handling of this all but incredible situation (against the background of the folk image of the devil as an essentially stupid fellow, easily tricked) shows a most ingenious interplay of chance and design: the poodle, evidently bent on no more than a bit of preliminary reconnoitering, has been forced to show his hand prematurely. Faust's self-confidence is heightened by the discovery that he has the visitor in his power. When his prodding questions bring out the fact that demons who invade the human realm are governed by strict rules of behavior, it is Faust who takes the initiative in broaching the idea of a pact, and it is Mephisto, caught off guard, who has to resort to a delaying action. Eventually Mephisto, apparently resigned to the situation, puts his captor to sleep by a ruse and makes his escape. Faust awakens in a state of redoubled frustration.

The next scene brings the great showdown, Faust's wager and pact with Mephisto. The time, the morning after; and Faust in a morning-after mood, a colossal hangover after the series of emotional shock waves that had battered him continuously for two nights and a day—the ups and downs of the blinding apparition called forth by his incantation; the great rebound of the suicidal venture, frustrated by the Easter bells; the lyrical exaltation of the Easter walk, brusquely turned into deepest despondency by memories of his part in the plague; the recovery of his buoyancy by the spectacle of the sunset; the serene atmosphere of high peace that prompted his turning to the gospel; the terrific excitement of the exorcism; the sense of mastery in his dialogue with the spirit of negation; the glimpse of a new approach to the cosmic mysteries; and finally, the sense of let-down and utter humiliation on awakening from his trance. All this has left him at a dead center of total exhaustion.

On this morning the tables are turned. The initiative has passed to Mephisto. Even before the smart cavalier enters the study, Faust's irritability is established as he is made to repeat the invitation to enter three times. He is in a devastated mood. There is no fight left in him. He is querulous, petulant, whining. His emotional tone is slack, unstrung. His harping on the theme of renunciation, his complaints about the staleness of his days and the terrors that haunt his nights mark him as the victim of an anxiety neurosis in the making. His attempts to wax lyrical in his laments appear forced, reminding us of the distorted tones of a worn-out record. Each of Mephisto's amused taunts and jibes makes him wince. Before long he flies into an uncontrollable rage that finds expression in a tirade of curses so all-inclusive as to leave no value intact. His foremost curse is leveled against the pride of his pretension to superman status. Next he reviles the sentimental softness that kept him from following through with his intended suicide. He then curses all the lure of the world of sense with its challenge and its invitations to pleasure. The climax is reached in the curse that he hurls against the highest boon of love, meaning, without question, not the love of the sexes, but the core of the Gospel message: "For God so loved the world. . . ." In the wake of this blasphemy he curses the other cardinal Christian virtues, faith and hope, topping off his tirade with a curse against patience, the virtue most alien to his impulsive temperament. With these curses Faust, so positive heretofore in his reverent affirmation of the creative process as divine, has yielded to the spirit of negation. His curses are an echo of the tempter's nihilism. They mark a turning point. Henceforth the infection of radical evil festers in Faust's blood.

Naturally, this violent swing of the pendulum provides for its own correction. In the remainder of this inexhaustibly rich scene Faust soon regains his balance. When Mephisto approaches him with a concrete proposal for their permanent association, with the forfeiture of Faust's soul in the Beyond as the price, Faust counters with a wager that shows him an alert and shrewd bargainer. The substance of the wager on which he conditions the pact is that Mephisto will never succeed in extinguishing the restless urge that makes Faust forever reach beyond the illusory satisfaction of the moment; that Mephisto will never succeed in lulling him into a sense of ease and contentment.

In the text of the play the crucial lines of the wager read as follows:

> *Werd' ich zum Augenblicke sagen:*
> *Verweile doch! du bist so schön!*
> Dann magst du mich in Fesseln schlagen,
> Dann will ich gern zugrunde gehn!
> Dann mag die Totenglocke schallen,
> Dann bist du deines Dienstes frei,
> Die Uhr mag stehn, der *Zeiger fallen,*
> Es sei die Zeit für mich *vorbei!*

(If you ever hear me say to the passing moment: / "Do linger, you are so beautiful!," / then you may clasp me in fetters, / then I will gladly perish. / Then may the funeral bell toll, / then your term of service is done. / Let the clock stop, the hour hand fall. / Let my time be over!)

Two lines, that formulate the condition, are followed by seven swift, short sentences that draw the conclusion. The four times repeated *dann* reverberates like the measured strokes of a gong. The words I have set in italics are destined to recur verbatim at the moment of Faust's death. Mephisto underlines the significance of the pronouncement with the reminder to Faust: "Mark your words well. *We* shall not forget!" There is superb irony in the fact that, when Faust has breathed his last, Mephisto misquotes a crucial word and has to stand corrected by his minions, who have remembered the exact wording.

After Faust has reluctantly gone through with the "farce" of signing the contract with a drop of his blood, he expatiates in a series of swiftly changing moods on the meaning of the momentous step he has taken. Dejection and elation spell each other off. The immediate vista is a mad, pointless whirl of dissipation. A moment later his energies rebound with the resolve, now that all prospects of an intellectual breakthrough have gone sour, to encompass in his individual person the totality of *experience* open to mankind, the whole gamut of the emotional life of the race, all its joys and pains, with ultimate annihilation as the end. Mephisto finds amusement in pointing out to him that he still persists in his aim to unite incompatibles, and once more Faust wallows in the trough of dejection. The impasse is broken by Mephisto's arrangements for the two of them to set out at once on a life of adventure in the world, leaving the musty study behind. As Faust goes to gather up some necessaries for the trip on the magic cloak, Mephisto regales the eager Freshman with his satirical wisdom.

Now follow the scenes of Auerbach's Cellar in Leipzig that night, and the visit next day to the witch's kitchen to accomplish Faust's physical rejuvenation. They need not detain us long. The roisterous atmosphere of the wine cellar, where Mephisto befuddles the drunken students with his magic tricks, may bring to mind the grosser aspects of Shakespeare's Falstaff scenes. It is entertaining in its triple perspective of the students' coarse antics, Mephisto's delight in leading them by the nose, and Faust's bored impassivity throughout.

In the witch's kitchen the situation is similar: Mephisto has a wonderful time enjoying first the grave nonsense of the animals that watch the boiling cauldron in the absence of their mistress, then in relishing the hysterical fury of the witch making her way down the chimney, and her consternation in recognizing the intruder as her master. Faust shows not the slightest interest in all the nonsense and obscenity. Only one thing catches Faust's attention, a magic mirror. It dazzles him with the elusive shifting image of the most beautiful woman the world has ever seen, Helen of Troy. He reluctantly leaves it to submit to the ritual hocus-pocus of the potion that is to rekindle in his veins the sexual fire of adolescence.

The stage is now set for the Gretchen tragedy, the absorbing theme of the last third of Part One. In the over-all drama of *Faust* the Gretchen action is only an episode, but it is developed with a spontaneity, a richness of delineation as regards the personality of Gretchen and her milieu, a depth of feeling, and a poignancy of tragic ruin that no sensitive reader is proof against. Thanks to Mephisto, who engineers the seduction, many of the scenes sparkle with infinite vivacity and humor. As a matter of fact, Mephisto's initiative and resourcefulness make him more and more the star performer, eclipsing the hero, whose unresolved tensions, unfolding in new situations but without major surprises, reduce him, dramatically speaking, to a more passive role. (This tendency, in fact, prevails throughout the greater portion of Part Two. Only at relatively brief intervals of special intensity does Faust come to the fore and take the lead. And it is only in the final act that Faust fully regains the undisputed summit of the dramatic protagonist.)

The Gretchen action develops swiftly. In the space of a few days Faust, fluctuating between carnal desire and adoration, has won the love and unquestioning trust of the artless girl. From now on we lose track of the passage of time. It is idle to ask how many days Faust spends alone, in the tranquil retreat of Forest and Cavern, enveloped by Gretchen's hallowed aura, welling over with grateful prayers to the Earth Spirit, to whom Faust attributes the new turn of his life, feeling a sense of brotherly intimacy with the birds and beasts of the wilderness, exploring the treasures of his own breast, and imagining himself in the company of the noblest spirits of bygone ages. It is idle to measure the degree of Gretchen's perturbation over her lover's disappearance by the calendar.

Mephisto brings Faust out of the clouds back to the work in hand. When the lovers meet again, Faust is put on the defensive by Gretchen's insistent questions about his religious beliefs, showing her concern for his salvation, and by her undisguised aversion for his companion. Gretchen's plain speaking is one of her most endearing qualities. In the matter-of-factness of her approach she is prosy and unimaginative, quite unlike the sentimental "romantic" heroines commonly met with in fiction. Faust is prompted to express his undogmatic pantheistic faith in exquisitely lyrical language, and Gretchen is half reassured. He is less successful in his embarrassed defense of Mephisto. The meeting ends with Gretchen's agreeing to doctor her mother's bedtime drink.

When the curtain rises again, events have taken their inevitable course. At the well Gretchen becomes reflectively aware of the harsh condemnation her own social class metes out to any girl caught straying from the straight and narrow path, and the double standard that prevails regarding the man's part in the affair. Before the icon of the Virgin she bares her prostrated soul. The next thing, her brother, stung by the wagging of loose tongues, ambushes the strangers serenading the sister whose beauty and virtue he had idolized. He is killed, and his dying words strike the poor girl's heart with fiendish cruelty. The killers have fled, the idyll is over.

Scattered hints, which no reader notices, show that all has taken place in one short month. Mephisto, accompanying Faust on his fatal tryst, alludes to the great adventure in store for them two nights later, the witches' sabbath on the eve of Saint Walpurga. The calendar date of this is fixed as the night ushering in the first of May. That night, as they trudge up the mountain, the Brocken, at the approach of midnight, Mephisto utters a couple of remarkably beautiful lines about the rising moon:

> Wie traurig steigt die unvollkommne Scheibe
> Des roten Monds mit später Glut heran.

(How dismally the imperfect disk of the red moon is ascending with its late glow.) The gibbous moon, rising late in the evening four or five nights after the full, places full moon about April 25. This is the second spring full moon. It fixes the date of the first spring full moon as around March 25. Inasmuch as Easter falls on the first Sunday after the first spring full moon, Easter must have been celebrated somewhere between March 26 and 31. We know that the time that elapsed between Faust's frustrated attempt at suicide and his rejuvenation in the witch's kitchen amounted to no more than four days. (On the eve of Easter, his vision and suicide attempt; on Easter day, the afternoon walk followed by the exorcism of the poodle in the study; on Easter Monday, the wager and pact with Mephisto, followed by the visit to Auerbach's wine cellar; on the next day, their visit to the witch's kitchen.) This places Faust's accosting of Gretchen somewhere between March 29 and April 3. From that point on to the night of Valentin's murder, April 28, the time stages of the developing love idyll are left vague.

Before we return to Faust we get one more glimpse of Gretchen in an early stage of her long martyrdom. From the scene in the cathedral we learn that her plight has infinitely worsened since her brother's death. Not only that the first stirrings of pregnancy fill her with forebodings, she bears a crushing burden of guilt on her mother's account, who faces a long period of purgatory, having died in her sleep (like Hamlet's father) without the ministrations of the Church. There can be no doubt about the circumstances: a precautionary overdose of the sleeping potion must have proved fatal to her mother—this on the very night of Valentin's murder. Had it occurred earlier, the fact would have had to be brought out in the play, and Gretchen's overwrought conscience would have made a later tryst unthinkable. When are we to suppose the scene in the cathedral to take place? As we know, the night of Walpurgis follows hard on the heels of Valentin's murder, only two days intervening. Perhaps the idea that we see Gretchen attending a requiem service for her mother and brother cannot be ruled out, but Gretchen's awareness of her pregnancy makes the assumption of a later date more likely. If so, Goethe did wisely in sacrificing the chronological sequence to the continuity of mood of the Gretchen action. The nine months of anguish that undermine her sanity are shrouded in obscurity. We see her for the last time in chains in a prison cell. Her mind is unhinged. She has done away with her baby. The executioner's sword awaits her at the dawn of day.

After the cathedral scene, a violent shift of mood and locale takes us to the witches' rendezvous on the Brocken with Faust and Mephisto as spectators and participants in the tumultuous annual convocation. This is a virtuoso performance of poetic genius. The language is strained to evoke a bewildering medley of eerie sound, light, and movement in the surge of the demonic elemental forces. Faust and Mephisto, their way lighted by a will-o'-the-wisp, are caught in the tugging updraft and the crush of the flying hosts and detached individuals, all straining to reach the summit for the celebration of the black mass. The modern theater, and particularly the film, finds a challenge in translating this feast of the imagination into a spectacle for the senses, but in accomplishing this it inevitably reduces the suggestive magic of the poetic word to a mere shadow.

In the carnival of obscene animal energy we never get to see the climactic performance on the summit, presided over by "Herr Urian." Mephisto's caprice shunts Faust away from the upward surging throng into the quieter byways of a camping area. At this sideshow we meet a group of motley characters, oldsters, has-beens, who got bogged down in their flight because the vital spark failed them. These impotents expatiate nostalgically on the good old days when they called the tune, and Mephisto gleefully apes them. From general satire, directed against types, the focus disconcertingly shifts to personal satire: Goethe lampoons a literary enemy, Friedrich Nicolai, the old warhorse of the German Enlightenment. The many topical allusions were relished by contemporaries in the know but are pointless without a detailed commentary today.

And what of Faust? He had felt the stiff climb among the knobby crags as a zestful challenge. To his inner eye the mountainside had unveiled itself as a living matrix of treasure in the making. Eagerly looking forward to the main spectacle, he had been drawn off to a sideshow. He had danced with a young witch but lost appetite when a red mouse slipped out of her mouth. Then he had spied the wraith of a girl, and Mephisto's warning to avert his eyes from the "Gorgon" had only served to rivet his gaze on the wide-open dead eyes and the gliding gait of the apparition. More and more it had taken on the semblance of Gretchen, and a red line, no wider than the back of a knife, circling her throat, had loomed as a portent of her fate. There we leave Faust, to turn to the anticlimactic conclusion of the "Walpurgisnacht" scene, with some final jibes against half-baked plays and amateurish performances.

Very abruptly the end of the Gretchen tragedy is now enacted. The discontinuity is extreme, as regards both the time and the form. The gap of nine months in Faust's life since his flight after Valentin's murder is a blank. Somehow Mephisto's magic must have succeeded in blocking Faust's memories of Gretchen and in stifling the voice of his conscience regarding her fate until the last night of her life. Then, learning what has happened to her and what awaits her, Faust breaks into violent recriminations against the satanic seducer, only to have has own guilt spelled out to him with pitiless matter-of-factness. The medium of this scene is prose—the rhetorical, exclamatory and at the same time long-winded prose of the Storm and Stress movement of the 1770's. Goethe left the scene "Bleak Day. Field." intact as a relic of his earliest work on the subject of *Faust*. The reference in the scene to the dog who amused himself during Faust's nightly strolls with playing practical jokes on harmless wanderers must belong to a phase of the composition before Goethe had hit upon the happy expedient of the exorcism scene as the means of introducing Mephisto to Faust.

Part One of *Faust* ends with the scene of the attempted rescue, an overwhelming finale. The personality of the wretched girl in the prison cell is completely shattered, but every fractured piece suggests the one-time perfection now irretrievably destroyed. In the wandering of her unhinged mind she bears a striking resemblance to Shakespeare's Ophelia, but with this difference: Ophelia, innocent victim of cruel fate, evokes a mood of pure pathos, while Gretchen, involved despite herself in fearful guilt, is a truly tragic victim. Physical dread and a desire to atone rend her bosom. Instinctively she senses the sinister aura of her one-time lover and shrinks from his touch. In a final flash of lucidity she throws herself upon the merciful judgment of God, and a voice from the Beyond proclaims her salvation.

The Gretchen episode was the first stage of Faust's career in the world of man outside the confining walls of the study. For Faust, the pure love of Gretchen will be forever imbedded in his memory as the deepest spiritual blessing vouchsafed to him by a kindly Providence, and as the ineradicable reminder of his darkest hour. When he finally departs from the earthly stage the intercession of Gretchen will weight the scales in the achievement of his redemption.

II

Part Two strikes the reader rather as a new beginning than the continuation of the *Faust* drama. The method, the perspective, the focus, the form in all its aspects, are radically new. Psychological drama, though not abandoned, is subordinated to symbolical drama. The Faust of Part Two is more a representative of mankind in its strivings and errings than an individual. The action is divided into five acts of such length as to preclude presentation on the stage in a single evening. The development is epic rather than dramatic. Instead of a forward movement focused upon the outcome of Faust's association with the forces of Evil, the scenes are crowded with pageantry and spectacles in many of which Faust's presence is unobserved or he is off-stage altogether. The versification is subtle and experimental in the extreme. The poetic style and vocabulary are full of innovations that it took German poetry generations to assimilate. The time of Part Two ranges over half a century. Yet of this total span only a minimal portion is accounted for by the action presented. In the present sketch the most fleeting glance at all but the final act must suffice. Only then, on the final day of Faust's life, does the dramatic action resume its forward thrust.

The first scene of act I shows us Faust asleep at the approach of sunrise in a smiling spring landscape. Ariel and his elfin host guard Faust's slumber. Their song helps to banish the images of horror and anguish from his memory. After this symbolical opening Faust awakens. In a grave and measured monologue in *terza rima* verse he communes with Mother Earth. As he drinks in the morning atmosphere, the dew, the myriad sounds of stirring life, the play of lights and colors, we participate through his lines in a process of recuperation amounting to a total rebirth. His reaction to the sunrise translates itself, in his reflective consciousness, into a grandiose symbol of the new approach to life on which he sets his course: blinded by the dazzling light, he turns his back upon the sun, and his gaze is caught by the iridescent play of a rainbow above the waterfall—a spectacle of enduring form despite the renewal from moment to moment of the vapor particles constituting its substance. The barren quest of the absolute is renounced in favor of the more profitable pursuit of exploring the infinite variety of the world of phenomena. This symbol of the rainbow recalls Plato's famous parable of the shadows of semblances thrown on the wall of a cave, as man's closest approach to cognition of reality, but it is zestfully affirmative rather than pessimistic. It is, of course, Goethe's own credo, and in a moment such as this the image of Faust completely blends with that of his author. Insofar as this insight is Faust's, it is one of those momentary flashes of heightened realization that illuminate the landscape of the mind for a fleeting moment, only to be pushed into the background by the preoccupations of daily life. (Strangely enough, there are moments in Part Two when even the voice of Mephisto loses its negativism and becomes indistinguishable from that of Goethe, as in the definitely good-natured send-off given the Baccalaureus, who storms ahead on the very quest of the absolute renounced by Faust, and with the imagery of light and darkness employed in reverse.) This is only to point out that the champions of strict consistency are hard put to it in their interpretation of *Faust Two.*

The scene now changes to the Imperial Court. There is a pleasure-loving young emperor, whose realm is fast drifting into a state of chaos. A satirical tone prevails in the presentation of the many woes that beset the government most inconveniently at a time when all thoughts are normally bent on pleasure. Into this pre-Lenten carnival atmosphere Mephisto and Faust make their entry. For them as for us readers, the bourgeois world has been left behind for good. Mephisto at once gains the emperor's favor in the mask of a court fool, who turns out to be more ingenious than all the grave ministers of the realm. His advice solves the most pressing problem of the moment—that of the exchequer. On the flimsiest security, indeed a phantom security, he gets the treasury to issue an unlimited supply of paper money. Henceforth nothing is allowed to interfere with the carnival mood. We are treated to a most elaborate mummery, itself an evening's entertainment, consisting for the most part of well-rehearsed gay and allegorical pantomime and song, but interspersed with features of dazzling pageantry that only the master magician could have improvised. The emperor himself participates as a masquer along with Faust and Mephisto. At the climactic moment His Majesty threatens to come to grief. Magic flames from a spring of liquid gold spurt up and and envelop the palace. But the ensuing panic is quelled at once by its promoter and the emperor expresses himself the next morning as jolly well pleased by the show. But, his appetite whetted by the quality of the entertainment, he asks Faust to conjure up Paris and Helen from the underworld as a spectacle for his court, and Faust, trusting in his companion's infinite resourcefulness, promises that it shall be done.

Dramatically speaking, the lavish pageantry of the night before is an elaborate device to trigger the main business of acts I-III. This is nothing less than to reenact one of the major episodes of the sixteenth-century *Faust Book* and achieve so staggeringly impossible a wishdream as the physical union of Faust with the all-time paragon of beauty, the fabulous Helen of Troy. Goethe seized upon this theme to symbolize the passionate dedication to the quest of beauty as one of the supreme drives of mankind. At the midpoint of his earthly career, Faust, dynamo of insatiable energy, is kindled with the passion to achieve in the here and now of the world of sense a union with the phantom of absolute beauty that resides in the shadowy world of Hades or in the realm of Platonic ideas. By a singular grace of the Powers his dream is vouchsafed fulfillment for one brief moment. The realization of the absolute takes tangible shape in the offspring of their union, the radiant boy Euphorion. He is the incarnation of the poetic spirit. But sired by absolutes, he, in his turn, is bent on the impossible. Bounding aloft from the cliff to try his wings, he plunges to his death, another Icarus, and Helen slips from Faust's embrace to rejoin her child in the Underworld.

Three long acts develop the story. In act I, Faust, coached by Mephisto in a scene of wondrous awe, penetrates into the realm of the "Mothers" and brings back the famous couple. As they are subjected to admiration and criticism by the court, uncontrollable jealousy and passion for her possession make Faust touch the phantom Helen. He is knocked unconscious by an explosion and carried off by Mephisto to be deposited in his old study.

In act II there is first a superbly humorous interlude: disguised in Faust's old mantle, Mephisto has a spirited colloquy with the erstwhile Freshman, now a sophisticated philosopher sporting a bachelor's degree. This scene reactivates our time sense. It places the action of acts I and II, along with the "timeless" moment of act III, at a point several years beyond the close of Part One. Together with act IV, all the second part except for the last act may be supposed to transpire in a single season.

We next follow Mephisto into an adjoining laboratory where Wagner, Faust's former assistant, now a professor with an enormous reputation, has been laboring for months on end to produce an artificial man, a homunculus, by the art of alchemy. Thanks to Mephisto's presence the miracle comes off: a sprightly mannikin in a test tube slips from Wagner's grasp to hover, weightless, in the atmosphere and greet daddy Wagner and cousin Mephisto with merry chatter. Hearing of Faust's plight, the little creature slips through the doorway to gaze on the unconscious form, and his supernatural intuition spells out the sleeper's vision—the divine swan embracing Leda to sire Helen. He knows that if Faust were to awaken in the study the shock would kill him. But the resourcefulness of our mannikin is equal to the emergency. It so happens, he says, that this very night is the classical counterpart of the witches' sabbath. All the creatures of classical myth are now gathering for their annual rendezvous in northeastern Greece. Let Mephisto carry Faust on his magic cloak, and himself will lead the way. Straightway they are off, leaving Wagner to attend to his laboratory. By this ingenious device Faust is transported to Greece. As soon as he sets foot on the sacred soil he awakens. His first words are: Where is she? He is possessed of only one thought, to find her. The three now strike out on separate paths to explore the inexhaustible world of wonders. Following each of them in turn, the reader is put through a most thoroughgoing refresher course in classical mythology. As for Faust, he learns from the sphinxes that the celebrated centaur Chiron is abroad and most likely to be of help in locating Helen. Luckily Faust encounters Chiron and, astride the restlessly trotting monster's back, he ventures to report his quest. The genial centaur, infinitely amused at this mortal man's harebrained whim, nevertheless takes him to the priestess Manto, who guards the approach to the Underworld at the foot of Mount Olympus. She hears Faust's plea sympathetically and promises to lead him down to the great goddess Persephone, who alone can grant it.

In this way it comes about that in act III Helen has actually been released from the Underworld to live again for a timeless moment. After long preliminaries of anxious suspense in which Mephisto, having donned the shape of a monstrous mythical hag, plays a sinister but helpful part, Helen and her retinue of maidens, just returned from Troy, find refuge from the bloody designs of Menelaos in a medieval castle built by Faust on Greek soil. Faust is pictured as the overlord of a victorious host of northern warriors that has established itself on the Peloponnesus. Faust's and Helen's exchange of greetings turns into a duet of mutual homage. Helen's union with Faust symbolizes a fusion of the genius of the Germanic north with that of Greek antiquity. The whole act—a phantasmagoria Goethe called it—is a *tour de force* of the poetic imagination without a parallel in Goethe's work. As anticipated above, the mirage of perfection is shattered by the death of their offspring, Euphorion.

If acts I-III were focused upon the experience of beauty—the aesthetic sphere—as a momentous enrichment of Faust's (and mankind's) expanding development, act IV introduces a new theme to engage man's restless imagination. It is the challenge of the physical environment, the will to understand and control the forces of Nature. It is man's will to power in the face of the inert or hostile elements.

The great turn had been prepared for, when Helen vanished. Faust is borne aloft by the garments Helen has left behind. Soaring with the clouds over mountain and sea, Faust's gaze is arrested by the spectacle of the tides, their ceaseless ebb and flow. It impresses him as a symbol of enormous power wasting itself in futile repetition. There dawns upon him the idea of a task, a project: to curb the sea, to reclaim a vast expanse of shore line by a network of dikes. This is a challenge to appeal to his own indomitable energies that have been idly wasting themselves. This is a job for Mephisto and his minions to execute.

Most of act IV is taken up with the machinery for acquiring the rights to the shore line as a sovereign fief from the Emperor, whom Faust had served. This cannot concern us here. But the Faust we meet again in act V has devoted, we must suppose, half a lifetime to this constantly expanding project. Faust has now become a great lord. His eye roams over a limitless expanse of newly created land, flourishing with human habitations, gardens, and woodland. He has built a palace with a high observation tower, and his fleets gather in a distant harbor from which a canal extends to the palace. To judge by Faust's and Mephisto's words, Faust's realm encompasses the world. We cannot suppress an uneasy feeling that this is more than a slip of rhetorical exaggeration: Has Mephisto's new obsequiousness of manner deluded Faust into a state of megalomania? Treasure is being brought from all parts of the earth, and the work goes on ceaselessly. But there is one feature to mar Faust's pride of absolute rule: on a high dune, landward from the palace, there dwells a very ancient couple with rights antedating his. Their thatched hut and tiny chapel shaded by a clump of hoary linden trees is a thorn in his flesh. They have refused his offer to sell on advantageous terms. Day after day the tinkle of the chapel bell exasperates him. Does it awaken uneasy echoes of the church bells that made him set down the poisoned chalice on that first Easter morning? Be that as it may, the tiny knoll sets limits to his craving for absolute sway. He chafes and upbraids his imagination for finding the knoll denied him pricelessly desirable. To Mephisto, returned from an overseas expedition, he confesses his sense of torment and his sense of humiliation in admitting to it, and he acknowledges that the couple are in their legal rights. But it all boils down to his prodding Mephisto to talk him into an act of benevolent violence. The order for their dispossession results in unforeseen catastrophe: the old couple die of fright as the door is battered down. A guest, who puts up a fight, is murdered, in the scuffle the hut catches fire, and Faust must hear his watchman on the tower report the fire that reduces the hut and the chapel to ashes and leaves charred hollow trunks where the lindens had stood. Faust is seized with remorse. Once again his impatience has got the better of him. Was not impatience his cardinal sin? On the day of the wager and pact, when in his bitterness he had uttered his all-encompassing curse, had he not saved up the curse on Patience as the final line of his tirade? But he persuades himself to take the calamity lightly; in place of the destroyed lindens he will erect a lookout tower ("Luginsland") and from there he will see the neat cottage which his generosity had assigned to the dispossessed couple. And when Mephisto and his three mighty henchmen return to report on their mission, Faust reacts in the manner typical of overlords: he puts the blame for the violence on them and dismisses them with his curse.

Of course, Faust had not intended the consequences of his rash command, but he might have anticipated them if his sense of frustration had not blinded him, and in any case he had committed a deliberate violation of human rights. Such unscrupulousness as to means is typical of persons who are accustomed to the exercise of great power. The bloody deed leaves a stain on Faust's great achievement. To dismiss it as a trifle in view of the immense benefits accruing to mankind from Faust's titanic project would be idle because these benefits were incidental to the exercise of his energy. Faust was no philanthropist. He envisioned the task as a great means to express himself. There was no altruistic motive, for better or worse, to color the project of that great egoist. But, first appearances to the contrary, Faust did not dismiss his responsibility lightly. His brief soliloquy, dwelling on his inveterate impetuosity, shows that his conscience is deeply troubled. And now as he is about to be assailed from another quarter, we see him give evidence of an ethical resilience that more than reconciles us to his faults. "Geboten schnell, zu schnell getan." (Ordered quickly, done too quickly.) Faust's repentance is sincere, but he does not waste his energies in morbid brooding over an act that cannot be undone.

Now comes the visitation of the four weird sisters, spectral apparitions that personify Want, Distress, Debt or Guilt ("Schuld" stands for both), and Anxiety. The first three find their entry to the palace barred. They have no power to molest a rich man. Not even "Schuld" in the sense of guilt; for objective wrongdoing must have an acute sense of wrongdoing as its subjective counterpart, to be troublesome. Anxiety, however, can slip through the keyhole, where other potential disturbances of tranquillity are barred. As the three depart, they hail the approach of Brother Death in the background. Faust has been troubled by the spectral images and their low spoken words which he has half divined rather than understood. But he clearly caught the last word uttered, Death, and knows it is a portent of the fact that his life has run its course. Frail as he is, at the outermost edge of the human life span, his mind, forever active and restless, finds the thought of death repugnant. "I have not yet fought my way to freedom," he protests. His ruminations revolve about the fatal misstep of his youth, his involvement with magic, the dread curse, the vilification of the world and himself, the curse that culminated in the blast against Patience, as he enlisted the services of the Evil One. If he could only undo it, he meditates, and the pathos of the fateful decision is fully upon him. Now (like the sorcerer's apprentice) he finds himself irremediably entangled in a web of apparitions and portents, a prey to forces he cannot control. At this moment his soliloquy becomes a dialogue with the spectral sister of whose entry he has become aware. He tries to dismiss her with an imperious command, but she refuses to budge. He reacts violently, but, about to have recourse to the magic powers with which he has saddled himself, he checks himself with the soft spoken admonition: "Take care, do not speak a magic word."

This line, spoken under his breath, is the significant turning point in Faust's personal drama. Though ever so late, with death at his door, for once he has not yielded to that impatience which was the fatal flaw of his personality. He has taken a first step to reverse the pattern of his responses to life. This is decisive. This is a metaphysical act in terms of Schiller's dictum: "The first step upward, ideally considered, is equivalent to traversing the whole road to the goal."

Now the weird sister announces her identity, and in three long passages of a whining, monotonous, staccato rhythm that suggest the wheedling persistence of a mosquito buzzing about the ear, she assaults the fortress of his will, hoping to reduce him to a bundle of nerves, prey to an anxiety neurosis. Three times he stands up to her assault maintaining the integrity of his personality in passages that rank among the finest in the play. His control never slips. He gives a thumbnail sketch of the course of his life, pronouncing an agnostic credo as to the Beyond, lashing out against the crooning tormentor, writhing under the pain of her relentless hypnotizing drone, but the integrity of his will is proof against her assaults. Let us not imagine for a moment that this is simply a rhetorical confrontation. The danger to Faust is very real. We turn back to the very first night of the *Faust* drama, where Faust, during one of his fluctuations between ecstasy and despair over his having been vouchsafed the vision of the Earth Spirit, lapsed into reflections about the power of "Sorge," Anxiety, to torment man with apprehensions of ills that never come to pass. That, to be sure, was the one passage among all those memorable first night monologues, which seemed least prompted by his personal desperate situation, approaching, rather, in the ring of its tone a mood of general reflection on human life. But two days later, at the time of Mephisto's second call that led to the wager and pact, Faust had exhibited a facet of his temperament that differed from anything we had observed heretofore. Whereas, on the preceding evening, he had replied to the riddling and the tantrums of Mephisto, the travelling scholar, with composure, superior raillery, and the active curiosity of a man in full command of that startlingly novel situation, this time he is completely out of sorts, he is petulant, querulous, whining, unnerved, pouring out lamentations about the emptiness of his days and the haunting, affrighting dreams of his nights, and bridling at Mephisto's jibes. The Faust of that mood, when at last provoked into uttering the all-embracing curse, showed all the symptoms of an anxiety neurosis. This lassitude, the show of a personality quite unstrung, was very different in kind from the bold superhuman gesture with which he had hailed the "Erdgeist," the dark, tense despair of his brooding after having been rejected, and of the euphoric serenity with which he had grasped the poisoned chalice. We see then that the danger of his succumbing to a neurosis that would have left him at loose ends was very real. It is in these terms that we must evaluate Faust's triumph over the specter of Anxiety on the last night of his life.

Anxiety is routed. Unable to enter the inner fortress of Faust's personality, she departs from the palace, but in doing so she exhibits her demonic power: she breathes upon him and casts a spell, making Faust go blind. "The run of men are blind all their lives," she comments; "now, Faust, it is your turn to become so at the end."

As a rule, commentators have tried to read a deep symbolism into the spell that reduces Faust to blindness, such as: Having been a man of clear-eyed determination all his life, he falls a prey to delusion in the end; he loses his faculty to appraise mankind realistically and surrenders to a utopian optimism. I think the whole attempt to read a symbolical meaning into Faust's blindness is a mistake. Rather, a mythical interpretation is in order. All is then both simple and humanly moving. Faust has matched his energies against an assailant from the non-human, infernal regions. Astonishingly enough, he has come off the victor. But is it customary, we ask, for a mortal to emerge from so unequal a contest unscathed? No, indeed, this would run counter to all tradition. He bears the mark of it on him for the rest of his life. The first analogical example that comes to mind is the biblical story of Jacob wrestling with the angel. Jacob triumphs, but his halting walk ever after serves as a reminder that the angel had touched his hip. Like everything biblical, the story of Jacob was so familiar to Goethe that he may have counted on the awareness of the analogy to come to mind automatically. We find something similar, in fact, in the story of the Fall where it is predicted that the seed of woman shall bruise the head of the serpent but suffer its sting in his heel. But we might also recall the unearthly expression indelibly stamped on the face of the Norse saga hero Grettir, after his wrestling match with the ghost Glam in the gravemound. We might recall the case of the great Pope Gregory whom medieval legend credits with having successfully importuned the saints and the Trinity to transplant Emperor Trajan, paragon of justice, but a pagan, from Hell to Heaven; but as a reminder that he should not be emboldened to try an idea of such lunatic rashness a second time, Gregory was smitten with a painful disease, the marks of which he bore for the rest of his life. In the case of Faust a peculiar pathos attaches to his being stricken with blindness as a compensatory penalty of his victory over the Demon: it happens to him at night, in the last hour of his life, and in the small span of time left him he possibly never registers any awareness of what has happened to him. The night closing in about him simply acts as a stimulus to heighten his fervor for pushing the task to which his life is dedicated.

We summarize: On this last night of his life, Faust has again been carried away by an excess of impatience to the perpetration of a highhanded act of injustice that resulted in destruction and murder. He has subsequently repented of this abuse of his power. Then, when assailed by the spectral demon of Anxiety, he had, in

the nick of time, remembered to check his impatience. The hypnotic crooning had prompted him to pass his life in review and, in
full acknowledgment of early decisions irretrievably made, he had
deeply repented of his cardinal sin of impatience that led to his all-
embracing curse and his involvement with the powers of darkness.
In this he had successfully countered the Demon's assault, but the
victory that left his personality whole has left its mark on his body.
The curtain now rises on the scene of Faust's death.

Faust's is a natural death, we emphasize, a death long overdue.
Faust has already felt the summons himself, and Mephisto, aware
of the impending end, has set his minions to work digging a grave.
Faust, afire with his task, aware that his physical energies are ebb-
ing, urges the expansion of his work force. The clanking of the
spades lifting the sods for his grave fires him to another vision of his
successful taming of the sea. Mephisto's sarcastic comment on the
upshot of the project, unheard by Faust, is ambiguous. Is he right
in his gleeful prophecy that the elements, in league with the demons,
will ultimately take over and reduce the whole expenditure of man's
energies to nothing—either because magic was enlisted to engineer
the project, or because in the long run no work of man can stand
up against the inexorable superior power of the elements? Or is he
again, as the spirit that forever negates, indulging that wish for
annihilation that expressed itself in a tantrum during his first dialogue with Faust? It does not matter. These malicious glosses of
Mephisto are confined to the material level. They have no bearing
on the spiritual values of the undaunted dying visionary.

During the few moments of life left him Faust continues to
grow. A moment ago we saw him reject—in principle—his lifetime association with magic and the infernal powers as a mistaken
approach. Now a breakthrough of another kind occurs. Whereas
the earlier one concerned his relation to Nature and the mystery of
the universe, this one concerns his relation to mankind. Faust's
social sense had not been developed. Social relations have played a
small part in his experience. Except for Gretchen, whom he both
worshiped and abandoned, he has never been close to any human
being. He has never had a friend or felt the need of one—a strange
lack indeed for a man who had programmatically set out to encompass the whole range of human experience in his person. In the
Emperor's court he remained aloof from the dignitaries. Since the

great idea of confining the sea dawned upon him, he has treated men only as means to his ends. His will had been supreme. They had only supplied the hands to carry out his plan. "Dass sich das grösste Werk vollende, genügt *ein* Geist für tausend Hände." (For the greatest work to be accomplished, one mastermind suffices for a thousand hands.) He had been a great benefactor for mankind, but all the benefactions accrued as an incidental to his sense of self-realization. It is in this regard that Faust's final utterance achieves a new breakthrough: for the first time he no longer thinks of man in terms of rule and obedience. He has a vision of a self-contained human society of free men, animated by the balanced operation of the two basic principles of competition and cooperation—competition as the drive directed against the nonhuman element, cooperation in the effective exercise of that drive in a society actuated by a common zeal. This is an idyllic vision, to be sure, an extreme simplification. The forces operating in human society will never range themselves to conform to so neat a design of polarity—certainly not in a democracy as we know it, and even though Goethe's eye dwelt with fascination on the new order taking shape in America. To a new direction, rather than to a goal achieved, Faust sets his sights. This is for him, at the last moment of his life, the embodiment of wisdom, the spirit that gives the stamp of value to collective human activity. Having outlined this creed in a phrasing which echoes the central formulation of the wager scene, though translated from statement to contingent hypothesis, Faust falls dead.

In breathing his last, Faust has uttered the key phrase of the wager that conditioned his pact with Mephisto. In the thousands of lines intervening, that situation has never been alluded to. Does its recurrence now stir an echo in Mephisto's ear? If so, he betrays no sign of it, as he shakes his head bemused by the unaccountable taste of this mortal. He admits, moreover, in plain words: Me he withstood so valiantly, now Time masters him at last. Then after further multiple echoes of the pact's phrasing, he concludes: "Es ist vollbracht," it is accomplished. The German "vollbracht" is a parodistic echo of Christ's last word on the Cross. Does the word here signify a burst of exultation or a sigh of relief? Be that as it may, the spectral grave-diggers cut in with a correction: "Es ist vorbei." Let time be past, over, done for me, were the words with which Faust concluded the rhetorically ringing lines of his wager.

This correction touches off a tantrum of nihilistic rage in Mephisto in which he rings the changes on that senseless word "vorbei."

Having recovered himself, he stakes his confidence on Faust's signature. He orders the hellish host that has gathered to keep a sharp lookout for the precious soul and snatch it at the moment it leaves the body. There follows a scene of magnificently farcical humor. Hosts of angels are circling above the grave; they sing and scatter roses that, falling on the devils, pain them with more than hellish fire. They take flight. Worse still, Mephisto's lascivious appetite is beguiled by the pleasing forms of the boy angels, and, his attention distracted, the soul is snatched and borne aloft.

The postlude that ends the drama with magnificent recourse to Catholic imagery lets us glimpse various levels of Purgatory— Purgatory, not as a place of torment, but as the unending process of purgation and purification on the part of individual souls and groups dedicated to the deepening contemplation of the divine mysteries. We hear the fervent chants of various fathers of the Church, bearing exalted names. We hear the voices of the very young, who come into mortal life only to leave it again at once. We hear a chorus of penitent women adoring the Blessed Virgin, and in their number there is one that bears the features of Gretchen. Her voice thrills with gratitude to the divine Mother for having heard her intercession for her wayward lover. All of this scene is designed to be executed after the manner of a richly orchestrated oratorio.

Faust's salvation is a highly unorthodox affair. Let the Lord make a defense of his tolerance to the theologians. Arrogantly erect to the last, no humble penitent sinner suing for mercy, Faust is nevertheless rated a sound and perfectible substance by the divine arbiter. On his credit side is his ceaseless striving to expand his personality, despite his constant lapse into error. Perhaps the realization of the part played by Gretchen in his redemption will temper his nature with a little of that sweet humility which is both a gift of divine grace and a visible sign of its bestowal.

PETER SCHLEMIHL

Peter Schlemihl, an immortal classic that charmed the reading public of Europe and America on its first appearance a century and a half ago, is the story of a man who got involved with the devil by selling him his shadow. That so great a poet as Hugo von Hofmannsthal nevertheless chose to omit it from his collection, *Deutsche Erzähler*, is due, I believe, not to any deficiencies on Chamisso's part, but rather to Hofmannsthal's own deep involvement with the motif of the shadow and its symbolism along totally divergent lines as developed in his *Die Frau ohne Schatten*, the text of Richard Strauss's opera, and later elaborated in a story bearing the same title. *Peter Schlemihl* should have been written by an American, because it is an illustration of the peculiarly American techniques of salesmanship as taught in the best manuals of the craft. *Peter Schlemihl* is a parable on the central Christian theme summed up in the words of Jesus: "For what shall it profit a man, if he shall gain the whole world, and lose his own soul" (Mark 8:36). *Peter Schlemihl* is a serious, realistic story built on fantastic premises; it is a two-act drama full of acute emotional tension and shot through with iridescent flashes of wit, humor, satire, and paradox. *Peter Schlemihl* is the psychological case study of an insecure individual beset by anxieties and phobias that shape up to a full-fledged psychoneurosis. He is cured in the end without benefit of the psychoanalyst's couch; he continues to bear the scars of his harrowing experience, but he has achieved an adjustment to conditions that guarantees him a life of satisfying concentrated activity and relative happiness. Making its appeal on so many counts, the story of Peter Schlemihl offers high entertainment to readers of the most various interests.

Peter's story takes the form of a personal confession addressed to his most intimate friend, Adelbert von Chamisso, the author. It is released to the public through the indiscretion of two of Chamisso's literary friends. The exchange of letters that heads the story in lieu of a preface must not be skipped by the discerning reader:

Reprinted from *Wert und Wort: Festschrift für Elsa M. Fleissner*, ed. Marion Sonnenfeld (Aurora, N.Y., 1965), pp. 32-44, by permission of Louis J. Long, president, Wells College.

they are an integral part of the intricate web of relationships that constitute the many-faceted charm of the story.

Peter Schlemihl is, on the face of it, a variant of the theme that received its most famous treatment in Goethe's *Faust*, the first part of which had appeared when Chamisso wrote his story. Among other, later treatments of the theme, Jeremias Gotthelf's *Die schwarze Spinne* (1842) deserves special mention. In all three cases the basic situation is the same: an individual or, as in Gotthelf's story, a community, gets involved with the devil, and in all three instances the devil is ultimately foiled in line with the tradition of folklore that shows the devil, for all his wiles, to be no match for the powers of good. But Chamisso's originality in the handling of the theme shows up at a glance. In Goethe's *Faust*, an individual of superman aspirations, contemptuous of the limits set to human existence, despairing of penetrating the ultimate mystery of being by ordinary means, enters open-eyed into a conditional pact and wager with the devil, with his soul as the stake. Faust's devil is a cavalier who hides his essentially evil design under an entertaining and often attractive mask of impish roguery. In Gotthelf's story of *The Black Spider* the community of peasants, tortured by impossible exactions of their overlords, is pressured into agreeing to the devil's terms, and he can afford to dispense with any attempt to conceal his identity. In *Peter Schlemihl*, on the other hand, the devil sets about ensnaring the soul of a simple, God-fearing man who would shrink in horror if overtly approached by the Evil One. He must accordingly go about the business of ensnaring Peter with the utmost circumspection. To this end, having first dazzled the unsuspecting Peter by a series of magical tricks, he approaches Peter as the deferential salesman bent first of all on putting his prospect at his ease. Though unable withal to overcome Peter's instinctive aversion to his sinuous, slimy, indefinable personality, he tempts him with the equivalent of an offer of something for nothing—a very large something indeed, an inexhaustible purse. The nothing he wants in exchange is the shadow that he sees Peter casting "with a certain disdainful nonchalance."

What is this shadow, what does it stand for? Readers asked this question of Chamisso when the story appeared, and interpreters have labored ever since to equate it with something positive and substantial. The conjecture most often voiced is that Chamisso equated the loss of Peter's shadow with his own loss of his homeland. Chamisso's family were refugees who fled from France in the wake of the Revolution. But Chamisso never endorsed this interpretation. Any attempt to see the shadow in terms of being rooted in a specific milieu must fail. It does not fit Peter's case. Peter's swap is an act of impulsive choice, and the gradual chain of involvement which Peter experiences could be deduced only from such a premise. The value of the shadow is given as a mere nothing according to all standards of human usefulness. A closer parallel might be found in Goethe's *Werther*. Finding himself inadvertently an uninvited guest at a social gathering of aristocrats, Werther suffers a most humiliating rebuff. He is taken aside by a well-wisher and informed that his presence is embarrassing to some of the highborn ladies—all this because, though attached to the Count's retinue and enjoying his personal benevolence, he has no "von" to his name, no magical three-letter word that serves as a card of admission to such company. But even such identification of the shadow with a specific social status is no equivalent for Peter's complete ostracism from all human society.

To read Peter's story in terms of an allegory is to take a false lead. We must take the shadow "for what it is worth." It is worth nothing in practical terms, but its absence makes Peter a marked man. In this way the missing shadow can serve as a symbol for anything that can produce such an effect on a man. The shadow in question, however, is not just an ordinary shadow. Since the devil has a hand in the business, it assumes magical properties. It can be manipulated, rolled up and unfolded for display like a substantial physical object. A second characteristic of equal importance is the fact that when Peter shows himself in the open, its absence is noticed by everybody at once. Such attention to an attribute of totally negligible value runs counter to all observable habits of human behavior.

These, then, are the fantastic premises on which Peter's story is built. By a free—if ill-considered—choice he has swapped his shadow for a very valuable consideration. By this choice he has lost his freedom of movement, his spontaneity. He can no longer be his natural self in the open. So far as he ventures to live among men, his whole personality will be geared to furtiveness and deception.

This basic situation, derived from fantastic premises, is the starting point for a development that unfolds with close adherence to realism and psychological plausibility. These same words would aptly describe Kafka's techniques in some of his most notable successes. *Peter Schlemihl* is in this respect a forerunner of *The Metamorphosis*.

Peter's story unfolds as a two-act drama. It is a contest of wills, a tug of war. The devil is the aggressor and Peter is on the defensive. For a long time Peter is unaware of the aggressor's long-range design. The supersalesman plots his course with wily calculation and infinite patience. A whole year elapses before he shows his hand. The tug of war runs its course in two distinct campaigns. The aggressor's initial strategy is, after exhaustive preparations, to close in on his unsuspecting victim with a double-pronged frontal attack calculated to achieve a total breakthrough. The plan, apparently foolproof, engineered with consummate ingenuity and executed without a flaw, nevertheless fails. A chance event, a circumstance beyond the range of foresight and calculation, at the last moment turns victory into rout. With Mephisto our salesman could vent his chagrin in the exclamation "Ein grosser Aufwand schmählich ist vertan!" [A lavish effort has been disgracefully wasted!] But his tenacity is not yet ready to give up the game as lost. In a second round he follows a strategy keyed to the new situation. He lays siege to the fortress, confident that a campaign of attrition will force its ultimate surrender. If this plan also fails, only an imperceptive reader will attribute the outcome to bungling. Such an imputation should bring a blush to the master salesman's cheek.

But in order to follow the moves deployed we must take a good look at Peter and follow it up by a second closer look.

While omitting any specific data on Peter's background, his story acquaints us very quickly with his circumstances and his personality. In the course of the first few pages we gather that Peter is a young man of good moral character, breeding, and education. He is very poor, but his dress and manner attempt to put on a brave show of respectability.[1] Bearing a letter of recommendation to Thomas John, a millionaire, he is enormously impressed by the

---

[1] "His newly turned coat." Thrifty Germans of the old school still make it a practice to have the tailor turn their worn woollens inside out. There may be nothing but the reversed position of buttons and buttonholes to indicate that the garment has been rebuilt.

display of wealth and aware of the gulf in social status it interposes between himself and those who enjoy it. For characterizing Peter's disposition, the language of modern psychology offers the handiest terms. Peter has an acute sense of inferiority. We may call it a complex because it shows up as insecurity in his social behavior. He impulsively toadies to his prospective patron by echoing his dictum that anyone not worth a million must be accounted a rogue. In stealing away from the garden party where he is out of place, Peter is apprehensive of being taken to task for walking across the grass. He overreacts to the uncanny stranger's compliments. In the course of this interview he fluctuates between a desire to shrink and hide from the eerie magician and an impulsive burst of condescension toward a man who apparently has lost his wits. He ends up with an equally impulsive lunge at the proffered bait. Without question, Peter suffers from ego-deficiency. Having no defined social status of his own, he overcompensates in his responses. We see this so well later, when Peter's image of himself is determined by the evil glances shot at him. Inner-directed by his moral education, he nevertheless succumbs to the pressure of the social environment to the point of lapsing into a state of hopelessly other-directed bewilderment. Eventually, the pressure of tacit social disapproval and the anguish over the outcome of his passion combine to make Peter fall prey to a full-fledged guilt psychoneurosis. This is what the salesman had counted on and waited for in order to apply the squeeze and close the pincers of his attack. But this is anticipating.

Now for that second closer look at Peter of which we spoke above. We have been seeing him as the artless simpleton entrapped by the wiles of a master salesman into a disastrous bargain. That is the surface version of Peter's story. But Peter's strange autobiography is a personal confession, addressed to his friend Adelbert von Chamisso, the author, and this friend is none other than Peter's double. As shown by the letters that introduce the story in lieu of a preface, Chamisso is playing a game—a game that abounds in wit, humor, hilarious fun, satire, irony, parody, and paradox. Chamisso, at the time of the writing, is a man of settled pursuits, a student of plant and animal science, chiefly concerned with the collecting and classifying of plants, but through Peter's mouth, at the close of the story, he also confesses to the more ambitious hope of contributing to the establishment of a "natural system"—not genetically, it is to be presumed, forty years before Darwin, but by ranging all the phenomena under observation in graduated series of typological relationships. In the story of *Peter Schlemihl* Chamisso delights in portraying his personality at a more youthful, immature stage of its development a decade earlier. He portrays his alter ego as involved in the turmoil of unattainable wishes and plunged into the vortex of a consuming passion that threatens his sanity and his integrity. Chamisso introduces Peter as his unmistakable double in looks and features, idiosyncrasy of costume, habits and disposition, including the gaucherie and lack of alertness that made him the butt of his friends' good-natured teasing.

The mask is fully transparent even to the present-day reader, who may never have heard of Hitzig, the biographer of Hoffmann, and is likely to associate Fouqué's name only with his immortal story of the mermaid Undine. One of its delightful devices is that Peter makes his confession with a straight face, with deep emotion and—tongue-in-cheek. The twinkle of his eye can be caught in any phase of his recital—in the puns and word plays, the literary allusions, the profound reflections, the dripping sentimentality of style in the recital of the love story, and in his half-hearted attempts to explain and excuse his unchivalrous conduct. A startling instance revealing Peter's double personality is his matter-of-fact account of that extraordinary dream of seeing Chamisso seated in his study among his plant specimens and skeletons, flanked by the tomes of the great authorities Haller, Linné, and Humboldt, but—dead. The heart of this Chamisso is stilled. It has forsworn the dance of devastating passion that will be the high point of Peter's confession. The mask is lifted to the limit at an early point of the story when Peter, appearing shadowless in public for the first time, finds himself "reviewed" and pelted with horse apples by the whole gang of "literary" juveniles. The wag in Peter is at his best in his sundry explanations of how he lost his shadow—the shadow that froze to the ground in the mythical cold of the Russian winter; the shadow sent out for repair because of damage suffered from the step of a heavy-footed lout; the shadow that faded out (and has not yet come back) along with the loss of hair and nails in the wake of a disease. This is in the best tradition of the great Baron Münchhausen. Contrast these admittedly ludicrous inventions of a desperate demented man with Peter's straight-faced account of the objects that successively came out of the stranger's pocket—tele-scope, rug, tent, plus three saddled riding horses. He concludes with guileless candor: "My dear Chamisso, you would not believe these things had I not seen them myself."

A fantastic story built on this premise, the identity of the nar-rator with the recipient of his confession, their thin disguise pene-trated at every moment by the flashing of impish lights—such a story, almost needless to say, calls for a double act of participation by the reader. The tense emotional drama will hold him in its grip. At the same time the witty double-play will afford no end of intel-lectual amusement. Like a light melody embroidering its graceful loops around a somber theme, the two attitudes will not interfere with or neutralize each other. They will rather afford that com-plex entertainment felt by the Romantic generation of German writers to be the essence of great literature.

With these preliminaries disposed of, we can turn our attention to the plot, the unfolding of the master salesman's grand strategy.

Knowing that Peter will repent of his bargain upon realizing that it brands him as a marked man, the cunning salesman disappears, leaving word that he will return for another business talk in "a year and a day." The phrase "über Jahr und Tag," originally a well-de-fined term of legal parlance, is a very vague measure of time in ordinary usage. That Peter takes the phrase literally and misses by one the count of the days elapsed is part of the same hypnotic spell to which he had succumbed in watching the stranger's sleight-of-hand manipulation of his inexhaustible pocket. This explanation is, of course, left to the reader's conjecture because Peter reports his error without suspecting that he has been tricked. We put it down as part of the devil's practice to deceive by telling the truth. What the devil counts on in his game is the force of habit. Within a year Peter will find it impossible to be without his wealth. At the same time the constant threat of exposure, the ever-present need to be on his guard, will undermine his personality, weak to begin with, and soften him up for the deal to be proposed. Peter's career as a man of wealth, it is true, got off to an auspicious start. But it could be foreseen that his short-lived flirtation with Fanny, during which he displayed a pose of self-confidence and ready wit quite alien to his bashful and impulsive nature, would end in disaster and precipitous flight. Thus, in his new place of residence, Peter finds himself in a tragi-comical predicament, passively forced to assume the role of the highborn man of mystery, Graf Peter, wrapped in an aura of gloom, a fraud against his will. That he now falls in love in earnest with a simple innocent girl and pins all his hopes on finding her a sympathetic partner of his loneliness might also have been predicted. That it did occur, enormously enhanced the tempter's prospects of success. If the force of habit is great, the motive force of a passionate love is without limit.

The devil plays his cards well. He engineered Rascal's betrayal of his master and the forester's three-day ultimatum to coincide with the time of his expected return. He lets the climactic day pass without showing himself, while Peter wears himself out with anxious waiting. The next day, when anxiety, anguish, despair, and desolation have driven Peter to roaming aimlessly on a deserted heath, the devil finds that the time is ripe at last for the frontal attack. Accosting Peter familiarly, he offers to extricate him from his predicament by the return of his shadow in exchange for the signature involving his soul. Peter demurs, not unexpectedly perhaps, but this is only the opening phase of a complicated battle of movement. Now the tempter comes forward with his offer to lead him unseen under the screen of his *Tarnkappe* to the forester's lodge and let him gaze his fill on the face of his beloved Mina. Again Peter declines, because he senses the trap, and he remains adamant in his refusal to commit his soul. But the tempter still has a whole bag of tricks up his sleeve. He produces Peter's shadow and carefully adjusting it to his own person, struts up and down with the shadow following him. This maneuver, while exposing Peter to sadistic torture, is dictated by a more practical design: Bendel approaches, having tracked his master like a faithful dog, but the tempter's business is with Peter alone, and Bendel must be removed from the scene. He accomplishes this with ingenious cunning. Ignoring Bendel's threats and impervious to the hail of blows from Bendel's stout blackthorn, he arches his shoulders and stalks away with measured step, continuing in this way until both he and Bendel have disappeared from Peter's sight.

Alone again, Peter spends the day and the night on the heath in aimless despair. The next day, the day that will irrevocably decide Mina's fate, sees the tempter execute his supreme maneuver. Of a sudden, startled by a sound, Peter sees an apparently masterless human shadow walking by. Instantly he makes a dash to capture it in the quixotic hope that it will cling to his person. But the shadow takes flight, and Peter exhausts his last energies in hot pursuit. As it makes for a wooded area, where it would be lost to sight, Peter redoubles his efforts. He gains on the shadow. It suddenly wheels about, and Peter collides with a solid body. The full force of the impact throws Peter to the ground, his arms locked around a man under him and visible. The denouement of this encounter represents the capital *tour de force* of Chamisso's wit. With lightning speed our guileless *ingénu* hero has grasped a desperately intricate chain of reasoning. "Now the situation resolved itself for me in the most natural way in the world." Obviously the stranger, carrying the invisible bird's nest that makes its bearer invisible but not his shadow (a requisite of folklore featured in the title of one of Grimmelshausen's novels), had dropped it under the force of the impact, thereby becoming visible. The nest must betray its location by a diminutive shadow. A glance at the ground, a quick grab, and Peter held in his hand the priceless nest that made him totally invisible since he had no shadow to begin with. The tempter had calculated only too well. Without wasting a thought on the identity of the stranger whose property he had unlawfully appropriated, Peter felt himself irresistibly drawn to the scene of his passion, now that he could do so without having to endure the odious company of the tempter. But events prove that he had walked into a trap. There is the stranger seated at his side, gloating over his misery, both of them screened by a magic net. And this time Peter would have infallibly succumbed to the combined pressure of love, heart-rending pity, a sense of honor and nervous exhaustion, had not "an event intervened in place of a deed," when the blood-stained pen was thrust into his hand to sign: Peter fell into a deep swoon from which he awoke only after Mina had been lost to him forever. In his confession Peter speaks of this event in sober and apologetic terms. To us it is clear nonetheless that he has been saved by the intervention of divine grace. The devil's frontal attack, launched with incredible cunning and patience to win the soul of a man who is weak but essentially good, has failed. With this, the curtain rings down on act one of the drama.

Act two of the drama can be passed in quick review. We can be certain to begin with that it can bring nothing to match the climactic tension of the first act. And as we watch the continuation of the contest, we are not likely to place our bets on the devil as the winner. That the devil does not give up after having suffered so stunning a defeat does credit to his tenacity. He still has a powerful hold on Peter by virtue of the inexhaustible purse. But after the loss of Mina he can no longer hope to further his ends by an appeal to Peter's noblest impulses. That he must alter his tactics to conform to a basically changed situation is evident. Having failed in his great frontal strategic thrust, he resorts to a strategy of attrition. Habituation, the motive on which he based his calculation from the outset, may yet bring his victim to terms, he reasons. He offers Peter the use of his shadow on a loan basis coupled with his own personal services, hoping thereby gradually to wear down that instinctive aversion to his slimy person which kept Peter from signing. The temptation to enjoy both the purse and the shadow exercises an enormous lure. Once more, in the course of their journeyings, our moral friend succumbs to the weakness of the flesh. He tries to abscond with the loaned shadow, but the ruse fails. He is put to shame by the observation of the complaisant servant that, while not making any profession of such high moral standards as Peter, he on his own part has simply followed the rules of decent behavior without resorting to violence or trickery.

There comes the moment of the second climax. Having had to listen to his companion's glib philosophical sales talk day after day, Peter is ready at last to face a showdown. Did the salesman have a signature from Mr. Thomas John, he asks. Oh, in the case of so good a friend that formality was altogether superfluous, he replies. What has become of him? Peter continues. By God, I want to know. At this, the devil reluctantly reaches into his pocket and draws forth the livid corpse of Thomas John whose lips utter the words: "Justo judicio dei judicatus sum; justo judicio dei condemnatus sum."

This denouement comes as a complete surprise. How is it possible that the devil, having played a superbly astute and infinitely tenacious game, should suddenly throw down his hand and call it quits? Is it possible that he writes off the pursuit of this particular soul as a bad investment, an investment of time and energy out of proportion to any possible yield? Or is he just a stupid devil after all who finds his tenacity outmatched by Peter's resistance? But does not this conclusion nullify the carefully built-up image of the devil as an aggressor who never lets go? Is it possible on the other hand, that the author, having run out of ideas, spoils the end of the story by a lame conclusion? Time and again I have known students to read this critical episode without raising an eyebrow. Does the foreign language operate as a barrier? I am persuaded that some of them, at least, read their comics with more discernment. However, even an interpreter like Benno von Wiese (*Die deutsche Novelle*, Düsseldorf, 1956) glosses over the scene without remarking on the tempter's incredible psychological inconsistency.

They have all missed the point, and yet the point is incredibly simple. Every child who has read the *Arabian Nights* knows that if you find yourself being carried aloft through space by a djinn and if in this plight you utter the words, "There is no power and no protection except in Allah the Sublime," the story will continue: "At these words a fiery dart fell from heaven and burned the djinn to ashes." It is an axiom of the game that if the devil is commanded something in the name of God, the infernal one must comply. Peter in his emotional outburst had inadvertently used the name of God. With that, the devil's game was up. This denouement was subtly prepared for at an earlier point of the story. When the devil first proffered the swap of Peter's shadow for his signature, Peter had replied: "If our bargain can be rescinded, well and good, in God's name." At this the tempter's brow had darkened.

Once more, divine grace, operating through the mechanics of a fortuitous outburst, has come to the aid of a good man. But in order to clinch the victory, Peter now has to rise to the great act of renunciation. There is no flinching from the decision. Casting the ill-gotten purse into the abyss, Peter now solemnly adjures the tempter in the name of the living God, to betake himself hence and show his face no more.

This is the end of the dramatic contest. The devil's frontal attack failed at the moment he thought victory in his grasp; his campaign of attrition has likewise come to naught. Both times divine intervention had mercy on the good man's frailty and saved his soul. But one cannot do business with the devil and expect to get off scot-free. Peter's shadow is lost to him forever. As the German phrase goes: "Er hat Haare gelassen." [He suffered the consequences.]

The story proper ends here. The appended sequel, centered on the divine gift of the Seven League Boots, an *Ersatz* (compensation) for the forfeited contact with human society, is a story of pure adventure. It is not lacking in exciting and hazardous incidents, but it is without a trace of the anguishing dramatic tension of the first story. It has the same fanciful touch, it is told with the same delightful attention to realistic detail in a miraculous setting, the same superb *Anschaulichkeit*, but it requires no analysis. The sequel is not a comedown in any sense, and the unity of personality is felicitously sustained. Here, incidentally, we have a rare instance, where a knowledge of the author's biography contributes to the inherent charm of the story. Peter's acquisition of the Seven League Boots projects a wish fulfillment on the part of his double. It turned out to be a prophetic anticipation of what was to happen. A few years after the writing of *Peter Schlemihl*, Chamisso participated in a great voyage of exploration as the expedition's official botanist. It took him to the polar regions, the South Seas, and the Andes. And like Peter, who wept at finding himself barred from exploring the reaches of the continent beyond the Indonesian archipelago, Chamisso too was denied setting foot on Australian soil. Like Peter, he had to learn that every human undertaking is doomed to fall short of fulfillment.

At the risk of appearing old-fashioned, we cannot take leave of our story without scrutinizing its moral. Peter himself, in his tongue-in-cheek manner, concludes with a moral tailored to his own state of social isolation. *Peter Schlemihl* is, among other things, a great satire on salesmanship and on business ethics generally. The warning "caveat emptor," let the buyer be on his guard, is sounded by implication all through the story. There are broad satirical references to the technique of getting rich quick by the practice of declaring bankruptcy. The whole story can be read as a negative illustration of the idealistic code of ethics formulated by Germany's greatest philosopher. Immanuel Kant found a variety of ways to word the ethical imperative. It is the second phrasing of the principle that most aptly applies to the circumstances of our story. In this phrasing the maxim reads as follows: "Always act in such a way as to treat your fellowman as an end in himself, never as a means only." No ethical precept has ever been devised that bears so directly on business ethics. It is the ABC of the businessman that he is performing a service, that he is enriching the lives of his customers by supplying existing wants and creating new ones. The compelling motive behind all this fine talk is invariably to make money. Even the businessman who serves genuine needs is bound to think of his transactions primarily in terms of profit. He is bound to think of his prospective customers primarily as means. If he also thinks of them as ends in themselves, that is a luxury that he can generously afford only on the basis of a sound balance sheet. We may generalize: The peaceful coexistence of the world of business enterprise and the realm of absolute ethics poses an antinomy that defies solution. Social life is a phenomenon with a built-in paradox.

The Kantian maxim, however, applies to the buyer as well as to the seller. It is no less unethical on the part of the purchaser to strike a profitable bargain by taking advantage of the seller's ignorance of the value of his offerings. Peter, surely, could not have swapped his shadow for the inexhaustible purse without feeling that he was taking unfair advantage of the eager salesman. Without question, it was this thought that implanted the germ of a sense of guilt in Peter's conscience that later blossomed into a full-fledged psychoneurosis of criminal involvement. (By contrast, an example of a rigorous—if quixotic—sense of rectitude comes to mind from Adalbert Stifter's famous novel *Der Nachsommer*. Here the white-haired Baron von Risach, the incarnation of mellow humane wisdom, tells his young protégé how he acquired the noble antique marble statue that graces the landing of the staircase in his "Rosenhaus." Seeing the statue in an Italian village, unvalued and exposed to the weather, he bought it from its owner under the impression that it was a plaster copy. But in the process of having it set up in his Austrian estate, its weight led to the discovery that it was a marble original, and the removal of the encrusted layers of paint and dirt confirmed the Baron's realization that he had inadvertently acquired a rare treasure. He forthwith proceeded to ascertain its true value and to recompense the unsuspecting owner with an adequate sum. Without this, he could not have enjoyed its possession with a clear conscience. This incident goes to show how, among the landed gentry of Europe, a stigma continued to attach to the mercantile profession long after the industrial revolution had set on its course.)

Perhaps the most ingenious feature of our whimsical story is the two systems of value presented. They may be ranged in a single mathematical series as (1) the shadow, (2) gold, (3) the immortal soul. In this series, the shadow appears as the equivalent of zero value, the inexhaustible purse is a finite value, and the immortal soul, which we can render as personal integrity, is of infinite value. In discussing this graded series of values, the devil deftly turns the three on the central axis to an angle of 180 degrees. The purse, the finite value, is left unchanged in its central position while the other two values are reversed. The shadow takes on the value of infinity, while the immortal soul, personal integrity, takes its place at the zero end of the scale. We remember how the glib salesman refers to the soul as this unknown quantity, this "X." A neater reversal of the values of the world and those of the spirit cannot be imagined. Consider the squeeze that the devil applies to Peter in trying to make him rescue Mina from Rascal's clutches. He appeals to Peter's warmest, noblest human impulses in order to induce him to agree to the absolute renunciation of his personal integrity in order to achieve a limited good. The motif of the sacrifice of self is posed here in its most paradoxical form. Peter's logic, of course, is too untrained to penetrate the maze of this dilemma. Speaking tongue-in-cheek as the simple man of feeling, he leaves the logic to us.

Chamisso returned to the problem of values in a delightful preface written for a new French edition of *Peter Schlemihl* in 1837. Having been pressed by curious readers, he tells us, to explain the meaning of the shadow, he gravely proceeds to quote section and paragraph from a French treatise on mathematical physics, to give a scientific definition of a shadow. Reducing the learned verbiage of the long quotation to simplest terms, we learn that a shadow, properly speaking, is a three dimensional object of solid geometry. The shape and size of this solid are determined, first, by the shape and size of the source of illumination and those of the opaque body that blocks the transmission of light and, secondly, by the distance that separates them. What we ordinarily refer to as a shadow is in reality only any one of an infinite number of possible cross sections of that solid, the real shadow. Therefore, Chamisso concludes his explanation, "Songez au solide," go for what is solid!

We would end here if a recent interpreter had not taken issue with Thomas Mann's delightful essay on Chamisso and doubted the ironic ring of this admonition. So we may be pardoned for spelling it out. Already in Imperial Rome the standard gold coin of the realm was known as the "solidus," the solid. Throughout the western world the term "solid" is still used to differentiate a well-founded business establishment from a fly-by-night venture. The rating of a business as solid comprises its evaluation in terms of plant, cash, other material assets and "good will"—the foundations of credit, the equivalent of the inexhaustible purse. Thus our tongue-in-cheek author has come full circle to fix the reader's eye upon the hypnotic dazzle of gold.

GERHART HAUPTMANN'S
RANGE AS DRAMATIST

IT IS EASIER, if more time-consuming, to write a book about a stimulating author than to say something worth while about him in a lecture. You do not wish me to take you on a Cook's Tour of Gerhart Hauptmann's vast production. It would be unspeakably tedious to enumerate each of his forty-odd dramas and his almost equally numerous novels, stories, verse epics, and other works and to affix to each some characteristic label. What do most of you know about Hauptmann? You all know of him as the author of a famous play about the Silesian weavers. A few of you who are old enough will recall his winning of the Nobel Prize for literature in 1912. And some of you know that he died a very old man in May 1946, having lived just long enough to have witnessed the death of his native Silesia, the sociological extinction of a branch of the German people that had developed its characteristic physiognomy over many centuries in conjunction with the specific landscape of its habitat. Hauptmann died when all but the last of its population had been swept as fugitives to the west of the Polish zone of occupation, a few weeks before the order for his own expulsion was to become effective.

But unless you happen to pursue professional interests in German or in comparative literature, you are not apt to know that more has been written about Hauptmann than about any other German author except Goethe; that to a wide and devoted following he came over many decades to be regarded as the incarnation of the poetic spirit. His appeal was broad, deep, and lasting. Publicity and contemporary popularity are no guarantees of enduring fame, but they are a factor to be taken account of in even the sketchiest treatment of some aspects of Hauptmann's career.

Except for a short period at the beginning of his career, Hauptmann's appeal has always been broad rather than specialized. Unlike his other great contemporaries in German literature, he had little, if anything, of the passion of art for art's sake in his make-up. He seemed always more concerned with the matter than with the

Reprinted from *Monatshefte*, XLIV (1952), 317-332, by permission of the University of Wisconsin Press.

manner of what he had to say. Except in the field of drama, he was an indifferent craftsman. One may be shaken to one's depths by the total pathos of a human situation projected by Hauptmann; one is rarely entranced in his work by a conscious experience of aesthetic perfection in the phrasing, in the rhythmic and melodic values of his linguistic material. He does not give to the trained ear the ecstasy of mutation achieved in the powers of language. He has none of the metallic density of Stefan George, none of the incorporeal incandescence of Rilke. His prose has none of the disciplined suppleness and brilliant phrasing that characterize Thomas Mann's mastery of narrative and essay. But what Hauptmann does in a comprehensive way is to penetrate to the heart of all that is human. Thus he encompasses the contemporary scene in accents which are compellingly authentic. But also in the grand manner of poets like Shakespeare he re-creates outstanding figures of history and myth to revel in an orchestration of passions of incomparably richer scope than the very limited range of modern civilized man.

The story of Hauptmann's youth is a saga of adventure which the old poet has himself recorded in great detail, taking full advantage of the perspective afforded by his subsequent rise to eminence. Born as the son of a hotel manager in a small Silesian spa (1862), he was largely left to his own devices as a youngster. Exceedingly alert and impressionable, he observed a great variety of town and country folk in pursuit of their callings, and visitors at the spa representing all classes of society. He associated with well-brought-up middle class companions, and he chummed and fought with ragamuffins of the gutter. While his adjustment to his home environment was happy on the whole, Hauptmann turned out to be very much of a problem child at school. Twice he had to repeat a year in the lower grades of the Breslau Gymnasium. According to his own account he spent these years in a state of unrelieved stupor, periodically accentuated by abject want. To escape from this hell he tried to fit himself for the career of a farm supervisor. He spent a year and a half doing chores on a country estate. The solitariness of this life made him turn inward and discover and nurse what he believed to be a spark of genius. On this diet of dreaming his ego was inflated to fantastic proportions. Believing himself destined for a career in the plastic arts, he persuaded his father to send him to the art school in Breslau. Again his temperament proved unamenable to discipline. Expelled from school, he was reinstated on the plea of one of his teachers. But at this time, not yet nineteen years old, he had the good fortune to win the love of one of five well-to-do orphaned sisters. Marie Thienemann, beautiful, serious, and young, believed in her fiancé's star, and from now on her purse supplied him with the means to see the world and find himself. He spent a term at the University of Jena, trying by voracious reading and eager discussion to overcome the handicap of many lost years. He took a Mediterranean cruise. In Rome he established himself in a sculptor's studio, afire with grandiose schemes to create a marble gallery of monumental figures. But having laid no foundation of solid craftsmanship, he literally saw his illusions collapse about his head. The shock of this deflation of his ego was cushioned by a severe attack of typhus. His fiancée, having come to visit him, nursed him back to health. They eventually returned to Germany and were married when Hauptmann was in his twenty-third year and had as yet given no proof of outstanding talent. He was convinced by now that imaginative writing was his field, and he had been wrestling rather ineffectually for some time with colossal themes from Roman and German antiquity. Settled now, first in the workers' quarters and then in the environs of the sprawling German capital, Hauptmann was soon caught up in the swing of a vigorous young literary movement that was imbued with a consciousness of pressing social problems and defined the field of vital poetry as the here and now. After much floundering, a summer's trip to his native Silesia led Hauptmann to discover the key to a treasure chest of literary materials stored up in the form of childhood memories. He went to work on a Silesian peasant drama. It was completed and performed in 1889. It evoked a storm of controversy. The spring of Hauptmann's productivity, once tapped, continued to flow steadily and abundantly. Hauptmann soon came to be recognized as the leader of the naturalistic movement. A theater, in step with the new art, aiming at the most exacting standards of performance and devoted to Hauptmann's personal cause, provided a highly effective springboard for his rapid rise to fame.

This early phase of Hauptmann's production commands our particular attention. When I said above that Hauptmann was by and large an indifferent craftsman, that statement requires qualification.

It does not hold for the early, spectacular phase of his career. On the contrary, Hauptmann's concern with living drama involved a very conscious craftsmanship, schooled by the great example of Ibsen. Hauptmann set out to advance the authenticity of dramatic representation of life beyond the point achieved by the great Norwegian master. He took over from Ibsen the medium of prose; the strict abandonment of the time-honored stage devices of the monologue and the aside; the imperceptible introduction and filling in of the exposition, the analytic technique, presupposing a long latent crisis which bursts into the open, reducing the play itself to the unfolding of a catastrophe that runs its course swiftly, in the space of a few days, or even a few hours. Thus Hauptmann's *Vor Sonnenaufgang* concentrates its five acts into two nights and one day. The catastrophe of *Das Friedensfest* fills one Christmas eve. *Die Weber*, dealing with conditions of prolonged, acutely intensified misery, presents but the chance touching-off of the spark and an outburst of pathetically blind, destructive, essentially futile mob fury—this in a space of probably not more than three or four days. But Hauptmann the naturalist is intent upon refining on Ibsen's quality of realism in a variety of ways. To a much greater degree than with Ibsen, the local setting, including the background of landscape, season, and weather, is integrally tied in with the dramatic action. The dramatic emphasis has shifted to the lower strata of society. Social stratification of great complexity is a background phenomenon of prime importance. The social group as such may stand in the focus of interest rather than a representative individual. Folk dialect, or rather folk dialects are employed, in meticulously authentic rendering, Silesian, Saxon, Berlin; and even the speech of characters of the bourgeois level takes on a variety of dialect shadings in response to the degree of nervous excitation evoked by the situation. The dramatic hero, no longer necessarily the focus of our sympathies, is replaced by the mere protagonist who happens to unite in his person a maximum number of the threads that make up the tissue of the segment of life presented. The concept of tragic guilt, so strong in Ibsen's heroes of often monumental individuality, is attenuated, dissipated, and replaced by the inescapable web of circumstance. Lastly, personality in terms of stable, static character, is replaced by multiple dynamic reactivity. As one might say, the matter of character is transmuted into energy. This last point may

tice is to do so by fair means wherever possible, but to take advantage of the solid reputation she has earned in order to resort to foul means wherever a special fillip is needed to speed the ship of her fortunes. The point is that she gets away with it, both in a small and a large way. A heart attack terminates her career at the moment when her lifelong ambition has been realized. She had been a washerwoman, a jewel of a washerwoman doing the work of two. But now her daughter is securely ensconced as a well-to-do member of the get-rich-quick section of the middle class. As we watch this spectacle, seeing through all of the mother's craft and scheming, we are as much moved to admiration by the adroitness and steadiness with which she plays the hazardous game as we may be shocked by the dubious means that lead to success in such a society. And if both sets of feelings are tempered by the melancholy realization that, measured by values of a more enduring sort, the game is not worth the candle, the general upshot of the spectacle is: such is life in a competitive modern society. We distinctly feel the career of the washerwoman as a symbol of the same drive and of analogous processes in all strata of our society. *Sansara* they would call it in India. Here is social satire of an all-embracing variety. It is philosophical, not doctrinaire political satire, I hasten to add; for Hauptmann, though leftish in his sympathies, never subscribed to any party line or believed in political action as efficacious for the solving of basic human problems.

Hauptmann made his literary debut in the heyday of naturalism. When he began to write, the air was thick with slogans and programs demanding a literature exclusively of the here and now and in step with advancing science. Hauptmann's early dramatic production was hailed by the adherents of the young movement as the fulfillment of their programs and slogans, and to us looking back it appears indeed as the exemplary embodiment of naturalism in drama. Theorizing had its share in this, unquestionably. But the essential fact is that the awakening of Hauptmann's creative genius occurred in felicitous conjunction with a very vigorous literary movement, and that his intimate contacts with both the humble elements of society and the intellectual middle class had stored away in his memory an apparently inexhaustible wealth of material waiting for the master hand to mold it. Hauptmann spoke the authentic language of the peasant and proletarian, and without resorting to spurious stage effects he voiced the pathos and the humanity of the underprivileged.

The fresh breeze of naturalistic doctrine first buoyed the wings of Hauptmann's nascent genius. As his prowess grew, he came to realize that it tended to restrict his flight to a very limited zone. It is important to see how Hauptmann first explored the border reaches of the permitted zone before resolutely venturing out on a bolder course. First he reintroduced the quality of imagination and the vehicle of verse into naturalistic drama, in his portrayal of the feverish hallucinations and the euphoria of a dying adolescent waif, in *Hannele*. All the material came out of the girl's background of experience: fairy-tale motifs, religious imagery, wish dreams of love, aggrandizement and revenge on her cruel stepfather were blended with compelling motivation. But how convey to an audience the singing of the blood in the rapture of delirium? The disconnected fragments of speech to be pieced together as the clinical record do not tell the story. All of us have been moved in dreams to wild joy and high laughter, and on awakening suddenly we would find our lips mumbling inane verbal fragments, grotesquely at variance with the emotions vividly remembered. There are states of mind, obviously, where the subjective experience and its observable behavioristic counterpart hopelessly fail to tally. Hauptmann, realizing this, projected a counterpart that would suggest the emotional tone of the girl's experience. At a certain climactic point of tension the prose turns into verse conveying a sense of ecstasy by the sweetness and purity of its strains and the richness of its rhythmic swell. This was a quasi-legitimate extension of the creative process into a field to which outward observation gives no access, a field which could only be known and suggested by the analogy of subjective experience. Having to choose between the alternatives of either being barred from the twilight zone of the mind altogether or of rendering it in a way that preserved its emotional value, the poet chose the latter.

Hauptmann's second venture of exploration into the borderland of the naturalistic zone was an attempt to apply the rules of the here and now to historical drama. In staging the German Peasant War of 1525 in his *Florian Geyer* he endeavored to create the illusion of the same degree of authenticity that applied to his portrayal of the nineteenth-century weavers. This was primarily a problem of language. Hauptmann wanted his embattled knights and peasants of Franconia to speak as they would have spoken in the age of the Reformation. The enormity of the undertaking becomes clear when you imagine a British author presenting Jack Cade's rebellion in the idiom of his day. A basically impossible task. For supposing that by the divination of genius an author versed in modern stagecraft did actually succeed in casting the peasant dialogue in an authentic mold, where is there a modern audience that could understand its vocabulary, its phrasing, its proverbialisms, its imagery? The dialect pronunciation of an age but little removed from Chaucer would present the least of the difficulties. Hauptmann labored for years on this ambitious attempt, poring over scores of volumes of fifteenth-, sixteenth-, and seventeenth-century documents (in the absence, alas, of phonograph recordings!), of literature, chronicles, broadsides and eye-witness accounts, excerpting countless phrases, figures, homely saws and sentences that to him harbored a latent vitality. He who had been a hopeless dunce at school began to spell out this language, then to master it—not as a trained philologist, of course, but as a poet with an uncanny genius of assimilation. It is safe to say that he ended up with a vastly more intimate knowledge of the language habits and the mentality of that remote age than the great majority of German Ph.D. candidates specializing in that field. In this case I speak with particular conviction. I have played the sleuth tracking down the sources of the language employed by Hauptmann in his *Florian Geyer*, sometimes helped by good hunches to the discovery of startling pieces of Hauptmann's linguistic material. It has been a source of amazement again and again to observe how he would contrive to discover a gem in a dustbin where philologically trained eyes would have seen nothing but dust. The completed play, a flat failure on the stage at its first presentation, has subsequently undergone a pruning process that simplified it and made it more manageable, and now it no longer defies successful presentation. It now draws a warmer response, to judge by reports, than Goethe's *Götz von Berlichingen*. And there is no question that once the thorny hurdle of its archaic language has been cleared, it has the vitality of real drama, quite unlike Ibsen's ambitious attempt to re-create the tragedy of Julian the Apostate. Ibsen, as little a trained scholar as Hauptmann, got mired in his sources, whereas Hauptmann brought his tragedy of the Peasant War into effective dramatic focus. I would maintain none the less that the stupendous labor lavished on the linguistic side of this recalcitrant subject was worth the effort only as a demonstration of the fact that this approach leads into a blind alley. It proceeded from mistaken premises. It was an attempt of heroic proportions to stretch to the limit the demarcation lines of the material amenable to naturalistic doctrine. That Hauptmann subsequently broke through the bars, after dashing his head against them, is a fortunate result of that experience. (The later Hauptmann has no scruples about having his Carolingians, his Greeks, his Spaniards, and his Mexicans express themselves in modern German verse and prose.) *Florian Geyer*, completed in 1895, was the first theme that, by material alien to his immediate experience, called powers of study and assimilation into play. Hauptmann wrestled with the material the hard way, the conscientious way. But in the pursuit of this task he discovered and developed capacities for assimilating and vitalizing large blocks of cultural tradition that are barred to the mere student of the here and now.

The gruelling grind of *Florian Geyer* earned Hauptmann his emancipation from dogmatic naturalism. Having explored the possibilities of the doctrine to its ultimate limits, having wrought his "master-piece," he could now feel himself a poet at large.

After *Florian Geyer* a new epoch in Hauptmann's life as artist begins. He now explores remote and diversified cultural climates. He tries a great many poetic media sanctioned by tradition. But from time to time he returns to the homely dialect prose of naturalism— a modern Antaeus drawing renewed strength from contact with Mother Earth.

One early, highly significant symptom of a growing emancipation from the straitjacket of naturalistic dogma must not go unnoticed. It concerns the phenomenon of rhythm in Hauptmann's prose dramas. Naturalistic dialogue, strictly speaking, can have no traffic with rhythmical regularity. Every person's speech has a distinctive phrasing of its own, just as it is distinct in its tempo and its variations of stress and pitch. But beginning with the comedy *Der Biberpelz* and continuing for a dozen years, Hauptmann's dramatic prose production is sustained by an undercurrent of regular rhythm. There are nine plays in which the prose dialogue, from beginning

GERHART HAUPTMANN'S RANGE AS DRAMATIST

to end, or with relatively small exceptions, is built on the pattern of four-beat units. The number of syllables is subject to great variation, but the number of stresses that constitute a rhythmic unit is four, or two plus two. With slight distortions of stress, pitch, and tempo whole prose plays can be read in strict rhythm, a kind of staccato singsong doggerel. A uniform vibration controls all the interplay of voices and temperaments, both dialect and standard speech. Without question, a very pronounced motor drive conditioned the fluency of Hauptmann's creative writing, and of the nine plays in question it can be said in the literal sense of the word that Hauptmann shook them out of his sleeve. Is this, then, verse in disguise? By no means. Not as though the irregular number of unaccented syllables mattered a whit. A regular, pulsing tempo is, however, only one quality constituting verse. True verse requires in addition the voicing of the unstressed syllables. In this dialogue, however, the unstressed syllables are unvoiced in the manner characteristic of colloquial prose, which reserves both stress and voiced pitch for the nodal points of the pattern. Do I need to say that no intelligent rendition of the dramas in question would accentuate the conditioning motor rhythm? The result would be intolerably monotonous. I am indeed sure that not one reader in a hundred ever becomes aware of the underlying uniformity of the pulse. I do not know, on the other hand, how and when Hauptmann became consciously aware of this motor drive. He must have become aware of it at one point and checked the tendency; for after *Und Pippa tanzt* (1906) this rhythmic pattern disappears from his prose plays. What is, then, the significant point of all this? It is that Hauptmann's creative writing was conditioned by very powerful motor impulses which tended in the direction of verse as their natural fulfillment.

Rhythm is somehow imbedded in the very heart of the expressive phase of language. I can listen without end to a record I happen to have of a Negro sermon on Christ's last entry into Jerusalem. It begins with subdued, relaxed accents, as though the voice were taking a stroll. By and by the pace quickens as the tension is tightened, and imperceptibly the voice is on the run. At the same time the melodic curve begins to expand. The voice reaches higher and higher with each new loop. The throb increases at a steady rate. Suddenly the voice, trying again and again, has leaped to the top of its register. The voice knows this, betraying its knowledge in a quaver of exultation. And now, glorying in its triumph, the voice repeats the swing of the identically pitched curve twenty, thirty, fifty times, to the accompanying chorus of muffled Amens and Hallelujahs. Then, quite suddenly, the voice snaps. A few low-pitched, relaxed, soberly articulated phrases conclude the sermon.

Hauptmann's first venture into the field of frankly imaginative dramatic writing, his verse play *Die versunkene Glocke* (1896), brought him the greatest popular success of his whole career. The fairy-tale setting, the red-haired elfin sprite teasing the mischievous satyr on the meadow and the mooning, melancholy merman in his well, have a haunting charm. And there is an irresistible pathos about the sad ending. The brief summer's idyll of love between the fairy girl and a mortal man who falls just short of superman stature is sharply terminated by a fit of rage on his part. She, bearing the human child in her womb, is fated to descend into the chilly well and become the merman's bride, emerging only once more to seal the fate of her broken lover with a tender, death-dealing kiss. Young people, in love for the first time, are likely to luxuriate in the pathos and sentiment of this sad fairy play. But the ease of its appeal makes the quality of its ingratiating effects suspect. The play is a medley of elements derived from literature and art. The folk-tale material is interwoven with easily recognizable strands from Böcklin's paintings, from Goethe's *Satyros* and *Faust*, Ibsen's *Peer Gynt, Brand*, and *Lady from the Sea*, Fouqué's *Undine*, Mörike's *Orplid*, Wagner's *Nibelungen*, Nietzsche's *Zarathustra*. The old Germanic gods of the *Edda* are present, and we hear the croak of Aristophanes' *Frogs*. And if the felicitous blending of all these secondary sources of inspiration is not in itself a fault, there is a more serious reproach: the planes of symbolic meaning, confusingly multiple, keep constantly interfering with one another. For besides being a fairy drama full of laughter and pathos, *The Sunken Bell* is a social drama of a man between two women, an individual challenging an outraged bourgeois society. It is a religious drama, a battleground between ascetic Christianity and sun-worshipping paganism. It is the tragedy of the artist who revels in divine inspiration but fails in the attempt to give embodiment to his airy visions. It is, furthermore, the tragedy of mankind as a whole; there is an irremediable flaw in man, the botched product of the evolutionary process. And it is lastly a seasonal myth, tracing the cycle from nature's awakening as heralded by the spring thunder, to the rigidity of winter blanketing the valleys with the leaden clouds that drift down from the *Riesengebirge.*

Ten years later, Hauptmann again gave free rein to poetic fancy in another fairy drama, *Und Pippa tanzt* (1906). Here the sprite around which the drama of mankind revolves is a wisp of an Italian girl, but a slight shift of focus transforms her, as it were, into the incandescent essence of an infinitely fragile goblet of Venetian glass. Except for a group of gamblers, riveted to the greed for gold, all mankind comes under the spell of this spark of the divine fire. The sophisticated business man has caught only a mild case of the infection and departs from the scene after a drastic cure, whereas the swashbuckling young poet, an egocentric, uncannily fluent illusionist, making up by bravado for lack of substance, seems fated to rescue Beauty from the clutches of the Beast. The Beast is an antediluvian, shaggy old monster of a glassblower, an incarnation of dumb force; yet a slight shift of focus makes us shudder to see behind the brutish mask the features of the Great God Pan. And there is an astonishing delicacy about the movements of his hulking frame, as he ministers to the shivering terrified girl whom he has carried off to his den in the winter night. Another figure of superhuman faculties is deeply involved in the drama—Wann, the sage, "ancient of the mountains," who dwells in a climate of the soul beyond the reach of coveting passion. He tries to abet the fortunes of the young couple with his wisdom, and when the beast-god is found to have stealthily entered upon the scene, the sage wrestles with him and paralyzes the brute. But even the wisdom of the sage is not proof against all contingencies. Matters come to a climax when the heart of the paralyzed monster pounds out a fearsome dance of death under his ribs, and his convulsive grasp snaps the stem of the fragile goblet in which Pippa's life resides. Here there is intricate allegory of a strangely exciting and moving quality. There is deep compassion for brute humanity, with its inarticulate longing for the divine spark. As for the youthful illusionist, so pathetically winning a figure with his inflated self-consciousness and sophisticated braggadocio, he is dismissed in the end with bloody irony.

Devoid in his modern self-sufficiency of all reverence for the cosmic forces between which life is suspended, wholly deaf to the appealing voice of suffering common humanity, he has comprehended nothing of the fearsome drama enacted about him. Having been blind to everything but his egocentric passion, he is stricken with physical blindness and thrust out into the cold with a beggar's staff for his only comfort. Pippa is, perhaps, the most sprightly and scintillating of Hauptmann's works; the most bizarre in its effects; one of the most enigmatic to interpret; yet conveying its essential message by a mastery of symbol and atmosphere. Unlike Hauptmann's early works, it is but lightly concerned with exposing the tawdry shams of the bourgeois world. It is concerned with eternal values. It celebrates the mystery of beauty as the divine spark to which everything human is responsive.

I despair of sketching in the little time left the range of Hauptmann's dramatic creation. He roamed over a wide expanse of mankind's cultural heritage to bring back treasure. From the Middle Ages Hauptmann recast the drama of the German Knight, Herr Heinrich von Aue, who is stricken with leprosy. From feeling himself the darling of the gods, he is reduced to the plane of Job, his personality disintegrating by degrees until, at the moment of supreme anguish, his cure is effected through an inner miracle, by means of a violent shock. He thinks he sees an apparition of the girl, supposedly dead, who had been the last link connecting him with mankind, when the overwhelming realization dawns upon him that it is her bodily presence which he is beholding. The ecstasy of this shock makes him confess: This moment is precious beyond compare; with such a moment in prospect I should beg on my knees to be vouchsafed a repetition of the unspeakable agony that has brought me hither. As the tone of feeling in *Der arme Heinrich* is essentially modern—in fact, Nietzschean—despite the medieval setting, I would single out as a more significant dramatic conquest of an alien climate his *Bogen des Odysseus* (1914), a drama of Odysseus' homecoming and his vengeance on Penelope's suitors. Here is an Odysseus stripped of the softening modulations of Homer's epic chant. He stands out stark as the archaic demigod in his capacity for suffering and in the inscrutable stealthiness of his guile. He wields the infallible bow of Apollo, and the immediacy of divine forces abetting him pervades the atmosphere. Whether by design or chance, this drama of Odysseus is a paradigmatic challenge to an older aesthetic that excluded the repulsive and the loathsome from dramatic representation. A little more than a hundred years earlier Schiller, echoing Lessing, had written:

> When Homer presents his Ulysses in beggar's rags it is for us to choose in what detail we are willing to visualize the picture and how long we care to dwell on it. But in no case is it vivid enough to be felt as distasteful or repulsive. If the painter, however, or worse, the actor, were to depict Ulysses faithfully on the Homeric model, we would turn away from the spectacle in disgust (*Schillers Werke*, Bellermann–Petsch, B. I. VII, 230).

It is precisely the repulsive that Hauptmann employs as a cardinal element in his archaic emotional pattern (and this links his poetic drama with the drama of naturalism!). The emotional range experienced by and in Odysseus transcends the range of the human on the hither side as well as on that beyond. It includes primitive and bestial elements of totemistic ancestral memory. This palsied, shrunken beggar, desiccated by the sun and pickled in brine, shakes with an ague that is both simulated and real, slobbers over old Laertes, his double, in filial rapture and the delirium of senile dementia. The afternoon of the homecoming (to the hut of the swineherd) is both the climactic moment of his tribulation and the supreme test of his elasticity, resourcefulness, and cunning. This is the tragic span of a demigod, far more at home in the extra-human climes of beast and god than in the median zone of man. Human drama, as distinct from this extra-human drama, grips us in the experience of Telemachus, the son, who had built up an idealized, a noble, a "classical" image of his celebrated father, believing him safely dead and devoting himself to the cult of his memory. When, by degrees, his reluctant eyes are confronted with the terrible truth that this loathsome but mysteriously magnetic beggar is indeed his father, his inner world collapses and he is all but annihilated. Seeing the shrunken beggar grow and expand to superhuman stature, Telemachus shrieks in terror:

> Er wächst! Er dehnt sich! er erfüllt das Haus,
> Und niemand ausser ihm kann drin noch atmen.

> [He is growing! He expands! He fills up the house,
> and no one except him can breathe in there.]

Brave, noble soul that he is, Telemachus is reluctant to discard his streamlined ideal of paternal greatness and embrace the infinitely more complex reality of the wily demigod in action. That Odysseus succeeds in winning over Telemachus to freely willed coöperation in his plan of retribution, hazardously improvised from moment to moment, is his greatest triumph. Throughout the action we never glimpse Penelope's presence. But her mysterious personality pervades the drama. Infinitely alluring, aloof, and enigmatic, she is the divine spider, *arachne*, who catches the youth of the land in the toils of her sinister web. When Odysseus has done his work and slain the four most prominent suitors (not in the palace, but in the hut of the herdsman Eumaios), his concluding words are a superb summation of the mood of archaic exultation:

> Was wird die Mutter sagen, Telemach,
> Dass ich ihr schönstes Spielzeug schon zerschlug?

> [What will mother say, Telemachus,
> now that I have smashed her prettiest toy?]

Another late drama, bearing the strange title *Indipohdi* (meaning: "no one knows") (1920), is as far removed as the play of Odysseus from the modern world and the life of the average man, but the climate of the soul here encountered has nothing in common with either. The central figure of *Indipohdi* is a sage named Prospero in frank acknowledgment of the debt owed to Shakespeare. The locale is an island of the Mayan civilization at the time of the Conquest. Prospero's fate parallels that of his Shakespearian namesake in his having found refuge, shipwrecked, on a strange volcanic island with no other survivors but his infant daughter. He too had lost a throne, but it was a son of glorious promise, a counterpart of David's Absalom, whose blind rage he had fled. And as in the *Tempest*, providential chance contrives a strange second encounter between the usurper and the aged exile who had fancied himself beyond the reach of those poignant memories of the past out of which he had distilled a contemplative wisdom. Despite himself, Prospero finds himself involved once more in the web of human passion and struggle. He is faced with fearful decisions in which the integrity of his personality is at stake. With reluctance he has acceded to the demand of the island population to assume the crown by virtue of the fact that he is revered by the priests as kin of their ancient gods, himself a white god. Even more reluctantly he has given an ambiguous promise to appease the angry deity of the volcano by restoring the ritual of human sacrifice which had been allowed to lapse by virtue of Prospero's influence. Now, as tension runs high over Prospero's delay in fulfilling his promise, circumstance places the ideal sacrificial victim in his grasp in the person of his usurper-son who, unwittingly, has once more challenged his father's authority and, unnerved in the face to face encounter by the power of Prospero's eye, has been taken prisoner. The hostile encounter between father and son has furnished the most impressive demonstration of Prospero's supernatural power. But Prospero spurns this easy solution of his dilemma. As all preparations for the sacrifice of the white prisoner are being put into effect with his sanction, he has inwardly willed his own sacrifice as the right and fitting solution. Just before the consummation of the sacrifice the priest, under instructions from Prospero, hands the son a scroll. He reads aloud his father's last will proclaiming him as his successor; and at the moment when the shock of this revelation prostrates the young man, Prospero is already beyond recall. We catch final glimpses of him as he makes his way up the mountain side through the eternal snow, to vanish in the mists that surround the crater.

In this play there is not the usual dramatic tension. In its acute phases, at any rate, the struggle of elemental passions is limited to the characters of the second and third dramatic level, particularly to Prospero's son and daughter, whose blood wells up in irresistible mutual attraction and turns the filial devotion of the young huntress into elemental rage bent upon the destruction of her father, whose purposes she is farthest from divining. But Prospero himself has long since come to dwell on a spiritual plane from which struggle and passion have been relegated as dominant concerns. He is the theoretical man, the poet, the seer. Having all but solved the problem of Archimedes (*dos moi pou sto*), having found, as it were, a foothold outside the life of changing shapes, he contemplates the scene of the awful ebb and flow of life, the mysterious loom of birth and death, the inexorably grinding mill of poignant lust and cruelty and fleeting sweetness, with a high tranquillity. To his contemplative gaze there is so little difference between the validity of the shapes of the world of sense and those conjured up by his creative imagination, that he surveys the totality of life from, as it were, the inner heart chamber of the cosmic agency that fathers the ceaseless process. He is both the creator and the totality of creation, solipsistically encompassing a world of the stuff of illusion. Even so things happen to remind him poignantly that, for all his soaring, he is himself an element of the mysterious grimly sublime process; the magic of his mantle is subject to definite limitations. And so he reverses himself in the end. No longer turning his back upon the world of human passion as merely a fitful spectacle without reality, his last words—if I read them aright—restore the validity of the experienced process and invoke an all-embracing love as man's truest approach to reality. Thus the dominant mood of this drama is the swell of a profoundly solemn, philosophical lyricism steeped in the reverence of worship, highly reminiscent of Goethe's *Faust* and Hölderlin's *Empedokles*, which latter furnished the prototype of self-sacrifice by way of the crater. This drama, lifting us above the tension of battling passions instead of entangling us as participants in the struggle, might well have been a great poet's valedictory to the world, and was, in fact, so intended. It is shot through, moreover, with an autobiographical flavor, the poet having, somehow, arrived at a point where the vast throng of shapes, spawned over a long succession of years by his fertile imagination, came to be felt by him, it would seem, as more real a universe than the world of sense reality. (His posthumous story *Mignon* is wrought of the same stuff.) It is an acknowlegment of the essential solipsism of imaginative creation.

Cosmic drama would seem more and more to have become the aging poet's prime concern. The roots of this preoccupation had, as we have seen, a long period of growth. The life process as such was a theme woven into the *Sunken Bell*. It was the very stuff out of which Hauptmann distilled the ecstatic martyrdom of the medieval knight, der arme Heinrich, the fragile iridescence of his Pippa, the passion-vindication cycle of the demigod Odysseus, the deep, rich orchestration of *Indipohdi*. It is once more the theme of the late tragedy of *Veland*, completed in 1925 but in process of growth over nearly thirty years. Veland, the Smith, (Wieland, Wölund) the Germanic demigod artificer, captured and maimed by a mortal king, has bided his time to wreak frightful vengeance on his captor and his kin before soaring aloft on the wings he has fashioned in his cavernous island smithy. Veland's case is very different from that of Odysseus. The wily Greek had only his genius of improvisation to rely on; here retribution is ground out with ultimate grimness according to plan. The acting out of the whole span of mental torture to which the king is subjected borders on the unendurable. It is made endurable only by the realization that, paradoxically, in the triumph of retribution—itself a measure of Veland's accumulated agonies—the avenger himself shares to the full the unspeakable torture endured by his victim. The slaking of his vengeance is in itself the most acute stage of the martyrdom of the god. And in full knowledge of the inevitability of this martyrdom, the gentle suasion of the Good Shepherd's strains that would tempt Veland's soul to another way of settling his score is dismissed as unavailing. It is fated that the cosmic tragedy of violence and retribution, of birth, struggle and torment, re-enact itself from eon to eon, involving even the collapse of All-Father's rule, until such time, perhaps, as the winged god's peregrinations may be destined to reach the confine of ultimate nothingness. In *Veland* life is envisaged under the aspect of total tragedy; and the affirmation of this pantragism (for protest is, in a measure, engulfed in affirmation) can find voice only in accents of ecstatic agony. With unmistakable intent Hauptmann designated the spectacle of *Veland* as a tragedy. None of his other dramas, except *Florian Geyer* and the very late tetralogy of the *House of Atreus* written in the shadow of the Second World War (and the posthumously published *Magnus Garbe*) is so entitled. And to reinforce its solemnity, he cast *Veland* in the meter of Greek tragedy, the classic trimeter, otherwise all but absent from his work.

I have chosen to give you a glimpse of certainly not inconsequential aspects of a great poet's work. I began by pointing out Hauptmann's significance as the creator and unchallenged master of German naturalistic drama. I continued by showing his emancipation from the confines of naturalistic dogma in his attempt to recreate the ultimate limits of what the elect of mankind have experienced in their highest tragic flights. In this Hauptmann remains a humanist in the comprehensive sense of the word; for only a narrow view would presume to restrict the term humanism to the experimental range of the common man. Time has prevented my giving you more than scattered glimpses, but enough, perhaps, to conclude that Hauptmann's genius is deeply religious. For it is not any special phase of human activity, but the whole organic mystery of life and death in its inexorableness, the relentless cruelty of its blind drive, its brief moments of ecstasy, on which he dwells. It is to this central mystery that Hauptmann recurs again and again, with fascination, rapture, awe, and that sense of reverence that prostrates itself before what is eternal and passes human understanding.

THOMAS MANN'S *GREGORIUS*:
DER ERWÄHLTE

1. The Approach

IN THE diary-like narrative that gives an account of *Doktor Faustus* as a work in progress (*Die Entstehung des Doktor Faustus: Roman eines Romans*, 1949) Thomas Mann tells of his reading the *Gesta Romanorum* and being fascinated by "the most beautiful and surprising of its stories," that of the birth of the sainted Pope Gregory. This story is turned into a musical puppet show by the composer Adrian Leverkühn in chapter xxxi of *Doktor Faustus*. At that time, according to the Diary, Thomas Mann was unfamiliar with the many medieval versions of the story, that of Hartmann von Aue in particular. "However," he goes on to say, "I liked it so well that I straightway took up the idea of some day taking the subject away from my hero and turning it into a little archaic novel of my own" (130).

Taking our cue from these remarks, we shall begin by turning to chapter xxxi of *Doktor Faustus*. (It is the last twelve pages of the chapter that concern us.) We expect that this chapter will supply revealing, if incomplete, answers to such questions as: What was the fascination of so bizarre a theme on Thomas Mann's creative imagination? And why did he choose to retell it in a way that puts the stamp of a very singular originality upon this latest product of his pen?

At the outset we learn, as we would expect, that it was a German translation of the famous medieval Latin prose collection of tales to which the composer was introduced by a friend (484). The hero of *Doktor Faustus* shares the reading habits of Thomas Mann, who makes no secret of the fact that he derives his knowledge of foreign literatures by preference from translations. That he used the translation by Dr. Johann Georg Theodor Grässe, which first appeared in 1842 and of which the third edition (1905) was available to me, is clear beyond doubt. The three and one-half page summary of

---

Reprinted from *The Germanic Review*, XXVII (1952), 10-30, 83-95, by permission of W. T. H. Jackson, editor.

this version[1] of the Gregorius story in *Doktor Faustus* (487-490), a very skillful condensation of the eighteen pages of Grässe's translation, not only contrives, despite the narrator's disclaimer,[2] to present a clear picture of the plot in all essentials, but we find, moreover, that all the numerous dialogue passages of the summary, given in quotation marks, literally reproduce dialogue passages of Grässe's with minimal deviations; and much of Grässe's phraseology is preserved in the narrative portions as well.

Despite this close adherence of the summary to the phraseology of the medieval tale, an occasional phrase crops up that gives a twist to the story quite foreign to the simple, piously edifying original. We must scrutinize these phrases. We must also remember in doing so that Thomas Mann is responsible for these twists in an indirect and complicated sort of way: he does not tell the story of *Doktor Faustus* in the first person. He interposes between author and hero the figure of an installed narrator, the crotchety, dry, and prudish philologist, Serenus Zeitblom, who writes the biography of his friend the composer Adrian Leverkühn, whose development he watches with a jealous fascination mingled with dismay at the nihilistic turn it is taking. This double focus of his vision also colors his summary of the Gregorius story. The puritanical smirk cannot escape us in his phrasing of the consequences of the incestuous love of brother and sister, "des Geschwisterpaars, von dem der Bruder die Schwester über Gebühr liebt, so dass er sie unbeherrschter Weise in mehr als interessante Umstände versetzt" (487) [of the sibling pair, of whom the brother loves his sister more than is proper, so that uncontrollably he puts her in more than interesting circumstances]. Again, when Gregorius' mother discovers, many years later, that she has been living in incestuous wedlock with her son, the narrator has the mother advert to dire possibilities, fortunately not come to pass, of which the *Gesta* story makes no mention: through the tablet the wife-mother learns "mit wem sie, gottlob ohne ihm auch noch einen Bruder und Enkel ihres Bruders geboren zu haben, das Lager teilt" (489) [with whom she shares her

---

[1] It differs in some important respects from Hartmann's version. Thus the fisherman's role in the *Gesta Romanorum* version, in chaining Gregorius to his rock, is conceived in terms of simple coöperation with no suggestion of malice.

[2] "Die Kette der Verwicklungen ist lang, und es erübrigt sich wohl für mich, die Geschichte . . . hier zu reiterieren" (487). [The chain of entanglements is long, and it surely would be unnecessary for me to reiterate the story here.]

bed, without however, thank heavens, having given him a brother and a grandson of her brother]. Here we pause to observe that Thomas Mann's imagination evidently communicates with that of the narrator by underground passages, for not only does a variant of these dire possibilities actually come to pass in Thomas Mann's own Gregorius novel—the mother bears her son-husband two daughters—but beyond this the saintly Pope's speculation dwells on the possibility that but for the grace of God the double incest might have been further compounded by an inadvertent carnal union of Gregorius with one of his own daughters. That possibility makes his thoughts stand still. "The world is finite," he concludes with a sigh of relief. A third and final instance of the narrator's injecting of his personality into the old story occurs in his reporting of the miracle of the automatic pealing of the bells of Rome, to which he appends the preciously phrased explanation: "zur Ankündigung, dass es einen so frommen und lehrreichen Papst noch nicht gegeben haben werde" (490) [to proclaim that there will never have been such a pious and instructive pope].

In introducing the Gregorius theme the narrator emphasizes, what we readily believe, that the quaint old story appealed to the composer's sense of the comic (484), that it stimulated his parodistic vein in the highest degree (485), and that he and his intimates were irresistibly rocked with mirth to the point of tears—all this with rather sour-faced reservations concerning his own, the narrator's, more restrained response.

Let us now follow Serenus Zeitblom's account of how the composer treated the theme in turning it into a musical puppet show.

The style of Adrian Leverkühn's puppet-play music was a reversion to the simpler manner of his earlier period. Such alternation between the invention of advanced idiom and the return to simpler modes is a phenomenon commonly observed in the development of creative production, Serenus Zeitblom observes (491). Here we have one of many obvious instances of a partial self-identification of Thomas Mann with his composer-hero Adrian Leverkühn.

This self-identification is also indicated in the analysis of the peculiar appeal of this type of story to the composer: it was an intellectual appeal, not without a dash of malice and disintegrating travesty, in reaction to the tumescent romantic music drama of the preceding epoch based on medieval themes. The narrator dwells on the "scurrilous" quality of the "erotic buffoonery" of the Gregorius theme and the "burlesque" effect, already inherent in the puppet-show medium (491). All this runs parallel to Thomas Mann's life-long ambivalent relation to Richard Wagner.

As particularly effective, invoking a mood compounded of laughter and fantastic rapture ("Ergriffenheit"), he stresses the scene of the final meeting between the Pope and his wife-mother (492). This is a patent anticipation of Thomas Mann's treatment of that scene in our novel—a treatment that achieves a unique blend of the burlesque with mirth of such celestial clarity as to dispel, for the moment at least, the grave reservations of more than one reader on the score of certain features of this ultra-conscious literary experiment.

The narrator finally gives us the gist of a discussion between Adrian Leverkühn and his friends—really an informal lecture on Adrian's part—emphasizing the paradigmatic quality of the Gregorius theme, thus handled, for the status of creative art in the contemporary world. This again is, clearly, a preview of Thomas Mann's own *Gregorius*: it is an attempt to bridge the gap between an exclusive, esoteric, intellectualistic art and an art that addresses itself to the widest possible public. The exclusive literary public of the nineteenth century has either ceased to exist or is about to cease to exist; hence art would move in a vacuum and be doomed to extinction unless it found a way of broadening its appeal. The art of the future, it is stated, will have to be much less pretentious than its nineteenth-century predecessor. In order to survive, art will have to achieve a new "innocence" and simplicity, discarding the preconceptions of a cultured class, making its appeal to humanity (*die Menschheit*, 492-496).

This view—a reflection of Thomas Mann's peculiar dilemma (writing as he does in a world in which the former cultured German *élite* with which he felt in close contact up to the time of his exile has been rapidly dwindling to the point of extinction)—is propounded only to be followed by its dialectic counterpart. Here the narrator, Zeitblom, clearly speaking with the other voice of Mann, for his own part emphasizes the view that true art can never forego its aristocratic quality. He is quite certain that the new style projected by the composer does not amount to a surrender of his prerogatives. On the contrary, it represents an instance of the most aristocratic condescension, a benevolent gesture that he could afford to bestow from the height of his consciousness of untouchable aloofness. Finally, as if again to nullify this reversal in part, he meditates on the quaver in Adrian's voice when he spoke of the need of art to be redeemed from its isolation, of its yearning to re-establish contact with simple humanity.

Here then we have, in advance, Thomas Mann's apologia, with all its ambiguities, for the *Gregorius* that he was about to write.

2. The Sources

Unlike Adrian Leverkühn, Thomas Mann did not write a musical puppet play based on the quaint, rude prose of the Gregorius tale in the *Gesta Romanorum*. He wrote a novel, and he modeled his work on the lines of a much earlier but vastly more artistic version—the Middle High German verse narrative of the Knight Hartmann von Aue, an acknowledged master of the courtly art and indeed the "normative" exponent of the cultural values of the upper stratum of society in a very short-lived age that achieved a felicitous fusion of secular and religious ideals, around the year 1200.

Most readers of Thomas Mann's Gregorius novel will be puzzled, mystified, amused, shocked, repelled, or entranced (perhaps all of these in turn) but never bored by the highly spiced dish that the author serves up to engage their palates. They will make up their minds on the quality of the entertainment without inquiring into the ingredients or into the recipe that binds them in so extraordinary a blend. The student, however, having partaken of the feast, will be eager to identify the materials that went into its making. Inasmuch as the story is frankly acknowledged to be the reworking of Hartmann's versified legend of some 4000 lines, he will scrutinize that elegant product of the age of chivalry and compare it with the performance of the twentieth-century master as regards the general plot, the development of incident and characters, the proportions of the whole, and the spirit of its message. He will find the plot of the novel preformed in all essentials in Hartmann's version, and echoes of Hartmann's phrasing and poetic diction will strike the informed reader's ear at countless turns of Thomas Mann's novel.

But apart from this the two works are as dissimilar as is conceivable.

Is all the elaboration and embroidery, then, which cannot be accounted for on the score of the Hartmann model, the product of Thomas Mann's unfettered fancy, or is it conditioned by other, secondary source material?

A moderate amount of probing reveals, indeed, the fact that Thomas Mann drew on a wide and highly diversified range of sources to stimulate his creative imagination. His *Gregorius* is studded with names and a bewildering host of archaic expressions of Middle High German, Old French, and Latin origin, leaving out of account for the moment the use of modern Low German idiom, archaic and modern English, Anglicisms, either studied or involuntary, and—a transitory phenomenon in present-day America—that unlovely "hash" of English and German which colors the speech of most recent immigrants from Germany, often to a grotesque degree. The composite flavor is enriched furthermore, by a highly spicy type of nineteenth-century *Fremdwort* from the French and occasional equally spicy elements of modern French vocabulary. It is to the names and archaisms of all kinds that the student's divining rod makes its most sensitive response.

So conspicuous as not to escape even the eye of the novice, as regards Middle High German literature, is the contribution derived from Wolfram von Eschenbach's *Parzival*. Among the proper names, chiefly personal and geographic, those lifted from *Parzival* stand out by their exotic flavor as well as their number. Whereas Hartmann's work had very little to offer in this regard, being very sparing in the use of proper names, a rough count reveals some forty names, chiefly of persons, countries, or cities that definitely owe their appearance in Thomas Mann's novel to Wolfram's *Parzival*, frequently in a spelling that suggests the use of Wilhelm Hertz's *Bearbeitung*,[3] and the great body of notes appended to that work. Thus the short form of the name Gregorius, Grigorss, derives from this source.

To mention a few of these exotic names, we find people named Feirefiss, Garschiloye, Jeschute, Klamide, Klias, Mahaute, Obilot, Plihopliheri, Rassalig, Schiolarss; countries like Anschouwe (also spelled Anschauwe), Assagauk, Gylstram, Rankulat, Waleis; towns

[3] *Parzival von Wolfram von Eschenbach*, newly revised (Stuttgart, 1897).

and castles like Beafontane, Bealzenan, Belrapeire, Dianasdrun, Halap, Ipotente; a boat named Reine Inguse, and a horse named Guverjorss. But in addition to these fanciful names, to which might be added precious fabrics like Achmardi and Pfellel, or the title of the master of court etiquette, Gurvenal,[4] Thomas Mann's *Gregorius* contains hundreds of terms, phrases, characteristic turns of expression, and boldly transplanted Middle High German words of every sort that derive from *Parzival*. The second chapter of the novel ("Grimald und Baduhenna," 17-23) leans so heavily on Wolfram in its detailed inventory of items connected with the life at court that the elimination of these borrowings would very largely destroy the atmosphere of the story. (Whether the author aims in any way at the creation of an authentic medieval atmosphere, is a question we are not concerned with at present.)

Along with Hartmann and Wolfram, the third great master of Middle High German knightly epic has left his unmistakable imprint on Thomas Mann's *Gregorius*: Gottfried von Strassburg's *Tristan* has contributed the name of his hero and his designation as the mourner (*der Trauerer*), the geographical name Parmenien, the courtly ethical code of "moraliteit," and an occasional Old French phrase. There are a number of echoes of the *Nibelungenlied* in the frequent employment of some of its characteristic epithets and the appearance of the name Herrad, but this name may have been lifted from the *Thidrekssaga* along with the sword Eckesachs. The passing mention of "Gutwetterkönig Orendel," on the other hand, does not warrant the inference that Thomas Mann so much as looked at that *Spielmannsepos*. He must have come across it in some book on Germanic mythology. A number of remarks on medieval medicine, including the "Tannewetzel," highly effective in its introduction and repetition as a mysterious agency causing a stroke, was also certainly gleaned from a secondary source.[5] The same would seem to be the case as regards such Old English names as Ethelwulf, Wiglaf, and Kynewulf, the appearance of Galfried (Geoffrey) of Monmouth as Gregorius' teacher at the abbey on

---

[4] Wolfram says of his hero Parzival: "in zôch dehein Kurvenâl" (*P.*, 144, 20), in allusion to the name of Tristan's master of etiquette. Wilhelm Hertz in his notes renders the name as Gurvenal. He attempts to derive it from an Old French equivalent of governor and reduce it to the status of a common noun.

[5] Lexer's large Middle High German dictionary lists the word in a number of forms, along with references to their occurrence.

Saint Dunstan Island, and the mention of the British King Vortigern in connection with the Saxon Invasion.

The derivation of the Old French material seems at first glance to offer a rather baffling problem. Some of the shorter phrases obviously derive from Wolfram and Gottfried, but some of the material extends over several lines and reveals itself to be rhymed verse, in a variety of dialects. An examination of the Old French versions of the Gregorius theme, one of which served Hartmann as his source, reveals no evidence of borrowing. Occasional words, phrases, and name forms seem to derive from Crétien de Troyes[6] but are more likely to stem from an annotated edition of Wolfram's *Parzival.* Is it possible, one wonders, that Thomas Mann could have taken the trouble to familiarize himself with a wide variety of twelfth-century French literature for the sake of enriching his work with a few special touches of color? This seems all the more improbable in view of the handy short-cut that led to the quaint archaic German prayers of the little boy Echo in *Doktor Faustus.*[7] In the case of the present work the longest and most difficult of the Old French passages provided the clue. It is the rather ghastly scene of the sister's seduction by her brother, preceded by his butchering of the whining dog between their beds. There a five-line Old French passage (which I first mistook for Provençal) is introduced by the words: "Dann murmelten sie, was man nicht mehr verstand und gar nicht verstehen soll" (44). [Then they murmured what one no longer understands and what one ought not to understand at all.] Failure to understand at first sight led to prolonged rumination and the discovery of rhyme. When the passage suddenly revealed its meaning, I began to suspect that it might be derived from an Old French Adam and Eve play. On an instant hunch I reached for Erich Auerbach's *Mimesis* and was rewarded by finding the passage verbatim together with a German translation at the head of the essay entitled: "Adam und Eva."[8] (Thomas Mann astutely omitted

---

[6] Klamidê is mentioned as a knight (this is the form in the Wolfram texts), but there is also a monk named Clamadex, a spelling found in some Crétien manuscripts.

[7] As shown by James F. White in "Echo's Prayers in *Doktor Faustus,*" *Monatshefte,* XLII (1950), 385-394, they all derive from Freidank's *Bescheidenheit* via the second volume of Samuel Singer's *Sprichwörter des Mittelalters* (Bern, 1946).

[8] *Mimesis: Dargestellte Wirklichkeit in der abendländischen Literatur* (Bern, 1946), 141-143; see also the English translation, *Mimesis. The Representation of Reality in Western Literature,* trans. Willard R. Trask (Princeton, 1953), pp. 143-145.

the name of Adam and he misspelled one word!) Finding this key passage led to further search in *Mimesis*. Two more of Thomas Mann's Old French passages, a line on page 47, and two rhyming lines on page 76, turned out to have been transplanted from a section of the Alexius legend (quoted and translated, *Mimesis*, p. 114), while another phrase, page 28, came from a selection from Crétien's *Yvain* (quoted and translated, *Mimesis*, pp. 123-125). This disposes of the most significant Old French passages. There can be no doubt that the shorter phrases still remaining to be identified would prove on closer search to be derived either from the same source or obtained in a similar way. No one, I hope, will be so absurd as to suspect a charge of plagiarism in the presentation of these findings.

The Latin phrases and sentences, on the other hand, of which there are a number, stem from miscellaneous sources. They are largely Church Latin. One Latin quotation, to be found on page 80, deserves a special note. It is a proverb of uncertain provenience used by Goethe as the motto for the fourth volume of *Dichtung und Wahrheit*.

Our search for sources takes a very different turn, again, as we focus upon the frequent imperceptible lapsing of the prose into rhymed verse in passages—mostly dialogue—that have to do with the spirit and exploits of chivalry. A foretaste of this device is presented in the undisguised four-beat couplet that concludes the first chapter with a delicious parodistic flourish:

> Es war ein Fürst, nommé Grimald,
> Der Tannewetzel macht' ihn kalt.
> Der liess zurück zween Kinder klar,
> Ahî, war das ein Sünderpaar!

> [There was a prince called Grimald,
> Tannewetzel made him cold.
> He left behind two children fair,
> ah, that was a sinful pair.]

(Here the German is spiced with French, Middle High German, and archaic elements, tied together by trite and humorous rhymes and dominated by the mysterious name of an agency no one has ever heard of.) And there are bits of dialogue, expressive of high resolve, that complete the rhyme by a weighty French word or phrase and strike the ear with an impact of unforgettable surprise, as in the summing up of the hairy Burgundian's suit: "Gebt Fraue doch den Frieden, dem Land nach so viel Lîden und reichet dem die Hand, der so nach Euch entbrannt, dem Werber kühn und viel zäh! Sie aber sprach: 'Jamais!' " (79). [My Lady, do give peace to the land after such suffering, and hold out your hand to him who is so enflamed for you, to the bold and stubborn suitor. But she said: Never!] Or when the *maire* concludes his report of the predicament of the ravaged land in the face of Sibylla's obstinate refusal to yield her hand to the ferocious suitor with the words: "Die Frau doch, was sagt sie? 'Niemalen de la vie!' " (150). [But the lady, what says she? Not as long as I live!]

We are not likely to be wrong in sensing the manner of Wilhelm Hertz' modernization of *Parzival* in these rhymes. In the account, on the other hand, of Gregorius' first exploit, which the *maire* of Bruges gives to Sibylla's seneschal (157-159), where despite himself, he repeatedly lapses into rhyme and under its spell mixes his report with fantastic hyperbole, the rhythms are those of the modernized *Nibelungenlied* and—in the rougher passages—of Scheffel's translation of *Waltharius*, which forms part of his *Ekkehard.*[9] Thomas Mann dipped into these works again, which must have been familiar to him from his school days, in the hope that they would contribute to the medieval-chivalrous flavor of his novel. No conscious search of a model can have been required, on the other hand, in the shaping of some alliterative lines effectively used, with slight variations, as a leitmotiv: The fishermen, challenged by the abbot to account for their strange find, report, "Sie hätten das Fass am Eingang zur Bucht mit frostiger Hand von der Freise gefischt" (92) [With frosty hands they had fished the keg from the turbulence at the entrance to the bay]; for the lilt of Wagner's Siegfried is plainly discernible. The longest rhymed passage is that of Sibylla's prayer (191-194). Some of its irregular rhythms suggest the Middle High German form of the "Leich." The substance of her prayer, however, contains so large an ingredient of Sibylla's personal experiences and hopes that it would be idle to look for a specific source in this instance.

---

[9] Two circumstances confirm this surmise: The name Patafrid, which occurs in Thomas Mann's novel, is also that of one of the combatants in the "Waltharilied." The motif of the gold coin baked into a loaf of bread was probably suggested by a simulated (really silver) loaf of bread filled with gold coin, mentioned in *Ekke-*

When the scene of the novel shifts from Northern Europe to Rome, Thomas Mann's imagination turns from the whole complex of medieval German poetry and its revival in more or less modern dress, to seek support in a totally different quarter. For everything that concerns the medieval Roman setting there was available a famous authoritative work, Ferdinand Gregorovius' *Geschichte der Stadt Rom im Mittelalter* (1859-1872) in eight volumes, and there is abundant evidence to show that it proved a bountiful source of background material. As was the case with Wolfram, the names of Roman persons and localities provide most immediate proof. Confining ourselves to names of persons alone, we find the second and third element of the name Sextus Anicius Probus in a great abundance of passages, such as: "Die Anicier aber waren die Häupter der christlichen Aristokratie in Rom" (I, 131) [The Anicians, however, were the heads of the Christian aristocracy in Rome], "die fürstlichen Paläste selbst der Bassus, Probus. . . , welche zum Christentum übergetreten waren" (I, 77) [the princely palaces, even Bassus, Probus . . . which had converted to Christianity]; Pope Gregory the Great was himself "ein Anicier" (II, 20), and he entrusted an abbot by the name of Probus with important missions (II, 57, 69). So much for Thomas Mann's Probus. The name of his friend, the Cardinal-Presbyter Liberius, also occurs in Gregorovius in a context too remarkable to be overlooked: a twelfth- or thirteenth-century legend connected with the founding of Santa Maria Maggiore has it that Bishop Liberius had a vision. Hastening to his friend to tell him about it, he learned to his surprise that his friend had been vouchsafed the identical vision (I, 108). Thomas Mann's two friends tell each other about the vision in Liberius' "Zetas estivalis," properly "Zeta" (nom. sing. fem.). But if we read in Gregorovius to III, 563, we find the "Zetas Estivalis, ein gekühlter Sommerraum" [a cooled summer room], mentioned as one of the twelve divisions of a typical South Italian palace of the later Middle Ages. In Thomas Mann's papal schism the two rivals are Symmachus and Eulalius. Gregorovius reports a schism in which one of the contenders was named Eulalius and his most influential supporter was the Prefect Symmachus (I, 176). All the choice epi-

---

hard (chapter v) and an accompanying note (note 85) referring to *Ruodlieb* as his authority for so curious an artifact.

thets which Thomas Mann's rival popes hurl at each other (" 'Ver-wüster der Kirche,' 'Wurzel der Sünde,' 'Herold des Teufels,' 'Apos-tel des Antichrist,' 'Pfeil vom Bogen des Satans,' 'Rute Assur,' 'Schiffbruch aller Keuschheit,' 'Kot des Saeculums,' 'scheusslicher und gekrümmter Wurm,' ") [devastator of the Church, root of all evil, herald of the devil, apostle of anti-Christ, arrow from the bow of Satan, Assur's scourge, shipwreck of all chastity, filth of the saeculum, abominable and misshapen worm] derive from invectives quoted by Gregorovius (IV, 138) in connection with another papal schism. The name Chrysogonus, tellingly employed by Thomas Mann in the matter of putting the foundling's gold out at interest, is repeatedly found in Gregorovius (I, 258, 263, 266) as is that of the "Praefect" Chromatius (II, 187); also, of course, such names as that of the Church Father Origines, some of whose doctrines were condemned by Emperor Justinian (I, 404) and the father of Western monasticism, St. Benedict of Nursia (II, 6), son of Eupro-bus (II, 7) and his sister Scholastica (II, 7). Gregorovius is also authority for the story of the release from hell of the pagan em-peror Trajan through the prayers of Pope Gregory the Great (II, 87), including even a characteristic element of the phrasing: God let the Pope know, according to Thomas Mann, that he accepted the *fait accompli*, "er möge sich aber nicht beikommen lassen, der-gleichen ein zweites Mal zu erbitten" (294) [let him not dare, however, to beg for such a thing a second time], corresponding to Gregorovius: "er solle sich nie mehr beikommen lassen . . ." [he ought never more to dare]. The miraculous joining together of the pieces of chain that fettered Saint Peter is also reported by Gre-gorovius (I, 213). Similarly many of the praiseworthy deeds per-formed by Gregorius during his papal term are echoes from widely scattered passages in Gregorovius. To be mentioned among these are the strengthening of the Aurelian walls of the City (I, 350, 426, etc.); the suppression of the Manichaean, Priscillian, and Pelagian heresies (I, 187, 224); the vindication of the papal au-thority over the bishops of Illyria and Gaul (I, 224). Thomas Mann's report that the Church of Saint Peter was built of materials taken from the Circus of the atrocious emperor Caligula corre-sponds to Gregorovius' statement that it was the Circus of Emperor Nero (I, 90), adding that the column of Caligula stood in its confines (I, 96). If it is noted among Gregorius' achievements "dass er . . . das Atrium von Sankt Peter mit Marmorplatten pflasterte" (293) [that he paved the atrium of Saint Peter's with slabs of marble], it cannot be chance which presents us in Gregorovius' text with the clause: "dass er das Atrium des S. Peter mit grossen, weissen Marmorsteinen 'wunderbar schön' pflasterte" (II, 178) [that he paved the atrium of Saint Peter's "wondrously beautifully" with great, white stones of marble]. The hymn sung by the populace on Gregorius' entry into Rome is Gregorovius' translation of a hymn of Prudentius (I, 74):

Ihr Völker jubelt allzumal,
Judäa, Rom und Graecia,
Ägypter, Thraker, Perser, Skythen,
Ein König herrscht ob allen! (290)

[O Peoples, jubilate together,
Judah, Rome and Greece,
Egyptians, Thracians, Persians, Scythians,
One King rules over all!]

One instance of a borrowing from Gregorovius is not without an embarrassing aspect and must be reported in some detail. During the ceremony of his coronation as pope, Gregorius is borne through the Cathedral. As Thomas Mann tells it: "Jünglinge . . . trugen ihn durch die Basilika, ganz umher, mit Frommen angefüllt wie sie war bis zum letzten heidnischen Marmorstück ihres Fussbodens: sei es dort, wo sie sich unter der hohen Decke des Mittelschiffs weit und lang ausdehnt und aus der Ferne der Apsis her die Augen mit musivischem Glanze blendet, oder dort, wo sie unter derselben Last der Dächer nach beiden Seiten in doppelten Säulenhallen die Arme breitet" (291-292). [Youths carried him through the basilica, all around, filled as it was with the faithful to the last heathen piece of marble in its floor: whether there, where it extends broad and long under the high ceiling of the middle aisle and blinds the eyes from the distance of the apse with mosaic brilliance, or there, where it spreads its arms to both sides in double-columned halls under the same burden of roofs.] This long sentence with its overextended coda gave me trouble at each reading. I had the feeling as though the author himself had been overcome by drowsiness under the influence of the automatic pealing of the bells, the music, and the incense. This puzzling deviation from the general pattern of Thomas

THOMAS MANN'S *GREGORIUS: DER ERWÄHLTE*

Mann's style was solved when I came in Gregorovius upon this translation of a highly florid passage from a letter of Bishop Paulinus of Nola to Senator Alethius whom he thanks for having been allowed to witness a most edifying spectacle in Saint Peter's: "Zu welcher Freude erhobst du den Apostel selbst, als du seine ganze Basilika mit dichten Scharen von Armen vollgedrängt hattest, sei es wo sie unter der hohen mittleren Decke weit und lang sich erstreckt, und aus der Ferne vom Apostolischen Stuhl her schimmernd die Augen der Eintretenden blendet und die Herzen erfreut, oder wo sie unter derselben Last der Dächer von beiden Seiten in doppelten Säulenhallen die Arme ausbreitet . . ." (ι, 94). [With what joy did you raise the apostle himself, when you had crowded his whole basilica with dense hosts of the poor, whether it be where it stretches broad and long under the high middle ceiling and from the distance of the apostolic chair blinds with brilliance the eyes of those entering and gladdens their hearts, or where under the same burden of roofs it spreads its arms from both sides in double columned halls.] The remainder of the sentence, extending over another six lines, also makes mention of the fountain adorned by a cupola supported by columns, corresponding to a similar ornament that is credited to Gregorius in the novel (293).

To mention a final instance of borrowing (many more could be added), we recall the long line of papal dignitaries who pass Sibylla and her daughters from hand to hand through an interminable succession of antechambers before her audience with the Pope. Without doubt the mien of these dignitaries was as impressive as their titles—the Nomenculator (305), the Cubicularius, Protoscrinarius, Vestiarius, and Vicedominus together with the Primicerius of the Defensors (307), and finally the Curopalata (308). While these fancy terms of rank sound as though assembled by Brentano, we meet many of them throughout Gregorovius' work, and all of them are enumerated and integrated into the papal bureaucracy in Volume ιι, pages 484-489.

3. The Transmutation

The quest of sources is an intriguing game that keeps the mind in a state of taut alertness. It is a legitimate literary enterprise as well when undertaken in the service of the basic question: in what manner and to what extent did the author achieve the transmutation of his materials into an integrated new work of art? This is particularly true of a work like *Der Erwählte*, inasmuch as it is not only the retelling of an old tale but involves beyond this the reworking of a great variety of diverse literary materials. The ideal approach for appraising the quality of the work before us, modeled as it is on a very old design and woven of literary strands of the greatest variety of texture and color, would presuppose a connoisseur's eye able to spot the provenience of every strand and knot of its tapestry. (Its effect is indeed that of a tapestry rather than a three-dimensional construct.) We are under no illusions of being able to satisfy this ideal standard; a great many questions regarding specific sources remain unanswered.

There is the name of the Duchess Baduhenna, for instance, Gregorius' grandmother, who died in childbirth. To discover that this name occurs just once, in the *Annals* of Tacitus, as the name of a sacred Frisian grove, probably standing for the goddess of a pagan cult,[10] is only mystifying, and mystification is doubtless intended. We should like to know the context in which Thomas Mann found it. Where did he pick up names like (the Irish) Flann, Gregorius' foster-brother, the dog Hanegiff, and Probus' wife Faltonia,[11] to mention a few? On what authority does he name an unknown tribe, the Haugens (87), along with the Saxons, Angles, and Jutes as the conquerors of Britain? Did he fake the name as he did those of the alleged Channel Islands, Saint Dunstan and Saint Aldhelm, an admission curiously conveyed by the Abbot's uncertainty and that of the natives regarding the name of their home ground (84, 88)?[12] Another thing, much more important, which we should also like to discover, is whether the milk that wells up from the udders of the Earth to nourish Gregorius on his rock for seventeen years by a concentrated vitamin diet, really derives authority from a myth of classical antiquity, or whether the old magician is here beguiling us by one of his most cunning tricks of sleight of hand. We suspect the latter, as the information to be found in Pauly-Wissowa on milk

---

[10] Hoops' *Realenzyklopaedie der germanischen Altertumskunde.*

[11] Anicia Faltonia Proba is mentioned in Procopius' *Gothic Wars*, according to Pauly-Wissowa, *Realencyklopaedie der klassischen Altertumswissenschaft*, as a pious descendant of the Anician clan at the time of Alaric.

[12] Baedeker's and Muirhead's *England* have not heard tell of them.

in the cult and ritual of the ancients would seem to offer not so much as a toe hold to the author's imagination for so bold a take-off.[13] It is time we turned from these obscure matters to the general question of how Thomas Mann used those sources on which we know him to have drawn directly and heavily.

Confining ourselves to the three main sources indicated, Hartmann's *Gregorius*, Wolfram's *Parzival*, and Gregorovius' *Stadt Rom*, let us see how Thomas Mann has worked them into his tapestry.

We begin with Wolfram because it is knots and tufts from Wolfram's *Parzival* that dominate in the introductory section of the story proper. As we find ourselves at the court of Grimald, Duke of Artois and Flanders, we move in an atmosphere that suggests both the reality of courtly life around the year 1200 and its reflection and embellishment in the idealized settings of the romantic epic of chivalry. The tone, to be sure, is that of fairy tale, and the specific playful flavor of the fairy-tale tone suggests the Märchen of Clemens Brentano rather than the smiling but more ceremonious decorum of Hartmann, Wolfram, and Gottfried. As regards the mode of life, however, the personnel, and the profuse inventory, these items are chiefly, though not exclusively, garnered from *Parzival*. The composition of the great body of ministrants, the twelve pages of high lineage, including two Saracens, the musical instruments, the exotic tissues, vestments, and entertainment, the furniture and floor coverings, the great fireplaces, the profusion of candles and candelabra in the great hall, the kinds of food and

---

[13] I am grateful to Konstantin Reichardt for referring me to Hermann Usener's "Milch und Honig" in *Rheinisches Museum für Philologie, Neue Folge*, LVII (1902), 177-195. On the first page we read: "Schon bei der Geburt des Dionysos hebt Philostratos es hervor, dass die Erde selbst sich an seinem Schwärmen beteiligen werde, indem 'sie ihm gewähre Wein aus Wasserquellen zu schöpfen und *Milch wie aus Brüsten* bald aus einer Ackerscholle, bald *aus einem Felsen* zu ziehn': es lässt sich nicht verkennen, dass dieser lebendigen und eigenartigen Schilderung die Worte eines alten Dichters zu Grunde liegen." [Even with the birth of Dionysos, Philostratos emphasizes that the earth itself would share in his adoration, in that it "would allow him to draw wine from springs of water and milk, as though from breasts, now from a clod of earth, now from a boulder"; one cannot fail to recognize, that this vivid and unique depiction is based on the words of an ancient poet.] This passage, referring to the nurturing of a god associated with all kinds of extravagance, is very different from the general anthropogonic myth to which Thomas Mann treats us. Nevertheless, the phrases italicized by me would seem to have fertilized Thomas Mann's imagination, whether he happened upon them in the above or in some other context. The article offers no further leads.

drink enumerated together with their containers and manner of presentation, the jewels, arms, and features of knightly sport—all these items unmistakably derive from *Parzival*, Books 1, 2, and 5 in particular. On pages 17-20, where this source is overwhelmingly in evidence, I count offhand some seventy-five names, words, and phrases that derive from *Parzival* in such a way that one or many specific passages could be quoted in substantiation of this claim. Their number precludes any such attempt. Let it suffice, therefore, to mention rather that the mincing walk of the pages, advancing in pairs, holding each other by the hand, and curtseying with crossed legs as they salute the ducal couple (17-18) is without any counterpart in *Parzival*. This should not surprise us, for it was not Thomas Mann's ambition to write a pseudo-authentic medieval tale. He was simply having his fun. Take his report of the story of Saint Sylvester for instance. Among other matters, the court minstrels sing "vom Glaubensstreit des heiligen Silvester vor Kaiser Konstantin mit einem Juden: der raunte einem Stier den Namen seines Gottes ins Ohr, und tot fiel der Stier zu Boden. Silvester aber rief Christum an: Da stieg der Bulle wieder auf seine Beine und verkündete mit Donnergebrüll die Überlegenheit des wahren Glaubens" (19) [of the religious contest in the presence of the Emperor Constantine between Saint Sylvester and a Jew. The latter whispered the name of his God into the ear of a steer and the steer fell to the ground dead. Sylvester, however, appealed to Christ. Thereupon the steer got to its legs again and with a thunderous roar proclaimed the superiority of the True Faith]. This way of telling the story is calculated to provoke hilarious mirth, whereas in *Parzival* it appears in a very serious context, just before the miraculous healing of Amfortas' wound; and it suppresses the point of the story as told in the *Legenda Aurea*: that it is a greater power which gives life than that which kills.

Thomas Mann's sense of fun is particularly in evidence in his manner of employing the proper names taken from *Parzival*: Belrapeire, the stronghold of Wolfram's lovely Kondwiramurs, becomes the residence of Duke Grimald (18); Bealzenan, the fabulous capital of Wolfram's Anschouwe, is here attached to the name of Herr Feirefiss who, as Sibylla's "Truchsess" [lord high steward], has nothing in common with Parzival's magpie-spotted half brother;

Wolfram's King Klamide here reappears as an ordinary knight and also as a monk (31, 123); Garschiloye, who is one of the twenty-five ladies in Wolfram's Grail procession, here becomes one of the ladies at court and derives "von der Beafontane" (32), a place associated in *Parzival* with the Lady Imane; Guverjorss, the battle steed of Wolfram's Klamide, here remains a horse, but Duke Grimald rides it (17); Wolfram's Reine Inguse (von Bahtarliez), a queen residing in remote parts, turns up as the name of a fisherman's boat; as for Wolfram's "Krieche Klias," the knight who missed out on the adventure of the Magic Castle, he turns up here as the Duke's Greek personal physician (38); the proud Lady Mahaute here lends her name to a shrewish fisherman's wife (93); the name of the charmingly sophisticated little girl Obilot whose colors Herr Gawan carries to victory, is here that of a knight from Gascony (37); Wolfram's coal-black knight Razalic, whose name reveals Arabic origin (Ras Ali = Prince Ali), is here transformed into a knight from Lorraine (32); and Schoydelakurt (to mention another instance without exhausting their number), in *Parzival* the magic garden of Mabonagrin, the terrible headhunter who makes an earlier appearance in Crétien's and Hartmann's *Erec*—Schoydelakurt (= joie de la cour) here appropriately becomes the endearing nickname affixed to the charming twins Sibylla and Wiligis (22). To more than remark that the lifting of these names from their context in *Parzival* shows an impish spirit of parody at work would be to labor the point. If Thomas Mann identifies himself with Wolfram in any respect it is in the playful spirit with which he manipulates the assortment of exotic proper names and in his use of linguistic material generally, derived from a great variety of old languages and dialects (of which more in the last division of this paper).

If we find that the climactic exploit of Gregorius, his combat with the Burgundian Duke, fails to conform to any of the conventional equestrian duels of Hartmann, Wolfram, or Gottfried as regards the fair observance of rules of the game, we will not be so foolish as to ascribe this deviation to negligence. And if we find the "gabylot," a rude peasant weapon put to infamous use in *Parzival*, mentioned in Thomas Mann's *Gregorius* as a weapon honorably employed by a knight's hand (28), or if we find the duel of Gregorius with the Burgundian Duke referred to, quite impossibly, as a "Holmgang" (176),[14] or the ruse of his flight, with the Burgundian in hot pursuit, as "einen langen puneiz,"[15] it might be rash to attribute these slips to ignorance on Thomas Mann's part. Who knows (and who will ever know!) whether these and similar "boners" are not conscious plants, in keeping with the clerical mask of the installed narrator, the Irish monk writing in Sankt Gallen, who is professedly bored with fighting and its technical vocabulary.

The initial part of Thomas Mann's story is deeply indebted to Wolfram, as we have seen, for a host of medieval courtly and exotic touches, applied with great verve. As the story progresses, such elements crop up more sparingly. To mention only one more such instance, it is Parzival's father riding into Kanvoleiz whose superimposed image we see when young Wiligis learns "wie man beim Lustritt in weicher Tracht ein Bein légèrement vor sich aufs Pferd legt" (28) [how when riding for pleasure in a supple costume one lays one leg casually in front of himself on the horse]. Quite different was the impact of Thomas Mann's avowed major source, Hartmann von Aue's *Gregorius*.

As already mentioned, Hartmann contributed the plot of the whole story, the design, the linear outline, with all its many twists and turns. Much of Hartmann's phrasing, moreover, has been preserved in the archaic coloring of Thomas Mann's language. A detailed comparison of Thomas Mann with his principal source, dwelling on the nature and extent of his elaborations (and prunings) will offer a grateful subject for a dissertation. Here we have to confine ourselves to a very cursory account of the most notable features inviting comparison.

Hartmann's legend has a long, gravely edifying introduction and conclusion, and much of his story is interspersed with long-winded reflections on human frailty and the cunning devices of the Tempter. These are either omitted by Thomas Mann or given a parodistic twist. Unlike his source, Thomas Mann effectively anticipates the glorious denouement in his very first sentence, filling our ears with

---

[14] Morold's fight with Tristan, on an *island*, is a "Holmgang," but the word, a common technical term of Norse saga, does not occur in Gottfried's *Tristan*.

[15] Hartmann uses this phrase (which means "a long charge") in his *Gregorius*, lines 1614 and 2118 (and perhaps elsewhere). Note the spelling "puneiz," whereas borrowings from Wolfram-Hertz are distinguished by capitalization of nouns and the substitution of "ss" for final "z."

the automatic pealing of all the bells of Rome, and he installs a narrator, not a knight but a monk, whose personality we shall discuss elsewhere. Hartmann passes over the initial phase of the story up to the incestuous union of brother and sister very briefly, and much of this is taken up with the cares of the dying duke regarding the future of his daughter. The death of the mother after giving birth to the twins is baldly reported, without any suggestion of the disconcertingly ironic response of Heaven to the couple's prayers for the granting of the long-delayed issue. Whereas Hartmann devotes less than a hundred lines to all this, Thomas Mann takes some twenty-three pages to develop the courtly setting, the personality of the parents, and the intimate life of the children, including the father's jealousy of his son. While Hartmann narrates the scene of cohabitation with the utmost courtly discretion, Thomas Mann turns the spotlight on a riot of elemental passion, both exciting and repulsive in its stark bloody cruelty, heightened by the proximity of the dead father's body lying in state (the son is getting even with his jealous sire), and deriving a peculiar piquancy from the symbolic Adam and Eve dialogue and the sister's artful poise and unabashed curiosity throughout the act of her violation. Here naturalistic detail is enveloped in an aura of surrealism that is without parallel in Thomas Mann's work, as regards the treatment of sex. Very notable in the development of pregnancy and the lying-in is Thomas Mann's delineation of Frau Eisengrein, that incarnation of efficient midwifery, whose counterpart in Hartmann's poem is no more than a perfectly conventional shadow. The exposure of the child at sea in a cask is told by both authors with comparable detail: the intimation of the child's lineage in the form of an intriguing riddle already appears in Hartmann's work (as in the Old French source that he did into German) and is harped upon with gusto, in keeping with the predilection of chivalric poetry for all forms of playful verbalization, inducing crosscurrents of tension and pleasure upon their resolution in a way quite foreign to the literary art of the nineteenth century. Hartmann also has the feature of the twenty gold pieces and the future disposition of the sum together with the fabulous growth of seventeen to a hundred and fifty in the course of seventeen years, when put out at interest. Thomas Mann's only addition here is the baking of the gold into a loaf of bread.

The account of the bereft Sibylla's grief permits of interesting comparisons. Both authors affect a systematic enumeration of her sorrows, but as regards her grief upon the news of her brother-lover's death and her reaction at his funeral, Hartmann has only a dry two lines, whereas Thomas Mann's account of her spirited bearing shows influence—*per contrarium*—of the *Gesta Romanorum* version. Hartmann makes much of the fact that the girl managed to survive despite four afflictions, whereas the grief of separation from his love sufficed to break her brother's heart—a circumstance showing, as Hartmann observes, the fallacy of the common assumption that women's emotions are deeper than men's. Thomas Mann, on the other hand, makes Wiligis appear rather in the light of a "softie." It was not from him, certainly, that Gregorius derived his faculty of concentration and his "festhaltende Hand" [tenacious hand].

As for the lady's subsequent fortune, her being importuned and made war on by an unwelcome suitor over a space of years long enough to allow her child to grow to manhood, Hartmann's rudimentary time sense skips over all this in twenty-three lines, in order to turn his attention to the fortunes of the infant. Thomas Mann sticks to the same sequence of the divided strands of the story, but he puts himself to considerable pains to clear the hurdle of implausibility regarding so long and tenacious a suit. We need not dwell here on the means by which he skillfully conveys to us the experience of duration.

Turning now to the fortunes of the child, we find this section of Thomas Mann's story introduced by a close-up view of the Abbot Gregorius as he approaches the shore of his island in the aftermath of a stormy night. He delivers himself of a six-page flow of interior monologue (83-89) in the process. Thomas Mann found nothing in Hartmann to suggest any of this detail. Why this rather long-winded though vivid enough introduction? Among a multiplicity of reasons to account for it we would mention (1) the installed narrator's partiality to one of his own cloth, (2) the author's desire to sketch in the geographical and historical Anglo-Norman background involved in the change of setting, (3) the sly superimposition upon the abbot's figure of another Gregorius, equally garrulous and equally snarled in his efforts to square the theory and practice of truthfulness—Bishop Gregory of Tours as he appears in Grillparzer's comedy *Weh dem, der lügt!*, and (4) the author's partial self-identification with the abbot in mentioning among his physical characteristics his prominent and rounded lower lip, a physiognomic trait mentioned just once (82), quite contrary to Thomas Mann's usage.

The delightful dialogue between the abbot and the fishermen, leading to the discovery of the foundling and arrangements for his care, though Thomas Mann's own in all its vivid humorous detail, is merely an elaboration of corresponding features of Hartmann's poem. Hartmann also supplied the model for the account of the boy's prodigious strides in monastic education, as he first becomes a "grammaticus," then studies "divinitas," and finally acquires proficiency "in legibus." (We appreciate the German knight's pride in this display of his Latin schooling involving the threefold, elegant variation of his construction.) As for the delineation of the antagonism, however, that developed between the high-spirited Grigorss and his plebeian foster brother Flann and the dreadful fist-fight that brought matters to a climax, Thomas Mann had to proceed entirely on his own: Hartmann's version is completely lifeless in reporting Grigorss' infliction of an accidental hurt during play upon his foster brother, who then runs crying to his mother, who releases a volley of foul imprecations and lets out the secret of Grigorss' being a foundling.

The conversation that ensues between Grigorss and the abbot, on the other hand, is of comparable length in both works. Hartmann devotes nearly 450 lines to it as compared to Thomas Mann's thirteen pages. The details of Grigorss' voyage again, including the fish as his coat of arms, of his reception at Bruges, of his preliminary exploits, his definitive triumph over the tenacious Burgundian, his conversations with Sibylla, her change of heart and her prayer, and the consummation of the marriage, are in overwhelming measure the creation of Thomas Mann's imagination. Once more a reminiscence from the *Gesta Romanorum* version contributed a characteristic touch. There, after listening to the representations of her council, urging her to marry and give the country an heir, the lady asks for one day's time to think it over. Thomas Mann has her speak of seven weeks and actually ask one week's "Bedenkzeit," despite the fact that she is madly in love—a tribute to her poise. Hartmann makes no mention of any "Bedenkzeit" [time to ponder] whatever.

Except for the fact that Thomas Mann has Sibylla bear her son two daughters, Hartmann making no mention of any issue, the course of the marriage follows along parallel lines in both works to the ghastly denouement, the separation, and finally the chaining of Gregorius to the barren reef by the fisherman who throws the key into the water.

A mere thirty-six lines suffices for Hartmann to cover Gregorius' seventeen-year period of penance and the miracle of his preservation, another indication of his rudimentary epic-time sense. This contrasts with an eight-page section of the novel in which Thomas Mann's humor achieves one of its greatest triumphs. With the gravest fairy-tale logic he demonstrates that Gregorius' preservation was not so much of a miracle after all. Given the premises about the milk of the Earth, presented on the authority of the ancients, all subsequent developments follow with the force of corollary deductions: exposure to the rigors of the hot and cold season together with the nutritive concentrate adapted to the status of the infant work their transformation of the immobile "Büsser" [penitent] into the horny, warty creature scarce bigger than a hedgehog, and the same line of analogous reasoning is invoked to account for the rapid restoration of his human stature after normal adult food has again entered his digestive tract. All this is told with so much precisely observed detail as to compel belief in the authenticity of these phenomena, and many a reader will at least be tempted to yield to a feeling that the miracle has been explained away in an entirely satisfactory manner. Thomas Mann makes very little, by the way, of the mental anguish suffered by Gregorius during his period of penance. Empathy concentrates rather upon the diminution of his sensitivity, as he shrinks by progressive stages, recalling to mind the "Herabminderungen" [diminutions] and "Gnadennarkosen" [merciful anaesthetics] of the desperately ill in the *Zauberberg*.

The last quarter of Thomas Mann's novel, which first takes us to Rome, shows the modern author emancipated to an even greater degree from his primary source as regards the elaboration of vivid scenes and the characterization of the saintly pope's wise administration of his office. Suffice it to say that the characteristic features of Hartmann's plot are preserved intact, including the papal schism, the revealing of Heaven's choice of a worthy incumbent of the apostolic seat to two pious Romans, their successful search for the saint, confirmed by the miracle of the key, the recovery of Gregorius' tablet, the automatic pealing of the bells of Rome during his triumphal entry into the City, and his interview, years later, with his mother, culminating in the assurance that all sins have been forgiven and even Wiligis' crime has been atoned for by the expiation of mother and son. The major accents, however, are Thomas Mann's own and would have been unthinkable in any previous version. What a difference between the medieval sinner's long-drawn-out remonstrances as to his unworthiness, when confronted on his rock by the Romans (Hartmann has him carry on in this vein for eighty-six lines) and the alert eagerness of the modern Gregorius to follow the call the instant he has become aware that Heaven has intervened in his favor! And who but a master of current psychology could have given the recognition scene between mother and son that sensational fillip—the mother's arch admission to her son that she had known her confessor's identity all along?

Despite the working of such utterly original touches into the old story's outline, the last quarter of Thomas Mann's novel shows an extraordinary manipulation of extraneous source material. Broadly speaking, everything in this last part, excluding the Penkhart episode, for which I am unable to account on the basis of any source, reveals the use of innumerable strands plucked from Gregorovius' *History of Rome in the Middle Ages*. The astonishing thing is not their use as such but the transformation they underwent in being worked into the new tapestry.

To mention the most astonishing thing first: Up to this point our story was enacted in a setting that reflected the age of chivalry in a very advanced stage—the turning point of the twelfth and thirteenth centuries. But what of the Rome to which Thomas Mann takes us now? This city of sparsely populated ruins, this vast marble cemetery of pagan glories, temples, and empty palaces, that are utilized piecemeal in the erection of Christian churches, transports us back to an era left many centuries behind.[16] This is the Rome

---

[16] I owe grateful acknowledgment to the late Curt von Faber du Faur, who was quick to perceive this and suggested Gregorovius as a likely factual source.

that has been sacked by Alaric and the Vandals, the Rome that has lived through its half-century of Gothic rule, the Rome that survives as a wretched dependency of the Byzantine empire, the Rome in which the papacy emerges as the spiritual authority of the West and the secular authority of a large part of the Italian peninsula. The heresies which the Pope's firm hand puts under control are those of the fifth and sixth centuries; his astute policy in facilitating the mass conversion of Mohammedans (296) surely takes us well into the era of the Crusades. Where then, exactly, are we to locate the career of our hero in point of time? What historical pope will bear identification with this legendary prince of the Church?

The answer is simple. In so far as the physical Roman setting is concerned, the time is from the fifth century to the ninth, reduced to an ideal point, and our pope has to his credit a variety of achievements distributed among successors to Saint Peter over a great many centuries. What happens to the historical setting in point of time is this: it undergoes a shrinking process, a reduction from a thirteenth-century to a fifth-century atmosphere, analogous to the transformation of the hero from a man to a horny little hedgehog. (At the very end, if you will have it that way, time reasserts its vitality and lets go in a prodigious stretch, as the characters suddenly assume the features of twentieth-century sophistication.) For the purposes of the story, the long succession of centuries that make up the medieval era are treated as though they were one undifferentiated point of fairy-tale time, after the manner of the sixteenth-century chapbooks and their playful imitation a hundred and fifty years ago by the German Romanticist Tieck in his *Kaiser Oktavianus.*

The jump from the era of knighthood in its age of flower to that of early medieval Rome is too evident to require laboring. We must take the time, however, to demonstrate by a series of samplings, what a diversity of events and personalities, separated by centuries, have furnished the strands for the Roman area of this modern tapestry of myth.

To begin with, the new pope's triumphal entry into the Eternal City (290 f.), which reads as though all of one piece, borrows its intimate geographic detail from Charlemagne's visit to Rome in the year 800. Our Gregorius approaches "auf der Nomentanischen

Strasse, an deren vierzehntem Meilenstein der Ort Nomentum gelegen ist, ein Bischofssitz" [on the Nomentanian Way, at whose fourteenth milestone the locality of Nomentum is situated, a bishop's see]. For Charlemagne's route the historian reports: "Am 14. Meilenstein auf der Nomentanischen Strasse lag damals noch der alte Ort Nomentum, schon seit dem vierten Jahrhundert Sitz eines Bischofs (Gregorovius, II, 537 f.). [At the fourteenth milestone on the Nomentanian Way there lay at that time the old locality of Nomentum, since the fourth century a bishop's see.] And further down the page we read in our novel: "Nicht durch das Nomentanische Tor, so liest man, zog er ein, sondern zog längs den Mauern hin und dann über die Milvische Brücke" [Not through the Nomentanian Gate, so one reads, did he enter, rather he went along the walls and then over the Milvian Bridge], which corresponds to the historian's: "Er hielt seinen Einzug wahrscheinlich nicht durch das Nomentanische Tor, sondern längs den Mauern hinziehend, überschritt er wohl die Milvische Brücke" (Gregorovius, II, 538). [In all probability he did not make his procession through the Nomentanian Gate, rather going along the walls he probably passed over the Milvian Bridge.] The two passages quoted, thirteen lines apart, are linked by descriptions that derive from another quarter. Regarding our hero we read: ". . . den Klerus, den Adel, die Zünfte des Bürgerstandes mit ihren Bannern . . . fand er zu seiner Bewillkommnung aufgereiht" (290) [. . . the clerics, the nobility, the guilds of the bourgeoisie with their banners he found lined up to welcome him]. This is modeled after the historian's: ". . . fand er alle Klassen des Volks vor der Milvischen Brücke zu seiner Bewillkommnung aufgereiht. Der Clerus, der Adel . . . die Zünfte des Bürgerstandes . . . standen dort mit ihren Bannern . . ." (Gregorovius, II, 534) [. . . he found all classes of the people lined up before the Milvian Bridge for his welcome. The clerics, the nobility, the guilds of the bourgeoisie stood there with their banners]. The passage just quoted, however, refers not to Charlemagne's visit in 800, but to Pope Leo III's return the year before, after his flight to the King of the Franks. As if this were not enough, elements of a third welcome found their way into the last, partially quoted sentence from Thomas Mann: ". . . die Schulen der Kinder, Palmen- und Ölzweige in den Händen . . ." (290) [the schools of children, palm and olive branches in their hands]. This passage derives verbatim from the historian's account of Charlemagne's first visit to Rome, at Easter 774 (Gregorovius, II, 393); and as our hero is greeted by the chant of the priests, "Benedictus qui venit in nomine Domini" (291) [Blessed be he, who comes in the name of the Lord], so there it was Charlemagne in whose honor these same strains resounded (Gregorovius, II, 394). However, to make our astonishment complete, looping the strand of the tapestry back once more, Thomas Mann separates these two features that he borrowed from Charlemagne's visit of 774 by a four-line hymn of welcome issuing from the mouths of the people. This hymn, the work of the poet Prudentius, takes us back nearly four centuries to Christianity's triumph over the pagan gods of Rome. The translation of the Latin hymn into German is, of course, Gregorovius' (I, 74).

It is not often, certainly, that we can peer over the shoulder of the weaver of myth in quite this fashion and see him work his needle and tie his tufts.[17]

Continuing now with the achievements of Thomas Mann's mythical Gregorius as our text (288-298) and comparing them with the record of events reported in Gregorovius' "History," we find the following correspondence: The repairing of the Aurelian walls (293) is credited by Gregorovius to Pope Symmachus, d. 514, to Belisar in the Gothic Wars, and again to the Popes Gregory II, d. 731, Gregory III, d. 741, and Hadrian, d. 795 (Gregorovius, I, 305, 349 f.; II, 244, 275, 319, 422 f.). The paving of the atrium of St. Peter's (293) is reported for Pope Symmachus (Gregorovius, I, 305) and again for Pope Domnus, d. 678 (Gregorovius, II, 178). Verbatim parallels regarding the consolidation of the Papal State (293) and the fortifying of the towns of Radicofani and Orte (293) take us all the way to Pope Hadrian IV, d. 1159 (Gregorovius, IV, 525).[18] The suppression of the Manichaean, Priscillian,

---

[17] Even the Pope's procession after his coronation, through the Holy City along the Via Sacra to the Lateran, including mention of the triumphal arches and the Jews of the Parione Region lined up to salute their new lord (292), is only an abbreviated version of the ceremony as reported in Gregorovius, IV, 613-615, and again in V, 10-13.

[18] "Er [Hadrian IV.] befestigte selbst Städte neu, wie Orta [*sic*] und Radicofani. . . . Viele [der einst mächtigen Barone] übergaben ihre Castelle halb oder ganz Hadrian, der sie ihnen dann als Lehn der Kirche zurückstellte, und so wurden Edelfreie zu pflichtigen Leuten (homines) des Papsts." [He (Hadrian IV) himself forti-

THOMAS MANN'S *GREGORIUS: DER ERWÄHLTE*

and Pelagian heresies (293) was achieved by Pope Leo I, d. 461 (Gregorovius, I, 224), who also forced the recalcitrant bishops of Illyria and Gaul (293) to bow to papal supremacy (Gregorovius, I, 224). Our pope's stern and effective measures against simony, the sale of Church offices (293), evoke the great figure of Gregory VII, d. 1085, as pictured by Gregorovius (IV, 31, 66, 74, 91, etc.). The feat of effecting by importunate prayers the release of the pagan emperor Trajan from hell (294) was credited by an eighth-century legend to Pope Gregory the Great, d. 604, (Gregorovius, II, 87). The same pope applied to Britain the principle of reconsecrating pagan temples in foreign lands (294-295) instead of destroying them (Gregorovius, II, 116-117). The miraculous fusion of the chains of St. Peter (297), on the other hand, takes us back to Pope Leo I (Gregorovius, I, 213).[19]

This use of history is not that of the scholar. All historical realism, all pretense of telling an authentic story in an authentic setting, has been cast to the winds. Unlike a nineteenth-century master like Conrad Ferdinand Meyer, whose superb craftsmanship aimed at a synthesis of literary art and historical truth, Thomas Mann gives free rein to his myth-making fancy. The merest hint in a source suffices for him to conjure up a series of scenes that have all the tension of drama and all the vividness and precision of the puppet stage. Compare the wonderful simultaneous vision of Probus and Liberius with Hartmann's colorless report of the divine message and its reinforcement by the brief mention of a similar heavenly communication in Gregorovius (I, 108). How those two friends, the short patrician and the long cleric, are alive in every word and gesture! How delightful the slight discrepancy in the vision vouch-

---

fied cities anew, such as Orta (*sic*) and Radicofani. . . . Many (of the once powerful barons) turned over their castles half or completely to Hadrian, who returned them then as fiefs of the Church, and so free nobles became beholden people (homines) of the pope.]

[19] This far-reaching pattern of correspondences would lead us to expect that each and every item of the mythical Gregorius' policies and achievements find its counterpart in the historian's work. It is disappointing, therefore, to find that three such items, all illustrating the pope's tolerance, progressiveness, and humane wisdom, are conspicuously missing. They are (1) our pope's repudiation of the Donatist heresy (293-294); (2) his handling of the case of the monk who performed a surgical operation (295-296); and (3) his decision regarding the polygamous status of Moslem converts in the Holy Land (296). Nowhere in his eight-volume history does Gregorovius mention any such issues.

safed to both in its exploitation of surprise, and how revealing of character! And how subtle the delight of recognizing in the aging patrician couple Sextus Anicius Probus and his wife Faltonia Proba a cousin of Serenus Zeitblom (whose peculiar dryness was much in evidence in *Doktor Faustus*) married to a very matronly Imma Spoelmann (*Königliche Hoheit*), who seems to be, borrowing a phrase from Viktor Mann's *Wir Waren Fünf* (1949) "ganz gefähr-lich gescheit" [really dangerously shrewd]! Such transparent use of masks that suggest a partial identification of their impersonators with Thomas Mann and his wife, leads us to the consideration of a new major topic: Thomas Mann's use of the mask.

4. The Mask

The work of Hartmann von Aue includes two legends. Besides *Gregorius* he left us *Der arme Heinrich*, the tale of a wealthy, valiant, and virtuous knight who is stricken with the dread scourge of leprosy at the height of his career and in his panic seeks a cure by accepting the offer of a half-grown girl to give her life for him on the operating table of a Salerno physician. Tragedy is averted at the last moment as the knight experiences a change of heart, is miraculously cured by the grace of God and then marries her, whom he had playfully styled his betrothed many years earlier. It is an interesting fact that both these legends were renewed in the twentieth century by the two most prominent exponents of literary art in Germany. But whereas Gerhart Hauptmann's dramatic poem, *Der arme Heinrich* (1902) plumbed the depths of tragic self-abandonment in the relentlessly pursued exposure of soul-searing anguish, ultimately turned into transcending rapture, Thomas Mann's prose version of *Gregorius* skirts the engaging of deeper emotions and develops his theme in a style of high intellectual humor. Of all of Thomas Mann's longer pieces, this is the lightest and most frankly humorous.

Both of these modern works are highly personal, though in very different ways. In drama the stage, occupied by the figures, leaves no room for a commenting author. Here the author can utter a confession only by having us sense his maximum self-identification with the hero, which is the case in Hauptmann's *Der arme Heinrich*. In Thomas Mann's novels, on the other hand, the author is commonly and pervasively present as the narrator, who not only tells his story but also speculates at length on all its aspects, involving the devices of his own epic technique. But as is already the case in *Doktor Faustus*, the author of the modern *Gregorius* chooses to veil his personality by installing a narrator who tells the whole story in the first person. Thomas Mann invents a mask with a personality of its own, which we equate with the author's personality at our peril. This fictitious self, which reports the story from beginning to end, allows him to project his personality in a stylized and teasing way without assuming full responsibility for the narrator's slant. Thus, in *Doktor Faustus*, something of the full personality of Thomas Mann is glimpsed only in the tension that exists between Serenus Zeitblom, the biographer, and his hero, the composer Adrian Leverkühn, and the latter is at least as much a projection of Thomas Mann's "real self" as the former. We note in passing that Thomas Mann does not use the device of a "frame" involving the introducing of the setting and characters by what appears to be a neutral author, who then allows the teller of the story to take over in the presence of a listener or a group of listeners. Such a framed form of narrative achieves very complex crosscurrents of tension between narrator, listener, and participating reader. It was developed with consummate artistry by Conrad Ferdinand Meyer, notably in *Der Heilige* and *Die Hochzeit des Mönchs*. In these works, however, the author turns out to be not a neutral voice but rather a stage director, reappearing as he does at significant intervals of dialogue to accentuate the visual aspects of the scene and turn the spotlight on the gesturing, play of features, and tone of voice of his characters. As often as not, these asides reveal the author as hiding behind a highly ambiguous mask. Thomas Mann felt, I dare say, that the possibilities of the framed story had been exhausted by these masterpieces. In his *Gregorius* he chooses, in a technically much less ambitious way, to don a mask at the beginning and wear it to the end.

Thomas Mann dons the mask of a Benedictine monk, not that of a medieval knight. In an ironically deliberate way that may strike us as tedious, the "spirit of narrative art," after weaving before the reader's eye as a kind of intangible vapor, settles into the shape of an Irish monk snugly ensconced in a nook of the library of the

monastery of St. Gallen to compose his new version of an oft-told
tale. He gives us concrete particulars regarding his person in all but
two respects: his remarks about the language in which he is writing,
or rather about the metamorphosis which it undergoes from day
to day (15-16), are just the waving of a magic wand in advance
of the show, and he drops no hint as regards the historical time
of his own existence. His references to his Irish monastic background tend to suggest a rather early medieval setting regarding his
own person—the sentiments of his Abbot Kilian, who believes in
combining the religion of Jesus with the cultivation of humanistic
studies (12), are those attributed by Gregorovius to St. Columban
(II, 91)—but we are disabused of this notion quickly by his taking
refuge in an "Abstraktheit" that refuses any commitment regarding the "when" of his writing (17). If we are on the alert, we have
already detected an intellectual climate about his person suggesting
the age of Erasmus: some pages back he introduced a Latin quotation that smacks of the *Epistolae Obscurorum Virorum*, involving,
it would seem, a dig at Luther in his disdainful reference to an
Augustinian monk as the purveyor of *such* sentiments in *such*
Latin (12). And his remarks on the following page about Saint
Peter and certain early decretals are a thinly veiled display of caustic
wit at the expense of the Church. For all the lip service that he
renders to the Church, this monk does not believe in the miracles
on which he embroiders. For the most part his skeptical barbs are
so finely pointed as to afford high amusement, but on occasion he
lapses into inanity. He cannot suppress a snicker when, for the second time, he reports the automatic pealing of the bells as "heilige
Heimsuchung und Kalamität" (288) [holy affliction and calamity]
and "hehre Plage" (289) [sacred torment], driving the population
to distraction by its incessant three-day droning and causing a run
on the supply of cotton with attendant profiteering. This destruction of the atmosphere of miracle, as regards not the teller of the
story but the populace for which it is staged, unmasks the monk
as a nihilistic destroyer of his own work, making it difficult to recapture the mood of suspended belief and to enjoy without reservation the celestial humor of the final scene of recognition. It was
evidently Thomas Mann's design to reveal himself under a Janus-
faced mask, as he did in *Doktor Faustus*. But instead of taking

offense at an occasional grimace like the above we should perhaps, after retracing the ground of Gregorovius' history, find it remarkable, rather, that this sort of thing is so rarely in evidence. For indoctrination in an attitude of cynical skepticism no better material can be found than the history of the medieval church. What would Flaubert and Anatole France have done without recourse to this arsenal!

The contours of the mask shift from moment to moment. If the narrator's familiarity with the detail of courtly medieval life tends to conjure up the figure of a contemporary of the high feudal era, the focus is impishly blurred by his reference to the *Summa Astesana* (97), a fourteenth-century work of casuistical edification that is read aloud in the refectory of the island monastery where Geoffrey (Galfried) of Monmouth (106), that famous twelfth-century faker of early British history, is included among the listeners. And when we find both the narrator and his characters versed in the subtleties of Freudianism—the fish as a phallic symbol (156)— and the intricacies of simultaneous planes of consciousness (257, for instance), the monkish mask is completely flung away.

It would be too much, on the other hand, to regard the mask as just a form of liability insurance covering the author as regards all features of the story except their modern verbalization. An atmosphere of duplicity hovers about the whole story, leaving us in doubt, at ever so many points, whether the peculiar flavor of a situation reflects the temperament of the installed narrator or that of the author. If we incline, perhaps too readily, to make the monk's suppressed desires responsible for the depiction of sex in the raw, we should not overlook Thomas Mann's constant striving for novel effects and his ambition to keep abreast of the times at all costs. Four and a half decades ago he had treated the theme of brother-sister incest in *Wälsungenblut* with exquisitely piquant discretion; it must have intrigued him to do it over again in the most modern manner and to fuse it with the point of one of his most advanced early stories, the butchering of the pet dog in *Tobias Mindernickel*. The disdain and hatred of the body as a device of nature to fetter the freedom of the spirit is again a characteristically monkish attitude, but it is paralleled by Thomas Mann's own dualistic approach to life. The monk's contemptuous or patronizing slant on the exhibition of brute force, feats of physical prowess, and indulgence in sport also has its counterpart in Thomas Mann's attitude, which finds a notable early expression in his drama *Fiorenza*. The sentimentality which colors the monk's narrative at a number of points, on the other hand, would seem to combine frank parody with the lack of restraint that is characteristic of an advanced phase of life. We should not forget, above all, that the same period of Thomas Mann's life, four decades ago, produced such divergent masks as that austere man of letters, Gustav Aschenbach in *Tod in Venedig*, and the exhibitionistic embezzler whose autobiography is presented in *Felix Krull*. As for the lengthy asides and musings on the form that his story is taking, including some of the finest passages Thomas Mann has done in this vein, the monk may be thought of as following the lead of Wolfram von Eschenbach's highly subjective manner, as in the casting of repeated commiserative glances in the direction of the "Nebenpersonen" (144, 146, 179) [secondary characters], who share all the hazards and none of the glory of the principals, but every reader of any discernment will recognize in these speculations the stamp of a style that first found full development in *Der Zauberberg*. As is well known, this style, in its shuttling back and forth between the story and observations on the tensions involved in its telling, is a fulfillment of Friedrich Schlegel's programmatic formulation in the "Fragmente" of the *Athenaeum*, the 238th fragment in particular.

The monk's figure, of course, is not the only mask through which we observe a conscious delineation of features that suggest the author. Can we fail to see the element of self-projection in the personality type of the hero? Gregorius' "festhaltende Hand" is the leitmotiv of most insistent recurrence throughout the work. As so often in the past, Thomas Mann has again coined a phrase that clamors for application to his own literary personality. It is enough to say that works of such scope as *Buddenbrooks, Der Zauberberg*, the *Joseph* series, and *Doktor Faustus* could not have found their way to completion without an equally "festhaltende Hand." But the author reveals himself under a third mask that harbors much subtler implications. In an earlier passage we no more than touched upon a limited identity that obtains between Thomas Mann and the Roman patrician, Sextus Anicius Probus. If we look at this more closely we shall be tempted to read into it a far-reaching symbolism that equates the age in which we are living with essential aspects of early medieval Rome. The account of Probus' circumstances and his domestic life (243-249) is full of symbolical overtones. The material decay of the monuments that stood for a thousand years of civilized rule parallels that of Europe in our own day. The old glories have crumbled in the wake of a series of savage wars and sieges. The far-flung domains of the Patrician, including 360 rooms and halls,[20] empty and abandoned for the most part, symbolize as well the crumbling of the ideological foundations which supported the material prosperity of a civilization that has fallen under its own weight. The number 360 is no gratuitous touch: a mathematical symbol of totality since the times of Babylonia and ancient Egypt, it casts an eerie light over the empty scene, and it suggests the author's personal tragedy as well as that of the modern era. How the intellectual and cultural premises on which the structure of Thomas Mann's early creative work was reared have been abandoned, one by one, under the onslaught of waves of political and social revolution! There remains, to be sure, an "Insel der Wohnlichkeit" (242) [island of comfort], providing sufficient comfort and even a degree of luxury, measured by ordinary standards, for the needs of the aging couple. This again suggests both a material and an intellectual plane of application. Most important, in its symbolic aspect, is the Patrician's acceptance and approval of the material decline that mirrors the collapse of institutions "weil seinen Augen Verfall, Zerrüttung und das Hinsinken des sehr Grossen unter der Wucht seiner eigenen Grösse als das Zeitgerechte, Notwendige und Gottgewollte erschien" (243) [because to his eyes decadence, ruin, and the collapse of the very great under the weight of his own greatness appeared timely, necessary, and willed by God]. And the aging couple reflects the same attitude as regards their reduced domestic setting: "So waren Probus und Proba es gewohnt und fanden es angemessen" (244). [Thus Probus and Proba were

[20] Improbable and superfluous, yet a fact: even this symbolic number derives from a source! Gregorovius quoted from the *Itinerary* of the twelfth-century Spanish Jew Benjamin de Tudela, who visited Rome: "Ausserdem sieht man den Palast des Königs Vespasian. . . . Dazu den Palast des Königs Galbinus, worin 360 Hallen, so viel als Tage im Jahr, drei Millien umfassend" (IV, 635). [In addition one sees the palace of King Vespasian. . . . Also the palace of King Galbinus, containing 360 chambers, as many as the days in a year, and three miles in circumference.]

accustomed to it and found it proper.] The names finally, Probus and Proba, impressively joined in this last quotation, were not selected by chance. Rather ostentatiously they label their bearers as exemplars of righteousness.

5. The Author's Relation to the Theme and to his Public

What was there about the Gregorius story that enticed Thomas Mann to get involved with it in a major way? A partial answer, the author's own, has already been quoted in our introductory pages. But there are many answers, just as there are many reasons for falling in love and many reasons for experiencing the growing hold of an attachment. In the case of such a man of letters as Thomas Mann, who is truly alive perhaps only when writing, all his reading tends to be a processing of literary materials; all his intake has an inherent urge to reappear as output, but this does not account for the author's impregnation with a specific theme which then draws nourishment from literary materials of unpredictable diversity. A more specific appeal may be found in the lightness of the Gregorius theme and the sparkle of its happy end after the arduous gestation of the sinister and daemonic *Doktor Faustus*. There must have been a peculiar incentive, moreover, in the projecting of such a feat as the retracing of an old story in all its ramifications and contriving despite this to transmute it into a superlatively personal product. But apart from such considerations, the theme must have had two aspects of compelling fascination for Thomas Mann, one of a material and one of a formal nature: the angle of incest and the angle of linguistic experimentation.

The treatment of incest is, of course, not peculiar to Thomas Mann. Among recent examples in German literature, Hauptmann's *Indipohdi* and *Die Insel der Grossen Mutter* come to mind for the brother-sister, and Schnitzler's *Frau Beate und ihr Sohn* for the mother-son relation. Yet there is the fact that *Wälsungenblut* (written in 1905), which is, everything considered, Thomas Mann's most amazing *tour de force*, was stillborn. As is well known, the already printed issue of *Die Neue Rundschau* in which the story was slated to appear was withdrawn from circulation and the German original has to this day appeared only in a limited bibliophile edition (1921), whereas French and English translations of the story have enjoyed a wider circulation. The brother-sister incest theme came to the fore again in *Joseph in Ägypten* where it is dwelt on at length as an element of the cultural background of that ancient civilization: Joseph's master, the eunuch Peteprê, is the offspring of such a union, once the general custom among the aristocracy, now an obsolescent practice adhered to only by the most conservative set. The fact that the Egyptian couple are twins links them most closely with the twins of *Wälsungenblut* and those of the present story. We cannot fail to notice that Sibylla and Wiligis are, as it were, a reincarnation of the pair in *Wälsungenblut*. As regards their figures, their manners, their poise, their obsession with a sense of their own exclusiveness, their preoccupation with the concept of "Ebenbürtigkeit" [equality of birth], the similarity is so striking as to preclude any element of chance. Thomas Mann was obviously at pains to make the Jewish twins of *Wälsungenblut* live again in the fairy-tale setting of *Der Erwählte*. As regards all their traits of personality they are removed as far as conceivable from the hereditary background of their ancestry. Compared with the florid, blustering Duke Grimald and his consort Baduhenna, they are a singular pair of biological sports, exotic, oriental in the delicacy of their limbs, features, and gestures and in the pale ivory of their complexions. They seem more like transplants from ancient Phoenicia. Do not both bear the badge of the moon goddess in the identical crescent pockmark on their foreheads? And does not this veiled allusion to Astarte also recall the allure of Joseph's narcissistic flirtation with pagan sensuous cults as he mirrors his exposed body in the well at dusk?

Turning now to the language of the story, we could fill pages with examples to demonstrate Thomas Mann's undiminished mastery of his literary medium as regards the right epithet, the felicitous phrase, the euphonious cadence, the incantatory power of the leitmotiv, and the unrivalled clarity of the visual focus. All this is not new and could be exemplified and analyzed just as well by random pickings from any of his novelistic works. Something absolutely new confronts us, however, in the linguistic experimentation that sets *Gregorius* apart from all the rest of Thomas Mann's work and from all modern literary experiments known to me.

It has been said that the physician is disqualified as a reader of

Der Zauberberg, the Egyptologist as a reader of *Joseph*. By the same rule the philologist would be disqualified as a reader of *Der Erwählte*. Of all people, it is certainly not he whom Thomas Mann had in mind in establishing communication with his audience, and the philologist is certainly the least qualified to judge the effect of the linguistic experiment on the ordinary reader. Yet even though his may not be the last word on the success of the fusion of polyglot elements, he alone enjoys the status of a connoisseur as regards the feature of linguistic experimentation.

The language of *Der Erwählte* is too fascinating a topic for scholars to pass by. There is material enough for a highly readable dissertation, given intelligence and discrimination. We do not propose to grapple here at length with so large a subject. We hope, instead, to throw considerable light on the quality of the experiment by asking: What considerations, impulses, motives prompted Thomas Mann to cast his novel in so odd a linguistic mold? For the answers to this question, of course, we turn to the work itself in its relation to the contemporary scene.

The first answer that suggests itself is the author's constant search for novel linguistic effects. His prodigious verbal facility impelled him to attempt something startlingly new. Like his Settembrini he has always enjoyed performing tricks of verbal prestidigitation: "wie er die Worte springen und rollen lässt . . . so elastisch wie Gummibälle" [how he let the words jump and roll, as elastic as rubber balls]. For the "Literat" [man of letters] all life boils down into "Stoff zu Worten" [matter for words], and here he refers to his figures, very significantly, as "seine aus Worten gesponnenen Gestalten" (195) [his figures spun from words].

James Joyce cannot but come to mind in this context. The name of Joyce has become a byword for verbal literary experimentation. Whether Thomas Mann read him or not, he must have been engaged in countless literary discussions about this boldest leader of the literary vanguard. Thomas Mann must have seen in Joyce a literary variant of the same fanatical zeal that carried Nietzsche's theoretical and moral speculations to the point of self-destruction, and his ambition must have prodded him to emulate, not the manner of Joyce, but the boldness of his departure from conventional norms. The same was the case in a different way with Hermann

Broch, whose great essay on Joyce[21] is to an astonishing degree a preview of his own *Tod des Vergil*.

Another contributing factor of no little weight is the fact that ever since *Der Zauberberg* Thomas Mann's reputation with the lay public has derived in large part from his fabulous skill in the manipulation of esoteric material. The impression is conveyed that he knows the history of the human mind inside out, from the remotest dawn of civilization to the present day, and that the tranquil eye of the sage encompasses the completely organized totality of human experience at every glance. Every hint that he drops seems like the distillate of fabulous lore. If the solidity of his background studies, literary, medical, philosophical, psychological, archaeological, mystical, mythical, musical, in his earlier works, smote the reader with a sense of faltering ignorance, the same impression carries over into *Gregorius*, where the whole medieval scene with its interests and mode of life, its orientation toward a life to come, its regulation by miraculous agencies and its literature recorded in a host of forgotten dialects, seems to lie before the author like an open book. This illusion is sustained despite (or because of) an ironic hint to the contrary when, having thrown at us a number of technical terms of the huntsman's language, including the verb "blatten" (28) [to decoy], the monk interrupts the flow of his narrative to remark: "Nie hab ich einen Gabylot in der Hand geschwungen, noch eine lange Lanze unter den Arm geworfen; auch habe ich nie auf einem Blatte blasend das Waldgetier betrogen und habe das Wort 'blatten,' das ich mit solcher Scheingeläufigkeit gebrauchte, eben nur aufgeschnappt. Aber so ist es die Art des Geistes der Erzählung, den ich verkörpere, dass er sich anstellt, als sei er in allem, wovon er kündet, gar wohlerfahren und zu Hause."[22] [I have never swung a gavelock in my hand, nor tucked a long lance under my arm; also I have never duped a woods animal by blowing on a blade of grass, and the word "decoy," which I used with such apparent facility, I just snapped up. But the type of spirit of narrative which I embody is such that it pretends to be well experienced and at home in everything that it relates]. There is a peculiar irony about the fact that the lay reader, accustomed to think of Thomas

---

[21] *James Joyce und die Gegenwart* (Leipzig, 1936).
[22] The "monk's" knowledge of "blatten" as a term of the chase derives from Bartsch's annotated edition of Wolfram's *Parzival*. See the note to *P*. 120, 13.

Mann as a second Leonardo, refuses to take this disclaimer seriously, seeing in it rather an artful touch to reinforce the personality mask of the monk, when, as a matter of fact, Thomas Mann's knowledge of medieval German literature is no more than skin-deep,[23] and not even as much can be claimed for his knowledge of the Romance literatures on the basis of the present work; his knack, nevertheless, of blending his German with medieval German and French words and phrases is prodigious. His introduction of elements of modern French into his German phrasing likewise achieves startling effects, as when Wiligis in a sentence of formal, archaic elegance refers to the predicament of his sister's pregnancy as "die Bredouille, in der wir uns befinden" (52) [the predicament in which we find ourselves], or when Sibylla expatiates to her brother, in the manner of Schopenhauer, on the aesthetic superiority of the male of the human species, as follows: "Wir neiden euch . . . euere Unterschiede, bewundern sie und sind in Scham gehüllt, weil wir in den Hüften breiter sind statt in den Schultern und folglich eine zu grosse Bauchfläche haben, auch einen zu umfangreichen derrière" (31). [We envy you . . . your differences, admire them, and are covered with shame because we are broader in the hips instead of in the shoulders and consequently have too large an expanse of belly, also too expansive a behind.]

But we have not exhausted the reasons that prompted Thomas Mann to strive in much of his narrative for the effect of a polyglot medley. (In the last third of the book this device is reduced to a minimum.) Without doubt the employment of elements of modern English is a feature of key significance. Whereas the mixing of French, medieval and modern, with German playfully parodies the courtly style of Hartmann and Wolfram, the use of English reflects the author's personal situation in a variety of ways.

Ever since his emigration from Germany Thomas Mann has

[23] The reader, who gained the impression from Thomas Mann's *Betrachtungen eines Unpolitischen* that he was completely at home among the masters of nineteenth-century German literature, experiences more than a mild shock in learning from *Die Entstehung des Doktor Faustus* that Thomas Mann had never read Gottfried Keller's great "Bildungsroman" *Der Grüne Heinrich* before his illness in 1946 (161 f.). In a later passage Thomas Mann has discovered that the novel exists in two versions, and is happy to inform us that the one version made its first posthumous appearance in 1926 (168 f.). Is it possible that he never knew that Keller drastically rewrote the work a quarter of a century after its first appearance and issued a new *Grüner Heinrich* ten years before his death—or could he have forgotten?

found himself exposed to a bilingual atmosphere that has both an amusing and a deeply disturbing aspect. He knew very little English on his arrival. His contacts with native Americans who did not speak German, though very numerous, have been, perforce, superficial. More intimate communication was limited to the host of German intellectuals in exile, to whom Thomas Mann was the outstanding symbol of the culture from which they were cut off. As everyone knows, such a group progressively succumbs to the pressure of the foreign language environment, regardless of the intellectual status of its members. But to a degree that scarcely finds a parallel in any earlier wave of German immigration, English usage has with this group encroached upon German idiom, and by now every conversation tends to shuttle back and forth between German and English.

Thomas Mann made use of this phenomenon with obviously humorous intent in all that part of the story which has the Channel Island as its setting. It is in evidence in the abbot's long monologue and in his conversation with the fishermen; in the dialogue that precedes the fist fight between Gregorius and his foster brother and in the final imprecations of Mahaute when her son comes home with a broken nose. In my opinion, this use of English and Anglicisms is the least successful feature of Thomas Mann's story. Taken as a whole, it does not achieve the status of make-believe credibility. Somehow these words and phrases, unlike the French and the medieval German, do not fall into place. Often their emotional charge strikes us as an utter misfit in their context. In this rare case, I think, Thomas Mann overreached himself in failing to gauge the reader's reactions. There will be a difference of opinion, no doubt, regarding individual instances (and I would not deny that English terms are happily employed on occasion). Thus expressions like "Grundwerk tun" (84) [do the groundwork], "an der anderen Hand gerechnet" (86) [figured on the other hand], and "Fallzeit" (87) [time of fall] aptly characterize the English mold of the abbot's thinking. But the hybrid coinage "smooth-lich," impossible for a German tongue to pronounce—"wie smooth-lich alles in unserer kleinen Gotteswirtschaft seinen frommen und wohleingefahrenen Gang geht" (84) [how smoothly everything proceeds on its pious and well-beaten path in our little establishment of God]—strikes me as offensive. Or when Flann admonishes his foster brother: "Tu nicht bosten und swaggern vor mir" (117) [Don't boast and swagger in front of me], and challenges him to act as "ein Mann und ein sossiger Kerl" (118) [a man and a saucy fellow] instead of putting on the manner of "ein slackichter, flimsiger Betbruder" (119) [slack, flimsy bigot], the spell of the scene, so masterfully handled in other respects, is rudely broken. To mention one more instance, the alternation in the fishermen's dialogue with the abbot of pure Low German dialect with a German-American broadside, "Puhr Pipels Stoff" (91) [poor people's stuff] is certainly not subtle. Even as a boy, we recall, young Gregorius felt ill at ease in using the dialect of the baseborn: "Wenn er mit achten und zehnen zu Besuch sass bei den Kätnern, gab er sich Mühe aus Höflichkeit, ihre Worte zu brauchen, doch waren sie falsch nun in seinem Munde und standen ihm unnatürlich, so dass die Gesichter sich verzerrten . . ." (106). [When at the ages of eight and ten he sat visiting with the farmhands, he tried out of politeness to use their words, but they were false in his mouth and were unnatural to him, so that their faces grimaced.] I would not put it beyond Thomas Mann that, sensing his own indifferent success with the use of low idiom, he wrote the above passage with an eye to forestalling adverse criticism.

It would be a mistake, however, to dwell exclusively on the humorous angle involved in the use of English. It reflects, besides, a very real predicament of the author. He is himself not immune to the insidious encroachment of English on his German, as he doubtless knows. The occasional cropping up of Anglicisms in the final *Joseph* volume and in *Doktor Faustus* has not escaped attention. In *Gregorius* likewise this tendency colors the narrator's own language, not only that of the characters. Thus we find him using "aufgebracht" (102) for "brought up," a usage that crops up again in the mouth of Grigorss' foster mother (126). "Überall" occurs repeatedly in a meaning that represents a cross between German "überhaupt" and English "at all" (104, 153). "Ausfigurieren" (235), standing for "ausrechnen" [calculate] or "mutmassen" [conjecture] can be accounted for only as a yielding to the pressure of our "figure out." It is funny to find Thomas Mann using "Substitut" (154) as an ersatz for "Ersatz." In a dialogue context that is not related to the Channel Island setting, we find literally transposed into German such common terms of our own language as "turning the cold shoulder" (33) or "not crossing a bridge before you come to it" (56). These cases, and many others like them, show that Thomas Mann's "Sprachgefühl" [feeling for language] is slipping. It should not be objected that some of these Anglicisms are deliberately planted: they may all be conscious and deliberate, for that matter. The fact is rather that they reveal a lack of concern for the inviolability of German idiom, a casual disregard of those safeguards with which every cultural language surrounds itself. I would even go so far as to say that Thomas Mann, as conscious a craftsman in the medium of language as the world has ever seen, here takes a rather malicious delight in nibbling away at the defenses which guarantee the integrity of his native language. We have not forgotten, surely, the tranquil affirmation with which Sextus Anicius Probus surveys the decay of the monuments of his native imperial Rome! The mood of an all-forgiving divine grace that pardons the blackest iniquity of the repentant sinner should not blind us to the fact that an ineradicable *ressentiment* against the spiritual core of that native heritage which repudiated the author is furtively woven into the tissue of this angelic story. On a lighter level, in claiming the absolute prerogatives of "der Geist der Erzählung," Thomas Mann doubtless identified himself with the sentiment of Pope Gregory the Great's famous dictum that the Holy Spirit refuses to submit to the trammels of grammar and syntax.

It is Thomas Mann's personal tragedy that his reputation as a writer has come to be determined by critics who, for the most part, either do not read the German text of his writings at all or who lack the background for appreciating the finesse of his language. For his royalties he has come to depend on a public that reads him only in translation. If the subtler implications of the German frame of reference of his writings are necessarily lost, as regards this larger public, the same is scarcely less the case with the new generation of German readers that has replaced the large intellectual elite of his following in the pre-Hitler era. That elite has disappeared as a class; only a sprinkling remains, and it dwindles from year to year. The support of intimate contact with his public has gone. It is Thomas Mann's personal tragedy that he now writes in a vacuum, much like Adrian Leverkühn. And like the hero of *Doktor Faustus* he oscillates between condescension and snobbish aloofness. One central fact, however, cannot be blurred by such melancholy reflections: It is still the hand of the master that guides the pen.

Appendix

By the author's kind permission a letter of Thomas Mann to Erich Auerbach is printed below. The correspondence which led to this letter was occasioned by Mr. Siegfried Mandel's communication to the *Saturday Review of Literature* which appeared in the issue of September 29, 1951. Mr. Mandel began by pointing out that Thomas Mann had used some lines from a portion of an Old French Adam and Eve play printed in Professor Auerbach's *Mimesis*. He contended, beyond this, that Thomas Mann was basically indebted to Erich Auerbach's book for the manner in which he revived the medieval tale of Gregorius and that, having admitted his dependence on the twelfth-century German poet Hartmann, he should have given credit to the living author as well. Professor Auerbach felt that there was no basis for Mr. Mandel's allegations beyond the possible use of a few lines from the Old French text quoted by him. He wrote to the editor of the *Saturday Review of Literature* to this effect and he sent Thomas Mann a copy of his letter.

Thomas Mann's subjoined letter, written without any knowledge of the contents of my essay, volunteers some highly interesting information to supplement the list of sources that have contributed to his shaping of the legend and in so doing corrects some conjectures I had hazarded regarding the originality of certain features of *Der Erwählte*. For the more serious student it will be a matter of great interest to discover for himself how Thomas Mann has woven into the very personal texture of Sibylla's prayer some sixty lines of the two medieval German poems he mentions. Their text is easily available in *Kleinere Deutsche Gedichte des XI. und XII. Jahrhunderts*, ed. Albert Waag ("Altdeutsche Textbibliothek," Vol. x).

Pacific Palisades, California
12. Okt. 1951

Sehr verehrter Herr Auerbach,

Gerade von Europa zurück, gehen die Wasser der Briefschulden mir bis zum Munde, so dass die simpelste Danksagung eigentlich nur zum halb artikulierten Geblubber wird. Auf vieles muss ich überhaupt verstummen, möchte und darf das aber in Ihrem Fall keineswegs tun, sondern muss Ihnen mein Vergnügen ausdrücken über Ihre gute, würdige Erwiderung an die Saturday Review und meine Erkenntlichkeit für die Mitteilung.

Vor allen Dingen hat es mich gefreut zu hören, dass Ihr so reiches und hochgelehrtes Buch in jenem angesehenen Blatt eine Würdigung erfahren hat, und dass eine englische Übersetzung im Erscheinen begriffen ist. Ihr Werk verdient es vollauf, nicht nur im deutschen Sprachkreise bemerkt, studiert und verarbeitet zu werden. Mit Ihrer heiteren Zurückweisung aber von Mr. Mandels Vorhaltung, ich hätte Sie, neben Hartmann (der es ja auch woandersher hatte) als Inspirator des "Erwählten" nennen müssen, sind Sie wohl wirklich im Recht. Es ist kaum Sache des Dichters, alle Quellen und Hilfsmittel eingestehend aufzuzählen, die ihm zum Werke gedient haben, und seine Abneigung, dies Werk als ein Mosaik entliehener Steinchen hinzustellen, wo er doch wünschen muss, dass der Leser es als den künstlerischen Organismus empfinde, der es ist, scheint mir berechtigt.

Ich bedurfte im Fall des "Erwählten" verhältnismässig geringer Vorstudien, um mein christlich-übernationales Mittelalter in die Luft zu spielen. Die ad hoc-Lektüre für den "Joseph" war, versteht sich, unvergleichlich umfangreicher. Immerhin wäre in einem Quellenverzeichnis und- Bekenntnis allerlei aufzureihen gewesen. Ich bin neugierig, ob Prof. Weigand alles ausgekundschaftet hat. Das Mittelhochdeutsche Element stammt natürlich von Hartmann direkt. Viele Namen und Einzelheiten, für den Germanisten auf der Hand liegend, aus Wolframs Parzival. Eine Parodie des Nibelungenliedes kommt auch vor. "Sibyllas Gebet," eins der mir liebsten Vorkommnisse des Buches, lehnt sich an die "Vorauer Sündenklage" (Mitte 12. Jahrhundert) und das sogen. Arnsteiner Marienlied an. Da von Ouwe Hartman die Ernährung des Büssers auf dem Stein unverzeihlich unrealistisch und obenhin behandelt hat, nahm ich die "Erdmilch" aus einer Schrift meines Freundes Karl Kerényi, des Mythologen, der die Kunde bei Epikur zuerst nachweist,—welcher das zullende Urmenschenkind aber auch schon von viel früher her hat. Bilderwerke über mittelalterliche Kunst haben geholfen. Das englische Plattdeutsch der Fischer von der nicht existierenden Insel St. Dunstan und Sprachscherze wie "Du Kauert, du lauernder, kauernder Pfaffenkauert" sind, wie so manches andere, meine persönliche Erfindung. Der altfranzösischen Sprachbrocken wegen, die das Sprachbild zu kolorieren helfen mussten, gab es eine Korrespondenz mit dem ehrwürdigen, nun verstorbenen Samuel Singer in Bern, dessen Altdeutschen Sprichwörtern ich schon die Gebete des kleinen "Echo" im "Faustus," leicht adaptierend, entnommen hatte. Er erteilte hilfreiche Auskunft. Ihr Buch mit dem Citat aus dem "Mystère d'Adam" kam genau zu dem Zeitpunkt, als ich das Kapitel von den "Schlimmen Kindern" schrieb. (Ein geheimer Magnetismus lässt Bücher sehr oft genau im richtigen Augenblick kommen). Die zwei Dutzend Worte, die ich aus dem alten Dialog herauspickte, waren besonders gut verwendbar, weil in der heiklen Situation ein dem Durchschnittsleser halb oder ganz unverständliches Gestammel sehr am Platze war. Ich schulde sie *Ihnen*, soweit hat Mr. Mandel durchaus recht. Aber sind sie nicht ganz hübsch und überraschend in den so anderen Zusammenhang eingepasst? Das Gefundene wird so doch gewissermassen zum Erfundenen. Ich bin froh, dass Sie in diesem Punkte denken, wie ich.

Mit den verbindlichsten Grüssen
Ihr ergebener
Thomas Mann

[Dear Mr. Auerbach,

Having just returned from Europe, I am so flooded with letters to answer that the simplest thank-you note actually becomes only a half-articulated blubber. There is much I simply must remain silent about, however in your case neither do I want nor may I do that, rather I must express to you my pleasure about your kind, estimable reply to the *Saturday Review* and my acknowledgment of notice about it.

Above all it pleased me to hear that your comprehensive and very learned book received a review in that respected journal, and that an English translation is in the process of preparation. Your work certainly deserves to be noticed, studied, and assimilated not only in German-speaking circles. Your cheerful rejection of Mr. Mandel's remonstrance that I should have named you—along with Hartmann (who got it from somewhere else, after all)—as inspiration for the *Erwählte* is probably really justified. It is hardly a poet's business to list avowedly the sources and aids which served him in his work, and his aversion to offer his work as a mosaic of borrowed pebbles—whereas he must after all desire that the reader receive it as the artistic organism which it is—seems justified to me.

In the case of the *Erwählte* I required comparatively few preliminary studies to project my Christian-supranational Middle Ages. The ad hoc reading for the Joseph novels, it goes without saying, was incomparably more comprehensive. At any rate, all kinds of things would have had to be included in a list of sources and acknowledgments. I am curious to know whether Professor Weigand has ferreted out everything. The Middle High German element comes from Hartmann directly, naturally. Many names and details, apparent to the Germanist, are from Wolfram's *Parzival*. A parody of the *Nibelungenlied* also occurs. "Sibylla's Prayer," one of my favorite incidents in the book, is modeled on the "Vorau Lament of Sins" (middle of the twelfth century) and the so-called Arnstein Song of Mary. Since Hartmann von Ouwe unforgivably handled the nourishment of the penitent on the rock with unrealistic perfunctoriness, I took the earth-milk from a monograph of my friend Karl Kerényi, the mythologist, who points out the lore first in Epicurus—who in turn leaned on a much earlier source for the primitive manchild sucking his pacifier. Picture volumes on medieval art were also helpful. The English Low German of the fishermen of the nonexistent island of Saint Dunstan, and linguistic tricks such as "You coward, you lurking, cowering priest-coward" are, like some other things, my personal invention. Because of the Old French linguistic morsels, which had to aid in the coloration of the language representation, there was correspondence with the venerable, now deceased Samuel Singer in Bern, from whose Old German proverbs I had taken the prayers of little Echo in *Faustus*, in slight adaptation. He rendered helpful information. Your book, with the quotation from the *Mystery of Adam*, came along at exactly the time when I was writing the chapter about the "Bad Children." (A secret magnetism allows books to arrive very often at exactly the right moment.) The two dozen words which I picked out of the old dialogue were especially well suited because in the sticky situation a stammer, entirely or half unintelligible to the average reader, was very appropriate. I owe them to *you*; in that respect Mr. Mandel is absolutely right. But did they not fit very nicely and surprisingly into such a different context? That which one finds becomes to a certain extent, after all, that which one invents. I am glad that you think on this point as I do.

> With the most cordial greetings,
> yours sincerely,
> Thomas Mann]

THOUGHTS ON THE PASSING
OF THOMAS MANN

AMONG THE innumerable pictures of Thomas Mann none is so arresting as the well-known photo-portrait that shows the young author at the age of twenty-five, in 1900. Visible to the knee, against a light background, the figure, slightly turned to the right, eyes the beholder with an attitude of grave nonchalance: both hands, thrust into the dark trouser pockets, holding back the tails of the buttoned cutaway to reveal a polka-dotted padded cummerbund; the broad black silk tie completely filling the space between the lapels and framing a white stand-up collar that along with the sliver of gleaming cuffs reinforces the note of sober elegance; the face, like the figure, immaculately groomed as to its broad moustache, slightly raised eyebrows and heavy dark hair, parted at the left and brushed back from a broad forehead that is modeled but not yet furrowed; the eyes with a look both dreamy and searching. The portrait seems to say what Thomas Mann wrote three years earlier in *Der Bajazzo*: "Seien wir ehrlich: es kommt darauf an, für was man sich hält, für was man sich gibt, für was man die Sicherheit hat, sich zu geben" (*Novellen* I, 77). [Let's be honest: the point at issue is what you take yourself for, what image you project, and with what assurance you project it.]

This is a young man's philosophy. Taken out of its context, it is the attitude of a man who feels himself poised on the threshold of an extraordinary career but as yet has no tangible achievements to back up his self-appraisal. It is underscored at the end of the story by the reflection that everybody is far too sedulously concerned with himself to find time seriously to have an opinion of anyone else: "man akzeptiert mit träger Bereitwilligkeit den Grad von Respekt, den du die Sicherheit hast, vor dir selbst an den Tag zu legen" (*Ibid.*, 95). [People accept with passive acquiescence the degree of self-respect that you have the assurance of displaying.] What counts is "Sicherheit," self-assurance. But self-assurance is only the visible correlate of an inner pleasurable intimacy with one's own person, "Selbstgefälligkeit" (*Ibid.*, 90), and

Reprinted from *The Germanic Review*, XXXI (1956), 163-175, by permission of W. T. H. Jackson, editor.

both the outer and inner aspect of personality, self-assurance and self-love, are contingent upon a regulated give-and-take relation between the individual and society. *Der Bajazzo*, the sketchy analytical autobiography of a man of diversified talent not channeled by any inner drive, a man who finds his life's sum amounting to abject failure,—this early tentative projection of the Christian Buddenbrook type bristles with psychological formulations of ethical problems after the manner of Ibsen and Nietzsche, such as: Is a bad conscience then nothing but festering vanity? ("eiternde Eitelkeit," *Ibid.*, 93). But the central proposition, the only one to engage us at the moment, is: "Es gibt nur ein Unglück: das Gefallen an sich selbst einbüssen. Sich nicht mehr zu gefallen, das ist das Unglück" (*Ibid.*). [There is only one misfortune: to have to suffer the loss of pleasure with oneself. No longer to be pleased with oneself, that is the misfortune.] Here we have a theme destined to find richest development in young Joseph, who mirrors himself in the well by the light of the moon, in the Goethe figure of *Lotte in Weimar*, and in the all-pervasive narcissism of the fabulous Felix Krull. We have a theme intimately lodged, as no one more clearly recognized than Mann himself, in the autobiographical core of Thomas Mann's own unfolding literary personality.

Perhaps all these trenchantly formulated *Erkenntnisse* sound a bit unconvincing as the self-searchings of so anaemic and futile a personality as the "Bajazzo," a decadent—twin brother of his creator only in the ambivalent prognosis "Held oder Narr" (*Ibid.*, 53) [hero or fool]. In the choice of such a hero the literary climate of decadence was doubtless a determining factor, no less than it was, a few years later, in the tracing of the theme of decline in the sequence of generations of the Buddenbrook family. But it is worth noting that, for all the fashionable pessimism of the age, the front that young Thomas Mann presents to the world, both when he poses for his picture and when he speaks in his own person, does not suggest resignation and decadence. We must not forget that terza rima *Monolog* of thirteen lines, one of his very rare poems, published in "Die Gesellschaft" in 1899 when he was engaged in the writing of *Buddenbrooks*. These lines, opening with a *topos* of modesty and self-depreciation, go on to breathe hope, ambition, self-assurance reflected in the judgment of others and envisage future fame in the dream of the slim laurel wreath that haunts his troubled nights, dispelling sleep.

Ich bin ein kindischer und schwacher Fant,
Und irrend schweift mein Geist in alle Runde,
Und schwankend fass' ich jede starke Hand.

Und dennoch regt die Hoffnung sich im Grunde,
Dass etwas, was ich dachte und empfand,
Mit Ruhm einst gehen wird von Mund zu Munde.

Schon klingt mein Name leise in das Land.
Schon nennt mich mancher in des Beifalls Tone:
Und Leute sind's von Urteil und Verstand.

Ein Traum von einer schmalen Lorbeerkrone
Scheucht oft den Schlaf mir unruhvoll zur Nacht,
Die meine Stirn einst zieren wird zum Lohne

Für dies und jenes, was ich hübsch gemacht.

[I am a childish and a feeble fop,
and erring my spirit sweeps all around,
and staggering I grab at any sturdy hand.

And still a hope bestirs itself at ground,
that something, that I thought and felt,
one day with fame from mouth to mouth will sound.

My name rings softly now throughout the land,
many mention me with tones of approbation:
people who have judgment and who understand.

A dream of a slender laurel crown
often at night scares off my restless sleep,
a crown which will one day adorn my brow in reward

For this and that which I accomplished nicely.]

The response to the idea of fame is a touchstone for distinguishing personality types. How apparently healthy and uncomplicated this, Thomas Mann's, frank admission of aspiration to fame. How different, as a literary posture, from the shrug with which fame is dismissed by young Rilke in the opening paragraph of his *Rodin* (1903): "Denn Ruhm ist schliesslich nur der Inbegriff aller Missverständnisse, die sich um einem neuen Namen sammeln" [For fame is, in the end, only the essence of all misunderstandings which gather about a new name]—a formulation to be repeated in *Malte*. Straightforward, secular aspiration versus saintly self-effacement! Or we may contrast Mann with the paradoxical extreme of the decadent's credo illustrated by the sculptor mentioned in Gerhart Hauptmann's *Vor Sonnenaufgang*: he believed in his art as long as the public ignored it; but when a jury awarded him the commission for a monument on the basis of a model he had submitted, he put a bullet through his brain.

It might have been mere cockiness, this self-assurance (Arno Holz comes to mind by way of example). The record rules this out. Sixty years after the writing of that poem, the "hübsch" of its concluding line—"Für dies und jenes, was ich hübsch gemacht"—has rather the ring of modesty. Or was it conscious understatement? We have our choice of interpretations, as we have it in the case of Mann's prediction, in the *Lebensabriss* of 1930, that, having equaled his mother's age, he would die in 1945 at seventy. Was this a settled conviction? Was it an apotropaeic projection, an oblique prayer to the Powers to grant him that extra measure needed fully to round out his life's cycle?

This is not the place for a glancing survey of Thomas Mann's large-scale achievements—that long series of works of the imagination, in the sustained density of their texture with scarcely a parallel in literary history, flanked as they are by smaller novelistic productions and a steady essayistic output, not to mention the flood of by-products that catered to the tastes and needs of the day. Let us limit ourselves, rather, to exploring in brief some aspects of his work as a continuous process of self-revelation.

It strikes one that in evoking literary or historical personages, whether in narrative or in essay, Thomas Mann has a way of identifying with his subject so as to give the impression of a double tracery: the structural outlines of the personality portrayed are somehow felt to correspond to the alignment of the author's own basic drives and responses. This, the reader's experiencing of a double tracery, holds true for a surprising number of sharply divergent types of personality. In *Schwere Stunde* (1905) the sketch of Friedrich Schiller suggests the delineating hand of a close twentieth-century kinsman, who creates with the same feverish glow in reckless disregard of his pitifully slim physical resources. In *Friedrich und die Grosse Koalition* (1915) it is the defiant amoralism of Nietzsche which seems to fuse author and subject into one personality. The centenary essay on *Lessing* (1929) sparkles with the vibrant clarity of the fearless destroyer of time-honored prejudice, come to life anew. In the many discussions on Wagner only an inner bond of deepest consanguinity can account, it seems, for the uncanny exhibition of the intricate fusion of an imperiously creative drive with the ruthlessly egoistic scheming of a master-seducer. But as time goes on, the identification with Goethe first begins to loom and then, gradually, to supplant all other personality types. The first, tentative indication of this came in the *Goethe und Tolstoi* essay of 1923, where the contrapuntal play with the paired figures of Goethe and Tolstoi, on the one hand, and Schiller and Dostoyevsky on the other, still tended to stress Thomas Mann's affinity with the "spirit" of the second pair as contrasted with the demonic life force, the nature-divinity of the first. But the dynamic equilibrium of the playful arrangement was in a state of flux; every contrast had an inherent tendency to turn into its opposite. Thus the surprise brought by *Lotte in Weimar*, in 1939, where the identification of the Mann personality-type with that of Goethe first fully asserts itself, to retain its dominance to the end, was somewhat tempered by benefit of hindsight. The identification with Goethe involved a gradual readjustment of focus as regards the features of Thomas Mann's mentality. His public had to submit to a course of reeducation.

The education of his public, in a more general way, is a sociological process of momentous significance as regards the age of Thomas Mann. A representative author and his public live in a state of symbiosis. We are on safe ground, I think, when we say: Supposing Thomas Mann had made his literary debut with a work written in the manner of the *Zauberberg*, he would have found only a small coterie of readers interested in esoteric literature. In view of the difficulties he experienced in getting *Buddenbrooks* accepted for publication without a drastic paring-down, it may well be doubted whether a book like the *Zauberberg* would have found a publisher at all at the turn of the century. The taste for Thomas Mann's involved manner had to be gradually inoculated into the public before Thomas Mann could hazard giving full rein to his imagination in the weaving of his intricate novelistic tapestries. Perhaps the matter can be most effectively stated in commercial terms: Before Thomas Mann could foist works like *Lotte in Weimar* and the *Joseph* series on an eager public, tremendous assets of goodwill had to be gradually accumulated. A long series of prior productions of ever increasing difficulty had first to be assimilated in order to pave the way for a willing reception of whatever he had to offer. Since we are concerned with the growing dominance of the Goethe *imago*, let us briefly recall some pertinent features of the *Lotte* novel.

Lotte was and remains an extraordinary performance, even for Thomas Mann. Its achievement as an intermezzo during the twelve years of patient work at the loom of his *Joseph* tapestry stamps it as such. As a novel it is structurally unique. There is no action, no complication, no development, no events to fill those 450 pages— just an inconsequential dinner party at Goethe's house on a September day of the year 1816 during which Goethe exchanged a few polite words with the woman after whom he had modeled the heroine of his *Werther* and whom he had not seen in the forty-four years intervening. This dinner party accounts for the greater part of the last fifth of the story. The preceding four-fifths are devoted entirely to exposition of the subject, Goethe—the first three-fifths to Goethe as seen through the eyes of others; the fourth to Goethe as seen from within.

The narrative, founded on fact, begins with the scene of Lotte Kestner's arrival, early one morning, at the leading Weimar hotel. As soon as the head waiter, an individual who prides himself on his "Bildung," learns the identity of the frail old widowed lady, he is thunderstruck. He showers the incredulous object of his fantastic veneration with a torrent of questions and perorations that turn his conducting her to her room into an exhausting, time-consuming ordeal for Lotte, who has to resort to strong measures in order finally to be left at peace for the two-hour nap she is badly in need of after a night in a coach. From then on she is besieged by a succession of interviewers and callers, for the news of her arrival has spread like wildfire through the little town. First the irrepressible Miss Cuzzle with her sketchbook takes three-quarters of an hour of Lotte's time with her chatter. Then, as she is on the point of going out, Goethe's secretary Riemer comes to make a ceremonial call. She is persuaded with difficulty to accord him two minutes, which turn into hours of densest exploratory psychological dialogue revolving about Goethe. As he leaves, Adele Schopenhauer, who has been patiently waiting in the anteroom, is ushered in, and again Lotte spends hours and hours in talking to this insider and in listening to her account of Goethe and his family problems. Finally Goethe's son August, who had been the central topic of Adele's narrative, appears in person, and again Lotte spends hours in exploring the personality of the young man whose features and manner move her as a powerfully evocative variant of her one-time adorer. Dialogue, dialogue, dialogue without end, interspersed with bits of author's narrative and comment! How many hours have ticked away in this fashion? Eight? Ten? Twelve? Has ever a person of robust constitution, let alone an infirm old lady, withstood so prolonged an ordeal of so packed a dialogue? The marvel of it, she remains alert all the time. To our amazement we notice that Lotte is as keen a listener and as ready a learner as Hans Castorp. How many memorable turns of speech dropped by her interlocutors turn up in her own mouth at unexpected points, in these conversations—and later! It is all a game, of course, this compression of the bewilderingly manifold aspects of Goethe and his milieu into one continuous flow of dialogue. The time here employed is of the quality of rubber: it will stretch indefinitely to suit the author's pleasure. And there is a point where Thomas Mann drops the pretense of the game (by mutual consent, shall we say, of author and reader?): After Adele Schopenhauer has already spent hours in give-and-take with Lotte, we are allowed to take in that part of her story which centers on August, not in its oral, interrupted rendition, but in the form of a well-composed, fluent narrative.

All this is a tour de force, a prodigious strain on the reader's capacity to play the game according to the time rules set by the author. Supposing we have succeeded in playing the game on the author's terms, we are now due for an intermission; we may settle down, after a day that allowed no room for food or drink, to a night's rest. But at seven the next morning—no, not the next but that very same morning, as we find out before the chapter is over—the piper again calls the tune. And what a tune it is!

With no warning whatever we find ourselves participants in a stream-of-consciousness monologue. There is no mistaking the identity of that inner voice: it is that of Goethe awakening from a deep dream vision to the life of the day. To try to intimate this monologue's contents would be sheer folly. What Thomas Mann attempted and accomplished with unparalleled success was to present in an extended moment the totality of Goethe's existence at the time of Lotte's visit—physiological, administrative, scientific, economic, poetic—the flow of multiple energies pulsing simultaneously in that dynamo of organic life. The movement of interests and ideas, creative sallies and musings on high moments of a living past, is as involved and apparently capricious as the planets' tracery of their epicycles in the heavens. The extended moment includes two substantial pieces of dictation (which are merely indicated) to two secretaries and a conversation with August, who has come to report to his father. Thus there are breaks in the interior monologue, but these are merely superficial. All the time we are held in the spell of that personality, which is never at rest for a moment. The duration of the extended moment amounts to three hours, we are told. But here again all ordinary measurement of time turns out to be a delusion.

Here we find ourselves at a point where we cannot avoid becoming personal. Is there any reader, be he ever so steeped in Goethe's productions and personality, who can take in at one stretch all the ultra-dense web of this chapter of eighty-eight pages? Personally I find this quite impossible. The spell of the experience holds one in a vise. The tension rises and rises. But at some point or other it snaps. Stimulation turns into protest: This overwhelms me. I cannot take it! There is a turn of the screw where the magic spell of empathy others itself and becomes sheer torture. The experiencing of this revulsion, this *Umschlag*, applies not to this chapter of Mann alone, but to much of Joyce, to Hermann Broch's *Tod des Vergil* and, doubtless, to others. It applies also, I confess, to Goethe's own "Klassische Walpurgisnacht" when I attempt to take it in in one sweep. As an objective criterion of literary art this purely subjective reaction probably deserves to be shrugged away as unworthy of objective criticism. I think nevertheless it is worth recording as a fairly recent development in the sphere of literary creation.

The dinner party given by Goethe in honor of Lotte, taking up most of the final fifth, makes no such demands. It is a straightforward account of a formal gathering where no one is at his ease. As to the host, the guest of honor carries away a sense of his chilling aloofness. The perfunctoriness of his hospitality is not intentional but due to preoccupation. There is no inner contact. What Lotte means to Goethe now, forty-four years after his infatuation was crystallized in *Werther*—"abreagiert" in the language of Freud—brings to mind Tonio Kröger's classic dictum: "Was ausgesprochen ist, ist erledigt." [What has been expressed is disposed of.] The inherent cruelty of the transitoriness of life's high moments is soberly registered.

We rebound from this to the unbelievable surprise of the final meeting of the principals in the carriage which Goethe had put at Lotte's disposal after her visit to the theater. What are we to make of this meeting, so out of keeping with what has gone before? Is it just a conventional happy ending, a sop for sentimental souls, in outrageous defiance of all probabilities? Is its palpable unreality a humorous author's trick for the benefit and at the expense of a gullible public?—You would not have us believe in this meeting as the organic conclusion of the story's cycle, I remember once saying to Thomas Mann. And I remember his concurring in what I urged, but in a curiously noncommittal way. What I now think was in his mind—he did not elaborate—is something like this:

Yes, such a meeting is a fantastic invention (and there are hints of this both in the playful interchange of the "Du" [thou] and the "Sie" [you]—reminiscent of the "Faschingsfreiheit" [carnival freedom] of the *Zauberberg*—and in the iambic lyricism of some of the dialogue). It is contrary to all the laws of probability. Goethe, aloof and withdrawn in the padded cell of his inner consciousness in order to channel all of his stupendous vitality into tangible work—it is most unlikely that a vibration coming from the real Lotte should strike his inner ear. But dare we rule out the very possibility? Would he be the incommensurable figure that he is if he were calculable? Would you not do well to reread, in the inner monologue, the two pages of Goethe's musings on "das Wirkliche" [the real] versus "das Mögliche" [the possible] (252-253)? Do you not recall teasing echoes of these (unheard) musings in the code language of Lotte's words addressed to Goethe in the carriage (447)? In other words: Given the total setting, this scene as a might-have-been is not to be dismissed as impossible.

We have dwelt on *Lotte in Weimar* as the first major work to suggest in a systematic way the idea of an archetypal likeness between Goethe and Thomas Mann amounting to inner identity. How could Thomas Mann have projected from within that welter of vital contradictions, if his own inner world had not also been of the stuff of the incommensurable? The spell of this suggestion pervades the *Lotte* so insistently that for moments we are apt to forget how unlike these two great representatives of the German spirit really were in ever so many respects. How different the controlled self-assurance of the young Thomas Mann from the effervescent emotionalism of the young Goethe! How different the pattern of their family life, how different their lives as a whole: Thomas Mann exclusively the man of letters; Goethe scattering, dissipating his energies in a thousand extra-literary activities. Whereas Thomas Mann's work *is* his life, Goethe's works *can* be viewed as the by-products of an enormously rich, diversified existence. Or think of Goethe's pioneering efforts in so many branches of natural science. In Thomas Mann's case we have nothing of this, we have instead the assimilation of vast amounts of ready-made scientific and scholarly learning and their transformation into thematic material for dialectical play in the tissue of his novels. Goethe's passionate curiosity centered on things, concrete phenomena, while Thomas Mann's curiosity, no less passionate, was concerned with the alchemy of turning things into words—images, sounds, rhythms. Goethe's works spring from the confessional urge, whereas in the case of Thomas Mann the core of personal, private experience is sublimated in a highly intellectualistic way. And let us not forget the prodigal wealth of unfinished fragments that mark every phase of Goethe's career as contrasted with the disciplined economy of Thomas Mann's production. Here the "Einheit des Lebens" [unity of life], underscored as regards Goethe, is exhibited as the unity of an all-absorbing literary drive. In both men this unity is nourished by an unwavering, mystical love of self.

The *Lotte* puts into Goethe's mouth a number of pages eminently worth recalling, but unfortunately too long to quote, that muse with approval on the many varieties of love of self, including autobiography and egocentrism, as higher forms of life-sustaining personal vanity (323-325). Here the trio, Goethe, Nietzsche, Mann, see eye to eye.

If we look closely enough in the *Lotte*, however, we come upon spots where even the inner identification of the author with his subject will not stand the scrutiny of the critical eye. I have in mind one of the many passages of the inner monologue where

Goethe comes back to the *Divan*. His musings dwell on the peculiar zest afforded by this engrossing task: there is an invigorating discipline about working one's way into a culture so foreign to that of the West as the Persian, but it is quite another thing for him, the Westerner, to be creative *as* a Persian. He muses on this two-fold challenge as "dies Sich-vergraben und Schürfen besessener Sympathie, die dich zum Eingeweihten macht der liebend ergriffenen Welt, sodass du mit freier Leichtigkeit ihre Sprache sprichst und niemand das studierte Détail vom charakteristisch erfundenen soll unterscheiden können" (335) [this burial of oneself and burrowing of frenzied sympathy, which makes you an initiate of the world gripped by love, so that you speak her language with a free ease and no one shall be able to distinguish the studied detail from the one characteristically invented]. No question, this passage makes its appeal on three levels. There is, first, Goethe speaking about his *Divan*. There is, next, Thomas Mann characterizing his venture into the culture of ancient Egypt. There is, finally, an unmistakable allusion to the task in hand, Thomas Mann's recreation of the living Goethe. So far, so good. But the concluding turn of the sentence quoted makes Goethe's mind revert to the *Werther*—a shift which we readily follow, having heard so much from Lotte and Riemer on the tantalizing relation of fact to fiction in this novel. And the thought of Werther brings the name of a disparaging early critic to Goethe's lips, pursed in scorn. "In meiner Jugend, der Werther macht' eben Furor, war Einer, der Bretschneider, ein Grobian, besorgt um meine Demut" (*Ibid.*) [In my youth—Werther was just causing a furor—there was one man, Bretschneider, a boor, concerned about my humility]. A bit of authentic detail, this, for Goethe knew Bretschneider since his foppish days at Leipzig. But now we must listen to the gathering impetus of the tirade that follows:

> Sagt mir über mich die letzten Wahrheiten, oder was er dafür hielt. Bild dir nichts ein, Bruder, mit dir ist nicht soviel los, wie dich das Lärmen will glauben machen, das dein Romänchen erregt! Was bist du schon für ein Kopf? Ich kenne dich. Urteilst meist schief und weisst im Grunde, dass dein Verstand ohne langes Nachdenken nicht zuverlässig ist, bist auch klug genug, Leuten, die du für einsichtig hältst, lieber gleich recht zu geben, als dass du eine Materie mit ihnen durch-discuriertest und zögst es dir auf den Hals, deine Schwäche zu zeigen. So bist du. Bist auch ein unbeständig Gemüt, das bei keinem System beharrt, sondern von einem zum andern Extremo überspringt und ebenso leicht zum

Herrnhuter wie zum Freigeist zu bereden wäre, denn beeinflussbar bist du, dass Gott erbarm. Hast dabei eine Dosis Stolz, schon unerlaubt, dass du fast alle Leute ausser dir für schwache Creaturen hältst, da doch du der Allerschwächste, nämlich zu dem Effect, dass du bei den Wenigen, die dir gescheit gelten, garnicht im Stand bist, selbst zu prüfen, sondern richtest dich nach dem allgemeinen Urteil der Welt. Heut sags ich dir einmal! Einen Samen von Fähigkeit hast du schon, ein poetisches Genie, das dann würkt, wenn du sehr lange Zeit einen Stoff mit dir herumgetragen und in dir bearbeitet und alles gesammelt hast, was zu deiner Sache dienen kann—dann gehts allenfalls, dann mag es was werden. Fällt dir etwas auf, so bleibts hängen in deinem Gemüt oder Kopf, und alles, was dir nur aufstösst, suchst du mit dem Klumpen Ton zu verkneten, den du in der Arbeit hast, denkst und sinnst auf nichts anderes als dies Object. Damit machst dus, und weiter ist nichts an dir. Lass dir keine bunten Vögel in Kopf setzen von deiner Popularität!—Ich hör ihn noch, den Kauz, war so ein Wahrheitsnarr und Fex der Erkenntnis, garnicht boshaft, litt wohl noch selber gar unter der Schärfe seines kritischen Einblicks, der Esel—gescheiter Esel, melancholisch scharfsinniger Esel, hatt er nicht recht? Hatt er nicht dreimal recht, oder noch zweieinhalbmal mit allem, was er mir unter die Nase rieb von Unbeständigkeit, Unselbstständigkeit und Bestimmbarkeit und dem Genie, das eben nur zu empfangen und lange auszutragen, Subsidia zu wählen und zu brauchen weiss? (335-336).

[He tells me the ultimate truths about myself, or what he thinks them to be.—Don't start getting ideas, brother. There's not as much to you as all that noise your little novel is causing might make you think! What kind of a fellow are you? I know you! Mostly you judge badly, and you know basically that your discernment is not dependable without long reflection. Also you're smart enough to admit right off that those people whom you think prudent are right, rather than to discuss a matter through with them and maybe stick your neck out and show your weakness. That's you! Also you're an unstable nature that sticks to no doctrine but jumps from one to the other extreme. You could be persuaded to become a pietist or a free-thinker, because you're so susceptible it's a fright. Besides, you have a dose of pride, in itself not allowed, to the point that you consider almost anybody besides yourself a weak creature, when you're the weakest of all; namely, to the effect that, in the case of those few whom you think of as clever, you're not at all in a position to judge yourself but rather you follow the general opinion of everybody. Today I'm going to lay it out for you. You do have a grain of ability, a poetic genius that goes to work when you have carried an idea about with you for a very long time, and when you have worked everything over and collected in your mind whatever can serve your cause—anyway, then it's all right, then something may come of it. Whenever you notice something, it sticks to your nature, or in your head, and everything that you pile up, you try to knead into that lump of clay you're working on. You think and reflect on nothing else but that object. That's the way you do it, and there's nothing else to you. Don't get any wild ideas about your popularity!—I can still hear him, that nut, he was such a nut for truth and a crank for knowledge, not at all malicious, probably even suffered himself under the sharpness of his critical insight, the fool—the clever fool, the melancholy, ingenious fool, wasn't he right? Wasn't he threefold right, or all in all at least two-and-a-half-fold, when he rubbed my nose in instability, unselfsufficiency, and determinacy, and in regard to the genius who is able only to conceive and gestate a long time, and to pick out and use subsidia?]

I have quoted the passage in full. To those who know Goethe and Thomas Mann it speaks an unmistakable language. As the passage starts out, this might be some Bretschneider giving a dressing-down to a cocky young Goethe whose inflated sense of self-importance rubbed him against the grain. But as it continues, the literary personality he so trenchantly defines with a malevolent animus is not that of young Goethe at all. At the time of his writing the *Werther* no one in his circle would have interpreted Goethe's literary physiognomy in terms of single-minded tenacity and slow, patient gestation. Herder, who knew him best, derided him as sparrow-brained. No, this is not Bretschneider depreciating young Goethe, this is some rival trying to take the wind out of Thomas Mann's sails, some "brother," who thinks he knows him inside out and airs his own superiority. Since Thomas Mann never had any intimates, there is only one person who could have attacked him in this way. Not quite in this way, to be sure: his rival's insight would necessarily have fallen far short of this retrospective self-revelation. Unquestionably the scene contains echoes of a jealous reaction to the great popular success of his *Buddenbrooks*. Now, nearly forty years later, the latent *élan* of the young man's emergent literary personality is dwelt upon with a sense of triumph.[1]

The page that follows contains a bitter prediction about the Germans that Goethe did not make but might have made—an agonizing echo of the Hitler madness. But the passage we have been analyzing cannot be read in terms of an upthrust of pent-up forces from the depths of Goethe's self.

Seen as a whole, the last phase of Thomas Mann, which dates from the completion of the sinister *Doktor Faustus*, is marked by

[1] In the above exposition there is an exemplary error in critical judgment on my part. Immediately after the publication of this essay Mr. Erich Neumann of the Thomas Mann Archive in Berlin very amicably called my attention to the fact that the whole Bretschneider passage is an almost verbatim reproduction of a letter from H. G. von Bretschneider to Friedrich Nicolai, dated October 16, 1775. The letter can be found in Heinz Amelung, *Goethe als Persönlichkeit* (Munich, 1914-Propyläen edition, supplementary Vol. I), pp. 128-130. See also *The Germanic Review*, XXXII (1957), 75-76.

an easing of tension, a relaxing of that turn of the screw with its often next to impossible demands on the sustaining powers of the reader's empathic response. *Der Erwählte* is light in a heady way, a sparkling draught of champagne that leaves no hang-over. *Felix Krull,* of which more in a moment, is playful throughout. As for the lightness of *Die Betrogene,* it was felt even as a letdown by many reviewers who did not know what to make of the master's new manner.

I have been quoted[2] as saying that *Die Betrogene* was written by Felix Krull with Thomas Mann looking over his shoulder. This statement warrants a little elaboration. There were readers, of course, who sought to probe into what they called the guilt of the heroine in order to see her organic dissolution in terms of a sternly moralistic retribution! But more commonly the old-fashioned technique gave rise to bewilderment. In the main, the story, except for its unmistakable twentieth-century ending that bristles with clinical vocabulary, was felt as a relapse into the carefree manner of the eighteenth century in its simple narrative style, its stiltedly artificial dialogues, and its extended use of such outworn conventions as the long, impeccably phrased soliloquies of the heroine. How was it possible for that most conscious craftsman, Thomas Mann, to revert to so timeworn a manner? Is this encroaching senility? The story itself supplies a different answer. We find it in a transparent dialogue between the emotive, blissfully effusive mother and her sophisticated, clubfooted, and inhibited daughter, the artist, who paints in the intellectual abstract manner. Why don't you for once, the mother pleads, paint something nice that will appeal to the heart—a fresh bouquet of flowers, compellingly fragrant, flanked by figurines, a gentleman blowing a kiss to a lady, and the whole mirrored in a lacquered tabletop? To which the daughter replies: Your imaginings, mother, run quite out of bounds. One cannot paint that way any more. The mother does not understand; so the daughter, in a vain attempt to make her understand, becomes very explicit: "Man kann es nicht," she insists. "Der Stand von Zeit und Kunst lässt es nicht mehr zu" (11). [You just can't. The condition of time and art no longer permits it.] This is Anna speaking to Rosalie. But we must be deaf

[2] By Erich Heller (unsigned) in the *Times Literary Supplement* (London), Nov. 11, 1955.

in one ear if we do not also hear the voice of Thomas Mann raised in amused protest against the insouciant manner of the very story in which this dialogue is imbedded. "Man kann es nicht." This sort of thing is altogether passé! You are taking me for a ride! To whom is Thomas Mann protesting? To whom can he be protesting if not to the incredibly talented imp of his creation? This facile elegance is not Thomas Mann's. The roles are reversed, the creature is in the saddle! This is Felix Krull as *spiritus rector*, guiding the redoubtable pen that gave him life in a piece of quasi-automatic writing with his master in the smilingly acquiescent role of the medium—up to a certain point!

Felix Krull, the confessions of a confidence-man, begun before *Tod in Venedig*, carried as a growing theme for more than four decades, was early referred to by its author as a parody on the German "Bildungsroman." The central idea—the artist and the criminal as twin brothers, both feeding on an excessive diet of the imagination—is already pointed up, as everyone knows, in *Tonio Kröger* and has its roots, no doubt, in a very deep stratum of Thomas Mann's psyche. When the first slim installment appeared (in 1923) the uncanny literary talent of that smooth scapegrace lent an extraordinary charm to his youthful escapades. The blending of vibrant vitality in his style with the fluent use of slick cliché added up to a self-portrait of compelling authenticity. Witness his posture in the scene after his father's suicide: There I stood, he reports "mit der Hand meine Augen bedeckend, an der erkaltenden Hülle meines Erzeugers und entrichtete ihm reichlich den Zoll der Tränen" [covering my eyes with my hand, beside the cooling shell of my sire, and paid abundantly a tribute of tears]. Does not this language glitter like the lacquered table-top of Rosalie's imagination?

If Thomas Mann's stylistic identification with his hero's uninhibited "Selbstgefälligkeit" [self-satisfaction] was a feat to be applauded, the spirit of parody takes an unexpectedly subtle turn in the ensuing course of the story. We note an ever-increasing tendency on the young man's part to become expansive in his descriptions, even to the point of tediousness, although he could not possibly ever be bored with himself. But a feature related to this, yet startlingly different, is the exhibition to which he treats us in the reproduction of his oral discourse. What reader does not remember the creeping sense of dazzled stupefaction at the elaborate, interminable periods in which Krull delivers himself on occasion to an unsuspecting stranger, as when, in Lisbon, he inquires for the location of a street, taking half a page to do it? Have we ever known any one to spin out the web of ingratiating oratory in that peculiar hypnotizing fashion? For all its strangeness it has a familiar ring. As we search in our memory we find the image of Thomas Mann's Joseph stealthily superimposing itself on that of our adventurer. Yes, this is the voice of Joseph echoing from its Egyptian spaces and their disregard of time into the milieu of pre-war Europe. What has happened? The creature, so light and full of verve at the outset, has drunk of his author's blood for so many years that a subtle transformation has been effected: First Thomas Mann writes like the budding confidence-man; now Felix Krull, for long stretches at a time, writes like Thomas Mann. First Thomas Mann creates Felix in a spirit of parody; now the creature parodies its author. Did Krull do this, by any chance, with an eye on secretary Riemer? This long-term member of Goethe's household tells in *Lotte in Weimar* that he became so adept in imitating Goethe's style that the recipients of letters from Goethe could not tell those dictated by the master from those of his own composition; he boasts, in fact, that the ceremonial turns of his style were more Goethean than Goethe's own.

Is it possible to speak of Felix Krull without recalling his greatest real-life prototype, Giacomo Casanova? Remember how Casanova fascinated the generation of Thomas Mann, becoming a major theme for Schnitzler and Hofmannsthal in plays and stories and leaving his imprint on Rilke's poems. To what extent Felix Krull's career is an "imitatio" of the adventurer *par excellence* would be an intriguing topic to dwell upon. Without doubt they have some striking fundamental features in common. Theirs is the same narcissistic "Selbstgefälligkeit" that irresistibly infects an overwhelming proportion of their acquaintances, men and women alike, and brings them under a kind of hypnotic spell. This same narcissism supplies the drive behind their incredible exploits and the element of hyperbole in their literary self-exhibition, making them both rank, untutored as they are, among the world's great storytellers. This narcissism allows both, with a degree of good faith, to profess a personal, a kind of custom-made morality: both can perpetrate the most unscrupulous acts on occasion without this engendering any deeper scruples within them as to their being essentially pleasing to God and man. Their sex life shows a similarity and a difference. In their relations with women both derive their greatest delight from giving pleasure to a partner stimulated to dizzying raptures of cooperation; neither would resort to fraud or force for the gratification of sexual desire. Both speak of the culminating act as the sacrifice (*das Opfer*).[3] But while Casanova makes a cult of his self-immolation and abandons himself to each successive love with the ecstasy of a new experience in which notes of tenderest sentiment mingle with the exhibition of incredible feats of potency, Felix Krull lacks this robust constitution and tempers his comparatively rare sexual orgies with self-preserving caution.

But the most fundamental difference between the two adventurers is to be found in the fact that Casanova's is an active, aggressive temperament that plunges headlong into the turmoil of life without any squeamishness regarding its gross and sordid aspects, whereas Krull is essentially a passive figure so far as real life is concerned. He finds his most exquisite gratification in the realm of the imagination. He did not cooperate actively during his birth, he tells us, and throughout his story, as far as we are able to follow its unfinished course, he is a *Sonntagskind* [Sunday's child, i.e. favored by fortune] on whom, for the most part, life bestows its gifts without his having to exert himself actively toward their attainment. Casanova experiences ups and downs of the most prodigious range; a grimy beggar today, ravaged by disease and hunger, he will turn up tomorrow a nobleman moving with the ease of one to the manner born in the sphere of aristocracy and royalty, secular and ecclesiastic, in Turkey as well as in Europe. Whatever happens to him, he always has a way of landing on his feet by virtue of an incredible robustness of constitution. Could we imagine Felix Krull surviving fifteen months of torture under the lead roofs of Venice and engineering his eventual escape with a tenacity of will that triumphs over stupendous obstacles? Comparing Felix Krull and Casanova as real characters—an unfair approach, to be sure—the eighteenth-century confidence-man dwarfs the nineteenth-cen-

[3] The term occurs frequently in the new German translation of Casanova's memoirs that began to appear in thirteen volumes under the imprint of Georg Müller, München, in 1907.

tury prodigy. The mere fact that Casanova writes his memoirs at seventy while Krull is through with life at forty points up the difference. If we evaluate the two as literary autobiographies, on the other hand, the scale tips decidedly in Krull's favor: Casanova's extremely uneven account cannot measure up to the stylistic mastery that Felix Krull acquired through the long years of mystical intimacy with his creator.

To our regret *Felix Krull* was left unfinished. What was committed to paper beyond the published first volume we shall doubtless see in due time. But our regrets are tempered by the consideration that Thomas Mann always had a major project in the works. Something was bound to be left unfinished even though in a sense it was there long ago. The themes were all there from way back, the variations, always startlingly novel, could go on *ad infinitum*. There are some lines in Goethe's *Divan* which for many years have haunted me as applying singularly, uniquely to Thomas Mann. They read as though written to hail his coming, to summarize his literary essence. To me they are the most fitting epitaph for a writer who, more than any other, rounded out his life's full cycle, transmuting the raw material of his earthly existence into works that live:

> Dass du nicht enden kannst, das macht dich gross,
> Und dass du nie beginnst, das ist dein Los.
> Dein Lied ist drehend wie das Sterngewölbe,
> Anfang und Ende immerfort dasselbe,
> Und was die Mitte bringt, ist offenbar
> Das, was zu Ende bleibt und Anfangs war.

> [That thou canst not end, that makes thee great,
> that thou never beginst, that is thy fate.
> Thy song is whirling like the starry vault,
> beginning and end the same for evermore,
> and what the middle brings is manifestly
> that which at the end remains and was originally.]

January 27, 1956

NOTE

An expanded German version of this essay was delivered under the auspices of the Allard Pierson Foundation in Amsterdam on March 21, 1956 and subsequently published in *Neophilologus*.

HERMANN BROCH'S
DEATH OF VERGIL:
PROGRAM NOTES

THE BOOK to be discussed[1] brings to mind a fascinating chapter of the fossil record of the evolution of life. Some two hundred million years ago, the geologists tell us, the Ammonites began to make their appearance among the crustaceans. Starting from modest and primitive beginnings, they were destined for a notable future. In the course of ages a million times beyond the span of human memory they grew in size and complexity, attaining to functional perfection of their communicating chambers and streamlined beauty of their spiral convolutions. They grew in numbers until they came to dominate the scene of teeming marine life. Then a change set in. The conservative classical form of the shell gave way to striking variations. It is as if the ingenuity of the race had suddenly abandoned itself to an orgy of formal experiments. The curves became more intricate and capricious, producing a bewildering variety of scallops and flutings, spirals and fantastic ornaments and an equally bewildering range of sizes and proportions. The whole genus seemed to be off balance, to be skidding erratically along the screen of evolutionary Time. Then, suddenly, when this giddy orgy seemed to have reached its climax the whole genus disappeared, as though a relentless hand had blotted it from the screen once and for all.

To us favored contemporaries of the atomic age, this and similar spectacles give food for thought, as we survey the proliferating forms of modern art, pictorial, musical, and literary. Talent runs to experimentation. The greater the talent the more fantastic is the range of experimentation. The destruction of traditional forms is accomplished by a form sense that has contrived to transmute the substance of subject matter into pure subjective

[1] Hermann Broch: *Der Tod des Vergil* (New York: Pantheon Books, 1945). Also published as *The Death of Virgil*, translated by Jean Starr Untermeyer. This paper, while making use of the English title, is based on the German text, and all page references are made with the German edition in mind.

Reprinted from *PMLA*, LXII (1947), 525-554, by permission of the Modern Language Association.

energy. Technical virtuosity seems obsessed by an auto-erotic mania. Has it become a patterned dance heading for chaos?

The *Death of Vergil* is a book of five hundred large octavo pages, divided into four chapters, each bearing the name of one of the four elements (water, fire, earth, air), and the captions: The Arrival, The Descent, The Expectation, The Homecoming. Three of the chapters have a number of subdivisions marked by a few blank lines and a larger initial letter, but not one additional word of articulating guidance.

I said that the book consists of four chapters. It would be more to the point to say, it consists of four movements, and the four movements constitute a verbal symphony of overwhelming proportions. This characterization is more than a metaphor. It describes accurately the sustained flow of its language broken by only three main pauses. Once this central fact has been grasped by the reader, he will have no difficulty in distinguishing differences of instrumentation, tempo, and volume; he will note solo parts and delicately blended voices of varying timbre, he will register the pulse of mounting tension and experience again and again the crashing climaxes of the full orchestra that leave him reeling as under the roar of the Day of Judgment.

Turning the pages of this book at random, a prospective reader would observe the extreme paucity of paragraph indentations. He might turn over ten, on occasion even twenty pages before finding a line for the eye to come to rest at. Supposing his curiosity led him to browse, he would scan the page for the beginning of a sentence, and as likely as not, he would fail to find one. Glancing over the next page, he might again fail to discern a full stop. This would induce a certain sense of uneasiness, if not alarm; for the eye should be expected to orient itself with ease among the clear bold type of this book. Perhaps he would then plunge into the text, right in the middle of a sentence, abandoning himself blindly to its lead. In following the guidance of the picked-up thread through the labyrinth, he might well ask himself whether he had been bewitched, plunged into an impenetrable jungle of the most fantastic verbal vegetation, groping his way forward through the lush and stifling growth, and arriving eventually, after innumerable dark and baffling turns, at a point of clearing where the suspended action of the lungs can function again: he would certainly be aware of an uncanny spell being woven.

This book is "a creation to the magic of which everyone must succumb who has experienced its spell." Thus Thomas Mann on the jacket.[2] That is a balanced and judicious statement, formulated I presume with deliberate intent. This becomes apparent when we rearrange the order of the sentence without altering its logical coherence. Thomas Mann says in effect: Whoever has come under the spell of this book must succumb to its magic. This statement presupposes or concedes the presence of a kind of magic. The elaboration is a neat tautology. Perhaps then the question poses itself: How does one come under the spell of this book?[3] Rather than attempt to answer such a question, let me counter with an objective test by which a reader can prove that he has truly come under the spell of its magic. Let him sit down with the *Death of Vergil* and read it from cover to cover at one sitting, as one sustained verbal symphony, punctated by three brief pauses. Let him summon the energy to conduct for himself the unbroken performance it calls for. It can be done in twenty-four hours, I think, and when preceded by a proper regimen of training, it should prove no more difficult than Charles Lindbergh's solo flight from New York to Paris.

That I have not altogether succumbed to the spell of this book may be gathered from this introduction. I account for this partly because I shrink from abandoning myself to its shattering cosmic violence; in part, however, I find myself rebelling against a certain feature of its hypnotizing magic, of which I shall speak at once,

[2] "eine . . . Schöpfung, deren Magie jeden gefangen nehmen muss, der in ihren Bannkreis gerät." This is rendered, perhaps a bit too loosely, on the jacket of the English version by: "A . . . performance, the magic of which must grip everyone who comes in contact with it."

[3] That Thomas Mann did not come under its spell would be a presumptuous thing for me to assert. But it must not be forgotten that a creative artist lives in a world of his own and casts spells and practices magic. He is not apt to surrender to a competitor's spell when the investment of an enormous amount of time is at stake. Artists are by inner necessity the most self-centered of humans. It is also well to remember that a public testimonial may differ considerably from an opinion confidentially expressed. We may take a leaf out of Broch's book to quote from an intimate literary conversation between Vergil and two close friends, one of whom having made a snide remark about Ovid hastens to add: "natürlich würde ich mich hüten derlei Urteile öffentlich kundzutun, denn, ob gut oder schlecht, wir Schreibenden gehören alle zusammen" (272) [naturally, I would guard myself against making such judgments publicly, for—whether good or bad—we writers all belong together].

and out of turn, simply because there will be no time to return to this later.

The master principle of literary development employed in this book is repetition, repetition on a grand scale, repetition as methodical as the pounding of a well-drill or a steam turbine, repetition that bludgeons and benumbs, repetition that never loses patience with itself, repetition that never betrays a flutter of nervousness, repetition that severely eschews every verbal shortcut, every acceleration of tempo, repetition as sure of its rightness as the repetitious pulse of the waves on the surface of the sea. This book proceeds at the slow but inexorable pace of the advancing tide on the beach. Rebel against its repetitious incantation, try to cut across the waves with your own dynamic initiative: you will only thrash about in a circle of foam spending your strength and your patience to no avail. If you would read this book at all you must resign yourself to letting it cradle you as it lists. I found this very difficult to do. Have I a right then to discuss this book at all? Am I qualified to judge it?

I admit at the outset that my attempt to project its essence is tentative and limited. I have seen it from without rather than within. I have walked all around this monstrous phenomenon of a book, glimpsing, measuring many notable features, but I have not locked embraces with it, and my spirit's ear has not penetrated to those innermost membranes which directly communicate the throb of its heart-beat. I have learned enough, however, to know that the work is the execution of a design of grandiose scope, planned to the last detail with a consummate mastery of the means employed. The author envisaged clearly what he wanted to say; he knew how to say it, and he impressed into the service of his project a disciplined and inflexible will. These are statements of fact, learned from wrestling with the book at painfully close range—facts that can be demonstrated by exact scholarly methods,[4] given sufficient time, facts that give me the right to qualify to some extent as an expert. Facts such as these, moreover, entitle the *Death of Vergil* to rank as a major work of imaginative creation regardless of whether one's personal taste finds it a source of rapture or torment.

It is cheap to make fun of what one does not understand. It is

[4] Most immediately by an analysis of the thematic material and its development.

dangerous to go into raptures over what passes one's comprehension. A prerequisite for judging any book, any artistic performance, from a high critical vantage point, is an intimate knowledge of its frame of reference. That frame of reference in this case would seem to be the great current of Christian mysticism which has developed from earliest times alongside the dogma, ritual and organized activity of the Church, sometimes encouraged by its leaders, more frequently frowned upon and persecuted. An intimate knowledge not only of the basic conceptions of mysticism, but also of the imagery and the phraseology employed to communicate states of mind that essentially refuse to conform to the vehicle of language is indispensable to a full understanding of Broch's *Death of Vergil*.[5] I confess that I have only a superficial acquaintance with the tradition of Christian mysticism. Hence I am not certain to just what degree Broch builds on this tradition. I know enough however to leave no doubt in my mind as to the fact that the thought of this book and its imagery and its language is not *sui generis*, not a mere product of the author's subjective imagination, but that it is based in a very real sense on forebears earnestly concerned with pursuing the goal of human salvation along a path that runs quite distinct from the orthodoxy of any church. I am not certain in all frankness either whether this book, like the *Divine Comedy*, is not primarily to be considered as inspirational poetry rather than as secular literature. Broch does not lure the reader by easy stages into the realm where his will takes command. He does not choose to be ingratiating. Except for giving reign to an extraordinary faculty of rendering light and sound and rendering them in terms of each other (synaesthesia) on the largest scale ever attempted to my knowledge, he does not court the reader's imagination. This book is concerned with the passion for cognition, for knowledge, for insight into ultimate reality. It expects the reader to concentrate all the faculties at his command

[5] Meister Eckhart (†1327), the fountain-head of German mysticism, comes to mind with his disciples Seuse and Tauler; Paracelsus in the sixteenth, Jacob Boehme in the seventeenth century; also the later Fichte (*Anweisung zum seligen Leben*). The work of a contemporary popularizer, Ernst Bergmann, *Die Entsinkung ins Weiselose* (Breslau, 1932), contains interesting leads, to be used with caution. German poets steeped in the mystical tradition include Angelus Silesius and Novalis, as well as many recent and contemporary writers of note, Hauptmann, Hesse, Stehr, Hofmannsthal, Rilke among them. Most of the latter have assimilated elements of mysticism in an eclectic way.

upon the task of following the exposition of very general ideas and their progressive interrelation. The task is sometimes rather grueling. The general ideas are distilled, to be sure, from a wealth of sensuous experience and remain permeated with an aura of sensuous associations. Yet the argument moves almost uninterruptedly in the stratosphere of airy abstraction. All human faculties are called into play, but intelligence, the faculty of logical abstraction and combination, is at the controls. Power is supplied by the drive of a will striving for the goal of ultimate reality, but intelligence charts the way. Perhaps the key-word most frequently met in the book (there are scores of such key-words) is *Erkennen* [discerning]. Our literary habits almost automatically tempt us to substitute *Erleben* [experiencing] and *Erlebnis* [experience] for *Erkennen* and *Erkenntnis* [discernment]. But although almost the entire action of the book proceeds in the interior of a poet's mind, we rarely meet the word "Erleben" in this volume. I think this is not a terminological vagary, but a matter of fundamental importance.

Broch aims at nothing less than to recapture by an act of spirit the unity of a fragmented universe: a unity that is the interpenetration of the here and the beyond, a unity that transcends time and space, embracing the totality of what has ever been or ever shall be in a single here and now. Broch pushes toward this goal by a series of escalations that take him through regions of mental anguish and inner desolation that chill the marrow, through an inferno of the soul as fearsome as that through which Dante passed. As in Dante's case the successive abysses of the Inferno into which the soul has plunged are followed by a Purgatorio to be endured before the soul is finally admitted to the Paradiso. It is not in his own person that Broch pursues in this book the insatiate passion for wholeness. He uses the historical figure of Vergil as the vehicle of his quest. But why? It was Vergil, we remember, who guided Dante through the infernal regions. But how could anyone, how could Vergil have qualified for this unique mission? Only by virtue, surely, of his having experienced that whole cycle of horrors in the flesh and come through it to ultimate triumph. Thus Broch reasoned, I am convinced, and with this deduction as his starting point he proceeded to grasp the tenuous thread of biographical tradition regarding Vergil and weave it into a tapestry of tortured hunger after the ultimate, of death and transfiguration.[6]

The plot of the narrative can be told in a few sentences. Vergil, the poet, dying of consumption, arrives by ship at Brundisium one autumn evening of the year 19 B.C. in the retinue of Emperor Augustus. Racked by fever during the night, Vergil passes his whole life in review; he weighs it and finds it wanting. As the climax to a number of shattering inner experiences he feels an imperative summons to burn all his manuscripts including the unfinished Aeneid. The next morning, Augustus, who has got wind of Vergil's intention, visits him and besets him with long and exhausting arguments. Vergil clings to his resolve with dogged tenacity, vainly trying to make Augustus understand. Then, after both parties have reached the verge of exhaustion, each standing his ground, the argument takes a sudden turn causing Vergil to yield. He has come to realize (with his heart and his head) that renouncing his heart's desire, the cherished sacrifice, constitutes at this stage a sacrifice on a higher plane, and he measures up to this supreme demand, because the spark of love has been kindled in his heart. Now he is at peace. He dictates his will. Then he dies.

To state the plot in this way prepares us for a major surprise. Having thought of the *Death of Vergil* as akin to a novel because of its enormous bulk, we suddenly realize that it conforms in all essentials to the classic type of the early Italian "Novella" of Boccaccio and his successors, as later defined by Goethe and Tieck. According to them, the "Novelle," insofar as it can be precisely delimited as a *genre*, has two characteristic features: First, it recounts an extraordinary incident. Secondly, somewhere in the course of the incident matters take a highly surprising turn. Well, here we have both. It is first an extraordinary, a unique occurrence for a

---

[6] It was certainly not the temper of Vergil's published work which gave Broch the cue for this book. Vergil's work does not manifest or even suggest that passion for the absolute with which Broch endows him. There are a great many quotations from Vergil's work and allusions to it interwoven with the narrative, but none of these many passages would have supplied the spark for conceiving of Vergil's personality in the terms of this book. He makes relatively little use even of the fourth Eclogue which the whole medieval church regarded as a prophecy of Christ and which is responsible for the unique position assigned by the Middle Ages to Vergil among the pagan poets. I would stress that Dante, rather than the Eclogues, Georgics, and Aeneid was responsible for the formation of Broch's creative Vergil complex. Broch came to focus upon his hero by a process of deduction as stated above.

successful poet to set about destroying his life-work. And second, the complete reversal of the situation from sacrifice as renunciation to renunciation of sacrifice gives the sharpest possible twist to an extraordinary situation. Thus the inner structure of this book of five hundred pages conforms to the structure of those *Decameron* stories, ten of which, told in succession, make up a day's pleasant entertainment. We feel transported into a world where midget dinosaurs, the size of a human hand, greet as first cousins monsters that weigh a hundred tons.

The events of the narrative follow the traditional record and run their course from Vergil's landing at Brundisium to his death, less than twenty-four hours later. The what of the story so briefly disposed of, it is obviously the how that matters. What is the tissue of the giant tapestry that Broch embroidered upon so simple a basic design?

Reducing matters to fundamentals, the work revolves about two problems. First, how does Vergil come to will the destruction of his work? Second, how is he prevailed upon to reverse his decision?

Given a poet who had devoted his whole life to the pursuit of his art, with unparalleled success, a poet who had been showered with honors and with wealth, a poet who enjoyed the friendship of the intellectuals and of the all-powerful head of the state, a poet revered by his contemporaries as next to divine, a poet on the point of adding the final touches to his greatest work which has been conceived and acclaimed in advance as a monumental imaginative counterpart to the awe-inspiring edifice of Imperial Rome,—given now the fact, vouched for by tradition, that this poet resolved on his deathbed to burn his master work and expunge his name from the annals of time, what "chain reaction" of mental processes could have led to this devastating culmination? What is the inner significance of this fantastic resolve?

The end-point, the goal, being fixed by tradition, it was the author's task to construct the course that led to it, to make this course appear plausible and the goal significant. The first 180 pages of this book are devoted to the working out of this problem (climax 189-192). There are a few pages of introductory narrative giving the setting and its historical background in broad outline, but very soon we are imperceptibly made a party to Vergil's state of mind, his feelings and moods, to his hyperaesthetic sensibility, to his disillusionment, also to the deepest aspirations which have fed the flame of his life since infancy—aspirations that have the character of a compelling urge, a categorical imperative. Imperceptibly the panorama of Vergil's mind comes to be unfolded from within, and the rhythmical flow of imagery and abstraction which at first seemed to proceed from the author is increasingly felt to be the pulsing stream of Vergil's consciousness.[7] From that point on, it is almost an exclusively inner drama that unfolds. This drama is harrowing in the extreme. Vergil is like a substance in the crucible of an invisible alchemist, subjected to tortures of the most ingenious devising in order to separate out the impurities and to distil eventually the subtlest divine essence from his soul. Vergil is tossed from one crisis into another. Each time the net result of his agonized self-searching is the stripping off of another layer of fraud, of self-deception, of sham values, leaving his ego finally reduced to an anonymous, naked shivering soul.

We must pass the stages of Vergil's inner collapse in brief review, merely as an attempt to grasp the articulation of the book. To suggest their psychological quality is quite beyond my power within the compass of this report.

Vergil's equanimity had received a severe jolt as he was being carried by slaves in a sedan chair through a milling crowd up the winding alleyways of the city's slum. Nauseated by filth, stench, and obscene abuse, he had been compelled to close his eyes. This gives an early intimation of how selectively he had filtered the elements of life despite his yearning to see life whole. After this harrowing prelude he finds himself lodged at last with his thoughts, having dismissed the ministering slave and a mysterious country boy who had clung to him after volunteering his services as guide to the party.

As he lies in his bed, in a state of high fever, hyperaesthetic and abnormally lucid, he probes again all the avenues by which he had attempted to encompass life as a whole, the avenues of science, the meditation of death, the creative activity of the poet. But approached from whatever angle, his quest had failed. It had been foredoomed to failure by its very nature. Even this realization, however, made the imperative of the fate-willed quest no less

---

[7] Even though it is largely stream-of-consciousness, as to subject matter, formally there is nothing chaotic or Joycean in the book at any time.

urgent and absolute. At bottom was the conviction that the world was hopelessly out of joint and that he, Vergil, was ordained somehow to piece together the fragmented parts. Hopelessly lost in a labyrinth of error, frustration, failure, stagnation, his mind reverts to his unfinished epic, the *Aeneid*, to find it too reflecting the same congenital qualities of imperfection inherent in all things. The thought of the poem becomes a magnet, as it were, drawing toward itself the whole weight of all his frustrations. In a world where everything is a symbol, the *Aeneid* becomes the supreme symbol of imperfection, and he is gripped with horror at the realization that it will never be completed. This is most important to realize. It is only because the *Aeneid* has become for Vergil the symbol par excellence of human limitation that its survival or destruction becomes the focus of the whole inner drama.

Stark terror climaxed the first cycle of his feverish thinking, a terror of soul[8] that had as its physiological counterpart a sense of suffocation. Here as in the succeeding crises we are kept aware, largely by rhythmical suggestion, of the drama of lungs and heart being enacted on the bed. The shock of terror has been a catalyzing agent, lifting Vergil above the plane of his conventional consciousness. Terror has flung open the portal admitting him to the "inner court" beyond which reality lies. Terror has opened up to Vergil great philosophical vistas: he experiences the mystical interrelation between Necessity and Freedom in the fate that has shaped him. He feels buoyed up by the hand of Fate that a moment ago had held him in a crushing grasp. But he is due straightway to be plunged into another abyss.

At the window to which he had dragged himself when terror made him bolt out of bed, he becomes a party, chiefly through the medium of sound, to a scene of drunken obscenity down below. Two men and a woman, typical representatives of the city-bred proletariat, bestial *and* sophisticated, engage in a quarrel that reveals the fragmentation of the world in its most devastating aspect. The scene culminates in peals of laughter, ribald, sub-human, chattering laughter, laughter of cosmic proportions, laughter that reveals itself as a demonic solvent reducing all divine and human values to primeval chaos, laughter the symbol of nihilism.

---

[8] We are reminded of "Angst" as a term of peculiar significance in the philosophies of Kierkegaard and Heidegger.

As this laughter recedes into the distance its grossness is muted by the atmosphere, and eventually a moment comes when it blends with the other sounds of the night into a harmonious effect. It has been incorporated into beauty. This is a frightening discovery. Vergil the devotee of beauty becomes aware of the precarious nature of beauty. Beauty is a mere matter of aspect. It is an unstable compound harboring within itself an ingredient of world-shattering laughter. Beauty creates a harmony that is pre-divine in its quality. It is indifferent to knowledge as cognition and indifferent to knowledge of good and evil. It flouts responsibility. It boasts of its civilizing refining function, but fully half of its appeal lies in the licensed outlet it gives to the lust for cruelty (tragedy). In thus analyzing the nature of beauty, at whose altar he worshipped, Vergil feels himself reduced to the level of the vile trio and implicated in the cosmic "perjury" of their laughter. The problem of beauty leads him to pose the question that strikes nearest home: What account can the artist give of himself in a world shot through with rottenness and fraud? He examines his own artistic creed and his performance, and he finds the former a tissue of false attitudes and hollow pretensions and the latter cold and stilted, lifeless and unconvincing. And he finds all these glaring shortcomings rooted in the artistic impulse and in the artist's disposition as such.[9] All this is familiar ground to those who remember how mercilessly nineteenth-century poets have been wont to expose the seamy side of art, the shoddy human quality of the attitudes that result in inspiring works. Tieck and Brentano had a thoroughly uneasy conscience on the matter. Nietzsche turned upon the artist with masochistic fury, and Ibsen brooded on the endowment of the artist as a curse that forever bars him from contact with life. In all this Broch's Vergil anticipates the anguish of an age that has lost faith in itself. He collapses at the bar of his conscience. He finds himself congenitally incapable of love, he has sidestepped involvement in all direct human bonds and obligations

[9] The condemnation of art is hedged by one reservation, pp. 150-151. Art is legitimate to the extent that it explores still uncharted regions of the human soul on the one hand and of the universe on the other, the two being linked by the mystery of correspondence, "das Geheimnis der Entsprechung." Every true work of art involves a permanent expansion of the sphere of mankind, for, according to Vergil-Broch's conviction, no element of experienced knowledge is ever lost. But for this reservation the reader would be haunted in all seriousness by the question: Why did Broch on his part not destroy the *Death of Vergil*?

in deference to his precious detachment. Humanly speaking, he has thriven on pose and make-believe all his life. And withal he has nourished the smug presumption of thinking that he or the likes of him could be ordained by fate to lead humanity out of its perjured state and reëstablish the covenant with the gods.

Stripped of his dignity and his merit, he feels himself to be a naked soul shivering in the void. The world has cast him out. All things have withdrawn their warmth and he is utterly alone.

But Vergil is fated to take one more headlong plunge before his self-annihilation is complete. He is caught up in a visionary state in which fantastic hosts of "pre-creational" entities swarm about him[10] and freeze his marrow with a sense of terror that is the ultimate escalation of the endurable. He feels himself become rigid with the rigidity of a coma from which there is no awakening (Scheintod). His heart has stopped beating. He is all but extinct.

This moment of self-abandonment when his existence hangs in the balance brings the turning-point. From out of the deepest core of his self there arises a summons to repudiate his past life utterly and all its works—his honors, his postures, his achievements, his name, all that old self mired in error, and save his soul. And this summons, welling up darkly, gathering momentum in an overwhelming chorus of sounds and voices as it rises to the threshold of consciousness, translates itself into the outcry: "Burn the *Aeneid*!" (p. 192).

This is not the end of Book Two, but it is a time to pause. The division of the work into four books cuts across the stages of the inner drama. Here we have arrived at the turning-point that dwarfs all others. The climax of anguished passion clamoring for the extinction of self spells Vergil's release from the horrors of his Inferno. Contrition ("Zerknirschung") has done its work. The divine mill of tribulation (con-tero,-trivi,-tritum) has crushed, ground and bolted the kernel of the soul to flour-dust.[11] Now grace becomes operative. A counter-movement, imperceptible at first, ensues to reconstitute the altered soul.

"Burn the *Aeneid*!" As the summons of the inner voice translates

[10] In some respects a close parallel to the sensations of Book Four, but experienced there as vision without a trace of terror.

[11] The original force of the image underlying the concept of contrition is impressively experienced in Strindberg's *To Damascus*.

itself into a cry from Vergil's mouth, he wakes up to become conscious of what it involves: A supreme sacrifice, demanded of him—nay, vouchsafed to him, rather, for it is fraught in his mind with implications of world-redeeming efficacy—a sacrifice to be performed with hallowed ritual, at the seashore, facing the rising sun. This is his first idea, but he realizes almost on the instant that this would be to continue the spurious old aesthetic play of posturing which he had seen through and found a participant in the world's "perjury." No, the summons must be carried out here and now, without any vestige of conventional trimmings. This realization is proof of his utter sincerity. His will is set to do it at once. Yet his will fails to be translated into the act willed. What stands in the way? Physical exhaustion for one thing, but more important: It is ordained otherwise. Fate had racked him in order to distill the act of will that envisaged the supreme sacrifice. At the same time Fate bars the acceptance of the proffered sacrifice as unavailing for the healing of the world's ills. Vergil comes to sense this in the course of a mystical inner dialogue in which the voice of the boyish guide takes part. The dialogue begins with the boy offering Vergil a cup of wine. Twice Vergil refuses, sensing temptation, unwilling to succumb again to the blandishment of intoxication. When it is offered a third time Vergil realizes the altered significance of the cup: the state of contrition invested by grace calls for the complete surcease of any exercise of will. Thus he accepts the proffered boon in grateful submission, to find himself transported by it into a new region of the spirit where he meets his poem reconstituted on a plane to which mortal speech has no access. Then he is lifted into a denser trance which is like a dream within a dream. In this sphere Vergil moves divested of individual memory and the guilt-tainted language of man. He has become a child again and the child experiences "the second memory" and "the second language" (223). There is an ineffable intermingling of forms without substance, disembodied essences in the pre-creational matrix of life. But as the vision proceeds the realm of pure form, ethically indifferent, is superseded by the assertion of forces which sunder the realm of indifference and establish clear-cut patterns of good and evil. The essence of the ethical imperative is Love, and Vergil perceives that only through Love can the world be made whole again. Now it is as if the breathing of all creation were hushed with a sense of waiting, building up to a tense expectancy of unheard-of things to come, until from the density of the supercharged silence words detach themselves, such as: the bringer of salvation—a hero of double origin, earthly by birth but divinely begotten—the salvation of the father—suffering the iniquity of fate to its ultimate extreme—the pure flame of sacrifice—the raising of the stone from the tomb—the future hallowed in the name of the father, hallowed in the name of the son and pledged to the spirit. Words like these, accompanied by the vision of a new star, for the first time clearly suggest the pattern of the Christian drama of the incarnation, atonement, and resurrection. Vergil hails the Son as the savior of the Father and of mankind. God needing to be redeemed as well as man—we note—is the one respect in which Vergil's vision departs from the conventional Christian pattern. The moment in the course of the world is at hand when the Covenant between God and Man will be reëstablished by virtue of a pure sacrifice untainted by mortal guilt. Vergil is indeed singled out to experience a first intuition of the salvation about to dawn, but even so much as for him to proclaim his vision of the new covenant transcends the scope of things ordained, let alone that he should qualify as the chosen vessel to bring it about. It is given to Vergil to see the dawn of things to come, but neither to herald it, nor to give it shape.

In the midst of this trance Vergil hears the summons to awaken; a summons that grows from an imperceptible murmur to an unearthly peal spanning the whole range of sensation (another pianissimo-fortissimo climax like that which terminated the preceding division). "Open thine eyes to love" (237) is what the summons conveys, translated into terms of human language. Vergil awakens from the trance to the sounds of dawning morning (a virtuoso passage!) only to feel himself wafted straightway into another visionary landscape dominated by the form of an angel who hails him in a voice blended of gentleness and finality with the words: "Enter thou into Creation that once was and again is. But as for thee, let thy name be Vergil, thy time is at hand."

This is the final moment in the flood of visions that made Vergil drink the cup of bitterness to its dregs, that plunged him from abyss to abyss, into unimaginable hells of anguish and self-annihilation to cleanse him of his taints, that wrung from his tortured soul the resolve, the act of will to destroy his work and his name, and thereby turned upon him the first faint ray of a divine grace becoming operative in a vessel prepared to receive it, thereafter expanding into a flood of light never before vouchsafed to mortal man, yet within certain limits, inasmuch as the acceptance of Vergil's sacrifice was inexorably ruled out as inefficacious for the achievement of the divine-human task of mutual redemption. Since the appearance of the angel with his message is the terminating point of this inner drama, let us pause for a moment to dwell upon the features of the angel. The angel suggests the biblical parallel of him with whom Jacob wrestled. The angel is the embodied essence of the ordeal. In confirming his name (he does not bestow a new one, he restores it as a boon to him who had willed the ultimate renunciation of self) he sets the seal of eternity upon a personality that has realized the ultimate sphere of its possibilities of expansion, remaining a finite, a human entity withal. And in saying: thy time is at hand, he announces that the hour of his death has arrived. Having heard this pronouncement, Vergil at last falls into a deep dreamless sleep in which his all but spent mortality accumulates the reserves with which to face the ordeals of his last day on earth.

Book Three, taken as a whole, presents a sharp contrast to Book Two. Book Two was a monodrama of 164 pages. Some of it was inner monologue. There were occasional traces of inner dialogue. By and large it was narrative making us a party through the medium of the author's words to successive states of mind experienced by Vergil as the fever burned in his veins, inducing general hyperaesthesia and an extraordinary quickening of his intellectual and affective powers. By contrast, Book Three presents a variety of scenes in which a number of real persons apart from Vergil participate: two friends of Vergil, a slave, the physician, Caesar Augustus, the friends again. Within these scenes, and in the intervals between them Vergil lapses into repeated states of semiconsciousness and delirium, states of incoherent wandering, tortured or ecstatic, often both. These states feed upon the material of the great visions of the night before, taking up fragments of them, processing them, elaborating them, recapturing for moments their ineffable clarity; but they cannot, in principle, carry him beyond that ultimate climax of insight attained during the visions of the night.

Book Three begins with a problem. Vergil's experiences of the night may be likened to a mathematical equation of the utmost complexity with the working out of which he has been charged by Fate. On the one side are ranged an appalling series of complicated ideational formulas, and on the other is the mysterious x, the meaning of his life. He solves the equation, to find that that staggering array of involved phenomena reduces the value of x to zero. Zero is the value which his life and his poetry adds up to when all the factors constituting its tissue are perscrutinized and resolved. It is an annihilating solution. But this zero is not an empty zero. It equilibrates the totality of phenomena ranged on the other side of the bars. It is zero, but it is also the whole complex formula plus the work that went into solving it. It is a zero that is meaningful to the highest degree. Now the problem of Book Three is to show what happens when this infinitely meaningful zero, the result of excruciating self-examination is thrust into the world of sense as an unrelated fact, a mere zero, dissociated from the spiritual mathematics of which it presents the upshot. What will the world say when presented with this finding? There can be only one reaction: baffled, utter, uncomprehending bewilderment.

This, of course, is only the first problem of Book Three. The further problem is to show how Vergil, baffled in the utter failure of his attempts to present the resultant zero as meaningful, badgered by total incomprehension, is finally induced by the stirring of a feeling within him to withdraw the object of the barren altercation and to yield. Book Three is climaxed by Vergil's renunciation of his resolve to burn his manuscript. We are held in suspense until the turning-point is reached when he gives up the struggle and presents his work as a gift to Augustus.—Let us now briefly review the events of Book Three in their sequence.

Scene 1. In the morning, when the sun is already high up in the heavens, Vergil awakens, reluctantly, but sufficiently conscious to see two intimates of former days who have come to visit him. The exalted tension of the night's visions is gone. His thinking is now on a reduced level. He remembers that the tortured self-analysis of the night had led to a devastating conclusion: the resolve to burn his manuscripts. But the dialectics that had followed upon the crystallizing of this resolve—the willing of the act here and now in pure simplicity without aesthetic trimmings, the rejection of his sacrifice by the Powers as inefficacious, the vision of the divine redeemer about to become incarnate—these culminating features of the night's experiences had been too exalted for his workaday memory to retain; all he knows now is the urge to proceed to the seashore and burn the manuscript of the *Aeneid* to the accompaniment of sacrificial rites. To his friends who enter he announces his purpose. Incredulous at first, they take his persistence as a symptom of temporary derangement. They expostulate and debate. They involve him in a discussion of current philosophies and literary personalities in order to convince him of the irrationality of his resolve. They are voluble. He utters but few words charged with deeper meaning that they do not understand. In the pauses and while they talk, concentrated echoes of the night's thoughts and visions stir in his memory and engage his attention more deeply than the superficial chatter of the men present in the room. Above all it is the theme of the newly found love that reasserts itself. Then he feels his strength waning and fear grips him anew. Realizing that he will never rise again to carry out his purpose, he tries to exact a promise from his friend to burn the manuscript of the Aeneid as the execution of his last will. By way of answer they rush out to summon the physician.

Scene 2. As Vergil is left alone, the outer scene recedes, but there is light within, and he finds himself involved in an inner dialogue that confirms and clarifies in human terms the mystical revelations of the night before. He is three people all in one, Lysanias the boyish guide, the nameless humble slave charged with ministering to his needs (whose physical presence in the room we sense by some snatches of discourse) and Vergil the poet. We now come to see clearly what symbolic character attaches to each of the other two. The boyish guide, who speaks the language of Vergil's native village is Vergil's childhood self.[12] In him Vergil has become a child again in the sense of the gospel. The Syrian slave, a Jew (without this being said in so many words), represents the lot of anonymity, of duty in the abstract, imperceptibly transformed into humility, service, help, self-effacing kindness, qualities that Vergil had come to experience when he willed the

---

[12] In other scenes the same figure is charged with other functions.

extinction of his work and his name and sensed the dawn of the new love. The three discourse in measured rhythms. They rehearse the origin of the world, the primal evil imbedded in its texture, the recurrence of titanic revolt and violence as misguided attempts to conquer the evil at the root of things. Against this recurrent failure the slave hails as the true hero him who comes divested of arms ("Jener ist erst der Held, der die Entwaffnung erträgt," 287). The passage may be read to contain overtones of pacifism, but in its context it points to Christ, for we hear again of the Son of the Virgin, who, one with the Father and the Spirit, is destined to invalidate the primal curse of domination, making all creation become a child again. Once more the boy hails the unique if limited part allotted to Vergil in the evolving drama of salvation:

> Du sahest den Anfang, Vergil, bist selber noch nicht der Anfang, du hörtest die Stimme, Vergil, bist selber noch nicht die Stimme, du fühltest das Schöpfungsherz pochen, bist selber noch nicht das Herz, du bist der ewige Führer, der selber das Ziel nicht erreicht: unsterblich wirst du sein, unsterblich als Führer, *noch nicht und doch schon, dein Los an jeder Wende der Zeit.* (287)

> [Thou sawest the beginning, Vergil, thou art thyself not yet the beginning, thou heardest the voice, Vergil, thou art thyself not yet the voice, thou feltest the heart of creation beating, thou art thyself not yet the heart, thou art the eternal guide, who himself does not reach the destination: thou shalt be immortal, immortal as the guide, *not yet and even so, thy lot at every turn of time.*]

But there is more than confirmation in these lines. Do they not project a vision of Dante and his guided tour through the realm beyond? Perhaps we were not prepared to glimpse vistas of so distant a future. But incredulity is dispelled when we turn back the pages of this dialogue, our ears alerted for such overtones. For as we read again that earlier give and take revolving about Vergil's destiny as "Führer" (280-281) so confidently proclaimed by the boy, we find enfolded even there the secret that has now come into the open.[13]

The inner dialogue of the vision reaches its climax in a fervent

---

[13] The ambivalence of the word "Führer" in the German version is designed to keep us guessing (as well as Vergil), especially as the delirious cry of the masses for a "Führer" earlier had stamped the word with its connotation of leader. The English version had to sacrifice this *double entendre*, rendering the term alternately by guide and leader.

prayer offered up by the voice of the slave to the Unknown God, a prayer into which Vergil pours the essence of his humility and of his longing to be vouchsafed participation in the salvation to be achieved by God incarnate.

Scene 3. It is high noon as he awakens from his trance, to be greeted by the entering physician. Vergil is now in a state of euphoria, a sure symptom of the approaching end. There is spirited banter and superior irony in his conversation with the physician. The scene, involving discussion of medical practice, is one of the most vivid in the book—a light interlude to what precedes and follows. It invites comparison with Thomas Mann's precise but neat factuality of descriptive detail. The well-groomed physician, a man of the world, radiating self-satisfaction and spicing the elegant fluency of his discourse with just enough technical lingo to flatter the patient's ears, would feel perfectly at home in the *Magic Mountain*. As the patient is fed, bathed with vinegar, and shaved under the physician's watchful eye, Vergil begins to feel his body like a foreign object, a mirror image of his physical self, divested of weight. His mind shows repeated traces of wandering. At his insistence his forelocks have been cut as is the wont with a sacrificial victim, for his mind is still focused upon the sacrifice.

Scene 4. Just as Vergil's mind had retreated into itself after the exhausting interview with his friends, so his strength is again depleted after the grooming that prepares him for the impending call of Emperor Augustus. He lapses into a state of delirium and experiences hallucinations in which actual goings-on in the sick-room are at times faintly discernible. There is a riot of imagery undergoing a constant process of kaleidoscopic transformation. Many significant themes developed during Vergil's hours of soul-searching come into view again, but transformed into airy visual and dramatic symbols and all but stripped of their conceptual content. This is a short scene but one that seems long by virtue of the phantasmagoria of changing elements, and the significance of the accompanying inner dialogue is not always easy to follow. Of one thing there can be no doubt: this scene is predominantly an assertion of sex. The stage is ruled by Plotia, the woman whose beauty Vergil admired, yet whom he refused to possess, though he owes his ring to her love. She has come to woo him. He kisses the points of her breasts and they are locked in all but complete embrace, even though the buttocks of the boy Alexis, of whom Vergil sang in his second eclogue, also assert their charms, and ithyphallic satyrs fill the background with their stamping dance. But the woman, Plotia, the eternal feminine, dominates the scene, while the voices of the boyish guide and the slave engage in a contest—the boy encouraging Vergil to yield himself up to the woman, whereas the voice of the slave sounds repeated insistent warnings, though without full effect. If I have understood these two competing voices aright, the boy, allied with Vergil's childhood self, encourages his yearning to succumb to the lure of the great womb of being, to yield up his soul and die now. Over against this, the voice of the slave represents the summons of duty; he hands Vergil a staff to signify that there must be no looking back upon the past and no relaxation so long as the Golden Bough,[14] symbol of Vergil's quest of ultimate truth, has not been found. But the sweet lure of yielding seems more powerful than any other consideration. Nevertheless the ecstasy of the embrace is abruptly halted by shocking and vulgar shapes that intrude upon the privacy of the lovers, and a moment later the vision is dispelled by the return of consciousness.

Scene 5. This scene is one hundred pages long, exactly one fifth of the whole. Its length is a measure, without doubt, of its importance. Here the Emperor and Vergil face each other in intimate dialogue. Their discourse is punctuated by silences filled with author's comment that elaborates Vergil's state of mind (stream-of-consciousness context without stream-of-consciousness form). Occasionally, too, an invisible audience participates in the drama. The woman Plotia, the boyish guide, the slave, all have their say. Their spirit voices tug at Vergil's heart-strings with insistent whispers. Judged by normal standards the duration of this scene extends over three or four hours at the very least, but when we learn subsequently that Augustus spent "far more than an hour" with Vergil (431) we realize that epic time in this book is the same highly elastic substance as which it appears in Thomas Mann's *Lotte in Weimar*. There, too, one day's time supported a sequence of dialogue that could not possibly have been equated with the movement of the hour-hand across the dial of the clock.

[14] First mentioned in a quotation from the sixth book of the *Aeneid* (148), it is one of the most persistent themes ever afterward.

The discussion between Augustus and Vergil spans a vast range of subjects, but all this ideation moves in orbits governed by a center of gravity: Vergil's resolve to destroy the Aeneid. Augustus steers a friendly but crafty course to bring this center of gravity into the open. Then, before he knows it, Vergil finds himself enmeshed in argument, in the attempt to explain in words the significance of his resolve. It does not make sense to Augustus, of course; for to him Vergil's words carry connotations that have meaning within his own finite frame of reference, whereas Vergil's words, to his own self, adumbrate his experience of the infinite. The discussion, a cerebral exercise on the highest plane for both parties, leads nowhere because the two friendly antagonists have no common ground and speak no common language. But for us the discussion builds up nevertheless to something very impressive. We throw the weight of our listening attention to Augustus rather than to Vergil, despite the fact that the density of Vergil's thought is incomparably greater than that of Augustus and that every theme woven into the texture of the night's visions recurs to Vergil. Vergil's thoughts, however profound, are but echoes of an experience in which we have already participated. Augustus, on the other hand, presents something new. He is the spokesman of finite reality, and not a chance spokesman. For, under the spell of the moment, he becomes superlatively conscious of the structure of the edifice of civilization and of his own function as its keystone. He may be said to evolve the consummate integration of the Roman world in this dialogue which is, ideally speaking, the crowning moment of his life. In the discourse of Augustus the finite world takes shape as a full-bodied entity, a structure of awe-inspiring grandeur of design.

Let me repeat, in this scene the two worlds, the world of finiteness and the world of infinity, face each other as mutually exclusive rivals. The two add up to two sharply contrasted ideological patterns, patterns that have contributed the scaffolding of much intellectual history. One hundred and fifty years ago Friedrich Schlegel's brilliant historical speculation, following in Schiller's footsteps, treading right on Schiller's heels in fact, captured the characteristic essence of the ancient classical world and the equally distinct essence of the world of Christianity by the device of a "magic" formula and a pair of symbols: the closed circle and the infinite line.

Antiquity spells perfection in limitation (Vollendung)—the closed circle; Christianity spells infinity (Unendlichkeit)—the infinite line. Classical antiquity, limited in its *Anlage*, developed its potentialities to perfection; the Christian world, on the other hand, universal in its scope, is never perfect, never fully realized, but infinitely progressive. Applied to poetry, this scheme led Friedrich Schlegel to his famous definition of Romantic, i.e., Christian as distinct from classical poetry, as "progressive Universalpoesie." Here in the *Death of Vergil* Broch applies the same touchstone to make the two spheres of being separate and emerge as mutually exclusive entities. The top concept in Augustus' finite world is the state. The top concept in Vergil's spiritual world is "Das Reich," the kingdom of Kingdom Come. There is a very simple way to give a suggestion of what the grand debate is about. Just think of Christ facing Pilate. Only instead of the shoulder-shrugging sceptic (What is truth!) let Pilate be an ardent believer in the political structure that he represents. Pilate asks Christ: Art thou the King of the Jews? And Christ gives answer: My Kingdom is not of this world. To quote for once, let us listen to Vergil's and to Augustus' definitions of piety. Vergil says:

> Frömmigkeit ist des Menschen Wissen um das Entrinnen aus seinem unentrinnbaren Einsamsein; Frömmigkeit des Blinden Sehen und des Tauben Hören, denn Frömmigkeit ist Erkenntnis in der Einfalt . . . aus der Frömmigkeit des Menschen sind die Götter geworden, und den Göttern dienend wird sie zur todesaufhebenden Erkenntnis der Liebe jenseits der Götter . . . Frömmigkeit, die Rückkehr aus den Tiefen . . . aufhebend das Irre, das Rasende . . . die erkenntnistragende Wahrheit . . . ja, das ist Frömmigkeit. (401)

> [Piety is the knowledge of man about his escaping from his inescapable solitude; piety is the seeing of the blind and the hearing of the deaf, for piety is cognition in simplicity . . . from the piety of man came the gods, and serving the gods it will become the death-suspending cognition of love beyond the gods . . . piety, the return from the depths . . . abolishing the confused, the maniacal . . . truth-bearing cognition . . . yes, that is piety.]

Contrast this with Augustus' formula:

> Die Frömmigkeit, das ist der Staat, das ist der Dienst am Staate, das ist die Einordnung in ihn; fromm ist, wer mit seiner ganzen Person und seinem ganzen Werk dem römischen Staat dient . . . ich brauche keine andere Frömmigkeit, und sie ist eine Pflicht, von der weder du, noch ich, noch sonst jemand ausgenommen ist. (402)

[Piety, that is the state, that is service to the state, that is alignment to it; he is pious who serves the Roman state with his whole person and all his deeds . . . I need no other piety, and it is a duty from which neither you nor I nor anyone else is exempt.]

As for Vergil, in the scene before us, he gropes his way closest to an intuition of the Christ, when prodded by Augustus' insistence that he stop speaking in riddles, that he be explicit about the work of salvation on which he has been harping, that he define that act of atonement which all creation has been holding its breath to see come to pass. Reacting to the strain of the challenge, Vergil gives utterance to the most coherent formulation of what his prophetic vision has been divining:

Den Menschen zur Liebe, der Menschheit zur Liebe wird der Heil-bringer sich selber zum Opfer bringen, wird er sich mit seinem Tode selber zur Erkenntnistat machen, zur Tat die er dem All entgegenwirft, auf dass aus solch höchstem Wirklichkeitsbild dienender Hilfe sich aufs neue die Schöpfung entfalte. (412)

[For the love of men, for the love of mankind the savior will sacrifice himself, with his own death will perform an act of cognition, an act which he will throw to the universe, so that from such succor in the service of the highest image of reality creation may unfold anew.]

Augustus does not understand (how could he?), rather he is more nonplussed than ever. A complete impasse has been reached. Augustus has long been restive. His patience has been sorely strained. Now, of a sudden his pique rises to exasperation. He bursts into a fit of anger and hurls a series of invectives against the dying poet. Vergil's self-depreciation is false, he rages. His humility is nothing but the inversion of a staggering, snobbish pride. He hates Augustus at heart, he has always hated him. Impotent himself, as concerns the world of affairs, he is consumed with jealousy at Augustus' success. Augustus' had been the reality, Vergil's had been the dreams of regal deeds. The eternal state has come into being. Its valid eternal symbol, due and promised, is likewise all but complete. Now Vergil has hatched his perfidious plan in order to belittle Augustus' achievement and rob him of his glory. Thus Augustus rants and raises his voice to a shriek.

Here we are at the turning point. A moment later, Vergil, having vainly protested his innocence of the charges, begs Augustus to accept the poem, promises to complete it for him upon his recovery, and asks him to take the manuscript to Rome for safe keeping. For ninety pages stone wall had been facing stone wall. Now a moment's burst of temper has achieved the solution.

What is the significance of Vergil's face-about? Was it physical exhaustion that drove him to yielding? That is too superficial an explanation. Was there perhaps some truth in the charges Augustus hurled at him in his tantrum? There can be no doubt of it. The evidence is furtively concealed in reams of inner monologue, but it can be brought to light. Last night on his arrival at the guest-house Vergil had resented the impersonal conventionality of the arrangements made for his comfort. Bitterness had risen in his gorge at the thought of Augustus—suave and smooth, crafty and elusive, calculating even in his most sentimental attachments. Yes, he had hated him. And what about Vergil's own ambitions? A bit of inner dialogue with his boyish guide had given them away too. When Lysanias insisted on hailing him as the "Führer" he had smiled. "Und da musste er lächeln": "Führer der Menschen zu sein, Feldherr, Priester und König, einst war's ein Knabenwunsch, und der Knabe sprach es nun aus" (281). [And at that he had to smile. To be the guide of mankind, commander, priest, and king, once it had been a boyish wish, and now the boy stated it.] So there is a grain of truth in Augustus' accusation: ". . . ja, du hassest mich, weil du selber voller Königsgedanken steckst, aber zu schwach warst, um auch nur den leisesten Versuch zu ihrer Ausführung zu unternehmen, du hassest mich, weil du gar keine andere Wahl gehabt hast, als deine Königsgedanken in deinem Gedicht unterzubringen . . ." (415). [Yes, you hate me because you are full of thoughts of kingship yourself, but you were too weak to undertake even the most tentative attempt to carry them out, you hate me because you have had absolutely no other choice than to set your thoughts on kingship down in your poem.]

'Königsgedanken' . . . we must retard our tempo for a moment. For once in this work a key word reveals a specific literary parallel. The word 'Königsgedanken' conjures up King Haakon and Jarl Skule from Ibsen's *Pretenders*. The "king-thoughts" are Haakon's, and Skule, too weak to evolve any king-thoughts of his own, steals the king-thought of his rival. The parallel cannot be passed over because, if we dwell upon this echo of one of Ibsen's boldest creations, we also become aware of the fact that it is no more than an echo.

Ibsen's whole tragedy is focused upon an ambitious soul in which a sense of impotent frustration has transformed admiration into festering hate that poisons the core of Skule's soul. Broch, on the other hand, did not write a psychological novel actuated by the desire to unmask the artist as the impotent victim of frustration, who takes his revenge on life (Heinrich Mann's formula). No, hatred and jealousy of Augustus' achievements in the factual realm was not the be-all and the end-all of Vergil's tormented self-analysis. But there was a grain of truth in the charges, and their sting touched Vergil acutely.

What, then, causes Vergil's face-about? If we persist in asking this question, we shall never find the answer. There is no motivation to cause Vergil's yielding. That yielding takes place in a realm in which causation does not function as an operative concept. Causation belongs to the psychological realm. This face-about is a metaphysical experience, a miracle, a mutation of the soul. Let us ask, rather, what has happened. "Immerzu durchbricht Liebe die eigene Grenze" (372) [Evermore love breaks through its own bounds], a voice had whispered to him when the obstinacy of argument was hardening two immutable positions from moment to moment. This is what happened: Love was born in Vergil's heart. He heard the cry of the kindred human soul through the ranting of the angry voice. For the first time in his life he felt touched by a simple sense of human fellowship, and he rose to the act of helpful, compassionate love. The night before he had seen the gleam of helpful love in his visions. It had conceptually dawned upon him that this was the pearl beyond price. It had been seen, but not had. It had lighted up the heavens to him as the star of Bethlehem, but its warmth had not glowed in his heart. Up to this moment he had remained wrapped within himself. In all his argument with Augustus he had been essentially concerned with saving himself. His very insistence upon destroying his work and deleting his name had been egocentrically conditioned. Suddenly all this is swept away like a cobweb. Love excogitated has been supplanted by love simply experienced. Love fills Vergil's heart, and even the realization that there was an element of craft mingled with the spontaneity of Augustus' passionate outburst does not dim its kindly radiance ever so slightly. Grace has become operative a second time. I have taken pains to point up the significance of Vergil's yielding. Broch presents the situation without comment, letting it speak for itself in its context.

The scene might have ended right there, with the resolution of the conflict achieved. Broch, however, appends a postlude, a few moments of intimate relaxation after the ending of the almost insupportable tension. Relaxation takes the form of a new argument, a childish dispute over the color of a certain horse's fetlocks that Vergil had cautioned Augustus not to buy, once upon a time long ago. The Emperor and the dying poet act like two boys. They shout at each other, getting more excited every time that each affirms his contrary recollection, until Vergil finally insists he will bet his life that the horse did have white fetlocks. Hold off, says Augustus, such stakes are beyond trifling. The argument is hushed at once and the eyes of each embrace the other in a moment of silent laughter not far from tears. Read by itself this little postlude of boyish exuberance is an insignificant trifle, but its position makes of it something profoundly moving. The two worlds, the finite and the infinite, have merged for one moment, fused by the power of mutual love. This little scene is by all odds the finest human touch in the book. In a book of many high points and intellectual climaxes, this is the supreme moment for the voice of the heart. Even so, the intellectual plane is never abandoned, for that moment of mutual love also achieves the rehabilitation of "laughter"—heretofore the vehicle of fiendish nihilism—thus guaranteeing the redemption of the world in the totality of its elements.

Scene 6. A moment later, at a sign from Augustus, friends, courtiers and slaves have thronged into the sick-room to hear Augustus announce the joyous tidings. The voice is no longer the voice of the friend but that of the statesman who had brought a very delicate negotiation to a gratifying conclusion. Only one more task now remains for Vergil to do on earth. He has at heart the liberation of his slaves, and he obtains Augustus' sanction to alter his last will to this end.

Scene 7. The best way to summarize this scene is to state its development in reverse. Toward the end of the scene Vergil has one last brief spell of lucid conscious functioning. This he uses first to acquaint his two friends with the provisions of the will previously drawn up. Then he dictates the precise stipulations for the manner in which the *Aeneid* is to be edited, and finally he adds the codicil freeing his slaves and remunerating them for their services. But before he rallies to perform his last duty on earth he has two prolonged sinking spells, and images of childhood alternating with echoes of the immediate past drift across the focus of his mind. Twice he is about to cross over into the beyond, twice he rouses himself by an anguished cry for help; the first an appeal to mother, the second to father. (Directly or indirectly, Bachofen's thought has sponsored this passage.) In this medley of images the slave, grown to giant stature and fused with the personality of the boy, calls the tune. He personifies Vergil's inner urge to complete the task assigned him before relaxing for the final slumber. The slave bids him summon the help of the ancestral forces of mother and father. The slave appeals to him to dismiss the last vestiges of rancor that poison his relation to the earthly—finite—phase of existence. His reluctance to embrace once more the spotty texture of life, shot through with imperfection, is acute. But the struggle resolves itself in a moment of ultimate triumph when his heart wells over with gratitude to the gods for life in its totality, life's imperfections as well as its blessings. In this total affirmation of life Vergil's personality becomes wholly integrated. This is the third, the crowning manifestation of divine grace. And its ultimate character is attested by the fact that the sprig of laurel left on the counterpane by Augustus has become the Golden Bough—symbol of final truth—that had been the object of his ceaseless quest. Now consciousness returns, and without a trace of fog he dictates the two pages of his will.

Then the world of sense recedes before the inner light. With his last audible breath Vergil bequeathes his ring—Plotia's gift, symbol of love—to "Lysanias—the child." With that the name Lysanias has revealed its deepest mystic meaning as signifying the liberator, the redeemer, the child to be born heralded by the star.

Book Four, Ether—The Home-Coming, tells the story of Vergil's passing into the Beyond. As life recedes—not abruptly, but by degrees, he does not regain consciousness. The forty-six pages of this book represent another sustained climax; for after all the toil and anguish of life, dying unfolds itself for Vergil as an effortless adventure, an adventure of such fabulous proportions as to satisfy the poet's desire for that ultimate of knowledge which he had pursued all his life. It is a thrill without parallel for Vergil, and possibly for the reader. Here the reader who has felt himself being ground to pulp in the implacable movement of the first three books, a speck of feeling-thinking matter locked in the inexorable vise of a glacier—here even the reluctant reader may possibly yield to the spell of a cosmic ecstasy.

Again there can be no attempt to suggest the quality of this spell. It could only be done by quoting. And as the rhythms of Broch's language lap over the pages like the infinite swell of the sea, quoting, to be effective, would involve the congressional prerogative of inserting the forty-six pages of this book into the record. Our task calls for the utmost reticence. We cannot afford to become excited or lyrical. The one service we can perform for the reader is to record the articulation of Vergil's supreme adventure, to expose its skeleton, to exhibit its inner logic as a sequence of precisely marked stages.

Vergil's quest of the Beyond proceeds in four clearly delimitable stages despite the fact that the transitions with one exception are as fluid as the crest of the tide. Stage 1, pp. 471-479; stage 2, pp. 479-489; stage 3, pp. 489-513; stage 4, pp. 513-516.

Stages 1-3 are embraced by a higher unity of progressive movement, whereas stage 4 represents an abrupt reversal of the course. Furthermore, since stages 1-3 are only the last phase of that same impulse which began with the first page of the volume, the whole of the *Death of Vergil* falls into two parts, namely Part I, pp. 1-516, Part II, pp. 516-519. Let us characterize each of the four stages of Book Four briefly.

Stage 1. Vergil, unconscious of his surroundings, feels relaxed. He has acquitted himself of his last task, and the voice of duty is stilled. As had often been the case earlier in the day when his mind was tempted to wander, he now feels himself moving swiftly forward in a barge, and the first two stages of his quest of the Beyond are experienced as a voyage over an infinite sea. (Cf. Meister Eckhart's characterization of life as *Überfahrt* [crossing].) Vergil himself occupies the middle of the boat, his friend Plotius Tucca plies the oars. At the stern there is an unseen helmsman[15] (Charon), and the prow is occupied by the figure of the boyish guide Lysanias. Now, as the shore of sensuous reality recedes, the images of his friends—Augustus, Horace, Lucretius, etc., the living and the departed—greet him for the last time, and it is here that dying bestows its first great new gift. Vergil's faculty of vision has been transformed. He no longer sees his friends from without but from within. With his mind's eye he beholds the essence of their personality, the "crystalline prototype" of their being, stripped of accidentals. The two phases of earthly being, the inner and the outer, have been merged in one essential image. Vergil is now moving in the realm of Platonic ideas. Specific memory is gone, in its place there is recognition of the pre-existential prototype. Experience as framed for man in the irreducible duality of the subject-object relationship is replaced by a sense of basic identity. (Schelling comes to mind along with Stefan George and the late Rilke.)

At this point one last faint echo of the world left behind finds its way to Vergil's swiftly moving barge. Is Plotius administering a last drop of moisture to the twitching lips of the form on the bed? This is the final farewell. The world of sense is now completely blotted out.

Stage 2 continues and completes the voyage in the median realm that separates the first infinity of the Hither from the second infinity of the Beyond. In an atmosphere where the twilight of the median realm gradually gives way to the utter purity of the light of absolute knowledge, the barge glides on noiselessly, but no longer so fast. As the speed diminishes, the size of the barge grows, and this transformation of speed into mass (Physicists: please note) continues until the course has come to a complete standstill and the barge has spanned infinity. When that point has been reached, the figure at the rudder has disappeared. Charon has done his work. Meanwhile the boyish guide at the prow had first stood in an attitude of straining forward. Then the ring on his hand (Vergil's bequest) had become a star to which his finger pointed. Finally Lysanias had taken to wing, and as he did so Vergil felt himself torn by a longing to follow and a flutter of homesickness for the infinity

[15] Vergil is facing forward, hence he cannot see the helmsman. But he does see some familiar faces left behind him. Such contradictions belong to the tissue of the dream.

left behind. Lysanias had steered his flight to a night-rainbow portal of seven colors, disappearing behind it, but in his stead the woman Plotia had appeared, now endowed with the boy's features, to continue as the smiling guide. All this imagery suggests that Vergil has entered the realm where time and space are one and where he, on his part, ceases to be Vergil, strictly speaking. For while the preceding phase retained the principle of individuation, personality is here reduced to the nameless human archetype. He is Vergil no longer, for individuality has been left behind along with his name. Vergil is now just a soul that has been guided into the haven of eternity. Hence the departure of the guide who in this last phase had most clearly suggested the function associated with Hermes, guide of the soul, in the ancient world. The substitution of the woman Plotia, at the end, poses a riddle to be solved in the next phase.

Stage 3. Now that the movement over the sea has come to a stop, Vergil sees unfolded to his view a landscape of beauty hallowed by peace. He sets foot upon it, walking hand in hand with the woman, both of them naked and innocent and devoid of shame. In the center of the landscape is a tree full of golden fruit. And the garden is filled with vegetation and animal life transcendingly peaceful.

This scene carries unmistakable echoes of the biblical Paradise; of Adam and Eve walking in the Garden; of the Tree of Life. It requires no discernment to note them. However, a sense of the familiar turns into startled surprise when further developments lead us to surmise that these echoes are more than echoes. When Vergil —Adam—falls into a deep sleep at the close of day and in his sleep experiences a mystical union with the woman, she entering into his flesh, his bones and his marrow; when he wakes up with the new dawn to find her gone, himself alone henceforth among animate creation, then the question may flash across the mind: Is not what Vergil-Adam experienced in his sleep for all the world like the creation of Eve in reverse? This suspicion aroused, we henceforth follow Vergil-Adam through the mazes of his wanderings with a detective's alertness. A hunch of further things to come gets support enough to emerge as a full-blown theory, and when the theory is confirmed, item for item, one feels a thrill of pleasure quite distinct from and added to that of participating in experiences of transcending weirdness.

Discarding circumlocution, we find this to be the case: In setting foot on the Garden of Eden Vergil-Adam is destined to experience the whole process of cosmic creation in reverse, cycle for cycle, as patterned by the story of Genesis, its scant outline filled in by the lush imagination of the poet-scientist. Phase after phase of organic evolution unfolds before us in reverse, in six gigantic stages, conforming to the six biblical days of creation; six times night closes in upon day; six times the light again dawns upon a world successively less familiar and more monstrous. Thus there is something apocalyptic about the movement of animal life toward the close of Vergil-Adam's first day alone: the four-footed creatures of the land are on the march. With an ever accelerated rhythmic tread they head toward the sea. They are progressively divested of their animal particularity, as the river valleys down which they are headed fold up behind them. And Vergil-Adam is caught up in the throbbing rhythm of their four-footed patter, he himself *being* all that which is taking its course to extinction, toward the womb of the sea, that is, from which the myriad varieties of teeming land life were destined to emerge. The process suggests a moving picture film in reverse. This would answer to the peculiar experience of time folding up. But we would have to add to it the reduction of the limitless simultaneous spaces of organic evolution into the focus of one eye. Thus we cannot follow Adam-Vergil on his eerie quest without the mystic's intuition as our vehicle.

On the next day (Genesis' fifth) the drama of the birds and the fishes unfolds in reverse. At the end of the third (Genesis' fourth), the sun, moon, and stars lose their luster and a diffused light dominates the jungle. The next day sees the dense mat of primitive vegetation gradually shrinking and fading out, and so on, until with the sixth day the "crater" of creation is finally reached. At the end of that day (Genesis' first), there is one final act of cosmic drama to be disenacted, as light—the light that had come forth in response to the word 'Let there be light,' is swallowed up in the vortex of primal night. (Meister Eckhart: "Gott ist die Urfinsternis" [God is the primeval darkness].) Through all this Adam-Vergil had continued somehow to *be*, no longer man, but himself the evolving whole, yet beholding it too, a functioning eye in the towering clod of clay to which Adam-Vergil had gradually been reduced.

Stage 4. When the first light is engulfed Adam-Vergil has returned with all creation into the vortex of primeval darkness, the womb of precreational godhead. This is the end, or should be the end. But there is a final act to come. With the systole complete, it is the diastole's turn. Once more light issues forth from the dark womb of godhead. Creation is re-enacted, and Adam-Vergil, participating in it all from the beginning, reassumes human form by degrees and ultimately stands reinvested in the specific personality of Vergil. And Vergil's gaze is directed along with all the animate creatures of the earth toward the east, focused upon a vision of the Mother and Child, radiating peace. Vergil thus beholds the Word that was in the beginning, the Logos, through which all things are created, and in the contemplation of the Logos, divested once more of all visual imagery, heard by the soul as a murmur swelling to strains of a cosmic harmony, the vibrations of the last long sentence finally come to rest.

To many readers this final stage, the reversal and the rebirth of Vergil, may appear like a gratuitous coda. But this is to overlook Vergil's unique place in the scheme of things. Though vouchsafed mystical reunion with the Godhead, he must issue forth again invested with that historic name and personality known to us as Vergil. It is foreordained, as we know, for him to function as Dante's guide in time to come. So the boy told him in words that passed his understanding. Let us ponder those words once more: "Unsterblich wirst du sein, unsterblich als Führer, *noch nicht und doch schon, dein Los an jeder Wende der Zeit*" (287) [Thou shalt be immortal, immortal as the guide, *not yet and even so, thy lot at every turn of time*]. "Führer . . . an jeder Wende der Zeit." [Guide . . . at every turn of time]. This pronouncement includes Vergil's relation to Dante, but does it not suggest something beyond? Is it not at the same time an index of Broch's appraisal of his own position? This fifth decade of the twentieth century is felt by Broch as the turning-point of an era. It takes little skill in reading between the lines to gather that Vergil's critique of society in all its aspects is a critique of our twentieth-century society, and that some of Vergil's apocalyptic visions have as their background the Second World War. Once again Vergil exercises his function of guide, as then to Dante, now to Hermann Broch. Without doubt the prophecy, "Führer an jeder Wende der Zeit" is made with pointed reference to the book before us.

It takes courage to compare oneself with Dante; courage to proclaim oneself as a seer who, with due allowance for the limitation involved in all symbolism, encompasses the totality of life in his vision and succeeds in restoring the unity of a fragmented world. Without a doubt Broch thinks of himself as another Dante, as the dispenser of a revelation, not as just another poet. Perhaps Broch's book is in essence but an orgy of auto-erotic cerebration. Yet its high seriousness cannot be denied. Supposing the improbable, that the world of man should continue to exist for another thousand years, it is by no means unthinkable that Broch's *Death of Vergil* should continue to stand as the twentieth century's towering monument of a mystically oriented spirituality.[16]

[16] Translation of Hermann Broch's letter of February 2, 1946 to Hermann Weigand.

(Complete letter except for first three paragraphs and the conclusion, which are personal.)

. . . Above all, I should like to tell you the story of how I happened on Vergil, since you concern yourself repeatedly with my choice of theme. Well, it was not a matter of choice at all, but pure chance. At Whitsuntide, 1935, I was asked to open the festival program of the Vienna radio with a reading of selections from my works. As a matter of principle, I am opposed to renditions of their works by poets, especially over the radio, for I know all too well how they bore everybody (and in my case, in addition, the speaker himself). So I went to the director of the literary section and proposed to him that he let me read on a more interesting topic, a topic with a historical and philosophic slant perhaps, such as "Literature at the End of a Cultural Epoch." But with this I had no luck. "No," said the director, "that is impossible. With a topic of this sort, we would trespass on the intellectual and scientific section of the organization and such an intermingling can't be handled by the bookkeeping department. You must by all means read something poetical." And since I realized that bookkeeping is one of the major deities of the age—the Fate of our age, in truth—I promised him to deal with my topic of literature and the end of a cultural epoch in the form of a short story. So I began to wonder how to solve this problem most conveniently, and it took very little thought for the parallels between the first pre-Christian century and our own to come to mind—civil war, dictatorship, and the dying away of the old religious forms. Even the phenomenon of emigration produced a striking analogy—Tomi, the fishing village on the Black Sea. Furthermore, I knew of the legend according to which Vergil had wanted to burn the Aeneid and—accepting the legend—I had a right to assume that a mind such as Vergil's must have been actuated by considerations of no mean weight to harbor so desperate an intention. Surely, the whole historical and metaphysical character of the age had something to do with it. With these matters in mind I decided upon my theme very quickly.

Just as quickly, of course, I took account of the fact that it was not Vergil who died in Tomi. But it would have been pointless to shift over to Ovid because of this circumstance. And thus I stuck to Vergil. As for Dante, he was no factor in the original outline of my project at all. This was not merely because I was planning only a short story for the radio. The fact is, I hate "literary" themes and motivations. The poet who invites Dante to sponsor his work commits an act of calculated literary snobbery which stamps his work as disingenuous from the outset. It is not possible to evoke the great spirits of the past deliberately. If they come, they come stealing in through the back door, sent by "Chance," by that chance which is so closely akin to "Miracle" that one is justified in regarding it as the source of all "authenticity." The fact that I hit upon Vergil by chance has something reassuring for me, confirming, as it were, my feeling that I have produced something more than mere "literature."

Thus the first draft, my short story for the radio, was a very rudimentary affair of some twenty pages. But it was only natural that even in writing the first draft the richness of the theme made itself felt. This feeling was so strong and compelling that I immediately interrupted my work on a novel that was all but completed. I expanded the original draft to approximately eighty pages, and since this format also proved inadequate to contain the well-nigh inexhaustible wealth of motifs, there was nothing else to do but make up my mind to grapple with this wealth on its own terms—without setting any time limit—and attempt to work up the whole material.

A further consideration contributed to this resolve. The menace to life of the Nazi movement was progressively gathering momentum. It was no longer possible to have any illusions on this score. In 1936, to be sure, this menace was not yet actual for us in Austria. And for that reason I, being bound by family ties, again and again postponed my flight, perhaps also succumbing to the lure that is involved in all danger. But at any rate, it was a state of affairs that compelled me more and more to face the preparation for death, a private preparation for death, as it were. This is in fact the aspect which the work on Vergil assumed more and more. And by virtue of this fact, as you quite correctly remark, the book developed a scope that was no longer commensurate with the figure and the work of the historical Vergil. It was no longer the dying of Vergil. It became the imagination of my own dying.

These years, including the time I spent in prison, were a constant, most intensive, concentration upon the experience of dying. That I was writing a "book" at the same time became a secondary consideration. The act of writing had to serve solely as a vehicle for fixing this experience. It was a means of clarification. It was thus an essentially private activity that no longer had the least thing to do with the creation of a "work of art," let alone any thought of its publication—this quite regardless of the fact that for external reasons (Hitler) I no longer envisaged any possibilities of publishing. And just as my writing proceeded without a thought of any possible impact on the outside world, in the same way I automatically excluded everything that I had ever taken into myself from without. That is to say, I excluded in a radical way everything that I had merely "learned"; concentration upon a single point forbade the use of any "literary material." When in spite of this the most varied symbols of death from ancient religions emerged from my subconscious to contribute to the work, I greeted this realization with an almost joyous surprise, since it confirmed not only the truth of these ancient symbols, but also that of my own visions. Even the experiencing of creation-in-reverse in Part IV of the book was not a deliberate trick. This phase of things too forced itself upon me automatically in the form of images which, though crowding in upon me chaotically at first, nevertheless ranged themselves in patterns of their own choosing. I had simply to accept them.

Inner necessity leads to plausibility, and plausibility is "cognition." To be sure, it was first of all a subjective plausibility and cognition—cognition of death—which I had achieved. It could not help being subjective, since an intimation of the mystical, even though this intimation points toward cognition, always emerges as a personal, in fact, a private experience. The prophet, of course, is a different case. His is the faculty and by virtue of this the prerogative to offer his visionary experience to his fellow-men as objective truth without qualifications. But is he whose experience does not measure up to prophetic grandeur, qualified, authorized, let alone obligated to speak in similar tones?

This is a specific Vergil problem—a problem not of the historical Vergil but of my Vergil. For the not-prophet becomes an artist,—a type of man, that is, who has ventured to make his homestead just across the border from the soothsayer's province, one whose mystical experience is too incomplete to call for direct religious utterance but that nevertheless craves for expression. Thus although art, insofar as it is true art, can never do without a mystical initial experience, it is nevertheless an "ersatz." Unlike prophecy it is not direct communication but rather a complicated apparatus of expression, using symbols, or, more correctly, generating symbols by putting certain units of expression into functions of equilibrium, and thereby investing them with "plausibility." A diamond in the process of being polished, shrinks in size, even though this treatment enhances its ornamental and commercial value. To make a long story short, the artist who engages in the work of polishing inevitably loses his unique, original cognitive trove. This is only a metaphor, to be sure, but it is an experience at the same time. The three years spent in polishing up the *Vergil* have in large measure blurred for me the experience of the cognition of death such as I had divined it—even though (or because) it has now perhaps been made accessible to others. There is a sense of being ill at ease about this, as in uttering a blasphemy—I have, as a matter of fact, tried to express this feeling in *Vergil*—and without doubt this blasphemous character adheres to art in direct proportion to the strength and genuineness of the mystical initial experience. The inadequacy of artistic expression is pointed up especially in an age like ours (and, in terms of my portrayal, that of Vergil), an age whose appetite for the stark and crass is intolerant of everything but the tissue of raw reality.

You are fully justified for that reason in asking the question why I exposed my *Vergil*—a work of artistic expression—to the public eye instead of burning it or at least keeping it to myself. The vanity of the artist, the ambition of the artist? Perhaps. But above all, a shrinking away from the failure to square an artistic obligation contracted: I came over to America with the unfinished *Vergil*, and I have experienced the confidence and helpfulness of so many people and institutions that I had to keep my promise,—this all the more as I am inviting the same confidence for the work of a politico-psychological nature on which I am now engaged and which is of definitely greater importance to me than the *Vergil*, because I hope that it may possibly help in a small way to prevent a repetition of the cosmic horror that we have experienced.

To be sure, one might object that a "sacrificium mentalis" can be justified on no count and that in spite of my sixty years I should have earned the means for my intellectual treatise by grinding lenses or washing dishes, but not by writing the *Vergil*. That may be true. However, when one is convinced, as I am, that in the world of today art no longer commands that dignified role which it once enjoyed (and will someday probably enjoy again), then it would have been an almost ridiculous gesture, a forced exaggeration, if I had put this view on exhibition and confirmed it by burning my book in public; it would have looked like a mania for originality at all costs. I resign myself to having left the book without its finishing touches because in this age of horror I could not afford to spend several additional years on a work which at each further touch would have become increasingly more esoteric. And I believe that with this book I have definitely finished my career as a poet. It seems to me that that is the utmost I was able to do for my conscience. This was, to be sure, a decision by no means lightly taken. For whoever has once been caught up in the current of art and moreover has come to master the technique of his profession (as I would claim for myself), has to muster a certain degree of courage to face such a farewell. It is a fairly painful farewell. It is not altogether simple, moreover, to change one's profession at the age of sixty. If I were to remain a "story-teller" I would certainly have an easy life ahead of me, with more assurance of success.

And with this—by a long round-about way—I finally touch upon your conjecture as though I had identified myself with Dante in writing the *Vergil*. I think I can claim that my attitude to the *Vergil* such as I have sketched here is most un-Dantesque. If ever a parallel with Dante occurred to me, it was at most by the idea of a Florentine radio network that possibly invited him, too, to a Whitsuntide lecture. So that subsequently in his case, also, the figure of Vergil may have stolen in accidentally by a back door of the poetic process. . . .

Very sincerely yours,

Hermann Broch

BIBLIOGRAPHY OF
THE WRITINGS OF
HERMANN J. WEIGAND

1919

1. "Heine's *Buch le Grand*," *JEGP*, xviii, 1-35.

1920

2. "Heine's Return to God," *Modern Philology*, xviii, 309-342.

1922

3. "Heine's Family Feud: The Culmination of his Struggle for Economic Security," *JEGP*, xxi, 70-106.

1923

4. "The Secret Mark of the Beast: A Study of Cryptic Character Portrayal in *Little Eyjolf*," *JEGP*, xxii, 18-53.

1925

5. *The Modern Ibsen: A Reconsideration.* New York: Henry Holt & Co. Pp. vii & 416. See also No. 61 below.

1929

6. "Warum stirbt Emilia Galotti?" *JEGP*, xxviii, 467-481.

1931

7. "Der symbolisch-autobiographische Gehalt von Thomas Manns Romandichtung *Königliche Hoheit*," *PMLA*, xxxxvi, 867-879. See also No. 60 below.

1933

8. *Thomas Mann's Novel "Der Zauberberg."* New York: Appleton-Century Co. Pp. ix & 183. See also No. 63 below.
9. "The Kohut-Rutra Collection of Heineana," *Yale University Library Gazette*, viii, 46-49.

1935

10. "How Censorship Worked in 1831: Heine's Amusing Bick-

erings and Baitings Sensationally Documented by an Un-published Manuscript of the Kohut-Rutra Collection of Heineana," *Yale University Library Gazette*, X, 17-24.

1937

11. "Heine Manuscripts at Yale: Their Contribution Concerning Him as Man and Artist," *Studies in Philology*, XXXIV, 65-90.
12. "Thomas Manns *Joseph in Aegypten*," *Monatshefte*, XXIX, 241-256.

1938

13. "Das Motiv des Vertrauens im Drama Heinrichs von Kleist," *Monatshefte*, XXX, 233-245.
14. "Die epischen Zeitverhältnisse in den Graldichtungen Crestiens und Wolframs," *PMLA*, LIII, 917-950.
15. "The Double Love-Tragedy in Heine's *Buch le Grand*: A Literary Myth," *Germanic Review*, XIII, 121-126.

1939

16. "Das Wunder im Werk Rainer Maria Rilkes," *Monatshefte*, XXXI, 1-21.

1941

17. "A 'Falsified Verse' in Kleist's *Homburg*?" *Modern Language Notes*, LVI, 321-324.
18. "Zur Textkritik von Hauptmanns *Florian Geyer*," *Monatshefte*, XXXIII, 198-202.

1942

19. "Das Vertrauen in Kleists Erzählungen," *Monatshefte*, XXXIV, 49-63, 126-144.
20. "The Two and Seventy Languages of the World," *Germanic Review*, XVII, 241-260.
21. *A Close-up of the German Peasants War*. Transactions of the Connecticut Academy of Arts and Sciences, 35:1. Pp. 1-32.
22. "Recent Studies of Germany's Classical Heritage," *Studies in Philology*, XXXIX, 580-595.
23. "Auf den Spuren von Hauptmanns *Florian Geyer*: I," *PMLA*, LVII, 1160-1195.

1943

24. "Auf den Spuren von Hauptmanns *Florian Geyer*: II," *PMLA*, LVIII, 797-848.

1946

25. "Zu Otto Ludwigs *Zwischen Himmel und Erde*," *Monatshefte*, XXXVIII, 385-402.
26. "*Wanderers Sturmlied*—'Neidgetroffen,'" *Germanic Review*, XXI, 165-172.
27. "Rilke as Letter Writer," *Yale Review*, XXXV, 368-370.

1947

28. "Broch's *Death of Vergil*: Program Notes," *PMLA*, LXII, 525-554.

1948

29. "Wagners Siegfried in *Florian Geyer*," *Gerhart Hauptmann Jahrbuch*, ed. F. V. Voigt, Vol. I, N.S. Breslau: Maruschke & Behrendt. Pp. 221-229.

1949

30. *Goethe: Wisdom and Experience*. Selections by Ludwig Curtius. Translated and edited by Hermann J. Weigand. New York: Pantheon. Pp. 299. See also No. 62 below.

1950

31. "Goethe's Friendship with Schiller," *Goethe and the Modern Age*. Bicentennial Lectures at Aspen, ed. Arnold Bergsträsser. Chicago: Henry Regnery. Pp. 50-74.

1952

32. "Thomas Mann's *Gregorius*," *Germanic Review*, XXVII, 10-30, 83-95.
33. "Gerhart Hauptmann's Range as Dramatist: a Lecture," *Monatshefte*, XLIV, 317-332.
34. "A Jester Scene at the Grail Castle in Wolfram's *Parzival*?" *PMLA*, LXVII, 485-510.

BIBLIOGRAPHY

1953

35. "Hermann Broch's *Die Schuldlosen*: An Approach," *PMLA*, LXVIII, 323-334.

1954

36. "Wolfram's Grail and the Neutral Angels," *Germanic Review*, XXXIX, 83-95.
37. "Trevrezent as Parzival's Rival?" *Modern Language Notes*, LXIX, 348-357.
38. "Illustrations to Highlight Some Points in Schiller's Essay on Poetry," *Monatshefte*, XLVI, 161-169.
39. "Zur Einführung," introduction in Hermann Broch, *Die Schuldlosen*. Zürich: Rhein Verlag. Pp. 5-26.

1956

40. *Three Chapters on Courtly Love in Arthurian France and Germany*. Studies in the Germanic Languages and Literatures, No. 17. Chapel Hill, N.C.: University of North Carolina Press. Pp. xii & 60.
41. "Thomas Mann zum Gedächtnis," Allard Pearson Foundation Lecture delivered at the University of Amsterdam, March 21, 1956, in *Neophilologus*, XL, 162-179.
42. "Thoughts on the Passing of Thomas Mann," *Germanic Review*, XXXI, 163-175.
43. "Hermann Broch," *Yale University Library Gazette*, XXX, 150-151.
44. "Heine in Paris: Friedrich Hirth's Commentary on the Letters 1831-44," *Orbis Litterarum*, XI, 175-193.

1957

45. "Thomas Mann and Goethe: A Supplement and a Correction," *Germanic Review*, XXXII, 75-76.

1958

46. "Zu Kleists Käthchen von Heilbronn," *Studia Philologica et Litteraria in Honorem L. Spitzer*, eds. Anna G. Hatcher and K. L. Selig. Bern: Francke Verlag. Pp. 413-430.

47. "The Edgar S. Oppenheimer Rainer Maria Rilke Collection," *Yale University Library Gazette*, XXXIII, 67-71.

1959

48. "Rilkes 'Archaïscher Torso Apollos,'" *Monatshefte*, LI, 49-62.
49. "*Oedipus Tyrannus* and *Die Braut von Messina*," *Schiller 1759/1959*. Commemorative American Studies, ed. John R. Frey. Urbana: University of Illinois Press. Pp. 171-202.

1960

50. "Schiller: Transfiguration of a Titan," *A Schiller Symposium*. In Observance of the Bicentenary of Schiller's Birth, ed. A. Leslie Willson. Austin: Department of Germanic Languages, The University of Texas. Pp. 85-132.
51. Reissue of No. 5, *The Modern Ibsen: A Reconsideration*. Dutton Paperback No. 54. New York: E. P. Dutton. Pp. vii & 416.

1961

52. "Rilkes 'Römische Sarkophage,'" *Dichtung und Deutung*, Gedenkschrift für Hans M. Wolff, ed. Karl S. Guthke. Bern: Francke Verlag. Pp. 153-162.
53. "Wetten und Pakt in Goethes *Faust*," *Monatshefte*, LIII, 325-337.

1962

54. Foreword to *Goethe: The Sorrows of Young Werther and Selected Writings*, trans. Catherine Hutter. New York: New American Library, Signet CP 140. Pp. vii-xvi.

1964

55. "Shakespeare in German Criticism," *The Persistence of Shakespeare Idolatry, Essays in Honor of Robert W. Babcock*, ed. Herbert Schueller. Detroit: Wayne State University Press. Pp. 105-133.
56. "Hamlet's Consistent Inconsistency," *The Persistence of Shakespeare Idolatry, Essays in Honor of Robert W. Babcock*, ed. Herbert Schueller. Detroit: Wayne State University Press. Pp. 135-172.

57. *"Flamenca.* A Post-Arthurian Romance of Courtly Love," *Euphorion,* LVIII, 129-152.

58. "Zu Rilkes Verskunst in den *Duineser Elegien,*" *Neophilologus,* XLIX, 31-51.

59. "Goethe's *Faust.* An Introduction for Students and Teachers of General Literature," *German Quarterly,* XXXVII, 467-486.

60. Republication of No. 7 above in English translation, "Thomas Mann's *Royal Highness* as Symbolic Autobiography," in *Thomas Mann. A Collection of Critical Essays,* ed. (and trans. of this item) Henry Hatfield. Englewood Cliffs, N.J.: Prentice-Hall. Pp. 35-45.

61. Republication of essay from No. 5, "The Master Builder," in *The Genius of the Scandinavian Theater,* ed. Evert Sprinchorn. New York: New American Library Mentor MQ 600. Pp. 555-582.

62. Reissue of No. 30 above, *Goethe: Wisdom and Experience.* Selections by Ludwig Curtius. Translated and edited by Hermann J. Weigand. New York: Ungar. Pp. 299.

63. Reissue of No. 8 above, *Thomas Mann's Novel The Magic Mountain.* Studies in the Germanic Languages and Literatures, No. 49. Chapel Hill, N.C.: University of North Carolina Press. Pp. xii & 184.

1965

64. "Goethe's *Faust.* An Introduction for Students and Teachers of General Literature (Part II)," *German Quarterly,* XXXVIII, 1-13.

65. "Peter Schlemihl," *Wert und Wort, Festschrift für Elsa M. Fleissner,* ed. Marion Sonnenfeld. Aurora, N.Y.: Wells College. Pp. 32-44.

INDEX OF NAMES AND TITLES

The Index includes the names of all authors, including those mentioned in footnotes, as well as the titles of all works mentioned in the essays. The names of characters have been set in small capital letters to distinguish them from those of historical or mythological persons.

INDEX